THE OXFORD SHAKE

General Editor · Stanley Wells

OXFORD WORLD'S CLASSICS

*For over 100 years Oxford World's Classics have brought
readers closer to the world's great literature. Now with over 700
titles—from the 4,000-year-old myths of Mesopotamia to the
twentieth century's greatest novels—the series makes available
lesser-known as well as celebrated writing.*

*The pocket-sized hardbacks of the early years contained
introductions by Virginia Woolf, T. S. Eliot, Graham Greene,
and other literary figures which enriched the experience of reading.
Today the series is recognized for its fine scholarship and
reliability in texts that span world literature, drama and poetry,
religion, philosophy and politics. Each edition includes perceptive
commentary and essential background information to meet the
changing needs of readers.*

THE OXFORD SHAKESPEARE

Cymbeline

EDITED BY ROGER WARREN

CLARENDON PRESS · OXFORD

1998

OXFORD
UNIVERSITY PRESS

Great Clarendon Street, Oxford OX2 6DP

Oxford University Press is a department of the University of Oxford.
It furthers the University's objective of excellence in research, scholarship,
and education by publishing worldwide in

Oxford New York

Auckland Bangkok Buenos Aires Cape Town Chennai
Dar es Salaam Delhi Hong Kong Istanbul Karachi Kolkata
Kuala Lumpur Madrid Melbourne Mexico City Mumbai Nairobi
São Paulo Shanghai Taipei Tokyo Toronto

Oxford is a registered trade mark of Oxford University Press
in the UK and in certain other countries

Published in the United States
by Oxford University Press Inc., New York

British Library Cataloguing in Publication Data

Data available

Library of Congress Cataloging in Publication Data

Shakespeare, William, 1564–1616
Cymbeline/edited by Roger Warren
(The Oxford Shakespeare)
Includes bibliographical references and index
1. Great Britain—History—Roman period, 55 B.C.–449 A.D.—Drama.
2. Fathers and daughters—Great Britain—Drama.   3. Married people—Great Britain—Drama.
4. Brittons-Kings and rulers-Drama.
I. Warren, Roger,   II. Title.   III. Series: Shakespeare, William, 1564–1616. Works. 1982.
PR2806.A2W363 1997   822'.3'-dc21   97–44999

ISBN 0-19-812927-0
ISBN 0-19-283350-2 (pbk.)

6

Typeset by Pure Tech India Ltd, Pondicherry, India.
Printed in Great Britain by
Clays Ltd, St Ives plc

PREFACE

I WAS fortunate to encounter *Cymbeline* for the first time in performance, at Stratford-upon-Avon in 1957, with Peggy Ashcroft unforgettable as the heroine; so from the start the play has been for me, not the eccentric experiment described by much criticism, but an absorbing theatrical experience, and I have tried to communicate something of that in this edition. The 1957 production was directed by Peter Hall; thirty years later he staged the play again, in the context of a season of late Shakespeare plays at the National Theatre, London. I was involved in its preparation, and working on every line of the text with the company for several months was an invaluable preparation for this edition. I have also learnt much from other productions, particularly from William Gaskill's at Stratford-upon-Avon in 1962.

I have also been fortunate in enjoying the stimulating advice and support of Stanley Wells as General Editor, whose generosity at all times has been unfailing, and of James Walker as music editor and, where necessary, composer. I am greatly indebted to Bruce Barker-Benfield of the Bodleian Library for helping to confirm the authenticity of Simon Forman's 'Book of Plays', so placing the first account of *Cymbeline* in performance on a firm footing. I should also like to thank Susan Brock, Christine Buckley, John Gough, Stella Lanham, Margaret Legge, the library staff at the Shakespeare Institute and the Shakespeare Centre, Stratford-upon-Avon, and all who have helped with suggestions and encouragement.

ROGER WARREN

CONTENTS

LIST OF ILLUSTRATIONS

INTRODUCTION

Theatricality

IN the scene which dramatizes the central crisis of her fortunes, the heroine of *Cymbeline* apparently dies, and her brothers speak over her body perhaps the most exquisite lyric in the language, 'Fear no more the heat o'th' sun', whose serene beauty has brought consolation to many a real-life funeral. The point is relevant, since that is its usual effect on a theatre audience too. But then, having fully absorbed that mood, the audience is jolted into participating in something radically different: the apparently dead heroine revives, to find herself beside a decapitated corpse dressed in her husband's clothes, which she takes to be her husband, and gives way to an expression of overpowering grief. This extraordinary scene, combining the extremes of lyrical beauty and psychological and physical horror, presents the technique of the play in its most drastic form: it at once engages the emotions of an audience and amazes them. Nowhere else in his work did Shakespeare invent such an extraordinary incident;[1] but the play contains other scenes scarcely less amazing: as the heroine lies asleep in the stillness of the night, the lid of a trunk in her bedroom slowly opens and a sinister figure emerges from it; and at the lowest point in the hero's fortunes, as he lies asleep in prison, the god Jupiter descends on an eagle's back to promise that he will be 'happier

---

[1] No source has yet been discovered for this incident. Perhaps a hint came from Heliodorus' *Ethiopica*, a Greek prose romance translated by Thomas Underdowne and published in 1569: in a darkened cave the hero, mistaking a dead body for his lover's, fell on it, 'and held the same in his arms a great while without moving' (p. 47). But this is some distance from a heroine waking beside a decapitated body wearing her husband's clothes. Still further is another proposed source, the anonymous play *Sir Clyomon and Clamydes* (published 1599, but probably written in the 1580s), where the heroine thinks her lover dead because she finds his shield and sword hanging next to a grave, although it is true that she would have killed herself had not 'Providence' descended to prevent her, promising 'thou shalt ere long thy knight attain' (l. 1564), as Jupiter promises Posthumus that he 'shall be lord of Lady Innogen' at *Cymbeline* 5.3.201; or even the moment in Edward Fairfax's *Godfrey of Bulloigne* (1600), certainly echoed elsewhere in the play (see the note to 5.3.207), where a decapitated body wearing Rinaldo's armour is mistaken for Rinaldo himself (8.52.3–8). As Edward Dowden laconically observes in the original Arden edition of *Cymbeline* (1903): 'after all Shakespeare may have been capable of a little original invention' (p. xxxiv).

much by his affliction made' (5.3.202), a phrase which aptly sums up the play's juxtaposition of contrasting emotions.

These episodes emphasize the fact that *Cymbeline* is the most overtly theatrical of Shakespeare's plays in the sense that its events and emotions are presented, even paraded, so openly before the audience; but although carried to an extreme here, the communication of startling events with great theatrical sophistication is one of the most striking of several links between this play and others written late in Shakespeare's career, roughly between 1609 and 1611.[1] The outburst of insane jealousy that suddenly takes hold of Leontes' mind and the coming to life of Hermione's apparent statue in *The Winter's Tale*; the dramatization of Prospero's magic as a series of theatrical shows in *The Tempest*; and the spectacular events that mark stages in the hero's career in *Pericles*, a play written somewhat earlier and published in a corrupt text in 1609: these clearly have much in common with the dramatic technique of *Cymbeline*. Together they form a group of plays more closely related than any others of Shakespeare's except the English histories; and their bold, overt theatricality has encouraged speculation that they might have been written in response to a specific Jacobean theatrical challenge.

In 1608, Shakespeare's company, the King's Men, occupied their indoor theatre, the Blackfriars, although because of an outbreak of plague they could not start performing there until late 1609 or early 1610. In the interim, suggests G. E. Bentley,[2] Shakespeare planned a new style of play that would take advantage of a theatre that was smaller, more intimate, and perhaps technically more sophisticated than their open-air theatre, the Globe, and one that would appeal to the more courtly audience that patronized the Blackfriars by employing a greater use of masque and spectacle. The descent of Jupiter in 5.3, for instance, may have been inspired by court masques of the period, some of them designed by Inigo Jones, who later provided a design for Jupiter on an eagle in Aurelian Townshend's masque *Tempe Restored* of 1632 (fig. 1). The King's Men, however, continued to play at the Globe, probably acting there in the summer months

---

[1] For further discussion of the date, see below, pp. 63–7.

[2] 'Shakespeare and the Blackfriars Theatre', *Shakespeare Survey 1* (Cambridge, 1948), pp. 38–50.

1. Jupiter on an eagle: Inigo Jones's design for Aurelian Townshend's *Tempe Restored* (1632).

and indoors at the Blackfriars in the winter; and while some episodes seem suited to an intimate theatre, others seem to need a larger space to make their full impact: these include the battle and especially the Jupiter scene, the very episode that might appear to be most influenced by the courtly, masque-oriented ambience of the Blackfriars. In this connection, it is salutary to remember that at roughly the same time, in Thomas Heywood's plays *The Golden Age*, *The Silver Age*, and *The Brazen Age*, Jupiter and other gods ascend and descend; and these plays were staged at the Red Bull, a popular theatre at the furthest social extreme from the Blackfriars.[1]

The first surviving reference to *Cymbeline* occurs in the manuscript 'Bock [Book] of Plaies and Notes therof' compiled by the

---

[1] For a discussion of the relation between Heywood's plays and *Cymbeline*, see below, pp. 65–7.

astrologer Simon Forman, who, probably not long before his death on 8 September 1611, recorded a performance that he saw, though unfortunately he does not say where or when. It could have been at the Blackfriars, but on 20 April 1611 he saw *Macbeth* and on 15 May *The Winter's Tale*, both at the Globe, so it is a natural assumption that he saw *Cymbeline* there too. Here is Forman's account in full; the spelling and punctuation are modernized, but the names of the characters in the play are left unchanged because two of them, 'Clotan/Cloten' and 'Innogen', provide important evidence for the forms of these names adopted in this edition of the play.[1]

Remember also the story of Cymbalin King of England in Lucius' time, how Lucius came from Octavius Caesar for tribute, and being denied, after sent Lucius with a great army of soldiers who landed at Milford Haven, and after were vanquished by Cimbalin, and Lucius taken prisoner, and all by means of 3 outlaws, of the which 2 of them were the sons of Cimbalin, stolen from him when they were but 2 years old, by an old man whom Cymbalin banished, and he kept them as his own sons 20 years with him in a cave. And how [one] of them slew Clotan that was the Queen's son, going to Milford Haven to seek the love of Innogen the King's daughter, whom he had banished also for loving his daughter. And how the Italian that came from her love conveyed himself into a chest, and said it was a chest of plate sent from her love and others to be presented to the King; and in the deepest of the night, she being asleep, he opened the chest and came forth of it, and viewed her in her bed, and the marks of her body, and took away her bracelet, and after accused her of adultery to her love, etc. And in the end how he came with the Romans into England, and was taken prisoner and after revealed to Innogen, who had turned herself into man's apparel, and fled to meet her love at Milford Haven, and chanced to fall on the cave in the woods where her 2 brothers were, and how by eating a sleeping dram they thought she had been dead, and laid her in the woods and the body of Cloten by her in her love's apparel that he left behind him, and how she was found by Lucius, etc.[2]

Forman is not writing a formal account for publication, but a series of impressions in a private memorandum book (hence the formula

---

[1] These names, and the modernization 'Giacomo' for the Folio's 'Iachimo', are discussed in Appendix A.

[2] The original is in the Bodleian Library, Oxford, MS Ashmole 208, fol. 206^r, reproduced in Appendix A. It has been suggested that the entire document (fols. 200–13) was forged by John Payne Collier in the 1830s; but Bruce Barker-Benfield of the Bodleian Library has kindly pointed out to me that an entry for it, slightly

'Remember . . . how'), but this is precisely what makes his account so valuable. It is one of the very rare examples of an eyewitness reaction to a performance by Shakespeare's company. His impressions are almost breathless in the repeated 'and's as he goes on from one event to another; this in itself bears witness to the impact that the play made on him in narrative terms. Perhaps taking his cue from the title, he begins with the 'historical' framework, which may possibly have made more impact in 1611 than it tends to do in modern performances,[1] before coming to the wager story. He surprisingly makes no mention of the descent of Jupiter, but that does not mean it did not take place; he has a habit of omitting striking events from the later stages of the plays he describes: he does not mention the apparitions in 4.1 of *Macbeth* or the statue scene in *The Winter's Tale* either.

But clearly Giacomo's emergence from the trunk and the princes' laying out of the body of the apparently dead Innogen were as memorable in the 1611 performance as they are in modern ones. Forman's vivid phrase 'in the deepest of the night' bears witness to the evocative impact of the language in the bedroom scene. He speaks of the burial scene taking place 'in the woods'; this may imply the use of property trees in the original performance (discussed further in the Commentary to 3.3.0.1), but 'the woods' may equally represent a general response to the verbal evocation of a rural world in the Welsh scenes comparable to his use of 'forest' for rural Bohemia in his account of *The Winter's Tale*, and possibly of 'wood' for 'heath' in his account of *Macbeth*.[2] Although Forman remembers most of the play accurately, there are slips. The plate in the trunk was to be a present for the Emperor, not for the King (1.6.187). And unless a phrase about Posthumus was accidentally omitted, Forman confuses, or conflates, Cloten

misprinted as 'Of Places [*sic*] and Notes thereof' but with the exact date, shelfmark and item-number, already appears in the Ashmolean section of E. Bernard's *Catalogi librorum manuscriptorum Angliae et Hiberniae* (Oxford, 1697), Tom. 1 Pt. i, p. 352 no. 8279.

[1] This aspect is discussed on pp. 61–3.

[2] It has been suggested, for example by Leah Scragg, 'Macbeth on Horseback', *SS* 26 (1973), pp. 81–8, that the latter derives, not from Forman's theatrical response, but from his reading, in this case the source of *Macbeth* in Holinshed's *Chronicles*. That cannot have happened with *Cymbeline*, since every detail comes from the play, and the play was not registered or printed until 1623.

and Posthumus when he speaks of Cloten 'going to Milford Haven to seek the love of Innogen the King's daughter, whom he had banished also for loving his daughter'; but even this may reflect a response to a theatrical point, for when Cloten does pursue Innogen in Posthumus' clothes, and she mistakes his headless body for that of Posthumus, the two characters become increasingly interconnected, a process described on pp. 50–1 below.

The other early performance about which we have information was at court on 1 January 1634, when, according to the Master of the Revels, it was 'well liked by the King', Charles I.[1] After the Restoration of the monarchy in 1660, the play was given in adaptations by Thomas D'Urfey, under the new title *The Injured Princess or The Fatal Wager* (1682), and later by William Hawkins (1759). David Garrick, however, restored much of the original play in 1761; Posthumus was one of his favourite parts. *Cymbeline* was then regularly performed until 1787, when the celebrated tragic actress Sarah Siddons first played the heroine in London, and on into the first half of the nineteenth century.[2] It was performed much less frequently in the second half of the nineteenth century and throughout the twentieth; and in the nineteenth century itself the real enthusiasm for the play came from poets and writers. It was one of the plays most frequently read by Keats;[3] Tennyson loved it so much that his copy was buried with him;[4] and A. C. Swinburne called the heroine the 'woman above all Shakespeare's women'.[5] But the cult of Innogen as a perfect woman that grew up in the nineteenth century seems to have had an adverse effect on performance: for example, the major exponent of the role in the middle of the century, Helen Faucit, was criticized for 'a monotonous ideal tenderness which scarcely changes throughout' (*The Spectator*, 29 October 1864). Monotony was however successfully avoided by the most famous Innogen of the nineteenth century, Ellen Terry in Henry Irving's production at the Lyceum Theatre, London, in 1896 (fig. 2).

---

[1] E. K. Chambers, *William Shakespeare*, 2 vols. (Oxford, 1930), ii. 352.
[2] Eighteenth- and nineteenth-century productions are listed in Maxwell's edition, pp. xliii–lv. More details about nineteenth-century performances are given in Russell Jackson's unpublished Ph.D. thesis, '*Cymbeline* in the Nineteenth Century', which can be consulted at the Shakespeare Institute Library, Stratford-upon-Avon.
[3] Caroline Spurgeon, *Keats's Shakespeare* (Oxford, 1928), p. 5.
[4] *Alfred, Lord Tennyson: A Memoir by His Son*, 2 vols. (1897), ii. 429.
[5] *A Study of Shakespeare* (1880), cited in Furness, p. 511.

2. A Victorian heroine: Ellen Terry in Henry Irving's production of *Cymbeline* at the Lyceum Theatre, London, in 1896.

Looking back on this performance when writing his *Preface* to the play thirty years later, Harley Granville Barker said that her delivery of the speech beginning 'O for a horse with wings!' (3.2.48–68) seemed 'to fill the Lyceum Theatre with dancing sunbeams'.[1] Contemporary accounts of the production make it clear that this effect was achieved by variety and lightness of touch; and she was encouraged in this by George Bernard Shaw, with whom she corresponded during the rehearsal period. Shaw's remarkable analysis of Innogen's speech beside the headless body is quoted in the discussion of that scene on p. 46 below; and he said of the character in general that she 'is an impulsive person, with quick transitions, absolutely frank self-expression, and no half

---

[1] *Prefaces to Shakespeare: Cymbeline*, revised edn. (1930), reprinted by Nick Hern Books (1993), p. 136.

affections or half forgivenesses'.[1] It seems to have been Ellen Terry's triumph to have realized these transitions on stage; and although Shaw affected to despise the play (even writing a jokey alternative final scene that was actually performed in London in 1937), his analysis of how it works reveals the shrewd understanding of a practical man of the theatre.

The variety, lightness of touch, and marking of transitions of mood apparently displayed by Ellen Terry have been essential elements in modern performances of the part, most notably Peggy Ashcroft's, first at the Old Vic, London, in 1932, and then, at the height of her powers, in Peter Hall's production at Stratford-upon-Avon in 1957. In this production Hall paralleled the play's range of reference (to ancient Britain, medieval Italy, Jacobean England) visually, in sumptuous designs by the Italian painter Lila de Nobili which drew on all those periods (figs. 3 and 8). When he returned to the play thirty years later, now at the National Theatre, London, he sought to unify the play's disparate elements by locating it firmly in the early seventeenth century, and presented it in the context of a special season of late Shakespeare plays, discussed on pp. 11–12 below. Other notable modern productions have included William Gaskill's at Stratford-upon-Avon in 1962 and Jean Gascon's at the Canadian Shakespeare Festival at Stratford, Ontario, in 1970: both used bare stages and very simple costumes to evoke a legendary Britain with outstanding success. Very different in approach were Robin Phillips's Ontario production of 1986, which set the play in the early 1940s, relating the psychological turbulence of the characters to a world of international strife; Bill Alexander's small-scale but intense production at the Other Place, Stratford-upon-Avon, in 1987; and the still smaller scale, imposed by the television screen, of Elijah Moshinsky's version for BBC television in 1983.[2] In their variety, these stagings served to emphasize that of the play itself, and have helped to focus the discussion of different aspects of the play in this introduction and in the commentary. They provide evidence, for example, about the question of whether the play might have been

---

[1] *Ellen Terry and Bernard Shaw: a Correspondence*, ed. Christopher St John (1949), p. 49.

[2] All the productions mentioned in this paragraph are discussed in greater detail than is possible in this edition in my *Shakespeare in Performance: Cymbeline* (Manchester, 1989).

3. Fidele: Lila de Nobili's design for Peggy Ashcroft at Stratford-upon-Avon in 1957.

written specially for a small, intimate theatre like the Blackfriars rather than for the larger open-air Globe, and also upon the influential critical claim that in *Cymbeline* Shakespeare was writing a consciously experimental play.

Theatrical Perspectives: Experiment and Intimacy

Developing Frank Kermode's view that 'we must assume [Shakespeare's] desire to experiment in a new kind of play, in which probabilities and personalities count for less than *coups de théâtre*',[1] Arthur C. Kirsch relates *Cymbeline* to dramatists active in the Jacobean theatres whose plays are written like that, particularly those of Marston or Beaumont and Fletcher:

---

[1] *Shakespeare: The Final Plays* (1963), pp. 21–2.

The most distinguishing feature of this dramaturgy is its deliberate self-consciousness. ... The play all the while calls attention to itself as a dramatic fiction [and] its dramatic effect is to keep the audience at least partially disengaged from ... the action and characters.[1]

What motivates this approach is critical bafflement at the play, a feeling that its events and the techniques with which they are presented cannot be accounted for in conventional critical terms : 'The salient fact about *Cymbeline* ... is that it is resistant to any coherent interpretation.' Kirsch's view is, essentially : this play is incomprehensible, so let us call it experimental.

It connects with an older view, first canvassed by A. H. Thorndike,[2] that *Cymbeline* is specifically influenced by Beaumont and Fletcher's *Philaster*. There are certainly similarities between the two plays, though I think they have been exaggerated. Setting aside trivial 'parallels' that are probably no more than common verbal currency, such as the 'stranger/strange fellow' joke that occurs in both plays (*Cymbeline* 2.1.32–3; *Philaster* 1.1.77–8), the chief similarities are that in *Philaster* a princess has two suitors, one vain and conceited (distantly resembling Cloten in *Cymbeline*), and Philaster, whom she loves, and who resembles Posthumus in *Cymbeline* not only in this respect but in his unreasoning jealousy, and in his physical violence both towards the princess and towards his devoted page, who turns out to be a lady in love with him. Here Philaster resembles the violent Orsino in *Twelfth Night* threatening to 'Kill what I love' (5.1.117), Viola/Cesario ; Beaumont and Fletcher are almost certainly echoing *Twelfth Night* here, and they may be echoing *Cymbeline* too, rather than the other way round. The situation is complicated by the fact that, while the plays were written at roughly the same time, it is difficult to establish which came first ; but since the resemblances are in my view slight, it is scarcely necessary to do so.

The point about theatrical experiment has been put more positively by Richard David in his account of *Cymbeline* in performance : 'at the end of his theatrical career Shakespeare was prepared to take hair-raising short-cuts in order to get his crucial situations onto the stage with the maximum expedition' ;[3] and it

---

[1] 'Cymbeline and Coterie Dramaturgy', *ELH* 34 (1967), 285–306.
[2] *The Influence of Beaumont and Fletcher on Shakspere* (Worcester, Mass., 1901).
[3] *Shakespeare in the Theatre* (Cambridge, 1978), p. 181.

is worth considering what light modern theatrical experience can shed on the claims that the theatricality of *Cymbeline* is experimentally sensational, designed to distance the audience from character and event, and that the play may have been planned for an intimate rather than a large theatre.

At the National Theatre, London, in 1988 Peter Hall staged three of the late plays—*Cymbeline*, *The Winter's Tale*, and *The Tempest*—as a group. Because of the happy accident that the smallest of the National's three auditoria, the Cottesloe, is roughly the same size as the 'Parliament Chamber' of the former Blackfriars monastery which was converted into the theatre,[1] the productions were initially staged there, but subsequently they were transferred to the large open-stage Olivier theatre, where more people could see them; so this provided an interesting opportunity to compare the same productions in small and large spaces.[2] These stagings did not attempt to reconstruct what the early performances might have been like, but rather explored three different aspects of the imaginative world of the late plays, drawing on the early seventeenth century for visual reference. Alison Chitty created a boldly simple, emblematic universe, a stage sloping back to a Jacobean façade containing a central classical doorway, and above it a huge circular disc representing the 'heavens', to use the seventeenth-century theatrical term (fig. 4). The heavens split apart to allow Jupiter to fly through; but in the relatively cramped conditions, there was no room for the eagle to be more than a flat image,[3] and the scene came fully into its own only in the open spaces of the Olivier, where, in a *coup de théâtre* matching that of the text, the circular heavens tilted behind Jupiter so that he and his now three-dimensional eagle appeared at the centre of a universe of brilliantly illuminated stars and planets. But such a

[1] Dimensions are given in E. K. Chambers, *The Elizabethan Stage*, 4 vols. (Oxford, 1923), ii. 490.

[2] There is an account of both the rehearsal process and the performances in my *Staging Shakespeare's Late Plays* (Oxford, 1990). The designer's sketch for the basic stage is reproduced on p. 22.

[3] If Harley Granville Barker's calculation that the acting area available at the Blackfriars was '10 or 12 feet in depth' by '46 feet in width' (p. 45) comes near the truth, space must have been tight there, too. Richard Hosley's estimate of 18 ft. 6 in. depth by 29 ft. width (allowing for on-stage spectators at the sides) gives slightly more room ('The Second Blackfriars Playhouse, 1596' in *The Revels History of Drama in English*, ed. C. Leech and T. W. Craik (1975), iii. 197–226; p. 210).

4. Posthumus (Peter Woodward) as a British peasant in the battle sequence, beneath the emblematic 'heavens' designed by Alison Chitty for Peter Hall's production at the National Theatre, London, in 1988.

scene might be expected to flourish in a larger space, and a yet more interesting discovery was that some of the intimate scenes seemed particularly cramped in the smallish theatre. The two scenes between Posthumus and Giacomo, for example (1.4 and 2.4), and still more the impact of the jealousy of Leontes in *The Winter's Tale*, had a large-scale power and psychological intensity that threatened to burst the bounds of the Cottesloe stage; they too grew and blossomed in the Olivier theatre, as if arriving in their natural environment.

But the Cottesloe is not the Blackfriars, and the Olivier is modelled, not on the Globe (even supposing that we possessed any hard evidence of what its stage was like), but on the Greek amphitheatre at Epidaurus. What other theatrical evidence is available on this question? Harley Granville Barker claims that 'one scene, at least, would be doubly effective at the Blackfriars' (p. 46), that in which

Giacomo emerges from the trunk in Innogen's bedroom. So this scene provides a useful test case. The Other Place at Stratford-upon-Avon is even more intimate than the Cottesloe. When Bill Alexander directed *Cymbeline* there in 1987, it was still virtually a corrugated iron hut rather than the purpose-built theatre which has since replaced it; and in the bedchamber scene, as Giacomo emerged from the trunk, he stepped, whether by accident or design, on a squeaky floorboard. He froze, and the audience with him: would she wake? We then became so much his accomplices that he hardly needed to raise his voice in the tense stillness to make all his points. Clearly, this performance supported Granville Barker's claim; but in his review of the production on its transfer to London, Michael Billington tempered his enthusiastic response with the thought that the play 'has a breadth and vision that sometimes cries out for a main stage' (*Guardian*, 24 March 1988).

It certainly got that at the Royal Shakespeare Theatre, Stratford-upon-Avon, in 1962. The designer René Allio covered the whole stage—floor, walls, proscenium—in white, thus making it appear even bigger. Into the neutral space thus created, large objects necessary for the action were moved or flown: the bed, the trunk, Belarius' cave, Jupiter's eagle. In this way the director, William Gaskill, placed the play within a frame which emphasized its theatricality, and not surprisingly the theatrical extremes came off strikingly: Jupiter descended on a huge copper eagle whose wings spanned half the width of the stage (fig. 5); Innogen's scene with Cloten's corpse, uncompromisingly positioned with its severed neck and dangling veins facing the audience at the very front of the stage, was played by Vanessa Redgrave with equally uncompromising power: there was no question of theatricality 'distancing' the audience from her plight here. Indeed, this production as a whole shed valuable light upon the function of that theatricality: rather than distancing the audience from the action and from the realities of the situations, as Kirsch and others argue, it acted as a kind of 'call to attention', its startlingness isolating and highlighting individual moments, almost putting them on display and holding them up to public scrutiny. That was certainly the effect of the bedroom scene: far from dissipating the intimacy of the scene amongst the wide-open spaces, the staging focused attention on Giacomo's sensuous tribute to Innogen, which Eric Porter delivered directly out into the house, dominating both stage and

5–6. Virtuoso theatricality in William Gaskill's production at Stratford-upon-Avon in 1962, designed by René Allio. Above: the descent of Jupiter (John Corvin); below: Vanessa Redgrave and Eric Porter in the bedroom scene.

audience with what Alan Brien called his 'fluid, unmannered clarity and control of dramatic poetry always tuned to wring every last syllable of sense from the lines without once losing the rhythm' (*Sunday Telegraph*, 15 November 1964). This staging demonstrated conclusively that the scene loses nothing when played with skill and sophistication on a large stage; and its handling of this scene drew attention to another important aspect of the play's technique: the overt theatricality is often combined with language of exceptional power and beauty actually to *focus* human emotions and realities, in this case Giacomo's reaction to Innogen's beauty and worth. More must be said about the language later on.

Romance

Another view locates the origins of the late plays not in Jacobean theatre conditions but in romance; indeed, the group is often given the generic title 'the Romances'. This is a description of comparatively recent date. Coleridge called *The Tempest* a 'romance'; Hazlitt considered *Cymbeline* 'a dramatic romance';[1] and Edward Dowden elaborated this in the original Arden edition of *Cymbeline* (1903):

there is a romantic element about these plays. In all there is the same romantic incident of lost children recovered by those to whom they are dear—the daughters of Pericles and Leontes, the sons of Cymbeline and Alonzo. In all there is a beautiful romantic background of sea and mountain. The dramas have a grave beauty, a sweet serenity. (pp. xi–xii)

All this, though true, omits the equally important reverse side of the coin: the darkness of the incest and the threats to Marina's chastity in *Pericles*; the psychological and physical violence of Posthumus to Innogen and the bloody events that occur within the 'romantic background' of *Cymbeline*; the jealousy of Leontes to the point of sadism in *The Winter's Tale*; the resentment and disillusion as well as the forgiveness of Prospero in *The Tempest*. But in fact such events are also to be found within the flexible

---

[1] Both are conveniently reprinted in Jonathan Bate's anthology *The Romantics on Shakespeare* (Harmondsworth, 1992, reprinted Penguin Classics, 1997, pp. 299–302, 528–34).

boundaries of 'romance'; indeed, the problem with the term, as Stanley Wells points out, is that 'it means so much that often it means nothing at all'.[1] But when Robert M. Adams bases his concept of romance more precisely upon the idea of a quest for discovery or self-discovery,[2] he is supported by the experience of modern productions, especially those which have staged the plays in groups. These have focused on spiritual journeys, which are sometimes also literal ones, as in Pericles' travels throughout the Mediterranean or Innogen's flight to Wales; Leontes' journey in *The Winter's Tale* is a psychological one through a 'wide gap of time' (5.3.155); and in *The Tempest*, Prospero has not only journeyed through space and time (twelve years) before the play begins, but relives both in 1.2, and uses the knowledge gained to bring his enemies into his power. The relation in romance between a far-flung, often episodic geographical action and a psychological journey is very relevant to Posthumus and Innogen in *Cymbeline*.

Partly because of the accommodating nature of romance, partly because of the way in which romance motifs are so widely disseminated among folk-tales and oral traditions, it is difficult to pin down precise examples of particular romances that might have influenced *Cymbeline*: for instance, the story of Snow-White has been ruled out on the grounds that no written version survives from Shakespeare's day; but it may have been in oral currency. A story in which the heroine, fleeing from a wicked stepmother, finds the cave of seven dwarfs, eats their food, is given sanctuary, apparently dies and is ritually mourned but then revives, seems too close to the action of *Cymbeline* for coincidence, especially when the birds gather to mourn Snow-White; compare Arviragus' allusion to the charitable robin at 4.2.225–30. Perhaps the point is that Innogen's adventures in Wales are the *kind* of events characteristic of folk-tales. But of written romance material, Heliodorus' *Ethiopica*, a Greek prose romance believed to date from the third century AD, which in Sir Thomas Underdowne's translation of 1569 was very popular in Shakespeare's day, and Edward Fairfax's *Godfrey of Bulloigne* (1600), a translation of Tasso's epic poem *Gerusalemme Liberata* (1581), are perhaps closest to the

---

[1] 'Shakespeare and Romance', in *Later Shakespeare*, Stratford-upon-Avon Studies, 8, ed. J. R. Brown and Bernard Harris (1966), 49–79; p. 49.

[2] *Shakespeare: The Four Romances* (New York, 1989), p. 16.

general tone of the play, and have certainly influenced particular details.[1] But romance comes in many forms, including drama; and an anonymous play called *The Rare Triumphs of Love and Fortune*, performed at court in 1582 and printed in 1589, not only brings together several characteristics of romance, but seems to have provided a specific stimulus for *Cymbeline*.[2]

The action of *The Rare Triumphs of Love and Fortune* is framed by a dispute among the gods, presided over by Jupiter, about whether Love (Venus) or Fortune has the greater power. Jupiter resolves to use their respective influences upon the two lovers in the play as a test case, and music punctuates the action to signal the 'triumphs' of Love (viols) or Fortune (trumpets and drums) as one or other gains the upper hand. They are ultimately reconciled, so ensuring the happy ending for the mortals.[3] It is surely a remarkable coincidence that in the opening argument Venus and Fortune speak in 'fourteeners' (long verse lines of fourteen syllables) whereas Jupiter speaks in shorter verse lines, the same contrast that differentiates the ghosts' speeches from Jupiter's in 5.3 of *Cymbeline*.

The two lovers who are used as guinea-pigs in Jupiter's experiment are the princess Fidelia (a name close to that assumed by Innogen in *Cymbeline*, with the same connotations of faith) and Hermione,[4] who, like Posthumus, was brought up at the court of Fidelia's father. There is even a close verbal link, though it could be accidental: Hermione is described (ironically) as 'a jewel of some price' (l. 387), Posthumus by Innogen as 'this jewel in the world' (1.1.92). Hermione is not, however, an orphan like Posthumus,

---

[1] See p. 1 n. 1, p. 21, and the Commentary to 5.3.207. Other commentators would add Sidney's *Arcadia* and Spenser's *Faerie Queene* as general influences.

[2] This was first identified as a source for *Cymbeline* by R. W. Boodle in *Notes and Queries* (1887), p. 405. Quotations here are from the Malone Society Reprint (Oxford, 1930). Bullough reprints extracts (pp. 90–103).

[3] This recalls the action of *A Midsummer Night's Dream*; so does the opening presentation of the cruel power of Love and Fortune, displayed in a series of theatrical shows that are mocked by the audience; and the jog-trot rhythms of the play as a whole are exactly the kind of writing that is parodied in the play scene of the *Dream*. Perhaps, then, Shakespeare came across *Love and Fortune* early in his career, rather than, as Nosworthy suggests (pp. xxv–xxvi), at the time of the opening of the Blackfriars.

[4] This probably prompted the use of the name in *The Winter's Tale*, where Shakespeare restores its proper use as a woman's name. Hermione was the cousin of Electra in Greek mythology.

but the son of Lord Bomelio, who was banished as a result of slander (like Belarius in *Cymbeline*); when Hermione is banished for loving the princess, the pair meet at Bomelio's cave. (This, incidentally, offers an important precedent for connecting the Posthumus–Innogen story in *Cymbeline* with that of Belarius and Innogen's brothers, which otherwise seem to have completely unrelated origins.) The lovers are pursued by Fidelia's arrogant brother Armenio, who, like Cloten, jibes at Hermione's inferior birth. Unlike Cloten, he is not beheaded, but struck dumb by Bomelio, who is also a magician.

There are strong hints for Prospero in *The Tempest* in this character, who uses magic books to seek revenge on his enemies; the 'comic' characters, like those in *The Tempest*, steal his 'fair apparel'; and Hermione burns Bomelio's books, as Caliban threatens to do in *The Tempest*. Bomelio then runs mad at the loss of these books; he can only be recovered, and Armenio's speech restored, if they are sprinkled with blood from 'the tenderest part' of Fidelia, her nipple (l. 1217). This bizarre detail is typical of the more fantastic moments of romance, and helps to put the bizarre moments of *Cymbeline* in perspective; the sprinkling of blood that restores Armenio's speech and Bomelio's senses may also be relevant in a general way to the bloodiness of Innogen's scene with the headless body in *Cymbeline*, and the fact that the blood needs to come from Fidelia's nipple is interestingly close to the way in which the privacy of Innogen's body is much intruded upon and to some extent 'besmirched'.[1] And Bomelio's view that 'A joy deferred is sweeter to the mind' (l. 1472) is of central importance in *Cymbeline*, summarized by Jupiter when he says that the happiness he promises will be 'The more delayed, delighted' (5.3.196).

A Retrospective Play

It is often claimed that in the 'Romances' Shakespeare was writing a completely new kind of play,[2] but in fact they grow out of, and develop, much of his earlier work. Journeys that end in lovers

---

[1] Michael Taylor's word in 'The Pastoral Reckoning in *Cymbeline*', *SS36* (1983), 97–106; p. 99. This article traces the 'element of punitive behaviour' in the Innogen–Posthumus relationship.

[2] For example by G. E. Bentley (see p. 2 n. 2), Philip Edwards (p. 45 n. 1), and Frank Kermode (p. 9 n. 1).

meeting, often after much hardship; family reunions; and the importance of forgiveness and reconciliation are present from Shakespeare's earliest comedies, and his two narrative poems, *Venus and Adonis* (1593) and *The Rape of Lucrece* (1594), influence much of the detail in *Cymbeline*. The sensuousness of *Venus*, and in particular the images from the rural world that express it, recur in Giacomo's equally sensuous tribute to Innogen's beauty in the bedroom scene (noted in the Commentary to 2.2.16, 18–19). That speech opens with a reference to Tarquin, the perpetrator of the rape of Lucrece; and in his poem on the subject Shakespeare makes the crucial point that it was the bragging of Lucrece's husband Collatine about his wife's qualities that drew Tarquin's attention to her in the first place: 'why is Collatine the publisher | Of that rich jewel he should keep unknown | From thievish ears...?' (*Lucrece* 33–5). This provides an interesting perspective on Posthumus' behaviour in the wager scene; and in *The Two Gentlemen of Verona*, Valentine's hyperbolically lyrical praise of Silvia (2.4.156–61) leads Proteus to abandon Julia and pursue Silvia to the point of attempted rape; when Proteus describes Valentine's praise as 'braggartism' (2.4.162), he provides further perspective on the behaviour of Posthumus. This combination of lyricism, extravagance, and sexual violence in what was probably Shakespeare's first play and in one of his last testifies both to Shakespeare's development of his own earlier work and especially to his enduring, almost obsessive interest in competitive sexuality (also a major concern of his Sonnets) and in the jealousy it provokes: from the slight but virulent case of Claudio in *Much Ado About Nothing* via Othello to Posthumus and Leontes in *The Winter's Tale*, this sequence of 'treatments of extreme possessive jealousy in men suggests that Shakespeare found it increasingly reprehensible, and more deserving of severe punishment'[1]— hence the sixteen-year penitence undergone by Leontes, and the nightmarish, near-suicidal experience of Posthumus in Act 5 of *Cymbeline*. By contrast, the creation of a rural sanctuary free from the constrictions of court life recurs from *A Midsummer Night's Dream* and *As You Like It*.

---

[1] F. H. Mares, ed., *Much Ado About Nothing*, The New Cambridge Shakespeare (Cambridge, 1988), p. 32.

But the play that most anticipates the *technique* of the late plays and of *Cymbeline* in particular is *Twelfth Night*. The drastic juxtaposition of extremes described at the start of this introduction is an extension of the dramatic method of the comedies, perfected in *Twelfth Night*. As Peter Hall, an experienced theatrical interpreter of both the comedies and the late plays, puts it : 'the comedy is rich because there is darkness and disturbance. The comedy is defined by tragedy, the folly and the illusions by sincerity, the joy by anguish.'[1] A persistent vein of melancholy and awareness of mortality shadows the revels in *Twelfth Night* and deepens the happiness achieved. It is as if Shakespeare feels that the resolutions of comedy endings must be put to the test of harsher experience if they are to be convincing. In *Cymbeline*, the happy ending is achieved after some very harsh experiences indeed. But allowing for the fact that Innogen's eventual happiness is hard won, she has a great deal in common with Viola in *Twelfth Night* : her candour, her humour which helps her to cope with tough situations, and her ability, like Viola, to 'Smil[e] at grief' (*Twelfth Night* 2.4.115 ; compare *Cymbeline* 4.2.53–5). The simplicity with which she expresses her sense of nothingness without Posthumus—'I am nothing ; or if not, | Nothing to be were better' (4.2.368–9)— represents a paring-down even of Viola's simplicity in the allegory of her sister which is the only way she can express what she takes to be her hopeless love for Orsino : 'A blank, my lord. She never told her love' (2.4.110). But like Viola, Innogen does not simply mope and pine, even in the severe crisis of the headless body scene : however intensely felt her desolation, she resists the impulse to kill herself, and, by agreeing to serve the Roman general as his page, she opts for life and so starts the play's upward movement towards its happy ending.

If Innogen in some ways represents an extreme development of the characterization of Viola, Orsino in *Twelfth Night* anticipates the far more explosive jealous rashness of Posthumus when he threatens to kill Viola/Cesario. And there is another interesting link when Orsino asks :

> Why should I not, had I the heart to do it,
> Like to th' Egyptian thief at point of death,

[1] *Twelfth Night*, The Folio Society (1966), p. 3.

> Kill what I love—a savage jealousy
> That sometime savours nobly.
> (5.1.115–18)

The 'Egyptian thief' is a character in Heliodorus' *Ethiopica*, the Greek romance mentioned earlier, who tries to kill a captive whom he loves when his life is in danger from a rival band; and when Posthumus strikes down the disguised Innogen at the end of *Cymbeline*, the incident was almost certainly inspired by another moment in the *Ethiopica*, where the heroine ran to the hero 'like a mad woman' and hung 'by her arms about his neck': 'He seeing her foul face, belike of purpose be-blacked, and her apparel vile and all torn, supposing her . . . a vagabond, cast her off . . . and at length gave her a blow on the ear' (p. 181).[1] The hero's violence to the heroine here, like Orsino's to Viola and Posthumus' to Innogen, shows a character in the grip of overpowering passion; and it is a useful reminder of the violence of much romance material, as well as of the psychological turbulence that makes a crucial contribution to the happy endings of Shakespearian comedy and 'romance'. One way of making a happy ending vivid and persuasive is to emphasize the contrasting things (even within the characters' own personalities) that threaten it. One extreme helps to define its opposite.

Style

The extremes of emotions and events in *Cymbeline* are equalled by the extremes of its language, which ranges from convoluted complexity to limpid simplicity. Sometimes the theatrical virtuosity is reinforced by verbal complexity, what James Sutherland calls 'a sort of impressionism',[2] but at other times, notably in the burial scene (4.2), it is offset by stylistic simplicity.

A good example of the 'impressionism' occurs in the scene in which Giacomo attempts to seduce Innogen. Realizing that he will not be able to win his bet by fair means, he resorts to trickery, trying to catch her off guard by using obscure sexual

---

[1] This source was first suggested by G. K. Hunter in Nosworthy, p. 183.

[2] 'The Language of the Last Plays', in *More Talking of Shakespeare*, ed. John Garrett (1959), 144–58; p. 147.

suggestiveness in order to imply that Posthumus is betraying her with prostitutes:

> It cannot be i'th' eye—for apes and monkeys,
> 'Twixt two such shes, would chatter this way and
> Contemn with mows the other; nor i'th' judgement,
> For idiots in this case of favour would
> Be wisely definite; nor i'th' appetite:
> Sluttery, to such neat excellence opposed,
> Should make desire vomit emptiness,
> Not so allured to feed.

$$(1.6.39-46)$$

Here Giacomo is drawing a distinction between Innogen and a prostitute, but without saying so directly, resorting instead to the imprecise phrase 'two such shes'. The drift of his speech is that Posthumus ought to be able to tell the two of them apart by looking at them, by judging between them, and even by his own desire itself. But his technique is to begin with the attention-grabbing but puzzling phrase 'It cannot be i'th' eye', then to use comparisons with apes, monkeys, and idiots which obscure rather than clarify the sense, and to build to a final comparison, not between two women, but between two vivid abstractions, 'sluttery' (the whore) and 'neat excellence' (Innogen), and ultimately to the extraordinary idea of the contrast between Innogen and the prostitute making even desire itself vomit—but vomit not substance but 'emptiness', rather than going ahead and feeding on, having intercourse with, the prostitute. Bringing out the sense in such a complex passage for the audience, while simultaneously bewildering Innogen, offers a stimulating challenge to the actor; most Giacomos rise to it, in the process demonstrating that the language has a perfectly legitimate function, rather than, as has sometimes been suggested, merely indicating that Shakespeare is wantonly 'playing with the play' or mocking the characters' failure to communicate with each other.[1]

At the opposite extreme is a direct verbal simplicity, as in Arviragus' phrase as he carries the apparently dead Innogen on stage at 4.2.198–9: 'The bird is dead | That we have made so much on.' Summarizing the response of most reviewers, Richard David cites

[1] For example by Frank Kermode, 'The Mature Comedies', in *Early Shakespeare*, Stratford-upon-Avon Studies, 3 (1961), pp. 211–27.

this moment and the lyric 'Fear no more the heat o'th' sun' that follows (4.2.259–82) as examples of 'the shattering effect of the simplicities that suddenly shine out from [the play's] complexities and obscurities'.[1] But of course the 'shattering effect' of such simple moments depends upon their arising from the play's complexities—another instance of the way in which the contrasting extremes of the play work: the one needs the other.

With this simplicity goes a lyrical evocation of the natural world. Although such language occurs frequently throughout Shakespeare's work, *Cymbeline* characteristically develops it in an extreme way, focusing on especially tiny aspects of the rural in order to express intense feelings with particular sharpness, notably when Innogen conveys her terror at awaking beside a headless body by pleading with the gods for a drop of pity—only a tiny drop, only as much (or as little) as the eye of the bird reputed to be the smallest:

> if there be
> Yet left in heaven as small a drop of pity
> As a wren's eye, feared gods, a part of it!
> (4.2.304–6)[2]

Sometimes these tiny images are reached by a gradual process of diminution. The most remarkable example of this is Innogen's imagining how she would have strained her eyes to follow the departure of Posthumus into banishment, had she been allowed to see it (1.3.17–22). First she visualizes him as small as a crow in the distance; then comes a phrase in which she characteristically corrects herself to define her meaning more precisely. To say that she 'broke [her] eye-strings' expresses her straining her eyes, but not sharply enough, so she adds the more vivid 'cracked them', with its suggestion of a sharper pain. The focus on Posthumus in the distance then narrows to the point of a needle, thence to

---

[1] *Shakespeare in the Theatre* (Cambridge, 1978), p. 188.

[2] Both the surprising quality and the tiny images are pushed further in Shakespeare's contribution to his collaboration with Fletcher, *The Two Noble Kinsmen* (1613), for example in the comparison of a short space of time to 'a dove's motion when the head's plucked off' (1.1.98), or in 'I had rather see a wren hawk at a fly | Than this decision' (5.5.2–3), or in the amazing picture of Arcite hanging from the horse that has thrown him: 'on his hind hooves— | On end he stands— | That Arcite's legs, being higher than his head, | Seemed with strange art to hang' (5.6.76–9). See Stanley Wells, *Shakespeare: A Dramatic Life* (1994), p. 384.

something so small as to be almost invisible, a gnat, and finally to nothing but air.[1]

Perhaps the most remarkable evocation of the natural world comes in Arviragus' speech over the body of Innogen/Fidele in the burial scene:

> With fairest flowers
> Whilst summer lasts and I live here, Fidele,
> I'll sweeten thy sad grave. Thou shalt not lack
> The flower that's like thy face, pale primrose, nor
> The azured harebell, like thy veins; no, nor
> The leaf of eglantine, whom not to slander
> Outsweetened not thy breath. The ruddock would
> With charitable bill—O bill sore shaming
> Those rich-left heirs that let their fathers lie
> Without a monument! —bring thee all this,
> Yea, and furred moss besides, when flowers are none,
> To winter-ground thy corpse.
>
> (4.2.219–30)

This speech depends for its effect as much upon a hypnotic rhythm as upon its exquisite language: Innogen is likened to the various flowers with which her grave will be strewn, first by Arviragus and then by the robin, whose charity is contrasted with human ingratitude; but as the speech proceeds, the language and rhythms convey a haunting impression that the body is itself becoming a part of the natural world evoked, especially in the final lines, where the body is covered with the protective moss of the winter landscape. The whole speech, as J. C. Maxwell says in his edition, carries subtle 'overtones of the cyclical processes of death and renewal' (p. xli).

This sense that Innogen's body is undergoing a kind of metamorphosis usefully draws attention to the work of another writer whose technique provides an illuminating parallel to Shakespeare's in *Cymbeline*. Ovid's *Metamorphoses* was one of Shakespeare's favourite books, to judge from the frequency with which he draws upon it in his work. Part of its fascination for Shakespeare seems to have been the close relationship it presents between human beings and the natural world: the characters are transformed into animals, birds, flowers, trees. And since, as Eugene

---

[1] There is a similar process of diminution at 3.3.11–13 and 5.4.471–4.

Waith points out, such transformations are inseparable from 'intense states of emotion . . . as if sheer intensity of feeling made [human beings] indistinguishable from other forms of life',[1] these transformations are of understandable interest to a dramatist who himself turns so often to the natural world for ways of expressing 'intensity of feeling'.

Innogen has apparently been reading Ovid's book in the bedroom scene, since at the end of it Giacomo says

> She hath been reading late,
> The tale of Tereus. Here the leaf's turned down
> Where Philomel gave up.
>
> (2.2.44–6)

Ovid tells the 'tale of Tereus' in *Metamorphoses* 6.424–674. Tereus raped his sister-in-law Philomela and tore out her tongue; in revenge, she and her sister Procne served Tereus with a cannibal meal consisting of his young son; as he pursued the sisters in frenzy, all the characters were turned into birds. Shakespeare constantly alludes to the story during *Titus Andronicus* as a parallel to that play's events; in *Cymbeline*, the rape of Philomela (Innogen had finished reading at the moment of rape, 'where Philomel gave up') is used not as a parallel but as a threat. Giacomo's speech begins and ends by evoking notorious classical rapes; this is what might have happened to Innogen too. She escapes both this and mutilation, which is reserved for Cloten and is the catalyst for her greatest emotional crisis when she wakes by his mutilated corpse. Ovid's treatment of the climax of Philomela's story is very relevant to that scene in particular. Waith's description of Ovid's characters at the moment of transformation as 'caught in some fantastic pose in the midst of their most violent actions' (p. 39) surely fits Innogen's embracing Cloten's headless corpse perfectly.[2] But as well as the violence and intensity, Ovid evokes a sense of amazement. At the climax of the 'tale of Tereus', for example, as Tereus and

---

[1] 'The Metamorphosis of Violence in *Titus Andronicus*', *SS* 10 (1957), 39–49; pp. 41–2.

[2] Another relevant example of a violent action expressed in a 'fantastic pose' occurs at *Metamorphoses* 9.216–20, possibly the inspiration for 5.4.262 (see the Commentary), where Hercules hurls his page Lichas into the sea: 'whirling him thrice . . . about his head, he hurled him far out into the Euboean sea, like a missile from a catapult. The youth stiffened as he yet hung in air'; he is then transformed into a rock.

Philomela are transformed into birds, Ovid provides the equivalent of a theatrical double-take; in Waith's rendering: 'You would have thought they were on wings; they *were* on wings!' And Waith concludes: 'We are left with these moments of wonder, caught in a series of vivid pictures' (p. 43). This fusion of 'intensity of feeling' with a sense of amazement in 'a series of vivid pictures' seems to me exactly what Shakespeare too achieves in the three virtuoso scenes with which this introduction began. The technique of both writers concentrates attention on individual moments which focus emotional realities to the point of isolating them and subjecting them to spotlit scrutiny, in a way particularly evident in William Gaskill's staging (see above, p. 13).

Ovid, of course, has to achieve this effect by language alone; Shakespeare does so by a combination of language and theatrical sophistication to create a self-sufficient dramatic universe. He draws upon very different sources (principally Holinshed's *Chronicles*, Boccaccio's *Decameron*, and the anonymous play *The Rare Triumphs of Love and Fortune*) to bring together at least three worlds which seem at first to have very little in common: Roman Britain, medieval-to-Renaissance Italy, and the Jacobean England in which he is writing. The result is a mythical world which is at once remote and recognizable.

The Wager Story

The story of the wager on Innogen's chastity has its origins in folklore. Myths and folk-tales always embody some deep-rooted human emotion, what Stephen Orgel calls 'the terrifying truths of the inner life';[1] and this one focuses the psychological insecurity inherent in any intimate relationship, a topic searchingly explored elsewhere in Shakespeare's work and summarized in the trenchant final line of Sonnet 92: 'Thou mayst be false, and yet I know it not.' The folk-tale of the husband who wagers on his wife's chastity in fact expresses less the confidence which the husband claims he feels than his lack of trust in his wife: she is being put to the test. Although at the start of *Cymbeline* the First Gentleman offers an ideal image of Posthumus as a heroic paragon (1.1.17–24), the process of the wager soon begins to modify that

[1] *The Winter's Tale*, The Oxford Shakespeare (Oxford, 1996), p. 17.

image. 'It might', says R. A. Foakes, 'be thought a hollow confidence in [Innogen] that drives Posthumus to brag so much that she is "more fair, virtuous, wise, chaste, constant, qualified, and less attemptable" than the rarest ladies of France'.[1] There is something, if not exactly sordid, at least spiritually mean, in making a bet on your wife's purity; this is emphasized when the Frenchman points out that Posthumus has got himself into trouble by making such claims before (1.4.32–58), and it is reinforced by Shakespeare's principal source for the wager story.

Although this story was in such wide currency as a folk-tale, the immediate impulse for Shakespeare was unquestionably the ninth tale of the second day of Boccaccio's *Decameron*. No English translation earlier than 1620 has survived, although since the printer of that translation pointed out that many of the stories 'have long since been published before', it is possible that Shakespeare knew a translation that has not survived. Otherwise, he must have read it in Italian or in one of the numerous sixteenth-century French translations of the *Decameron*, for simply to read straight through Boccaccio's story reveals its illuminating closeness to *Cymbeline* not merely in events, but more crucially in tone and attitude.[2] Like Posthumus, Bernabò, the husband in the *Decameron*, maintains that he is 'blessed with a wife who was possibly without equal in the whole of Italy,... endowed with all the qualities of the ideal woman,... the most chaste and honest woman to be found anywhere on earth'. This provokes the mockery of Ambrogiuolo, the equivalent of Shakespeare's Giacomo, who asks whether the Emperor had granted him the privilege of such a perfect wife: 'Faintly annoyed, Bernabò replied that this favour had been conceded to him, not by the Emperor, but by God, who was a little more powerful'. This clearly suggested both Posthumus' claim that Innogen is 'only the gift of the gods' and Giacomo's ironic response 'Which the gods have given you?' (1.4.81–2); but perhaps the close relationship with Boccaccio emerges still more clearly in the way that Shakespeare adopts, for Giacomo particularly, the bantering tone of passages that he does not in fact use; for example, Bernabò, proposing the wager, extravagantly offers,

---

[1] *Shakespeare: The Dark Comedies to the Last Plays* (1971), pp. 108–9.
[2] Quotations are from the excellent translation of the *Decameron* by G. H. McWilliam, Penguin Classics, revised edn. (1995), pp. 165–78.

'in order to convince you of my lady's integrity, to place my head on the block' if Ambrogiuolo succeeds in seducing his wife; Ambrogiuolo takes the wind out of Bernabò's sails, as Giacomo often does Posthumus' (1.4.84–5, 129–32; 2.4.95–8, 105), by replying: 'I wouldn't know what to do with your head, if I were to win. But if you really want to see proof of what I have been saying, you can put up five thousand florins of your own, which is less than you'd pay for a new head, against my thousand.' When Boccaccio says that by the end of their dispute 'the passions of the two men were so strongly aroused that, contrary to the wishes of the others, they drew up a form of contract . . . which was binding on both parties', he might be summarizing the development of Shakespeare's scene. Posthumus' bragging about Innogen needles Giacomo, who is specific about his motivation: 'I make my wager rather against your confidence than her reputation' (1.4.106–7); and in the process he releases Posthumus' touchiness and inner insecurity about his wife's sexuality. Boccaccio provides an interesting perspective on the behaviour of both Bernabò and Posthumus when he has the narrator of the following story mock the 'foolishness of such people as Bernabò'. The model for Posthumus, then, is a stupid man who doesn't trust his wife and has a lot to learn.

If Shakespeare's Giacomo reflects Boccaccio's Ambrogiuolo in his ironical, worldly manner, an unexpected undercurrent of powerful feeling is released in the bedroom scene in both versions. When Giacomo emerges from the trunk and compares himself to Tarquin (2.2.12–14), the allusion arouses expectations of rape; but it is important not only to the characterization of Giacomo but to the tone of the play as a whole that such tragic potential is not fulfilled. As Granville Barker puts it, catching not only Shakespeare's tone but Boccaccio's too, 'no tragically-potent scoundrel, we should be sure, will ever come out of a trunk' (p. 92). But equally, both Boccaccio and Shakespeare emphasize the powerful temptation that the sleeping heroine's naked beauty offers. Both Ambrogiuolo and Giacomo run enormous risks: Ambrogiuolo draws the bedclothes completely off Zinevra, in the process discovering that 'below her left breast there was a mole, surrounded by a few strands of fine, golden hair'; and Boccaccio adds: 'on seeing how beautiful she was he was sorely tempted to hazard his life and lie down beside her'. But he doesn't do so; nor does Giacomo,

7. The equivalent of Giacomo in Boccaccio's *Decameron* emerges from the trunk: a 'comprehensive' illustration, showing various stages of his emergence, starting from the bottom left-hand corner (a detail from a *cassone*, School of Giovanni Toscani).

though he is so overwhelmed by Innogen's loveliness that he cannot resist kissing her (2.2.17), even at the risk of waking her.

But Shakespeare develops Giacomo's response beyond the sensuality presented by Boccaccio into a lyrical celebration of Innogen herself, her beauty and her worth:

> 'Tis her breathing that
> Perfumes the chamber thus. The flame o'th' taper
> Bows toward her, and would underpeep her lids
> To see th'enclosèd lights, now canopied
> Under these windows, white and azure-laced
> With blue of heaven's own tinct.
>
> (2.2.18–23)

And when Shakespeare uses one of those tiny aspects of the natural world discussed on p. 23 above to describe the mole on

the heroine's breast mentioned by Boccaccio, the image simultaneously celebrates Innogen's physical beauty and expresses the
intense sensitivity of Giacomo's response to her, a sensitivity
which her husband, the ostensible romantic hero, has not so far
displayed:

> On her left breast
> A mole cinque-spotted, like the crimson drops
> I'th' bottom of a cowslip.
>
> (2.2.37–9)

But Shakespeare also develops other implications of the situation
presented by Boccaccio. If Giacomo celebrates Innogen, he also
preys upon her: he is in a way a voyeur. She is not raped by
him, but she is arguably soiled by his invasion of her privacy;
and since he shares his reactions with us, we become his accomplices.

Some performances emphasize Giacomo's intrusion more than
others. At the National Theatre in 1988, for instance, Tim Pigott-
Smith drew aside the bedclothes and kissed the mole on Innogen's
breast, as Giacomo subsequently tells Posthumus that he did
(2.4.137), and his infatuation with Innogen intensified his scorn
in that later scene for the husband who seemed not to value her.
Again, Boccaccio provides an illuminating perspective, this time
as a contrast. In his version the husband refuses to accept any of
Ambrogiuolo's evidence until the mole is mentioned, when 'he felt
as though he had been stabbed through the heart'; but Shakespeare, developing Posthumus' rashness, impetuosity, and insecurity from the wager scene, has him leap so quickly to believe
circumstantial evidence that Philario has to intervene: 'This is not
strong enough to be believed | Of one persuaded well of' (2.4.131–
2). In this version, the mole is merely a confirmation rather than
the crucial revelation that it is in Boccaccio. Tim Pigott-Smith
edged the point by asking Posthumus contemptuously 'You *do*
remember | This stain upon her?' (2.4.138–9), implying that a
man so ready to believe the worst of such a wife might in fact not
have remembered.

The climax of this scene is Posthumus' frenzied soliloquy, and
the stylistic modulations in it offer both opportunities and difficulties for the actor. In the opening lines (2.4.153–60), Posthumus
seems to express his shock by taking refuge in generalizations

about female frailty;[1] at ll. 161–71 he becomes more specific, drawing a contrast between Innogen restraining him from his 'lawful pleasure' with a 'rosy . . . pudency' (modesty), yet allowing Giacomo to mount her like a rutting German boar; then he switches back to a general denunciation of women which culminates rather surprisingly in his assuming the role of a satirist *writing* against them:

> I'll write against them,
> Detest them, curse them, yet 'tis greater skill
> In a true hate to pray they have their will.

With that couplet the soliloquy seems to be over; but then Posthumus adds a single line as a parting shot: 'The very devils cannot plague them better' (ll. 184–7). Many actors disregard these tricky fluctuations of tone and deliver the whole speech as one great curse, which robs it of point and effect. A conspicuous exception was Patrick Allen in William Gaskill's production of 1962.

Allen brought to the speech a sense of outrage and indignation which suggested less heartbreak than humiliated confidence, that same confidence which had stung Giacomo into making the wager in the first place (1.4.106–7). The cynicism and misogyny came across as the reaction of a limited man less concerned with Innogen herself than with the collapse of his image of her; and the modulations of tone emphasized the character's insecurity and rashness: this was exactly the kind of man who would suddenly instruct Pisanio to kill Innogen, and just as suddenly repent his folly *before* learning that she was innocent (as the soliloquy with which he reappears in 5.1 makes clear that he has done). This interpretation made excellent sense of the anticlimactic last three lines: their satirical rhetoric seemed rather hollow; it carried a hint that beneath his rage Posthumus' heart was not wholly in his attack on her, which helped to motivate his later repentance. Patrick Allen's delivery of the whole speech precisely embodied the 'overwrought heroic folly' which G. K. Hunter thinks characterizes Posthumus.[2] The critical view of Posthumus presented by both actor and commentator here is very much in accord not only

---

[1] Compare Leontes' view, as jealousy overcomes him, that 'there's comfort in't, | Whiles other men have gates, and those gates opened, | As mine, against their will' (*Winter's Tale* 1.2.197–9).

[2] *All's Well That Ends Well*, The Arden Shakespeare (1959), p. lvi.

with the writing but with Boccaccio's comments on the husband at the end of his version of the story. Just before revealing who she is, the disguised heroine criticizes a husband who paid 'more attention to another man's falsehoods than to the truth that years of experience should have taught him'. This emphasizes the lack of trust that lies at the heart of this story; in the case of Posthumus and Innogen the 'years of experience' were not of course spent as husband and wife, but were years spent by two people who had known each other since childhood and who had been brought up together. Indeed, it could be argued that Posthumus' insecurity derives in part from having to make the difficult transition from their being childhood sweethearts to becoming adult lovers, and then having that new relationship rudely disrupted by the King.

Or it may derive from something else. When Posthumus says of Innogen that

> Me of my lawful pleasure she restrained,
> And prayed me oft forbearance, did it with
> A pudency so rosy ... that I thought her
> As chaste as unsunned snow
>
> (2.4.161–5)

Anne Barton takes him to mean, not that Innogen was showing restraint within marriage, or 'married chastity' as Shakespeare calls it in his poem 'The Phoenix and Turtle' (l. 61), but that she was actually a virgin, literally chaste, and that the secret marriage had not been consummated. This argument depends upon the exact meaning of Posthumus' subsequent remark that Giacomo

> found no opposition
> But what he looked for should oppose, and she
> Should from encounter guard.
>
> (2.4.169–71)

Anne Barton argues that 'opposition' here 'does not seem to be an abstraction—his wife's honour, for instance—nor a vague allusion to the vagina' but 'is a specific reference to the hymen'.[1] The claim is perfectly possible, but none of the supporting evidence she adduces—from Shakespeare himself, from both Catholic and Pro-

---

[1] 'Wrying but a little', in *Essays, Mainly Shakespearean* (Cambridge, 1994), 3–30; p. 24.

testant writers condemning voluntary abstinence within marriage as an evil, or from the claim that the Posthumus–Innogen marriage was a 'hand-fasting' only, that could the more easily be annulled (see 1.5.78)—unequivocally clinches it.[1] The obvious dramatic gains would be to intensify both Posthumus' rage that Giacomo has enjoyed what he himself has not enjoyed, and, as Barton points out, his generosity in forgiving her while still believing her guilty, since there would be more to forgive. Indeed, part of Barton's motive is to excuse Posthumus for his murderous fury, and to 'rescue' Innogen 'from charges of prudery' in 'restraining' him (p. 29). I think she needs no such excuse; that any criticism is directed not at her but at Posthumus for a sexual demandingness that now, apparently humiliated, drives him to interpret her restraint as the behaviour of a professional 'tease'; and that when he says that Giacomo 'found no opposition | But what he looked for should oppose', he simply means that Giacomo anticipated pleasurable physical 'opposition' to penetration, and that her behaviour was a mere prelude to intercourse ('encounter').[2] In this ferocious passage, Shakespeare hardly seems to be aiming to excuse Posthumus' behaviour, any more than Boccaccio excuses Bernabò's. A wager unthinkingly undertaken has turned very sour.

Widening the Wager Story

Shakespeare's working-out of the wager story sticks less closely to Boccaccio, although his description of the wild place where the

[1] It could just as easily be argued, since Innogen's eyes (or her eyelids) are blue (2.2.23), that she is pregnant, by analogy with Sycorax in *The Tempest* ('This blue-eyed hag was hither brought with child', 1.2.270) and Webster's pregnant Duchess of Malfi ('The fins of her eyelids look most teeming blue', 2.1.65); that Pisanio realizes this and therefore gives her the drug (3.4.189–92); and that her illness in 4.2 derives from her pregnancy. I don't actually believe any of this; but the point is that it is no more susceptible of proof or disproof than Barton's speculation that Innogen is still a virgin.
[2] When Barton has to get round the problem of how, if Posthumus didn't consummate the marriage, he knew about the mole on, or under, Innogen's breast (2.2.37–9; 2.4.134–9) by explaining that contracted couples were allowed 'to engage in a good deal of sexual play so long as actual intercourse did not occur' (p. 28), this odious mixture of technical chastity and titillation seems to me to put Innogen in a far worse light than the supposed 'prudery' from which it is intended to 'rescue' her.

hero's servant takes the heroine to kill her but eventually to spare her, 'a lonely spot with precipitous crags and trees all round it', may initially have suggested the play's movement to Wales. Even in Boccaccio's version, the tightly knit, perhaps rather limited world of intrigue broadens out into a story of wandering; but this expansion is more noticeable in other versions of the story, particularly in a rather garrulous prose tale called *Frederick of Jennen* (i.e. Genoa), and in a medieval French miracle play, *Otto King of Spain*, one of several such plays using versions of the wager story. *Frederick of Jennen* itself provides evidence of the widespread popularity of the story, since it is a translation of a Dutch version which in turn derives from a German one. First printed in Antwerp in 1518, and reprinted in London in 1520 and 1560, it was obviously popular;[1] and although it is clear that the suave sophistication of Boccaccio's version was the immediate influence, several details equally clearly derive from *Frederick*.[2]

The opening stage direction of the wager scene (1.4), for example, brings on stage, as well as the speaking roles of Giacomo, Philario, and the Frenchman, a Dutchman and a Spaniard who are given nothing to say. Since their nationalities were probably recognizable through distinctive costuming, their presence helps to give the impression of a cosmopolitan gathering, and precisely this mixture of nationalities is found in *Frederick of Jennen*, whereas in Boccaccio the merchants are all Italian; so perhaps this is a tiny hint that Shakespeare, in adopting this detail, is inclining to a somewhat wider view of the material. It is surprising that there is no conversation at all between the equivalents of Giacomo and Innogen in Boccaccio; there is a short exchange in *Frederick*, but of the surviving versions of the wager story, only the French miracle play *Otto* provides any dialogue that corresponds to Shakespeare's,

---

[1] That Shakespeare was familiar with it early in his career is established by the fact that, instead of the mole on the heroine's breast, *Frederick* gives her a 'black wart' on her left arm (Bullough, p. 69), and Dromio of Syracuse in *The Comedy of Errors* (*c.*1594) mentions as an identifying mark 'the great wart on my left arm' (3.2.148–9).

[2] These details are closely studied in W. F. Thrall, '*Cymbeline*, Boccaccio, and the Wager Story in England', *Studies in Philology*, 28 (1931), pp. 639–51, and in Bullough, pp. 15–19. Bullough reprints *Frederick* on pp. 63–78, from which the quotations here are taken.

as J. P. Collier pointed out in 1839.[1] The equivalent of Giacomo thus slanders Otto to his wife:

I come from Rome, where I left your lord, who values you less than the stalk of a cherry; he is having an affair with a whore whom he loves so much that he is unable to leave her. This made me leave Rome to come and tell you, for it gives me great distress and rage; and because he has acted so badly I have fallen deeply in love with you.

One might feel that Shakespeare needed no such prompting to work out that a good way for Giacomo to slander Posthumus was to suggest that he was involved with other women, were it not for the curiously exact correspondence between the claim of Giacomo's equivalent in *Otto* that he will only need to speak with any woman on *two* occasions in order to seduce her, and Giacomo's own claim that he will need 'no more advantage than the opportunity of a *second* conference' to seduce Innogen (1.4.123–5). There is nothing like this detailed dialogue in the corresponding scenes of *Frederick*; on the other hand, whereas the hero in Boccaccio shows no remorse on hearing of his wife's death, his equivalent in *Frederick* repents 'that he spake not with her before that he caused her to be put to death', a hint for Posthumus' repenting his rashness in 5.1.

Perhaps more significant is the way in which both *Frederick* and *Otto* widen the scope of the action from the private, triangular relationship of the central characters to involve public issues. 'Frederick' is the name that the heroine in the prose story assumes when she disguises herself as a man. Taking service with the King of Cairo, [s]he is made 'lord protector and defender' of his realm, defeats his enemies in battle, 'and slew them down afore him like a lion'. In *Cymbeline*, it is not Innogen-as-Fidele herself, who takes almost no part in the culminating battle, but her husband 'the lion's whelp', her brothers, and the Britons whose courage they have revived, who win the battle and who 'grin like lions | Upon the pikes o'th' hunters' (5.3.38–9); the point is that *Frederick* provides Shakespeare with a precedent for expanding the wager story into a story about international warfare.[2] *Otto* does this too,

---

[1] Cited in Furness, pp. 474–7. Collier speculates that *Otto* might have come to Shakespeare's notice as a late-surviving English miracle play based on the French one.

[2] Another prose tale, *Westward for Smelts*, sets the wager and the disguised heroine's wanderings against the background of the Wars of the Roses. But as it

and goes further: the Virgin Mary descends from heaven, accompanied by singing angels, to comfort the heroine and to advise her to adopt male disguise; God himself descends, again accompanied by music, to advise the husband to find and forgive his wife; the husband defeats the Giacomo figure in single combat; the reunion of husband and wife leads to international peace. There are obviously several striking resemblances to *Cymbeline* here; but the most important is the general one that Boccaccio's limited story is given a wider context both here and in *Frederick of Jennen*; and since, as suggested on p. 18 above, *Love and Fortune* links the story of a princess and her banished husband with that of a cave-dwelling hermit, Shakespeare may not seem so eccentric as is usually suggested in linking the Posthumus–Innogen story with others which initially seem to have nothing to do with it. He may have taken the hints in *Frederick* and *Otto* to expand the scope of the play beyond the sexual intrigue he found in Boccaccio by placing it within a wider context. That context was provided primarily by Holinshed's *Chronicles*.

'In a great pool a swan's nest': Rome and Britain

It is part of the virtuosity of the play that the wager story is balanced against two others: those of the war between Britain and Rome, and of the two stolen princes, which, like the wager, derive from various sources, partly from myth and folklore, partly from widely separated sections of Holinshed's *Chronicles*. Once the wager plot has got the play going, the momentum is sustained by the other two plots, with Innogen the character who moves between them and holds them together: she is central to the play in every way.

Posthumus and Innogen are not simply a husband and wife separated by an Italian intriguer and the husband's lack of trust: Innogen is the heir to the crown of a mythical ancient Britain, and the breakdown and eventual re-creation of their private relationship is reflected in the public world by the collapse and restoration of relations between Britain and Rome, a restoration to which both Innogen and Posthumus make crucial individual contributions.

was not entered in the Stationers' Register or printed until 1620, its slight resemblances to *Cymbeline* may derive from the play itself.

The peace between them leads at the very end to peace between the two nations.

Posthumus' soliloquy in which he reacts to his apparent betrayal marks the culmination for the time being of the wager story; Innogen expresses her corresponding reaction in the long and complex scene with Pisanio, 3.4. Both in the process try to cope with the apparent faithlessness of the other by generalizing about the frailty of the opposite sex (2.4.171–87; 3.4.53–64). But whereas Posthumus' response results in murderous violence, Innogen's is characteristically more positive. She has, of course, the advantage of being guided by the compassionate Pisanio who, in a process traced in the commentary to 3.4, gradually 'educates' her mind and encourages her to rise above thoughts of death to a new life as a page-boy—and perhaps outside Britain. She responds to this suggestion with an image that places Britain in a universal context:

> Hath Britain all the sun that shines? Day, night,
> Are they not but in Britain? I'th' world's volume
> Our Britain seems as of it but not in't,
> In a great pool a swan's nest.
>
> (3.4.137–40)

This beautifully expresses the view of ancient Britain presented in the play—independent, yet related to the Roman empire. Most of the pseudo-historical material comes from Holinshed's *Chronicles*, as may be demonstrated by a brief summary of the relevant sections of Books 1–4 of the First Volume.[1]

Drawing on the twelfth-century chronicler Geoffrey of Monmouth as well as on the more historically factual accounts of Bede and of Julius Caesar in his account of his two invasions of Britain in *De Bello Gallico*, Holinshed presents the early history of Britain as a mixture of fantasy and something resembling fact, which may well have acted as a spur to Shakespeare's treatment. Ancient Britain ('Albion') is a fantastic landscape peopled with giants, into which come the Trojan hero Brutus, who rechristens Albion 'Britain' after his own name, and his wife Innogen. Brutus was a grandson of Silvius Posthumus, and either the grandson or

---

[1] Shakespeare probably used the 1587 edition, from which the quotations here are taken. Most of this material is conveniently assembled in Bullough, pp. 38–46.

great-grandson of Aeneas, who escaped the sack of Troy and founded Rome. So already, in the mists of prehistory, Britain's origins are associated with Rome's. Brutus divided Britain into three, christening Wales 'Cambria'. After his death and those of his descendants, Britain was divided between five kings, including Cloton, King of Cornwall, whose son, Mulmutius Dunwallon, made laws, and 'ordained him . . . a crown of gold, and caused himself with great solemnity to be crowned, according to the custom of the pagan laws then in use', so that 'some writers' call him the first King of Britain. In 72 BC, King Lud rebuilt Brutus' city Troynovant, 'so that it was called . . . Lud's town, and after, by corruption of speech, it was named London'. Mulmutius' crowning is mentioned at *Cymbeline* 3.1.57–9, Lud's town at 3.1.32, 4.2.101, and 5.4.482.

During the reign of Lud's brother (or son) Cassibelan, Julius Caesar demanded tribute, which was refused. Holinshed makes use here of Caesar's own account in Book 4 of *De Bello Gallico*, but is reluctant to allow too much credit to Caesar or too much criticism of the Britons, claiming that Caesar 'maketh the best of things for his own honour'; so, though he admits that Cassibelan submitted to Caesar, he adds that 'our histories far differ from this'; and he draws on both Caesar and Bede for the information that Caesar's ships, 'being taken with a sore tempest, were either beaten one against another, or else cast upon the flats and sands, and so broken' (echoed at 3.1.24–9). Cassibelan was succeeded by Lud's younger son Tenantius; Cymbeline (Cunobellus) was his son.

The most significant event that took place during Cymbeline's reign was the birth of Christ, and this may be the reason why Shakespeare chose this king's reign in which to set a play ending with international peace (and to name it after him),[1] although, as Robert M. Adams points out, 'Shakespeare neither mentions nor alludes to the fact' in the play itself.[2] More relevant to the facts of the play is Cymbeline's relationship with Rome : 'being brought up in Rome and knighted in the court of Augustus, [he] ever showed himself a friend to the Romans, and . . . was loath to break with

---

[1] Brian Gibbons argues that Spenser's reference to the concurrence of Cymbeline's reign and Christ's birth in *The Faerie Queene* 2.10.50, and indeed Canto 10 as a whole, provided Shakespeare with 'a mythical but also a religious idea of providence in history' (*Shakespeare and Multiplicity* (Cambridge, 1993), p. 30).

[2] *Shakespeare : The Four Romances* (New York, 1989), p. 78.

them' (echoed at 3.1.68–70). Partly for this reason, Holinshed is uncertain if Rome's tribute was denied by Cymbeline, or by his son Guiderius, who succeeded in AD 17. Guiderius was killed in battle; his brother Arviragus succeeded him, and perhaps married the daughter of the Roman emperor Claudius, although Holinshed suspects that this may be 'but a feigned tale'.

It is evident from this summary that Shakespeare drew on Holinshed's account, not only for events and passages of dialogue, but also for the names, and forms of the names (see Appendix A) of several major characters. He may also have read a little further, for Holinshed reports the possibility that Arviragus may have been the same person as Prasutagus, the husband of the British queen Voadicea (our Boadicea or Boudicca). In his account of Voadicea's rebellion against the Romans, Holinshed gives her a speech rallying her troops in which she describes Britain as 'this island, which for the quantity thereof may well be called a main [i.e. main land] . . . environed about with the ocean sea, dividing us from other nations, so that we seem to live upon another earth, and under a several heaven'. The insular patriotism of this speech, together with the passages describing the shipwreck of Caesar's navy quoted above, may have influenced the Queen's defiant celebration of Britain,

> which stands
> As Neptune's park, ribbed and paled in
> With oaks unscalable and roaring waters,
> With sands that will not bear your enemies' boats,
> But suck them up to th' topmast.   (3.1.18–22)

It has often been thought surprising that the Queen should be given this ringing expression of patriotism, whereas elsewhere she is presented as an archetypal malignant stepmother or as a wicked sorceress from a fairy tale. But the point is surely that in *Cymbeline* patriotism is subjected to a more critical scrutiny than, for example, in John of Gaunt's celebrated view of England as 'this blessèd plot' (*Richard II* 2.1.40–64). The insularity of the Queen's anti-Roman sentiments is set in sharp contrast to Innogen's larger view of Britain as a swan's nest floating in the pool that represents the rest of the world, the view that eventually prevails in the harmony between Britain and Rome at the end of the play.

Furthermore, just as the play complicates the image of Posthu-

8. The Queen as a black-clad enchantress (Joan Miller) with the two lovers (Peggy Ashcroft and Richard Johnson) in Peter Hall's production, designed by Lila de Nobili, Stratford-upon-Avon, 1957.

mus as an ideal hero or of Giacomo as a worldly-wise seducer (or a potential rapist), so the Queen has several different 'faces', as the strikingly different ways of presenting her in performance emphasize. Sometimes the sinister aspect predominates, as in the black-clad enchantress seen at Stratford-upon-Avon in 1957 (fig. 8); sometimes the glamorous, glowing with all the colours of the rainbow (Stratford 1974); sometimes the political, as in the Medici Queen Mother of the BBC television version. To these images may be added another, from Holinshed. In the woodcut illustrating Voadicea's oration in the 1577 edition of the *Chronicles*, there is a similar mingling of historical periods to that found in the play:

9. A barbarian Queen: Voadicea (Boadicea) encourages her troops (from the 1577 edition of Holinshed's *Chronicles*). Apart from the hare which she is holding, a fertility emblem, her appearance may give some idea of how the Queen in *Cymbeline* was originally presented.

'barbarian' costume, Roman armour, Elizabethan doublets and weapons (fig. 9). In particular, Voadicea herself wears a free-flowing robe and cloak bearing a strong resemblance to those worn by Tamora in the famous Peacham sketch of a scene from *Titus Andronicus*. Was this a standard image of a barbarian queen? If so, and if the drawing represents how Tamora was actually dressed on stage, the image of Voadicea may possibly give some idea of how the Queen in *Cymbeline*, and perhaps Innogen too, may have appeared in the original performances.[1]

However that may be, this illustration is a further reminder that what Dr Johnson stigmatized as Shakespeare's 'imbecile' 'confusion of the...manners of different times' (p. 307) does not lack precedents. But Shakespeare certainly carries it, as he carries most other things in this play, to an extreme. Why does he do it? Brian Gibbons argues that Shakespeare is creating 'a new kind of drama intended to be as inclusive as possible', and he puts Johnson's negative view of the play's historical 'confusion' in a positive way:

In terms of the representation of historical periods Shakespeare offers a dramatic narrative which presents a Jacobean audience with a mirror of its own...manners and topical allusions...while also relating it to the cultural past in the European Renaissance in Italy, beyond that to the

[1] Jean Wilson juxtaposes the Holinshed and Peacham illustrations in *The Archaeology of Shakespeare* (Stroud, 1995), p. 111.

medieval world of chivalry, thence to ancient Rome and Brutan Britain, and beyond that again to the primeval wilderness of prehistory.[1]

Gibbons here provides a useful summary of the sheer range of the play; and he goes on to point out that it is Innogen who 'gives the audience a guide through these time warps'; but noting that her 'dream and subconscious life are as important as her waking life, in which, indeed, she twice suffers a kind of death in the course of the play', Gibbons also emphasizes the links between those three virtuoso scenes with which this introduction began: 'Shakespeare arranged three major scenes concerning an unconscious figure, spaced at significant points and with obvious ... interconnections', two focused on Innogen (2.2, 4.2), one on Posthumus (5.3). The theatrical potential of the first of these, the bedroom scene, has been touched on more than once. The second, the 'burial' of Innogen and her revival beside the headless corpse, is at once her central crisis and the central episode of the whole play. The event itself is so extraordinary that one feels it must have been Shakespeare's starting-point, that it was, so to speak, what he wrote the play for. There is nothing in the wager story or in the Holinshed material to suggest that the narrative might develop in this way; and yet Shakespeare prepares for this climactic episode from much earlier in the play.

'None but Milford way': From Court to Country

Innogen's arrival in the rural world is fleetingly anticipated in the opening scene, when she longs for a world far removed from the restrictions of the court where differences of rank would not threaten her marriage to Posthumus:

> Would I were
> A neatherd's [cowherd's] daughter, and my Leonatus
> Our neighbour shepherd's son.
>
> (1.1.149–51)

This longing is intensified when she receives Posthumus' letter summoning her to Milford Haven in 3.2. Her excitement to get there is communicated in one of those vivid evocations of the natural world discussed on pp. 23–4 above, as she imagines

---

[1] *Shakespeare and Multiplicity*, pp. 14, 22, 24–5, 45.

horses capable of running more swiftly than the sands through an hourglass:

> I have heard of riding wagers
> Where horses have been nimbler than the sands
> That run i'th' clock's behalf.
>
> (3.2.71–3)

This excitement builds to her ecstatic cry 'Accessible is none but Milford way' (l. 82); and the effect is that the audience first see the rural world through Innogen's eyes before they see it for themselves in the next scene.

The language of that scene swiftly sketches the topography, an open landscape in which Belarius seems as small as a crow from the distance of the mountains, and which provides a safe refuge for the 'sharded beetle' as much as for 'the full-winged eagle' (3.3.12–21) and for the human inhabitants. Here Belarius has lived

> at honest freedom, paid
> More pious debts to heaven than in all
> The fore-end of my time.
>
> (3.3.71–3)

The moving simplicity of these lines strikes a note that has not been heard so far in the play, for all its range and variety: contentment. But that is Belarius' view of the rural world. The princes seem chiefly aware of its restrictions, equally vividly evoked by Arviragus' speech about the wind and rain pounding on their 'pinching' cave in the 'freezing hours' of 'dark December' (3.3.37–9). This powerful speech is a reminder that the countryside of this play is no utopia; it is far removed from the idealized landscape of literary pastoral. In the harsh winter weather there can be no pretending: here people are forced to come to terms with themselves and others—and this is precisely what happens to Innogen when she arrives here: in this place that she has longed for, she experiences the two greatest crises of her life, first the realization in 3.4 that her husband tried to have her killed, and then in 4.2 her awaking by the body that seems to be his.

But between those two experiences comes her first scene disguised as a boy, 3.6. It is worth emphasizing the astonishing variety of Innogen's role. Since the start of the play, she has been variously the separated and then the betrayed wife of Posthumus;

the image of perfection, the 'Arabian bird' instinctively recognized by Giacomo and celebrated by him in the bedroom scene; the princess of a mythical Britain who glimpses her country's relationship to the larger world of the Roman empire in the 'swan's nest' speech at 3.4.137–40; and now she displays yet another 'face' and becomes what Peter Hall, rehearsing the scene at the National Theatre in 1988, called the 'witty boy-girl from Shakespearian comedy'.[1] The comparison is exact: like Viola in her 'ring' soliloquy at *Twelfth Night* 2.2.17–41, Innogen combines humour and direct address to the audience in order to involve them still further in the realities of her situation; this helps to ensure that they go through her greatest ordeal, beside the headless body, with her.

Her soliloquy opens with a one-liner—'I see a man's life is a tedious one'—which could simply be a statement of exhaustion, but which most actresses deliver in a way that brings out its humorous potential, a statement of the ironical discrepancy between the princess she once was and the boy she now is; and this tone is developed when she describes her meeting with the two beggars of whom she asked the way to Milford: 'Two beggars told me | I could not miss my way' (3.6.8–9)—as people always do when giving you directions. Most actresses exploit the comic value of this enduring modern parallel. Humour rounds off the soliloquy too: as Innogen enters the cave, she draws her sword, but hopes that she will encounter only an enemy who 'fear[s] the sword' as much as she does—a momentary echo of Viola again, in her reluctant duel with Sir Andrew Aguecheek. The dramatic gain is clear: both actress and audience are allowed a relaxation of tension before such emotional demands are made upon them in the headless body scene. This is an excellent example of the way in which the extreme contrasts of the play work in dramatic terms.

Such contrasts also operate in the headless body scene itself (4.2), where the most horrific scene in the play is preceded by the most beautiful, the lyrical celebration of Innogen by her brothers. What is its effect on an audience, beginning with the moment when Arviragus enters carrying her in his arms (4.2.196)? The stage direction in this edition is substantially that in the First Folio text, which may be Shakespeare's own;[2] its most crucial feature

---

[1] Cited in my *Staging Shakespeare's Late Plays*, p. 59.
[2] But see the account of the text, pp. 67–74 below.

is that it refers to Innogen as 'dead', not, as some conscientiously literal-minded editors insist in their emendation, 'as dead'. The Folio's phrase surely provides an important clue. Shakespeare is indulging in theatrical sleight of hand. In 1.5, the Doctor told the audience that he had substituted a harmless drug that would give the impression of death, like that given by Friar Laurence to Juliet, for the poison which the Queen asked for; the Queen then gives this drug to Pisanio, and Shakespeare reminds us of its provenance earlier in this scene: 'Pisanio, I'll now taste of thy drug' (4.2.37–8). And yet the reaction of an audience, in all the productions I have seen or been involved in, has been the same: a hushed, tense stillness in which, so to speak, they seem to suppress that factual knowledge and respond instead to the theatrical experience: to all intents and purposes, as the Folio says, Innogen is dead.

Such a reaction seems to me essential if the scene is to have its full impact. The power of the celebrated lyric 'Fear no more the heat o'th' sun' derives partly from the fact that it is at once specifically relevant to Innogen herself in its detail, since if dead she would be beyond the reach of a 'tyrant' like her father (l. 266), 'slander' like Giacomo's or 'censure rash' like Posthumus' (l. 273), and yet expressed in general terms which make it seem applicable to everyone. In this way, the language lures the audience further into the experience of apparent death and funeral ritual, and then, when they have experienced these to the full, takes them beyond even that point to share in Innogen's revival and to endure with her the waking nightmare beside the headless body.

The whole scene, hovering so strangely between death and life,[1] raises in acute form the question of whether Shakespeare is simply playing with the play, manipulating not only the emotions of the characters but those of the audience as well, providing a kind of exploitative sensationalism like Beaumont and Fletcher's in *Philaster*. Arthur Kirsch thinks he is: 'We experience [Innogen's] sufferings, but always with [a] dispassion ... [that] is frequently ironical'.[2] Richard David, on the other hand, summarizes

---

[1] It is easy to see why this and the other late plays should have provoked allegorical readings; for an aptly caustic account of some of these, see Philip Edwards, 'Shakespeare's Romances: 1900–1957', *SS* 11 (1958), 1–18, especially pp. 6–12.

[2] '*Cymbeline* and Coterie Dramaturgy', *ELH* 34 (1967), p. 299.

the experience of most performances when he says of Susan Fleetwood's handling of the waking soliloquy at Stratford-upon-Avon in 1974 that she involved 'the audience in the nightmare quality of the experience and in its power, so that detached and critical spectatorship was impossible' ; and he provides a valuable summary of the technique of the late plays in general and of this one in particular : 'the artifice, though Shakespeare resorted to it more openly and even with more self-conscious bravado than before, is used to enhance rather than to contradict the reality of the basic human situations presented.'[1]

Innogen by Cloten's Corpse

As Richard David suggests, the theatrical virtuosity (or 'bravado') of this scene is a means to an end : Shakespeare uses the situation he has artfully contrived in order to subject Innogen to a purgatorial experience, the crisis of her spiritual journey. It is worth analysing in some detail how he does it.

As modern performances have demonstrated, Innogen's speech is cunningly constructed so that the actress does not have to release the full intensity of her passion all at once. In a letter of 6 September 1896 to Ellen Terry while she was rehearsing the part in Henry Irving's production, Bernard Shaw shows a dramatist's grasp of how this speech is written for acting, of its gradations and its careful pacing. Here is part of his moment-by-moment analysis of the first half of the speech :

you sit up, half awake, and think you are asking the way to Milford Haven ... You lie down to sleep again, and in doing so touch the body of Cloten, whose head (or no head) is presumably muffled in a cloak. . . . Then in rousing yourself sufficiently to get away from this vaguely apprehended person, you awaken a little more [and realize] that the bedfellow is covered with flowers. You take up a flower ... It is *bloody* . . . But it is quite clear that you must not know that 'this bloody man' is headless, as that would utterly spoil the point later on. . . . When you utter the prayer 'If there be yet left in heaven as small a drop of pity as a wren's eye, feared gods, give me a part of it,' I suppose you kneel and cover your eyes with your hands in the hope that when you remove them your prayer will be answered and the nightmare gone. You take down your hands and dare to look again.

---

[1] *Shakespeare in the Theatre*, pp. 186, 127.

'The dream's here still. Even when I wake it is without me and within me, not imagined—felt'.[1]

For this *tour de force* Shakespeare brings together the principal stylistic features of the play: its use of extremes in Innogen's comment on the combination of blood and flowers: 'These flowers are like the pleasures of the world, | This bloody man the care on't' (4.2.297–8); its impressionism in the image of an arrow which is made of nothing and shot at nothing (l. 301), perfectly catching the insubstantial quality of dreams, and so expressing her half-sleeping, half-waking state; and that characteristic image of something very tiny from the natural world of which she is now a part, as she asks the gods for 'as small a drop of pity | As a wren's eye' (ll. 305–6).

Her realization that the body is headless is followed, in the same line, by another: 'The garments of Posthumus?' (l. 309). There follows the precise identification of the various parts of Cloten's body with those of Posthumus. The usual way of playing this is exemplified in an extreme and unnerving form by Helen Mirren in the BBC television version: she nods with an increasing, terrifying certainty as she makes the identification of each bodily part. This episode was handled quite differently by Geraldine James at the National Theatre in 1988. She made the identification in a flash, from the clothes, and then turned away in horror, only half-looking at the body as she provided the corroborating evidence that 'confirms it home' (l. 329). This interpretation had the advantage, not only of corresponding with Innogen's habit of making a point and then correcting or amplifying it (compare 1.3.17–22) but, in her impulsive leaping to the wrong conclusion, of forming an interesting parallel with her husband's equally impulsive readiness to believe the worst in 2.4. It is customary for Innogens to play the rest of the speech—from her attack on Pisanio (l. 313) onwards—in a flood-tide of passion, as Peggy Ashcroft did at Stratford-upon-Avon in 1957, and Vanessa Redgrave there in 1962. Geraldine James, however, discovered more variety in the passage. Like Ashcroft and Redgrave, she poured out her passion at 'Where is thy head? Where's that? Ay me, where's that?' (l. 322), cradling the body in her arms, her face very close to the

---

[1] *Ellen Terry and Bernard Shaw: a Correspondence* (1949), pp. 45–6. Shaw's slight misquotations have been retained.

10. Innogen (Geraldine James) embracing Cloten's corpse: National Theatre, 1988.

bloody neck (fig. 10); but then she modulated from passion to invest the words 'Pisanio might have killed thee at the heart | And left this head on' (ll. 323–4) with a very telling tenderness, the intimacy of which prepared for her treatment of the end of the speech.

What does 'Give colour to my pale cheek with thy blood' (l. 331) imply? The Oxford Shakespeare *Complete Works* inserts the stage direction '*She smears her face with blood*'. When it is played that way, for example by Helen Mirren in the BBC television version, it emerges as a powerful but grotesque moment, supporting those who see the virtuosity of the speech as an experimental exercise. But most actresses have brought out what Richard David, in the passage about theatrical 'bravado' cited on p. 46 above, calls 'the reality of the basic human situations presented'. That is certainly how Vanessa Redgrave and Geraldine James played it, cradling the body in their arms and burying their faces in the severed neck, bloodying themselves in the process. There seems no reason why Innogen should dip her fingers in her husband's neck, every reason why she should embrace him. This perfectly fits Caius Lucius' later description of her 'Or dead or sleeping on him' (l. 357), and gains further support from *Venus and Adonis*, a poem much echoed in the play, where Venus embraces the dead Adonis, 'And stains her face with his congealèd blood' (l. 1122). For these reasons, the stage direction in this edition suggests that Innogen should embrace the body.

A tender rather than a grotesque treatment of the body also provides a better transition to Innogen's statement of her sense of complete nothingness without her husband, in her reply to Caius Lucius' questions: 'I am nothing; or if not, | Nothing to be were better' (4.2.368–9). This sense of desolation was memorably and movingly expressed by Vanessa Redgrave who delivered it very slowly, 'one broken word at a time'.[1] This is her most negative moment in the play; but in the next lines, her wide-ranging tribute to Posthumus is not only moving in itself but serves to reinstate her earlier view of her husband and so to purge his betrayal from her system:

> There is no more such masters. I may wander
> From east to occident, cry out for service,
> Try many, all good; serve truly; never
> Find such another master.
>
> (4.2.372–5)

This is a good example of the way in which something that is factually untrue can nevertheless reveal emotional truth, for although the body is Cloten's, Innogen's restored faith in her husband is at least partially justified since, as we discover when he reappears shortly (5.1.2–7), he has forgiven her while still believing her to be guilty. And Innogen's expression first of deep negation and then of recovering faith begins a process which culminates in her agreement to serve Caius Lucius as his page. After burying and mourning the body, she will then turn to something more positive: 'And leaving so his service, follow you' (4.2.394).

[1] John Russell Brown, 'Acting Shakespeare Today', *SS 16* (1963), 143–51; p. 151.

Innogen's decision to turn away from despair and to opt for life marks the turning-point of the play. After her horrific experience by the corpse, she might well have followed the example of an earlier heroine, Juliet, who finds herself in a similar situation and kills herself. That Innogen does not do so makes important points both about her personality and about the nature of the play. Innogen undergoes tragic experiences, and expresses a full range of tragic emotions, without having to suffer a tragic outcome. This emphasizes that *Cymbeline*, like the late plays in general, engages with tragedy but in the end looks beyond it: the vision is a broader one. To this vision, Innogen's decision is crucial. By choosing life rather than death, she initiates the upward movement of the play, not only paving the way for reunion with her husband, but also, by joining the Romans and serving Caius Lucius, ultimately preparing for the wider reconciliation between Britain and Rome.

At the end of the scene, Cloten is carried from the stage like a military hero. However ironical this may be, Cloten's body has become so associated with Posthumus' during this scene in Innogen's mind, and, because they have gone through the experience with her, in the audience's too, that this funeral ritual has the effect of exorcizing the Cloten-like aspects of Posthumus just before he reappears, to some extent a changed and chastened man. In this respect, the moment marks the climax of a process that has begun earlier in the play.

The opening scene contrasts the two of them in extreme terms, Posthumus as a nonpareil, Cloten as 'a thing | Too bad for bad report' (1.1.16–24); but as the process of the wager story dents Posthumus' ideal image, it also brings out in him a latent violence towards Innogen which includes humiliating her in front of her father:

> O that I had her here to tear her limb-meal!
> I will go there and do't, i'th' court, before
> Her father.

(2.4.147–9)

There is a remarkably similar combination of violence and public humiliation in Cloten's plan to rape Innogen in her husband's clothes:

when my lust hath dined—which, as I say, to vex her I will execute in the clothes that she so praised—to the court I'll knock her back, foot her home again. (3.5.140–3)

Cloten makes that last threat even more specific, and closer to Posthumus', when he repeats it in his soliloquy as he arrives in Wales: 'all this done, spurn her home to her father' (4.1.17–18).[1] This soliloquy, in which Cloten wears Posthumus' clothes, insists on the physical closeness between them, so that Posthumus' garments fit Cloten perfectly. 'Why', asks Frank Kermode, 'give Posthumus the body of a paragon, and then allow Cloten's equal to it?'[2] To pose the question is to suggest the answer. The two characters are alike physically, but also to some extent temperamentally. That is surely the basic reason why Cloten is made to dress in Posthumus' clothes, and why Innogen is given such a detailed identification of the body.[3] Cloten is ultimately used as a scapegoat: just as Innogen undergoes tragic experiences without enduring a tragic consequence, and a 'death' without actually dying, so with Posthumus: Cloten dies in his place, purging the Cloten-like aspects of his personality, even if the process is, as we shall see, an incomplete one.

Posthumus—and Jupiter

The first half of Act 5, up to the start of the final scene, is concerned almost exclusively with Posthumus. Shakespeare needs to restore him to the centre of the action after an absence of two entire acts, and in the process he puts him through an ordeal similar to that just undergone by his wife. This is done in a theatrically radical, risk-taking way typical of the technique of this play, in a series of soliloquies, or speeches that have the effect of soliloquies (the account of the battle in 5.3 is technically addressed to a lord),

---

[1] For further points of connection, and for evidence that Cloten cannot be dismissed as a total 'clotpoll' any more than Posthumus is wholly a nonpareil, see the Commentary to 2.3.64–73 and 3.5.70.

[2] *Shakespeare: The Final Plays* (1963), p. 26.

[3] The resemblances between Posthumus and Cloten have also been discussed, for example, by Homer Swander, '*Cymbeline* and the "Blameless Hero"', *ELH* 31 (1964), pp. 259–70; James E. Siemon, 'Noble Virtue in *Cymbeline*', *SS* 29 (1976), pp. 51–61; Michael Taylor, 'The Pastoral Reckoning in *Cymbeline*', *SS* 36 (1983), pp. 97–106.

interrupted only by the battle and by the Jupiter scene, which is itself, on one level, an externalization on stage of what Posthumus is dreaming about. The text of Act 5 shows some signs of disturbance,[1] so that Posthumus may not have been intended to have had quite so many soliloquies; but it is possible to account for this section of the play as it stands. First, by communicating so directly with the audience to such an extent, Posthumus involves them in his purgatorial journey, as his wife involved them in hers in the previous act. Second, Posthumus' theatrical isolation reflects his psychological isolation. Obsessive jealousy, and the self-absorption and lack of trust of the other person that lies at the heart of it, isolate those who yield to it. The most striking example is provided by Leontes in the contemporaneous *Winter's Tale*; though surrounded by other people, he is cut off from them in the nightmare grip of a treacherous world that exists only in his own fevered imagination. Posthumus is isolated by the consequences of a similar mistrust, and tormented by what it led him to do to his wife.

Posthumus engages with the audience, the only people with whom he can now communicate, as soon as he arrives back on stage. After addressing the 'bloody cloth' which is the emblem of what he believes he has done to Innogen, he directly addresses at least a part of the audience in his second line:

> You married ones,
> If each of you should take this course, how many
> Must murder wives much better than themselves
> For wrying but a little!

$$(5.1.2-5)$$

There is an interesting mixture of tones in these lines, as there was in his soliloquy when we last saw him, in 2.4. On the one hand is the cynical assumption that even wives 'much better than' their husbands nevertheless betray those husbands, even if that should be viewed indulgently, as 'wrying but a little'; on the other, the phrase itself makes the point that Posthumus has forgiven Innogen while still believing that she is guilty, and repents his rashness in ordering her death. The cynical element in the lines connects with that in his earlier soliloquy, and helps the actor to maintain some continuity between the two halves of the part, as well as

---

[1] See the discussion of the text, pp. 74–5 below.

making the psychological point that however repentant he may be, no one's personality changes overnight. Posthumus is still recognizably the same man; and his rashness and violence return in his urge towards self-destruction during the following episodes.

This impulse emerges particularly in his long account of the battle between the Britons and the Romans (5.3.3–51). A peculiarity about this speech is that it describes in detail what the audience has already seen. Although another possible explanation of this duplication is offered on p. 74 below, the text as it stands suggests that the battle scene (5.2) presents the facts as seen from the outside, whereas Posthumus reinterprets them from the viewpoint of a participant—though, in his chastened state, he makes no mention of his own contribution to the victory, a discrepancy which an audience can pick up, since they have just seen the events for themselves. And while the battle is staged in a simple, almost stylized way, Posthumus' narration is very complex indeed, feverishly excited to the point, sometimes, of incoherence (see the Commentary to ll. 46–8). It is based on a passage of Holinshed's *Chronicles* widely separated from the account of the foundation of Britain from which most of the pseudo-historical material derives: it comes from a part of the History of Scotland upon which Shakespeare had already drawn for *Macbeth*, and tells how, in the battle of Luncarty (near Perth) between the Scots and the Danes in AD 976, an old man called Hay and his two sons reversed the rout of a Scots army by defending a narrow lane against the full might of the Danes.[1] Holinshed, like Shakespeare, presents the event as something at once providential—'the appointment (as is to be thought) of almighty God'; compare 'the heavens fought' at 5.3.4—and ferociously realistic, especially when Posthumus describes how the Britons began

> to grin like lions
> Upon the pikes o'th' hunters. Then began
> A stop i'th' chaser; a retire; anon
> A rout, confusion thick . . .

$$(5.3.38–41)$$

The animal imagery is striking: the rejuvenated Britons are like lions baring their fangs, and the Roman army, halted in its tracks,

---

[1] The relevant passage is given in Bullough, pp. 46–50.

is seen as a horse thrown back on to its haunches ('A stop'); as elsewhere in the play, comparisons to animals, and particularly horses, are used to express moments of heightened intensity (3.2.48, 71–3; 5.4.233).

The language of this speech suggests a man in a state of feverish excitement, partly because of the experience of going through the battle itself, partly because Posthumus is enduring a kind of purgatory similar to his wife's beside the headless body. But whereas she is purged by that experience to the extent of avoiding suicide, he still seeks death (5.3.66–83). It is a measure of the difference between them. There is a difference of another kind between Posthumus' ordeal in this sequence and Innogen's in the preceding one. Both offer virtuoso challenges to the two actors; but whereas the poetic impact and verbal precision of the burial–headless body sequence supports the heroine at every turn, the actor of Posthumus has a much harder task, virtually alone on stage to deliver huge speeches that vary greatly in quality. And this question of the unevenness of the writing leads directly to the problems of the Jupiter scene (5.3.124–244).

Shakespeare's authorship of Posthumus' vision of his ghostly family and of Jupiter has often been questioned, on the grounds that it is a detachable episode and that the ghosts' speeches in particular are written in a style thought to be unworthy of Shakespeare; but, in addition to noting numerous verbal parallels with the rest of the play and with Shakespeare's other work,[1] it is possible to approach the question of the scene's integrity from another angle. Jupiter's speech in particular has been cited several times in this introduction because its suggestion that happiness is only achieved after enduring great trials, thus making it more appreciated (5.3.195–6, 202), seems to summarize so precisely the experience of the play; if the scene is an interpolation by another hand, it fits with remarkable neatness into the play as a whole. And the theatrical *tour de force* of Jupiter's descent on his eagle matches those of Giacomo emerging from the trunk in Innogen's bedroom and Innogen waking by the headless body.

Perhaps it is less profitable to argue about the authorship of the scene than to ask *why* the ghosts' speeches are written so oddly—if

---

[1] Some of these parallels are noted in the commentary. See also G. Wilson Knight, *The Crown of Life* (1947), pp. 168–202.

you like, so badly. It has long been recognized that the way in which they are laid out in the Folio text (as in this edition) disguises the fact that the basic rhythmic unit of the ghosts' speeches is the rhyming 'fourteener', so called because it is a long line of fourteen syllables. There are also three isolated half-lines (ll. 128, 141, 156), presumably to provide variety and to emphasize specific points. The fourteener was an old-fashioned verse form occurring, for example, in the anonymous play *Love and Fortune*, one of the sources of *Cymbeline* (discussed on pp. 17—18 above), and in Arthur Golding's translation of Ovid's *Metamorphoses* (1567), parodied in the play scene of *A Midsummer Night's Dream*. It was probably chosen because it sounded archaic, evoking a world even more remote than Cymbeline's Britain, perhaps to suggest that this is how Posthumus thinks of the family he has never known. Alternatively, the moments of near-doggerel may be intended to represent the strangeness of a dream.

What sort of dream is Posthumus having? This partly depends upon how the ghosts' speeches are delivered, and it so happens that Peter Hall's production at the National Theatre in 1988 suggested two radically different approaches. At an early rehearsal, the speeches were spoken slowly, steadily, marking the short-line layout as printed in this edition, with a simple dignity that evoked a world of heroic antiquity; but in performance, they were treated as fourteeners and spoken very rapidly, with the rhythms exaggerated and underpinned by hectic violin figurations that suggested a very troubled nightmare indeed, as Posthumus writhed and buckled in torment on the floor, especially at the isolated half-line referring to 'Sweet Innogen' (l. 156). But it is possible for these half-lines to suggest pathos rather than torment: Stanley Wells remembers that that was the effect at Stratford-upon-Avon in 1962 when Posthumus' mother described the child that was torn from her as 'A thing of pity' (l. 141).[1] The experience of the National Theatre's versions suggested that the lines sound less threadbare, less like doggerel, when they are delivered simply, without calling too much attention to their origin in the fourteener; and this has influenced my decision to print them substantially as they appear in the Folio text.

---

[1] 'Staging Shakespeare's Apparitions and Dream Visions', the first Globe Theatre lecture, Globe Education (1990), p. 12.

In the introduction to the edition of the play accompanying his BBC television production, Elijah Moshinsky describes the headless body and Jupiter scenes as 'therapeutic dreams' for the central characters.[1] The language certainly supports this view: when Innogen wakes beside the body, she describes her experience in terms of the insubstantiality of dreams:

> 'Twas but a bolt of nothing, shot at nothing,
> Which the brain makes of fumes.

> (4.2.301–2)

And when Posthumus awakes, he describes the cryptic prophecy that Jupiter has left with him in similar terms, expressed in that terse, thornily complex style characteristic of the impressionism of much of the play's language:

> 'Tis still a dream, or else such stuff as madmen
> Tongue, and brain not; either both, or nothing,
> Or senseless speaking, or a speaking such
> As sense cannot untie.

> (5.3.239–42)

What Moshinsky calls the 'therapeutic' aspect seems clear in the Innogen scene, allowing her to exorcize the Cloten-like aspects of Posthumus and her reaction to them, restoring his original image before they meet at the end of the play; but Posthumus' reactions are more ambiguous, perhaps reflecting the way in which his dream is both encouraging and disturbing. On the one hand, he describes his glimpse of his dead family as 'this golden chance' (l. 226); on the other, this positive reaction is mingled with disappointment at waking to 'find nothing' (l. 223), and bewilderment at Jupiter's prophecy. But by the end of the speech he has come to feel that, strange as the prophecy is, it is no stranger than what has happened to him in the 'ordinary' course of his life so far: 'Be what it is, | The action of my life is like it' (5.3.242–3). For Elijah Moshinsky, these lines summarize the experience of the whole play: 'the confusion of the play is like life: it's bizarre and emotionally penetrating, and psychologically intense. And very lifelike' (BBC edition, p. 26).[2]

---

[1] *Cymbeline*, The BBC TV Shakespeare (1983), p. 17.
[2] Moshinsky's view is shared by R. A. Foakes: 'In an analogous sense we may say of the play as a whole that it is like the action of our own lives' (*Shakespeare : The Dark Comedies to the Last Plays* (1971), p. 118).

But if the vision of his family and Jupiter is rejected as an interpolation, then Posthumus' comment on it inevitably has to be rejected as well; yet this is in some ways the most character-istically Shakespearian speech in the play. There are also larger problems in performance when the scene is omitted or when the descent of Jupiter is replaced, for example, by lighting effects and a taped voice, as at Stratford-upon-Avon in 1979 and 1987. Unless Jupiter actually descends and makes a big, even sensational impact, this Act 5 sequence is deprived of its natural climax, and the rhythm of the whole play noticeably falters: the elaborate final scene becomes much harder to play, because the rhythmic pre-paration for it is missing. But when the Jupiter scene is staged in all its theatrical virtuosity, as for example by William Gaskill at Strat-ford-upon-Avon in 1962 and by Peter Hall at the Olivier theatre in 1988, it emerges as a theatrical climax equivalent to Innogen's scene by the headless body: both these episodes mark important stages of the purgatorial journeys of hero and heroine, and so prepare for the larger climax of the final scene, and the reunion of husband and wife within it.

The Final Scene — and James I

The final scene is yet another theatrical *tour de force*, bringing together the various plots and containing some twenty-four revelations. What performance demonstrates is the way in which the complexities of the narrative are manipulated to throw maximum emphasis on the human situations at its centre, which become a series of highlighted moments, held as if spotlit: Giacomo's elaborate repentance, the reunion of husband and wife, then of brothers and sister, the moving parting of Belarius from his foster-sons, and ultimately the reconciliation between the Britons and the Romans. The technique of this finale thus mirrors that of the whole play.

Giacomo's retrospective account of the wager scene (5.4.153–209) carries to new extremes the tortuous language that he used in his attempt to catch Innogen off guard in 1.6, discussed on p. 22 above. This complexity implies an inner turbulence, reflecting the remorse which he has already expressed in his soliloquy after being defeated in battle by the disguised Posthumus (5.2.1–10). He provides a revealingly distorted account of what happened in the wager scene, whitewashing the behaviour of Posthumus, who was certainly not 'as calm as virtue' in that scene, and who did in fact 'disprais[e] whom we praised' (5.4.173–4). When the listening Posthumus reveals himself and denounces Giacomo as an 'Italian fiend' (5.4.210), he likewise distorts the facts: Giacomo is no more a 'fiend' here or in his earlier behaviour, however disreputable, than Posthumus was 'as calm as virtue' earlier on—or now. In their highly-wrought state, intensified by the traumatic battle that they have been through, both exaggerate their views of each other (and of themselves, as in the rest of Posthumus' speech at 5.4.210–27).

It is in this state of near-frenzy, believing that he has killed Innogen for no reason, that he strikes her down. It is true that she is disguised as a boy, but yet again the theatrical device brings out something truthful about their relationship: this is the climax of his violence to her in the play. As he does so, he asks 'Shall's have a play of this?'; and for those who see the play as self-consciously mocking its own artifice, this is a key moment, comparable to the scene in Beaumont and Fletcher's *Philaster* in which the heroine is wounded by the hero but protected by a country fellow who in his turn molests her (4.5.85–108): in this view, both scenes exploit attacks on women for purposes of pure (or impure) sensation, titillating the audience with gratuitous (potential) sex and (actual) violence. I think this is a key moment too, but for the opposite reason that Shakespeare is emphasizing human realities rather than distancing them. It is, for example, utterly characteristic of Posthumus that at the very moment of reunion with Innogen he should treat her with violence, however unconsciously—and equally characteristic that in the next line it should be the ever-compassionate Pisanio who intervenes to help her, serving to emphasize the important theatrical point that Innogen spends much more time on stage with Pisanio (1.3, 3.2, 3.4) than with Posthumus. It is only in this scene and the opening one that hero and heroine appear on stage together, and this is perhaps in itself an image of their relationship: it exists and does not exist; they know and do not know each other; and for much of the play Pisanio acts not only as Innogen's loyal supporter and counsellor, but as a surrogate for Posthumus' better qualities, as Cloten is for his worse ones. When Posthumus realizes whom he has struck, his intensity is expressed (and perhaps his physical movement is reflected) in another of those vivid phrases alluding to horses, this time the disease that makes them unsteady: 'How comes these staggers on me?' (5.4.233). And when their reunion finally takes place, Innogen uses an image as extravagant as his behaviour (in order to comment on it?), suggesting as she embraces him that he should throw her off a rock into the sea:

> Think that you are upon a rock, and now
> Throw me again.[1]

In responding, Posthumus turns to the natural world for an image already used by Belarius at 3.3.60–1:

> Hang there like fruit, my soul,
> Till the tree die.
>
> (5.4.262–4)

These lines are justly famous; but their expression of something indissolubly linked depends for its full effect on the contrast with his striking her only a few moments before: the more violent he was then, the more overwhelming this moment seems now. Once again, the play's technique of contrasting extremes is in full operation.

Powerful and moving though this reunion is, and 'The more delayed, delighted' (5.3.196) for the audience as well as for the participants, it is not the only emotional climax in the scene: as in the final scene of *Twelfth Night*, the reunion of the siblings usually has at least as much impact in performance as that between the lovers. In William Gaskill's 1962 production, for example, Vanessa Redgrave's delivery of

> O my gentle brothers,
> Have we thus met? O never say hereafter
> But I am truest speaker. You called me brother
> When I was but your sister, I you brothers
> When ye were so indeed
>
> (5.4.375–9)

'held the audience by its large impression of new-born wonder and spontaneous joy'.[2] And this testimony to the emotional impact of

---

[1] 'Rock' is the Folio's reading, often disputed. For a justification of retaining it in this edition, see the Commentary to l. 262.

[2] John Russell Brown, 'Acting Shakespeare Today', *SS* 16 (1963), 143–51; p. 150.

what might seem matter-of-fact lines is especially interesting since Gaskill's was a staging which emphasized the overt theatricality of the play. Again like the finale of *Twelfth Night*, this scene insists on such apparently prosaic identifying details as 'Guiderius had | Upon his neck a mole, a sanguine star' (5.4.364–5), matching that of his sister, which was earlier used as a more dangerous kind of identification. These lines can draw laughter from an audience; but far from diminishing the tenderness and joy of the family reunion, that laughter can enhance them by contrast, as it can in the similar revelation at *Twelfth Night* 5.1.240–6.

Performance also regularly brings out the emotional quality of Belarius' blessing as he takes leave of his foster-children:

> The benediction of these covering heavens
> Fall on their heads like dew, for they are worthy
> To inlay heaven with stars.

(5.4.351–3)

Cymbeline completes that last line with the comment 'Thou weep'st, and speak'st', implying that Belarius delivers the blessing in a voice choked with emotion, as Michael Gough does in the BBC television production, with the two princes clinging to him, reluctant to be parted from him, even if they are heirs to a kingdom.[1] But there is nothing sentimental about this episode. Just as the reunion of Posthumus and Innogen is preceded by his striking her, so this tender moment for Belarius, shared in the same line by Cymbeline, is preceded only a few moments earlier by Cymbeline's threat to kill him. All Cymbeline's old wrath at what he takes to have been Belarius' treason, despite the passage of twenty years, and despite the fact that Belarius has just helped to save his kingdom, pours ungratefully out: 'Take him hence, | The whole world shall not save him' (5.4.321–2). At the end of the play, Cymbeline is very ready to blame the Queen for the war with Rome (5.4.463–4), but even with her influence removed, he still remains to an extent the choleric tyrant that he was at the beginning. He shows, as Posthumus does earlier, that no one changes overnight. But Cymbeline learns from Posthumus himself, whose forgiveness of Giacomo—a significant difference from other versions of the wager

---

[1] Compare John Russell Brown's account of Paul Hardwick's 'affecting' handling of the episode at Stratford-upon-Avon in 1962 (see the previous note).

story—prompts him to show magnanimity, rather late in the day, to the Romans, another indication of the way in which personal relationships in this play influence public ones.

Stanley Wells suggests that the conclusion of Underdowne's translation of Heliodorus' *Ethiopica*, already cited in this introduction as an influence on the play, provides a parallel to the tone of *Cymbeline*, its characteristic mingling of the extremes of happiness and sadness.[1] Heliodorus says that the gods' will

was that this should fall out wonderfully, as in a comedy. Surely they made very contrary things agree, and joined sorrow and mirth, tears and laughter, together, and turned fearful and terrible things into a joyful banquet in the end; many that wept began to laugh, and such as were sorrowful to rejoice, when they found that they sought not for, and lost that they hoped to find; and to be short, the cruel slaughters which were looked for every moment were turned into holy sacrifice.

'Many that wept began to laugh': this phrase helps to emphasize the part played by laughter in the final scene of *Cymbeline* as well, to some extent on the stage, and also in the audience. This is not, in my experience of performances, laughter at a play mocking its own artifice, but the laughter which comes from the release of long-pent-up tension. Certain lines seem strategically placed frankly to invite such a release: the Doctor's 'I left out one thing which the Queen confessed' (5.4.244) is one example, and Guiderius' blunt revelation about Cloten,

> I cut off's head,
> And am right glad he is not standing here
> To tell this tale of mine
>
> (5.4.296–8)

is another: Guiderius is simultaneously 'young prince and young savage', as Granville Barker puts it (p. 71). This laughter coexists with, and emphasizes by contrast, the hard-won happiness of the central characters. The Doctor promised the audience at 1.5.42 that whoever took his drug would 'be more fresh, reviving'. That is the effect of the end of the play, both in the characters' personal relationships and in the renewed peace between Britain and Rome.

That peace, Stanley Wells goes on to say, may have reminded the original audiences 'both that the reign of King Cymbeline

---

[1] *Shakespeare: A Dramatic Life* (1994), pp. 358–9.

spanned the time of universal peace—the *pax Romana*—during which Jesus Christ was born in Bethlehem, and that their current king, James I, who liked to be known as Jacobus Pacificus, prided himself especially on his achievements as a peacemaker who had brought about the union of the British isles'. Emrys Jones argues that these two facts help to explain why Shakespeare chose to set his play in the reign of Cymbeline, and in particular why the Roman army travels to and from Britain, not via the south of England, where Julius Caesar invaded, but via Milford Haven in Wales—'not, on the face of it, the directest route', as Jones dryly observes.[1] Milford Haven obviously becomes the focus for events in the second half of the play; Jones points out that it had a wider significance outside it. Milford Haven's resonance for sixteenth- and seventeenth-century audiences was that it was the port at which Henry Tudor (Shakespeare's Richmond in *Richard III*) landed in 1485 to establish the Tudor dynasty, of which Elizabeth I was the last representative, and to which James I was keen to present himself as the natural successor, genetically (both his parents were direct descendants of Henry VII) and symbolically, inheriting Henry's role as unifier and peacemaker. He called himself a 'Western King', and Jones suggests that in the final peace tableau Cymbeline is a mirror of James, 'the great Western King...magnanimously radiating Peace'. That would help to explain why Cymbeline is characterized so slightly (though his tendency to tyranny might discourage too direct an equation with James), and why the Queen is made 'conventionally grotesque after a fairy tale fashion' rather than a figure of genuine evil, thus avoiding the risk of any equation with James's own queen. It seems likely that the international peace with which the play ends was intended to appeal to James, who saw himself not only as the bringer of peaceful unity to Britain but as the peacemaker of Europe; but the very fact that Cymbeline and the Queen are, theatrically, the least successful (and the least central) of the major characters makes it improbable that the entire play was

---

[1] 'Stuart *Cymbeline*', *Essays in Criticism*, 11 (1961), pp. 84–99. Other studies relating the play to James I's court include: Bernard Harris, '"What's past is prologue": *Cymbeline* and *Henry VIII*' in *Later Shakespeare*, Stratford-upon-Avon Studies, 8 (1966), pp. 203–33; David Bergeron, *Shakespeare's Romances and the Royal Family* (Kansas, 1985); Brian Gibbons, *Shakespeare and Multiplicity* (Cambridge, 1993), pp. 25–9.

written to evoke the court world of James, as Jones implies when he says that 'the dramatist has evoked a body of knowledge, shared by the audience, which doubtless provided a kind of inter-pretative key to events on the stage which, without such a key, appear insufficiently motivated, almost incoherent'. This intro-duction has suggested that no such 'key' is needed, since the play creates, arguably to a greater extent than many of Shake-speare's other plays, its own self-sufficient theatrical world, requiring no explanation beyond itself. If it did, it would not work as well as it does in modern performance. The connection with James I, therefore, seems to me a 'grace note', rather than an issue of central importance. It may, however, help to shed light on the complex question of when the play was written.

Date

The sole surviving reference to *Cymbeline* in Shakespeare's lifetime is Simon Forman's account of the performance he saw;[1] it is unfortunately undated, but it must have been before 8 September 1611, the day on which Forman was drowned. But how long before? At least since Dowden's view in his edition of 1903, quoted on p. 15 above, it has been generally agreed that *Cymbeline* was written in close proximity to *The Winter's Tale* and *The Tempest*, but it is not easy to establish a chronology. It used to be assumed that the natural order was *Cymbeline*, *Winter's Tale*, *Tempest*, but this was based purely upon evaluative judgements about relative qual-ity: Shakespeare 'fumbled in *Cymbeline*, did better in *The Winter's Tale*, and only in his last attempt achieved full success' is a repres-entative statement of a view still encountered.[2] Gary Taylor, however, points out that tests based upon the frequency of collo-quialisms in the verse and upon rare vocabulary suggest that *The Winter's Tale* may be the earlier of the two (*Textual Companion*, pp. 101–9, 131–2). But these tests can as easily imply the close proximity of the two plays as the precedence of either, and this proximity is what we should expect from the similarities of tech-nique and subject matter discussed at the start of this introduction, particularly between the obsessive jealousy of Posthumus and Leontes, and the fact that the punishment of Giacomo's equivalent

---

[1] See above, p. 4.
[2] E. M. W. Tillyard, *Shakespeare's Last Plays* (1938), p. 1.

in Boccaccio's version of the wager story (his naked body is smeared with honey and consumed by mosquitoes, wasps, and horseflies), though not used in *Cymbeline*, crops up in Autolycus' threats to the young shepherd in *The Winter's Tale* (4.4.784–92).

Indeed, J. M. Nosworthy in his Arden edition argues that the composition of the two plays was 'more or less simultaneous or, at any rate, that both had been written, revised and prepared for the stage before either was actually performed, with consequent cross-fertilisation' (p. xvi). Stanley Wells objects, privately, that no dramatist writes two major works at the same time; but in view of the prolonged outbreak of plague that kept the theatres closed from August 1608 to late 1609 or even early 1610, it would be surprising if Shakespeare had not been at least thinking about the new works that would be needed when they reopened. The enforced closure would have provided him with the opportunity for reading or rereading[1] the wide variety of material that he draws on for *Cymbeline* in particular.[2] But to plan works is not necessarily to complete them, and either *Cymbeline* or *The Winter's Tale* could still have been unfinished after the period of closure. And other evidence suggests a date of 1610 for *Cymbeline*.

In June 1610 James I's elder son Henry was invested as Prince of Wales, and the investiture was celebrated at court with many entertainments between 31 May and 6 June. One of these, Samuel Daniel's masque *Tethys' Festival*, performed at Whitehall on 5 June 1610, provides a good example of the symbolic overtones of Milford Haven for the Jacobean court, discussed in the previous section. Milford is described as

> The happy port of union, which gave way
> To that great hero Henry and his fleet,
> To make the blest conjunction that begat
> O greater and more glorious far than that.
> (149–52)[3]

---

[1] See p. 34 n. 1, and J. P. Brockbank, 'History and Histrionics in *Cymbeline*', *SS 11* (1958), 42–9; p. 43.

[2] The often-canvassed similarities between *Cymbeline* and Beaumont and Fletcher's *Philaster* shed no light on the question, since there is no agreement upon which influenced the other (if either did), and the date of *Philaster* is uncertain: the Revels edn. (1969) suggests mid-1609 (pp. xxvii–xxviii). See the discussion on p. 10 above.

[3] Samuel Daniel, *Complete Works*, ed. A. B. Grosart, 5 vols. (1885), iii. 314.

As James's own theatrical company, the King's Men were presumably involved in some of the entertainments celebrating the investiture, and Geoffrey Bullough speculates that *Cymbeline*, with its focus on Milford Haven, 'may well have been composed, or adapted, for production at that time' (p. 7). He also points out that the King's friend Sir James Hay was made a Knight of the Bath during the investiture, on 4 June 1610 : he was descended from that Hay who, with his two sons, turned the Danes' rout of the Scots at the Battle of Luncarty into victory (see above, p. 53); the Hays were so proud of their ancestor's achievement that their coat of arms alluded to it, and Bullough argues that 'the King and his courtiers would recognize the Hay ancestry in the feat of Belarius and the two boys' (p. 12). But it is also possible that the ennobling of Hay *reminded* Shakespeare of the story of Hay's ancestors which he had already encountered in his reading for *Macbeth*, and this would push the composition of at any rate the last act of *Cymbeline* later than 4 June 1610; but probably not much later. In July 1610, Arabella Stuart, who had a claim on the English throne, married William Seymour and was imprisoned in the Tower, where she died. The similarity to the marriage of heir to the throne and commoner in *Cymbeline* would have made the choice of subject tactless after July 1610 for a play that might be seen at court. But the chief evidence for 1610 comes from a theatrical source far removed from the court.

The title-page of Thomas Heywood's *The Golden Age* says that it was 'sundry times acted at the Red Bull', a popular public theatre. This play is the first of a series about the four Ages of classical mythology : Gold, Silver, Brazen, and Iron. There seems to have been some irregularity about the printing of *The Golden Age*, since in an epistle to the reader Heywood speaks of the play 'coming accidentally to the press . . . without . . . title for acknowledgement'. His phrase 'at length having notice thereof' implies that he found out about the imminent publication in time to insert his epistle and a title-page stating his authorship. This may explain why the title-page has two dates on it : a printer's date of 1611 (supported by the play's entry in the Stationers' Register on 14 October 1611) and, after a Latin epigraph, 1610. The latter may tell us when Heywood wrote it, since in his epistle he says that *The Golden Age* is 'the eldest brother of three Ages that have adventured the stage, but the only yet that hath been judged to the press'. This suggests that the first three plays of the series had been written and performed, but that *The Silver Age* and *The Brazen Age* had not yet been published: they eventually appeared in 1613 (*The Iron Age* not until 1632). Working backwards from a publication date of late 1611 for *The Golden Age*, and allowing time (just) for the other two plays to be written and performed as well, supports a date of 1610 for the composition of *The Golden Age*.

What has all this to do with *Cymbeline*? At the end of *The Golden Age*, Jupiter '*ascends upon the eagle*' to the heavens. Jupiter is the central character of *The Golden Age*, so this ascent is an appropriate climax. The descent and ascent of Jupiter in *Cymbeline*, however, though anticipated verbally in the play, are not central in the same way, so Shakespeare might seem to be borrowing a spectacular effect from the Red Bull; but other evidence points decisively in the opposite direction. There are numerous borrowings from Shakespeare's earlier plays in *The Golden Age*, of which the most blatant are 'I'll kiss thee ere I kill thee' (Act 1, page 18,[1] clearly echoing 'I kissed thee ere I killed thee' at *Othello* 5.2.368) and the Clown's borrowing the Jupiter/gibbet-maker wordplay from the Clown in *Titus Andronicus* (*Golden Age* Act 3, p. 45; *Titus* 4.3.79–80). The most extensive of these occurs in Act 4 of *The Golden Age*, where Heywood dramatizes the legend of Jupiter seducing Danaë in the form of a shower of gold, here a matter of bribing the four crones who guard her. The ensuing bedroom scene provides a good example of how beds were brought on stage in theatres of the period: '*Enter the four old beldams, drawing out Danaë's bed, she in it*' (p. 67; Innogen's bed was probably 'drawn out' at the start of *Cymbeline* 2.2). Jupiter then has a long description of the sleeping Danaë which contains these lines:

> Charming sleep,
> Death's younger brother, show thyself as still-less[2]
> As death himself....
> O thou more beauteous in thy nakedness
> Than ornament can add to—
> How sweetly doth she breathe, how well become

---

[1] Quotations are from Heywood's *Dramatic Works*, ed. R. H. Shepherd, 6 vols. (1874), vol. 3. Since there are act divisions but no line numbers, acts and page numbers are given here.

[2] A slip for 'stir-less'?

> Imaginary deadness! But I'll wake her
> Unto new life.   (p. 68)

This was surely inspired by Giacomo's speech over the sleeping Innogen, especially by

> 'Tis her breathing that
> Perfumes the chamber thus....
> O sleep, thou ape of death, lie dull upon her
>   (2.2.18–19, 31)

and by Giacomo's being carried away by Innogen's beauty and needing to check himself (2.2.23). Perhaps, too, Heywood's 'I'll wake her | Unto new life' echoes the Doctor's remark that those who take his drug will appear to die only 'To be more fresh, reviving' (1.5.42), and indeed the episode of Innogen waking beside Cloten's corpse. It might be argued that Shakespeare borrowed from Heywood, but Heywood's indisputable echoes of Shakespeare's other plays suggest that he was the borrower. This is the more likely in that, although *The Golden Age* is closely based upon Heywood's own poem *Troia Britannica* (published 1609), there is no model for Jupiter's speech in the poem. The inspiration seems to have come from *Cymbeline*.

If so, and if the information about 1610 on the title-page of *The Golden Age* does reflect its date of composition, *Cymbeline* must have been written and performed by autumn 1610 at latest. This accords with the other evidence discussed, slight as that is.[1] It also helps to clarify the play's relation to *The Tempest*. Gary Taylor remarks that 'although we cannot be positive that [*The Tempest*] followed *Cymbeline*, that does remain the most probable interpretation of the data at our disposal' (*Textual Companion*, p. 132); a date of autumn 1610 for *Cymbeline* confirms that 'interpretation', since, as Taylor says, *The Tempest* 'is indebted to sources which were not available before September 1610'.

The Text

Cymbeline first appeared in print in the First Folio edition of Shakespeare's plays in 1623. It was entered in the Stationers' Register

---

[1] A further contributory crumb is Emrys Jones's point that '1610 was the only year, of this period, in which all the European states were at peace' (see p. 62 n. 1),

on 8 November 1623, together with the fifteen other plays not previously registered for publication. The text is generally clean, presenting few major problems. An important exception is the spelling of the heroine's name; the reasons for believing the Folio's 'Imogen' an error, and so for emending it, are given in Appendix A. It is customary to differentiate the compositors of the First Folio by letter: *Cymbeline* was set by Compositor B, except for five pages (Folio page numbers 372, 374, 376, 378, 381; signatures zz4^v, 5^v, 6^v, aaa1^v, 3), set by Compositor E. Although Compositor B was experienced, and responsible for setting about half the pages of the First Folio, he could be careless. Compositor E was the least experienced of the Folio compositors, and was probably an apprentice.[1] Since both were prone to error, the clean text they provided suggests that the copy for it is unlikely to have been Shakespeare's manuscript, as his handwriting seems to have caused compositors problems, but was probably a scribal transcript. If so, a strong candidate for its preparation is Ralph Crane.

Crane was a professional scribe known to have worked for the King's Men.[2] Because of the fortunate survival of certain plays, notably Thomas Middleton's *A Game at Chess*, both in the dramatist's manuscripts and in transcripts by Crane, we have a great deal of information about Crane's scribal characteristics and about how he handled an author's text. Drawing on such evidence, modern scholarship has concluded that Crane prepared the copy for the first four plays in the Folio volume (*The Tempest*, *The Two Gentlemen of Verona*, *The Merry Wives of Windsor*, *Measure for Measure*) and for *The Winter's Tale*; and J. C. Maxwell in his edition of *Cymbeline* suggested that it too shows some of the features of Crane's transcripts (p. 126). These can be conveniently considered under three headings: punctuation, spelling, and stage directions.

Crane's punctuation was heavy. His transcripts show a liberal use of parentheses (i.e. round brackets), hyphens, apostrophes, capitalization, and colons; all are frequent in *Cymbeline*. The most thorough examination of Crane's work, to which this discus-

---

though this will carry greater or lesser weight depending upon the extent to which one thinks that the final peace tableau was specifically designed to reflect James I's 'strenuous peace-making policy'.

[1] Further information is available in Charlton Hinman, *The Printing and Proof-Reading of the First Folio of Shakespeare*, 2 vols. (Oxford, 1963), i. 180–226.

[2] Further details are provided in *Textual Companion*, pp. 20–2.

sion is greatly indebted, has been carried out by T. H. Howard-Hill. He made two comparative tests on the punctuation of *Cymbeline* and of known or probable Crane texts. The first test involved calculation of the proportion of sets of parentheses to Folio lines, 'a rough but consistent measure' of likely Crane presence: the proportion that he found in *Cymbeline* was a set of parentheses every 24.79 lines, close to the proportion for *The Tempest* (23.88) and of one of the *Game at Chess* transcripts, the Archdall manuscript (21.21). Howard-Hill adds: 'It is also worth noting in the general context that the Folio texts with the highest proportion of parentheses to lines are the rigorously edited texts' of *The Winter's Tale* (parentheses every 4.78 lines), *Merry Wives* (12.57) and *Two Gentlemen* (18.24).[1]

His second test concerned the frequency of 'hyphenated-prefixes in words beginning with "a, ante, be, de, dis, en, enter, for(e), in, ore, ont, over, re, un, under, up"', a good indication of Crane's influence'. Examples of such prefixes in *Cymbeline* would be 'fore-end' (3.3.73 / TLN 1632) or 'out-craftied' (3.4.15 / TLN 1685).[2] Howard-Hill compared the frequency of these in the five comedies attributed to Crane and in *Cymbeline*, *Twelfth Night*, *Coriolanus*, and *Antony and Cleopatra*; this test 'places *Cymbeline* third (i.e. amongst the Crane copy comedies)'. These two tests provide strong evidence of connections with the other plays showing signs of Crane transcription; and the material about round brackets has been supplemented by E. A. J. Honigmann, who emphasizes Crane's 'partiality for placing single words in brackets, a less common phenomenon than the use of brackets in general'.[3] Honigmann's calculation of the number of occurrences of these in the Folio plays generally agreed to be set from Crane transcripts yields an average of 41; my count of those in *Cymbeline* is 32 (interestingly close, incidentally, to Honigmann's count of 34 in the Folio text of *Othello*, a play of similar length, which he is proposing as another Crane transcript).

---

[1] 'Shakespeare's Earliest Editor, Ralph Crane', *SS* 44 (1992), 113–29; p. 128 n. 51.

[2] For convenience of reference, quotations in this section are keyed both to this edition and to the through line numbering (TLN) provided by Charlton Hinman in *The Norton Facsimile of the First Folio of Shakespeare* (1968, reprinted 1996).

[3] *The Texts of 'Othello' and Shakespearian Revision* (1996), p. 59.

As far as hyphens are concerned, it should be borne in mind that, as Howard-Hill points out elsewhere, the 'greatest number of the hyphenated-compounds are simple adjective-noun compounds [e.g. "Wedded-Lady" (1.6.2 / TLN 594)] which do not reveal Crane's influence with certainty' because they 'are not uncommon in printed texts' of the period.[1] Even 'Milford-Hauen' may reflect Crane's habits; Simon Forman's manuscript account of *Cymbeline* has 'Milford Hauen' unhyphenated as in the modern form. More elaborate hyphenated compounds are a distinctive feature of Crane transcripts. Examples in *Cymbeline* are 'not-fearing-Britaine' (2.4.19 / TLN 1164), 'rich-left-heyres' (4.2.227 / TLN 2536), 'scarce-cold-Battaile' (5.4.470 / TLN 3801); and I suspect that the hyphen in 'wild wood-leaues' (4.2.391 / TLN 2722) was not simply wrongly positioned (for 'wild-wood'; see the Commentary), but that the phrase in the copy read 'wild-wood-leaves', and only the second hyphen survived into the Folio text. On the other hand, there are no occurrences of such Crane characteristics as hypenated verb plus pronominal object (e.g. 'sty-me' at *Tempest* 1.2.344 / TLN 481)— but nor are there in *Measure for Measure*, one of the plays confidently attributed to Crane transcription—nor of 'pre-thee' for 'prithee'; but as Howard-Hill points out, 'no single manuscript shows all the characteristics which are now called Crane's'.[2]

Crane is inconsistent in his liberal use of apostrophes to represent elisions. Sometimes he uses them to mark colloquial ellipses. Examples in *Cymbeline* might include ' 'Please your Highnesse' (1.1.80 / TLN 94); 'y'are worthy of' (1.4.110 / TLN 430–1); and the abbreviation 'I'ld' or 'Il'd' for 'I'd' (e.g. 'such a welcome as I'ld giue to him' at 3.6.70 / TLN 2165). But others seem merely idiosyncratic, such as 'Whil'st' (e.g. 1.6.81 / TLN 687; 4.2.220 / TLN 2529), or are in the wrong place to indicate the elision: 'ta'en' (i.e. 'taken') is misrepresented as 't'ane' at 2.2.41 / TLN 948 (where the inexperienced Compositor E is almost certainly following his copy), and as ' 'tane' (e.g. at 3.4.108 / TLN 1785), set by Compositor B.[3] Another feature of Crane's

---

[1] *Ralph Crane and Some Shakespeare First Folio Comedies* (Charlottesville, 1972), hereafter *Comedies*, pp. 91, 40.

[2] *Comedies*, p. 9.

[3] To complete the picture, there are six occurrences of 'tane' with no apostrophe, which may be evidence of Crane reproducing what was in Shakespeare's

punctuation was the 'Jonsonian elision', whereby an apostrophe marks an elision, yet the syllable to be elided is nevertheless printed as well. There is no example of this in the Folio *Cymbeline* as it stands, but I think it probable that 'My Brother weares thee not the one halfe so well' (4.2.203 / TLN 2506), which appears to have an extra syllable, implies that there may have been a Jonsonian elision in the copy, i.e.: 'My Brother weares thee not the'one halfe so well'. Another such elision may have been responsible for the reading 'number'd', which this edition assumes is an error for 'unnumber'd' (1.6.36 / TLN 632), if the copy read 'Vpon the'unnumber'd Beach' and the inexperienced Compositor E omitted the wrong letters.

The question of Crane's spellings is complicated by the fact that spelling was not standardized in the seventeenth century: a word could be spelt in different ways in the same sentence by an author or by a compositor, particularly if space was tight in a 'justified' line. But when allowance is made for this, and also for the pre-ferred spellings of Compositor B where these are known,[1] several of Crane's characteristic spellings can be detected in the Folio text of *Cymbeline*. His known spelling 'ceiz'd' for 'seized' (2.2.7 / TLN 913) occurs elsewhere in the Folio only at *Measure for Measure* 2.1.23 / TLN 473 ('ceizes'). The Riverside edition of Shakespeare's works points out that 'one typical Crane spelling, *dampn'd*, has been changed to *damn'd* in the process of stop-press correction' (1.6.104 / TLN 716), so that one piece of evidence for Crane does not survive into the corrected state of Folio p. 374 (sig. zz5^v). Several idiosyncrasies noted by Howard-Hill (*Comedies*, pp. 66–7) occur frequently in *Cymbeline*, particularly the insertion of an extra letter in mid-word. As well as 'dampn'd' just noted, an internal 'a' occurs in numerous spellings ('cloake', 'cloathes', 'yoake'), an internal 'w' in 'valewation' (for 'valuation' at 4.4.49 / TLN 2850) and 'Continew'd' (5.4.381 / TLN 3700), and a doubling of the medial 't' in 'Brittish', 'citties', 'pittie/

manuscript, since 'tane' appears to have been at least *a* Shakespeare spelling, occurring in the pages of the manuscript play *Sir Thomas More* that are attributed to him, and in the 'good' Quartos where there may be 'show-through' of Shakespeare's preferred spellings (see p. 72 n. 1).

[1] Some of these are conveniently listed and discussed by W. S. Kable, 'Compositor B, The Pavier Quartos, and Copy Spellings', *Studies in Bibliography*, 21 (1968), 131–61, and by T. H. Howard-Hill, *Comedies* (see p. 70 n. 1), pp. 165–72.

pitty'.[1] Crane's invariable spelling of 'gift' as 'guift' is also the spelling in all five occurrences of the word in *Cymbeline*. And although 'go' has been established as Compositor B's preferred spelling, Crane's preference 'goe' survives in the first stage direction for the battle: '*They march ouer, and goe out*' (5.2.0.4 / TLN 2894–5). This survival in spite of B's preference is interesting because it is in the stage directions of Act 5 that Crane's influence is most strongly felt.

These stage directions are much fuller than elsewhere in the play, although they coexist with terse one-word instructions like '*Ascends*' for Jupiter at 5.3.207 / TLN 3149, and '*Vanish*' for the ghosts at 5.3.216 / TLN 3159. The extended directions resemble several elaborate ones in *The Tempest*, *All is True* (*Henry VIII*) and *The Two Noble Kinsmen*. Where they differ from those in *All is True* and *Kinsmen*, but resemble those in *The Tempest*, is in showing signs of Crane's phrasing as well as Shakespeare's. We know from Crane's transcripts of Middleton's manuscripts of *A Game at Chess* that he often rewrote stage directions from the point of view of a spectator, usually expanding them to help a reader visualize what is going on, and perhaps to reflect a contemporary staging. John Jowett has subjected the stage directions in *The Tempest* to careful scrutiny, and demonstrated that they probably expand and reword what Shakespeare originally wrote. Phrases like '*with a quient deuice*' (*Tempest* 3.3.52.3–4 / TLN 1584) or '*to a strange hollow and confused noyse, they heauily vanish*' (4.1.142.1–2 / TLN 1807–8) are unhelpfully vague for theatrical purposes, and almost certainly reflect Crane's phrasing rather than Shakespeare's.[2] The stage directions for the battle in *Cymbeline* are not vague in that way, but they seem 'literary', descriptive rather than theatrical: '*he vanquisheth and disarmeth Iachimo, and then leaues him*' (rather than something like '*They fight. Iachimo falls. Exit Posthumus*'), and particularly, after Giacomo's soliloquy, '*The Battaile*

---

[1] But since internal 'w' and doubled medial 't' also occur in the pages of *Sir Thomas More* attributed to Shakespeare and in the 'good' Quartos where Shakespearian spellings may 'show through', perhaps these habits should be attributed to Shakespeare as much as, or rather than, Crane (see *Shakespeare's Hand in 'The Play of Sir Thomas More'*, papers by A. W. Pollard, W. W. Greg, E. M. Thompson, J. Dover Wilson, and R. W. Chambers (Cambridge, 1923), pp. 113–41, 230–42).
[2] 'New Created Creatures: Ralph Crane and the Stage Directions in "The Tempest"', *SS 36* (1983), pp. 107–20.

continues' (5.2.0.5–7 / TLN 2896–7; 5.2.10.1 / TLN 2908). At the same time, the curt sound cues that usually accompany battle scenes, '*alarums*', '*excursions*', and so on, are absent; they are supplied editorially in this edition. Similar sound cues are missing elsewhere, notably for the formal state meeting between Cymbeline and Caius Lucius (3.1.0.1); these too have been supplied editorially. Possibly, in rewriting these directions for the reader, Crane accidentally omitted sound cues that were present in Shakespeare's manuscript; but I suspect that, here as elsewhere, Shakespeare 'did not specify ... in his foul papers ... anything so obviously appropriate'.[1]

There is still stronger evidence for Crane's presence in Posthumus' ghostly vision of his dead family (5.3.123.1–8). In the Folio, this begins: '*Solemne Musicke. Enter (as in an Apparation) Sicillius Leonatus ...*' (TLN 3065–6). John Jowett says of '(*as in an Apparation*)': 'exactly the same words occur, again within brackets, in at least two of Crane's transcripts of *A Game at Chess.* ... Middleton's wording was "*like an Apparition*".'[2] Crane's favoured round brackets occur three times in this stage direction; and as Jowett has found only one example of these brackets within stage directions in the Folio outside texts based on Crane transcriptions, at *King John* 5.2.0.1 / TLN 2250, they strongly suggest Crane annotation here. There is probably Crane phrasing too. '*Solemne Musicke*', which opens this stage direction, and which also occurs at 4.2.187 / TLN 2482, on three occasions in *The Tempest*, and in the scenes of *All is True* attributed to Fletcher, is unlikely to be Shakespeare's phrase. His preference was '*Still music*', as for example at the entry of Hymen in *As You Like It* 5.4.105.1 / TLN 2682. In view of the doubts cast upon Shakespeare's authorship of Posthumus' vision, I should emphasize that I am not suggesting that this direction does not substantially represent what Shakespeare wrote, merely that Crane annotated and perhaps modified it. This evidence, taken together with that provided by punctuation and spelling, makes it probable that Crane was the scribe who prepared the copy for the Folio text of

---

[1] Stanley Wells, *Re-Editing Shakespeare for the Modern Reader* (Oxford, 1984), p. 82.

[2] 'New Created Creatures', pp. 113–14. Jowett adds: 'The distinctive spelling "Apparation" is probably Compositor B's: it occurs twice in his stint in the stage directions of *Macbeth*.'

Cymbeline, even if it is less decisive than that for his transcription of the five Folio comedies confidently attributed to him.[1]

The Folio text of Act 5, however, raises problems of a different kind. The first is that the text as we have it appears to present the battle twice over: the audience sees it acted out in 5.2, and then hears about it again in Posthumus' long narration (5.3.3–51). It is possible that these are alternative versions. After writing 5.2, Shakespeare may have decided to present the battle instead through Posthumus' eyes, thus contributing to the general 'rehabilitation' of Posthumus as a hero that takes place from his reappearance in 5.1, both by restoring him to the centre of the action and by increasing his heroic stature. Perhaps Shakespeare intended to delete the rest of 5.2 after Giacomo's soliloquy, replacing the events with Posthumus' description of them, but then either failed to make the revision or to mark it sufficiently clearly.[2] The weakness of this argument is that there is no sign of textual disturbance at this point, so it is probably safer to conclude that the duplication is deliberate, Shakespeare choosing to show the audience the battle from the outside and then from the viewpoint of a participant.

There are, on the other hand, definite signs of textual disturbance later in the act. Act 5, Scene 3 in the Folio's version ends, after the arrest of Posthumus by the British captains, with this stage direction:

[1] Drawing primarily upon the varying spelling of the exclamation 'O'/'Oh' in the Folio text of *Cymbeline*, Gary Taylor and John Jowett argue that the Folio copy was based on an earlier transcript of Shakespeare's manuscript prepared by two different scribes, the first copying the play up to 2.4.152/TLN 1336, the second thereafter; the first, it is argued, wrote the exclamation as 'O', with a single 'oh' at 1.6.68/TLN 671; the second preferred 'oh', but used 'O' at 4.2.25/TLN 2275 (immediately after an 'Oh' in the previous line), 5.1.26/TLN 2883, 5.3.296/TLN 3243, 5.4.47/TLN 3307, and 5.4.382/TLN 3702. These differences cannot be compositorial, since they do not coincide with the different pages set by Compositors B and E (*Shakespeare Reshaped* (Oxford, 1993), pp. 248–59). This strikes me as an uneconomical hypothesis, particularly in view of Crane's 'habitual mixture of these spellings' (Howard-Hill, *Comedies*, p. 97). Indeed, the varying between 'O' and 'oh' may itself provide further evidence of Crane's presence in *Cymbeline*.

[2] A tiny shred of evidence in support of this may be found in Simon Forman's reference to *three* Britons (not four) defeating the Roman army (see p. 4 above). That is what he would have heard if Posthumus' narration had replaced the battle, since Posthumus suppresses his own contribution to the victory (5.3.28).

Enter Cymbeline, Belarius, Guiderius, Aruiragus Pisanio, and Romane Captiues. The Captaines present Posthumus to Cymbeline, who deliuers him ouer to a Gaoler. (TLN 3029–31)

The first sentence seems suspiciously similar to the one that opens the final scene, as if that scene were about to begin here. The second sentence presents no impediment to this view, since Posthumus could simply have been in the custody of a jailer until his intervention at 5.4.209. But then the Folio starts a new scene with the direction '*Enter Posthumus, and Gaoler*', when they are still on stage; and one line is spoken by a second jailer, to whom no further reference is made in stage directions or dialogue. Clearly something has gone wrong here. J. M. Nosworthy in his Arden edition records a conjecture by Alice Walker that the curious stage direction ending Folio 5.3 'looks almost like a note for an intended scene' (p. 161); but what would there be for the scene to do (and the play is already very long)—unless this was a reminder for the scene that we actually have, perhaps to be written after an interval of time? If so, it might subsequently have been started on a fresh page, perhaps headed 'Posthumus and Gaoler', which was then mistaken for a stage direction by the Folio copyist. Once again, Shakespeare's motivation for the addition of 5.3.95–298, if that is what happened, seems to have been to increase the centrality of Posthumus in the scheme of the play by giving him, not merely the conversation with the Jailer, but the spectacular vision of Jupiter.

If this scene did start on a fresh sheet, or if the entire scene was written on separate sheets marked to be inserted between 5.3.94.5 / TLN 3031 and the start of the final scene, that raises once more the possibility of interpolation : if the scene was separated from the main body of the play, might it not be by a different author? Had the entry of the ghosts opened the scene, instead of coming twenty-nine lines into it, that might have been a possibility; but it is preceded and followed by soliloquies for Posthumus, and his conversations with the Jailer, whose authenticity is not in question. The whole scene must stand or fall together; if it was an interpolated afterthought, it was an interpolation by Shakespeare himself. So in the end the hints of textual disturbance support rather than question Shakespeare's authorship of the scene.

That does not, however, quite dispose of the difficulties of this act. Placing the whole burden of Act 5 up to the final scene on

Posthumus' shoulders after he has been offstage since the end of Act 2 is asking a great deal of the actor. I have suggested that Shakespeare may have intended to revise the early part of Act 5. I think that this act, and perhaps earlier sections of a very long play, would have benefited from the kind of revision and consequent tightening that is evident in the Folio text of *King Lear*.[1] Such authorial revision might have forestalled the severe cutting in several modern productions; it is one thing for Shakespeare to revise and adjust the proportions of his play, another for modern directors to do so for him.

This issue was raised in an extreme form by the most recent production at the time of writing, Adrian Noble's at Stratford-upon-Avon in 1997, which cut about 1,000 lines—nearly a third of the play. It also provided further evidence about issues of the play discussed earlier in this introduction, which will conclude with a brief account of it. Noble translated the play's overt theatricality into that of a very different theatrical tradition, Japanese kabuki, so that the play was presented within a (largely oriental) fairy-tale framework. The combination of the severe cutting and the artificial frame had the effect of simplifying the wager plot in particular. With so much of the material omitted, Posthumus had no opportunity to explore the dark emotional mistrust underlying the wager: he could only be the victim of a machiavellian trickster. Yet Noble included, perhaps perversely, both the battle *and* Posthumus' account of it, somewhat shortened, without offering any theatrical solution to the duplication.

Not for the first time in a production of this play, however, the Welsh scenes were particularly effective. This was partly because, at least to start with, they were less heavily cut, but still more because they emphasized how the humour they contain brings out the warm humanity of the relationship between Belarius and the princes, and especially between the princes and Innogen, a performance of limpid clarity from Joanne Pearce which had the great merit of communicating very directly not only with the other characters but with the audience too. Building upon the success of these scenes, the family reunions at the end were very convincing, Joanne Pearce radiant in her delivery of her answer to

---

[1] Evidence for this is set out in, for example, *The Division of the Kingdoms*, ed. Gary Taylor and Michael Warren (Oxford, 1983).

Cymbeline's 'Thou hast lost by this a kingdom': 'No, my lord, | I have got *two worlds* by't' (5.4.374–5); and when she asked Posthumus 'Why did you throw your wedded lady from you?' (5.4.261), the question seemed to apply not merely to the immediate situation, but to his lack of faith in the first place—making it the more regrettable that this had not been more fully explored.

By now Noble's strategy was clear. As in his production of *The Winter's Tale* at the same theatre in 1992, the centre of gravity lay with the rural scenes rather than with the court ones, which were ruthlessly cut back in both plays in order to focus on new life and reunion. But this one-sided emphasis obscured the crucial point that both plays depend upon making the most of contrasting extremes: the greater the impact of the sexual mistrust and violence, the greater the effect of the positives that are set against it, as the most successful stagings of *Cymbeline*, William Gaskill's in 1962 and Peter Hall's in 1988, made clear. It is no accident that both productions used very full texts. They recognized that some sense of sprawl is the price to be paid for the play's range and achievement in creating its own mythical world, and that it needs space and time to unfold and to make its full impact.

EDITORIAL PROCEDURES

THIS edition follows the Editorial Procedures established for the series by Stanley Wells and summarized in Gary Taylor's Oxford Shakespeare edition of *Henry V* (1982), pp. 75–81. In accordance with them, passages from Shakespeare's contemporaries quoted in the introduction and commentary are also modernized even when they are taken from editions using old spelling; as Taylor says, 'If modernizing is valid for Shakespeare's text it is equally valid for passages quoted only to illuminate that text'. Where old spelling is relevant, for example in the collations, the early use of u, v, i, and j is retained, but not long 's'.

Stage directions such as 'aside' or 'to' a character are all editorial, and are not collated; nor are act and scene divisions, except on the few occasions when those of the Folio text are not followed. All changes in directions for stage action are listed in the collations, but where the specified action is clearly implied by the dialogue, the change is neither bracketed in the text nor attributed to an earlier editor. Disputable directions (for example, '*She embraces the body*' at 4.2.333.1) are bracketed. Speech-prefixes are silently normalized.

Quotations from the Bible are normally from the Geneva Bible of 1560; those from classical Latin works are from the Loeb editions. References to other works of Shakespeare are from the Oxford *Complete Works*, Compact Edition (1988). References to works by Shakespeare's contemporaries are to major modern editions (wherever possible, to the Revels plays series).

I have often adopted punctuation lighter than that required by strictly grammatical modern usage, in order to preserve the shape and rhythm of the verse lines as much as possible.

Abbreviations and References

The following references are used in the introduction, in the collations, and in the commentary. In all bibliographical references, the place of publication is London, unless otherwise specified.

EDITIONS OF SHAKESPEARE

F, F1	The First Folio, 1623
F2	The Second Folio, 1632
F3	The Third Folio, 1663
F4	The Fourth Folio, 1685
Boswell	James Boswell, *Plays and Poems*, 21 vols. (1821)
Cambridge	W. G. Clark and W. A. Wright, *Works*, The Cambridge Shakespeare, 9 vols. (Cambridge, 1863–6)
Capell	Edward Capell, *Comedies, Histories, and Tragedies*, 10 vols. (1767–8)
Collier	John Payne Collier, *Comedies, Histories, Tragedies, and Poems*, 'The Second Edition', 6 vols. (1858)
Craig	W. J. Craig, *Works* (1891)
Dowden	Edward Dowden, *Cymbeline*, The Arden Shakespeare (1903)
Dyce	Alexander Dyce, *Works*, 6 vols. (1857)
Furness	H. H. Furness, *Cymbeline*, A New Variorum Edition (Philadelphia, 1913)
Globe	W. G. Clark and W. A. Wright, *Works* (1864)
Hanmer	Thomas Hanmer, *Works*, 6 vols. (Oxford, 1743–4)
Hudson	H. N. Hudson, *Works*, 11 vols. (Boston, 1851–6)
Hudson 1881	H. N. Hudson, *Works*, 20 vols. (Boston, 1880–1)
Ingleby	C. M. Ingleby, *Cymbeline* (1886)
Johnson	Samuel Johnson, *Plays*, 8 vols. (1765)
Knight	Charles Knight, *Comedies, Histories, Tragedies, and Poems*, Pictorial Edition, 55 parts (1838–43)
Malone	Edmond Malone, *Plays and Poems*, 10 vols. (1790)
Maxwell	J. C. Maxwell, *Cymbeline*, The New Shakespeare (Cambridge, 1960)
Neilson–Hill	William Allan Neilson and Charles Jarvis Hill, *Complete Plays and Poems* (Cambridge, Mass., 1942)
Nosworthy	J. M. Nosworthy, *Cymbeline*, The Arden Shakespeare (1955)
Oxford	Stanley Wells and Gary Taylor, *Complete Works* (Oxford, 1986; Compact Edition, 1988)
Pope	Alexander Pope, *Works*, 6 vols. (1723–5)
Pope 1728	Alexander Pope, *Works*, 10 vols. (1728)

Rann	Joseph Rann, *Dramatic Works*, 6 vols. (Oxford, 1786–94)
Riverside	G. B. Evans (textual editor), *The Riverside Shakespeare* (2nd edn., Boston, 1997)
Rowe	Nicholas Rowe, *Works*, 6 vols. (1709)
Rowe 1714	Nicholas Rowe, *Works*, 8 vols. (1714)
Singer	Samuel W. Singer, *Dramatic Works*, 10 vols. (1826)
Singer 1856	Samuel W. Singer, *Dramatic Works*, 10 vols. (1856)
Steevens	Samuel Johnson and George Steevens, *Plays*, 10 vols. (1773)
Steevens 1778	Samuel Johnson and George Steevens, *Plays*, 10 vols. (1778)
Steevens–Reed 1793	George Steevens and Isaac Reed, *Plays*, 15 vols. (1793)
Theobald	Lewis Theobald, *Works*, 7 vols. (1733)
Theobald 1740	Lewis Theobald, *Works*, 8 vols. (1740)
Warburton	Alexander Pope and William Warburton, *Works*, 8 vols. (1747)

OTHER WORKS

Abbott	E. A. Abbott, *A Shakespearian Grammar*, 2nd edn. (1870)
Bullough	Geoffrey Bullough, *Narrative and Dramatic Sources of Shakespeare*, vol. 8, Romances (1975)
Cartwright	Robert Cartwright, *New Readings in Shakespeare* (1866)
COD	*The Concise Oxford Dictionary*, 7th edn. (Oxford, 1982)
Daniel	P. A. Daniel, *Notes and Conjectural Emendations of Certain Doubtful Passages in Shakespeare's Plays* (1870)
Douce	Francis Douce, *Illustrations of Shakespeare* (1807)
Granville Barker	Harley Granville Barker, *Prefaces to Shakespeare: Cymbeline*, revised edn. (1930), reprinted by Nick Hern Books (1993)
Fairfax	Edward Fairfax, *Godfrey of Bulloigne*, ed. K. M. Lea and T. M. Gang (Oxford, 1981)
Heliodorus	*Ethiopica*, translated as *An Aethiopian History* by Thomas Underdowne, The Tudor Translations (1895)
Henslowe's Diary	*Henslowe's Diary*, ed. R. A. Foakes and R. T. Rickert (Cambridge, 1961)
Kellner	Leon Kellner, *Restoring Shakespeare* (1925)

Mason	John Monck Mason, *Comments on the Last Edition of Shakespeare's Plays* (Dublin, 1785)
OED	The Oxford English Dictionary, 2nd edn., 20 vols. (Oxford, 1989)
Onions	C. T. Onions, *A Shakespeare Glossary*, 2nd edn., with enlarged addenda (Oxford, 1953)
Plutarch	*Shakespeare's Plutarch*, ed. T. J. B. Spencer, Penguin Shakespeare Library (Harmondsworth, 1968)
Ritson	Joseph Ritson, *Remarks, Critical and Illustrative, on the Text and Notes of the Last Edition of Shakespeare* (1783)
Schmidt	Alexander Schmidt, *Shakespeare-Lexicon*, 2 vols. (Berlin and Leipzig, 1923)
Seymour	E. H. Seymour, *Remarks . . . upon the Plays of Shakespeare*, 2 vols. (1805)
SR	Stationers' Register
SS	*Shakespeare Survey*
Sutherland	James Sutherland, 'The Language of the Last Plays', in *More Talking of Shakespeare*, ed. J. Garrett (1959), pp. 144–58
Textual Companion	Stanley Wells and Gary Taylor, with John Jowett and William Montgomery, *William Shakespeare: A Textual Companion* (Oxford, 1987)
Thirlby	Styan Thirlby's unpublished conjectures (mainly manuscript annotations in his copies of early eighteenth-century editions)
Tilley	M. P. Tilley, *A Dictionary of the Proverbs in England in the Sixteenth and Seventeenth Centuries* (Ann Arbor, 1950)
Tyrwhitt	Thomas Tyrwhitt, *Observations and Conjectures upon Some Passages of Shakespeare* (Oxford, 1766)
W. S. Walker	W. S. Walker, *A Critical Examination of the Text of Shakespeare*, ed. W. N. Lettsom, 3 vols. (1860)
Wright, *Dialect Dictionary*	Joseph Wright, *The Dialect Dictionary*, 6 vols. (1898–1905)

Cymbeline

THE PERSONS OF THE PLAY

CYMBELINE, King of Britain

THE QUEEN, his second wife

INNOGEN, his daughter by a former queen, later disguised as the page Fidele

POSTHUMUS LEONATUS, her husband

CLOTEN, the Queen's son by a former husband

PISANIO, Posthumus' servant

CORNELIUS, a doctor

HELEN, a lady attending Innogen

Two LORDS attending Cloten

Two GENTLEMEN

Two British CAPTAINS

Two JAILERS

PHILARIO, Posthumus' host in Rome

GIACOMO, an Italian gentleman
A FRENCHMAN
A DUTCHMAN
A SPANIARD
} Philario's friends

CAIUS LUCIUS, Roman ambassador and later general of the Roman army

PHILHARMONUS, a soothsayer

Two Roman SENATORS

Roman TRIBUNES

A Roman CAPTAIN

BELARIUS, a banished lord living near Milford Haven, Wales, under the name Morgan

GUIDERIUS } Cymbeline's sons, but known as Belarius' sons Polydore
ARVIRAGUS } and Cadwal

JUPITER, King of the gods
SICILIUS Leonatus, Posthumus' father
His wife, Posthumus' MOTHER
Posthumus' two BROTHERS

} Apparitions

Lords, ladies, musicians, messengers, soldiers

Cymbeline

I.I   *Enter two Gentlemen*

FIRST GENTLEMAN

You do not meet a man but frowns. Our bloods
No more obey the heavens than our courtiers
Still seem as does the King.

SECOND GENTLEMAN   But what's the matter?

FIRST GENTLEMAN

His daughter, and the heir of's kingdom, whom
He purposed to his wife's sole son—a widow   5
That late he married—hath referred herself
Unto a poor but worthy gentleman. She's wedded,
Her husband banished, she imprisoned. All
Is outward sorrow, though I think the King
Be touched at very heart.

SECOND GENTLEMAN   None but the King?   10

FIRST GENTLEMAN

He that hath lost her too; so is the Queen,

Cymbeline] *Cymbeline King of Britaine* F (*table of contents*); THE TRAGEDIE OF CYMBELINE F
(*head-title; and running titles, alternating with 'Tragedy'*); *Cymbeline* SR
   1.1.2 courtiers,] BOSWELL (*conj.* Tyrwhitt); Courtiers: F   3 King] KNIGHT (*conj.* Tyrwhitt); Kings F

1.1.1–70 This exchange establishes the style
for much of the play: condensed, elliptical, 'impressionistic' (see Introduction,
pp. 21–2). It also gives the audience a
great deal of information very swiftly.
   1 **but frowns** who does not frown (*OED, but,
   conj.* 12b)
1–3 **Our . . . King** Our dispositions do not
reflect the influence of the heavens more
completely than our courtiers reflect the
behaviour of the King. That the heavens
influence our dispositions is as much a
Renaissance commonplace as the scepti-
cal opposite view that the heavens have
no influence on us at all. The two atti-
tudes are represented by Gloucester and
Edmond at *Tragedy of Lear* 1.2.101–30.
   1 **bloods** Blood was supposed to be the seat
   of the emotions.
   3 **Still** always

3 **King** F has 'Kings', which may be correct
   (i.e. the courtiers reflect the King's looks).
4 **of's** of his
5 **purposed to** intended for
   a widow That this refers to the Queen, not
   to her *sole son*, is obvious, but the
   wrenched syntax, using a parenthesis
   referring not to the immediately preceding word but to one used earlier in the
   sentence, is characteristic of much of
   Shakespeare's late style.
6 **referred** given (*OED v.* 10)
9 **outward** external (contrasted with
   touched at very heart in the next line)
10 **touched at very heart** deeply wounded
   ('struck to the heart'). Cymbeline's
   anger is real, unlike the courtiers' *outward* scowlings). A similar idiom occurs
   at *2 Henry IV* 2.4.8–9: 'It angered him to
   the heart.'

87

That most desired the match. But not a courtier,
Although they wear their faces to the bent
Of the King's looks, hath a heart that is not
Glad at the thing they scowl at.
SECOND GENTLEMAN   And why so?   15
FIRST GENTLEMAN
He that hath missed the Princess is a thing
Too bad for bad report; and he that hath her—
I mean that married her, alack, good man,
And therefore banished—is a creature such
As to seek through the regions of the earth   20
For one his like, there would be something failing
In him that should compare. I do not think
So fair an outward and such stuff within
Endows a man but he.
SECOND GENTLEMAN   You speak him far.
FIRST GENTLEMAN
I do extend him, sir, within himself,   25
Crush him together rather than unfold
His measure duly.
SECOND GENTLEMAN What's his name and birth?

---

13 **bent** inclination. Compare *Winter's Tale*
1.2.180: 'To your own bents dispose
you.' *Bent* in this sense was a relatively
recent usage—*OED*'s earliest example is
from 1586 (*sb.*² 6a)—and seems to be a
metaphorical version of the literal sense
of bending in a certain direction.

15 **glad at** Usually emended to 'glad of' on
the grounds that 'glad *at*' does not occur
elsewhere in Shakespeare; but the *glad
at/scowl at* echo (and contrast) may be
deliberate; *OED a.* 3b cites 'He that is glad
at calamities' (Proverbs 17: 5) from the
Authorized Version of the Bible (begun in
1607 and published in 1611, almost
exactly contemporary with the play).

17–18 **hath her . . . married her** Characters
in this play, especially Innogen, as at
1.3.17, often correct themselves, defining what they mean more precisely. Perhaps the Gentleman thinks that to say
hath her of a husband and wife is too
sexually suggestive and needs modifying.

18 **alack** alas

19–20 **such | As to** Another example of ellip-
tical style: *such as* seems to invite a

phrase like 'cannot be equalled', but
then the speaker searches for something
more emphatic, the hyperbolical *to seek
through the regions of the earth*, in order to
express Posthumus' uniqueness.

22 **him . . . compare** whoever might be compared to him

23 **outward** external appearance
stuff substance, what a person is 'made
of' (*OED sb.*¹ 3b)

24 **Endows** enriches, furnishes (the word
Philario uses to describe Posthumus' outward and inward qualities at 1.4.7)
speak him far praise him highly (with the
implication of modern 'go too far')

25 **extend . . . himself** only praise him as far
as he deserves it

26–7 **Crush . . . duly** minimize his virtues
rather than do them justice. The image
is probably drawn from torture, which
could both crush limbs and stretch
(*extend*, l. 25) them on the rack. This is
the first of a series of violent, punitive
expressions used of Posthumus and Innogen and of their relationship.

FIRST GENTLEMAN

I cannot delve him to the root. His father
Was called Sicilius, who did join his honour
Against the Romans with Cassibelan   30
But had his titles by Tenantius, whom
He served with glory and admired success,
So gained the sur-addition 'Leonatus';
And had, besides this gentleman in question,
Two other sons who in the wars o'th' time   35
Died with their swords in hand; for which their father,
Then old and fond of issue, took such sorrow
That he quit being, and his gentle lady,
Big of this gentleman, our theme, deceased
As he was born. The King he takes the babe   40
To his protection, calls him Posthumus Leonatus,
Breeds him, and makes him of his bedchamber,
Puts to him all the learnings that his time
Could make him the receiver of, which he took
As we do air, fast as 'twas ministered,   45
And in's spring became a harvest; lived in court—

30 Cassibelan] F2 *throughout the play*, *Cassibulan* F1

28 **delve . . . root** trace his ancestry completely (*delve* literally means 'dig')
29–31 **Sicilius . . . Cassibelan . . . Tenantius** The names of three British kings in
Holinshed. This *Sicilius* is obviously not a
king, but a professional soldier. *Cassibelan*
is subsequently identified as the king who
agreed to pay Rome tribute, the cause of
the war later in the play; F2's spelling
agrees with Holinshed's.
29 **join his honour** allied his soldierly
virtue
31 **by** from
32 **admired** wonderful
33 **sur-addition** surname
Leonatus 'born of a lion': the meaning
is spelled out at 5.4.444–6. See Appendix
A.
37 **fond of issue** Either 'doting on his children' or 'despairing of having further
children', since *fond* can mean 'foolish',
often to the point of despair, as Nosworthy points out.
38 **quit being** died
gentle Probably both 'noble' and 'kind'.

39 **Big of** pregnant with
40 **The King he** The insertion of a pronoun
after a noun as the subject of a sentence is
common in Shakespeare (Abbott §243).
41 **calls him Posthumus** —because he was
born after the death of his father. For the
spelling, see Appendix A. The name is
stressed on the second syllable.
42 **Breeds** educates
of his bedchamber i.e. a personal servant.
To be a Gentleman of the Bedchamber
was a sign of royal favour, especially at
the court of James I.
43 **Puts to him** makes available to him
learnings education
time age, time of life
44 **make . . . of** enable him to understand
44–5 **he took . . . ministered** he absorbed
education as easily as breathing, was an
apt pupil
45 **fast** as fast
46 **spring . . . harvest** he learnt so quickly
that he ripened, became wise, even in his
youth (*spring*)

Which rare it is to do—most praised, most loved;
A sample to the youngest, to th' more mature
A glass that feated them, and to the graver
A child that guided dotards. To his mistress,   50
For whom he now is banished, her own price
Proclaims how she esteemed him; and his virtue
By her election may be truly read,
What kind of man he is.

SECOND GENTLEMAN   I honour him
Even out of your report. But pray you tell me,   55
Is she sole child to th' King?

FIRST GENTLEMAN   His only child.
He had two sons—if this be worth your hearing,
Mark it: the eldest of them at three years old,
I'th' swathing clothes the other, from their nursery
Were stol'n, and to this hour no guess in knowledge   60
Which way they went.

SECOND GENTLEMAN How long is this ago?

---

52 him; and his virtue‸] F; him‸ and his virtue; CAPELL   59 clothes the other,] ROWE;
cloathes, the other F

47 **rare** This word occurs frequently in the
play, usually to emphasize the exceptional qualities of Posthumus or Innogen
(as at 1.6.16, 175; 3.5.77; 4.2.209;
5.4.160, 382); here it is used more col-
loquially to mean 'splendid, fine' (*OED
a.*[1] 6a and b).

48–50 **A sample . . . dotards** Posthumus acts
as an example (*sample*) to the young, the
middle-aged, and the old, to the point
where it seems as if a *child* is acting as a
model to those who are in their *dotage*.
Perhaps there is a biblical echo: 'a little
child shall lead them' (Isaiah 11:6).

49 **glass** mirror or model of behaviour
that feated them The adjective *feat* means
'neat, graceful' as in the description of
Innogen as 'So feat, so nurse-like' at
5.4.88. So if *feated* is not an error, the
phrase probably means 'showed them
how to behave well, elegantly'. *OED* suggests 'constrained them to propriety'
(*feat, v.* 3).

50 **dotards** old fools
To his mistress Perhaps 'as for his mistress'; or perhaps another grammatically
wrenched sentence, beginning 'To his

mistress he was', and then shifting to
her own price | Proclaims . . .

51 **her own price** what she paid for Posthumus (in giving up the kingdom for him).
This is the first of many phrases that
represent their marriage in terms of mer-
chandise, e.g. ll. 120–2, 147–8, and Giacomo's subsequent wager.

52–4 **and his . . . he is** Capell's rephrasing
(see collation) is arguably clearer, but F
makes good sense: the fact that Innogen
chose him demonstrates his quality, with
the phrase *What kind of man he is* in
apposition to, and enlarging upon, *his
virtue*, in a way characteristic of
the play's 'defining' style (see note to ll.
17–18).

53 **election** choice (of Posthumus)

55 **pray** I pray (a polite way of starting to
make a request)

57–8 **if . . . it** Perhaps this is a way of drawing
the audience's attention to an important
piece of information.

58 **Mark it** take notice of it

59 **swathing** swaddling (baby-clothes)

60 **no guess in knowledge** (there has been)
no well-informed guess

FIRST GENTLEMAN Some twenty years.
SECOND GENTLEMAN
  That a king's children should be so conveyed,
  So slackly guarded, and the search so slow   65
  That could not trace them!
FIRST GENTLEMAN   Howsoe'er 'tis strange,
  Or that the negligence may well be laughed at,
  Yet is it true, sir.
SECOND GENTLEMAN I do well believe you.
FIRST GENTLEMAN
  We must forbear. Here comes the gentleman,
  The Queen, and Princess.   *Exeunt*   70
     Enter Posthumus, the Queen, and Innogen
QUEEN
  No, be assured you shall not find me, daughter,
  After the slander of most stepmothers,
  Evil-eyed unto you. You're my prisoner, but
  Your jailer shall deliver you the keys
  That lock up your restraint. For you, Posthumus,   75
  So soon as I can win th'offended King
  I will be known your advocate; marry, yet
  The fire of rage is in him, and 'twere good
  You leaned unto his sentence with what patience
  Your wisdom may inform you.
POSTHUMUS   Please your highness,   80

---

70 *Exeunt*] *Exeunt* | *Scena Secunda.* F   70.1 *Posthumus, the Queen*] *the Queene, Posthumus*
F   *Innogen*] OXFORD, *throughout the play*; *Imogen* F

64 **conveyed** stolen
66 **Howsoe'er 'tis strange** however strange it
  may be
69 **forbear** withdraw
69–70 **Here . . . Princess** Although the
  Folio text marks a new scene after the
  Gentlemen's departure, the action is
  clearly continuous, so much so that
  Oxford brings Posthumus, the Queen,
  and Innogen on stage before l. 69; but
  presumably the Gentleman can see them
  offstage and announces their imminent
  arrival, so that the exit overlaps with the
  entry. His line even provides a hint as to
  how they appear, with the Queen soli-
  citously between her stepdaughter and
  son-in-law, and F's direction for their

entry is here modified to be consistent
with it.
70.1 **Innogen** For the spelling and significance of the name, see Appendix A.
71 **daughter** i.e. stepdaughter
72 **After the slander** according to the ill
  repute (that stepmothers hate their step-
  daughters)
75 **your restraint** 'your prison', or more generally 'what restrains you, your house-
  arrest'
76 **win** win over
77 **marry** a mild oath (a reduction of 'By the
  Virgin Mary')
79 **leaned unto** inclined towards, accepted
80 **inform you** invest you with
  Please if it please (a polite phrase)

I will from hence today.

QUEEN   You know the peril.
I'll fetch a turn about the garden, pitying
The pangs of barred affections, though the King
Hath charged you should not speak together.   *Exit*

INNOGEN

O dissembling courtesy! How fine this tyrant   85
Can tickle where she wounds! My dearest husband,
I something fear my father's wrath, but nothing—
Always reserved my holy duty—what
His rage can do on me. You must be gone,
And I shall here abide the hourly shot   90
Of angry eyes, not comforted to live
But that there is this jewel in the world
That I may see again.

POSTHUMUS   My queen, my mistress!
O lady, weep no more, lest I give cause
To be suspected of more tenderness   95
Than doth become a man. I will remain
The loyal'st husband that did e'er plight troth.
My residence in Rome at one Philario's,
Who to my father was a friend, to me
Known but by letter, thither write, my queen,   100
And with mine eyes I'll drink the words you send
Though ink be made of gall.

98 Philario's] ROWE; *Filorio's* F

81 **the peril** Posthumus is banished on pain
of death (l. 128).

83 **barred** separated (perhaps by prison bars,
picking up the language of ll. 73–5; compare *Winter's Tale* 3.2.96–7: 'from his
presence | I am barred, like one infec-
tious')

85 **O dissembling courtesy** This phrase
comes as a shock, exploding the Queen's
apparent solicitude, and instantly
establishing Innogen's uncompromising
candour and dislike of hypocrisy.

86 **tickle** flatter

87 **something . . . nothing** somewhat . . . not
at all

88 **reserved . . . duty** apart from the respect I
owe my father. She respects him, but will
not give in to his irrational rages.

90 **hourly** continual

92 **this jewel** i.e. Posthumus himself. This is
the language of lovers; compare Sonnet
131.3–4: 'to my dear doting heart | Thou
art the fairest and most precious jewel.'

94–6 **give cause . . . man** i.e. in weeping

96 **doth** does. 'The original northern form
does superseded *doth, doeth* in 16–17th
c. in general use; the latter being liturg-
ical and poetic' (*OED, do, v.* 2c).

97 **plight troth** take vows of marriage

98 **Philario** The spelling and significance of
this name are discussed in Appendix A.

100 **thither** there

102 **ink . . . gall** Ink was made of bitter oak-
gall. The phrase is a commonplace,
occurring for example in Middleton and
Dekker's *The Roaring Girl* (1611): 'Love's
sweets taste best when we have drunk
down gall' (3.2.156).

Enter the Queen

QUEEN   Be brief, I pray you.
If the King come, I shall incur I know not
How much of his displeasure. (*Aside*) Yet I'll move him
To walk this way. I never do him wrong   105
But he does buy my injuries to be friends,
Pays dear for my offences.   *Exit*
POSTHUMUS   Should we be taking leave
As long a term as yet we have to live,
The loathness to depart would grow. Adieu.
INNOGEN Nay, stay a little.   110
Were you but riding forth to air yourself
Such parting were too petty. Look here, love,
This diamond was my mother's. Take it, heart,
        She gives him a ring
But keep it till you woo another wife,
When Innogen is dead.
POSTHUMUS   How, how? Another?   115
You gentle gods, give me but this I have,
And cere up my embracements from a next
With bonds of death! Remain, remain thou here
        He puts on the ring
While sense can keep it on; and sweetest, fairest,

107 *Exit*] *not in* F   113.1 *She gives him a ring*] *not in* F   117 cere] F (seare)   118.1 *He puts on the ring*] *not in* F

104 *Aside* Although this term was in use from the mid-1590s (*Textual Companion*, p. 80), it is always added editorially in this edition. It simply indicates that lines are spoken directly to the audience, almost as mini-soliloquies, but not they are hurriedly thrown away, as *aside* often suggests in nineteenth-century and subsequent drama.
   move encourage
106 **does . . . friends** takes my wrongs as acts of friendship, benefits (or, less likely, 'repays injuries with kindness so as to remain friends with me')
109 **Adieu** goodbye. Originally French, it came to be regarded as an English word and pronounced as such: 'adew'.
110 Incomplete lines in a verse passage, as here, often suggest some theatrical point. Perhaps Posthumus leaves quickly on

Adieu, and Innogen rushes to stop him; perhaps they embrace; perhaps both.
110 **Nay** Literally 'No', but often, as here, having the force of an exclamation or an intensifier.
111 **but** only
   to air yourself for exercise
112 **too petty** inadequate
113 **heart** An endearment: 'dear heart', or similar.
117 **cere up** wrap in cere-cloths (i.e. in grave-clothes). If F's 'seare' is a misprint for 'seale', the phrase would mean 'seal me up with wax, like the *bonds* (l. 118) on a legal document'—only these are *bonds of death*. Either way, Posthumus is making an extreme protestation of fidelity.
118–19 **thou . . . it** Both refer to the ring; presumably he addresses the ring, then Innogen.
119 **sense** the capacity to feel

As I my poor self did exchange for you   120
To your so infinite loss, so in our trifles
I still win of you. For my sake wear this.
    He gives her a bracelet
It is a manacle of love, I'll place it
Upon this fairest prisoner.
INNOGEN   O the gods!
When shall we see again?
    Enter Cymbeline and Lords
POSTHUMUS   Alack, the King!   125
CYMBELINE
Thou basest thing, avoid hence, from my sight!
If after this command thou freight the court
With thy unworthiness, thou diest. Away,
Thou'rt poison to my blood.
POSTHUMUS   The gods protect you,
And bless the good remainders of the court!   130
I am gone.   *Exit*
INNOGEN   There cannot be a pinch in death
More sharp than this is.
CYMBELINE   O disloyal thing,
That shouldst repair my youth, thou heap'st
A year's age on me.
INNOGEN   I beseech you sir,

122.1 *He gives her a bracelet*] *not in* F   127 freight] F (fraught)

120–4 The language changes from that of commerce (*exchange . . . loss . . . win*) to that of imprisonment (*manacle . . . prisoner*). To call a bracelet *a manacle of love* is to use the language of love poetry (as in Marvell's 'The Fair Singer' (*c.*1650), who will make the poet's 'fetters of the very air I breathe'); but *manacle* also suggests the desperate situation, and the harsh straits into which this relationship will be drawn.

122 **still win of** always gain advantage over

125 **see** meet

126 **Thou** In seventeenth-century English, *you* is the polite term, *thou* the familiar or abusive one. So far, all the characters have addressed each other as *you*, even the two lovers; Cymbeline's *Thou* expresses his contempt for Posthumus.

126 **thing** An abusive term which Cymbeline keeps using (ll. 132, 151). Compare Leontes' insult to his wife at *Winter's Tale* 2.1.84–5: 'thou thing, | Which I'll not call a creature of thy place'.
avoid hence begone

127 **freight** burden, weigh down. *Freight* is identical in meaning to F's 'fraught' (*OED v.* 1), from parallel roots.

130 **remainders of** those people remaining at court

131 **pinch in death** intense pain (even) in death

133–4 **That shouldst . . . me** who should restore me to my youth, you add an extra year to my age. L. 133 is two syllables short, but octosyllabic lines are common in Shakespeare, and emendation is unnecessary.

134 **beseech** implore

Harm not yourself with your vexation.   135
I am senseless of your wrath; a touch more rare
Subdues all pangs, all fears.
CYMBELINE   Past grace, obedience?
INNOGEN
Past hope and in despair: that way past grace.
CYMBELINE
That mightst have had the sole son of my queen!
INNOGEN
O blest that I might not! I chose an eagle   140
And did avoid a puttock.
CYMBELINE
Thou took'st a beggar, wouldst have made my throne
A seat for baseness.
INNOGEN   No, I rather added
A lustre to it.
CYMBELINE   O thou vile one!
INNOGEN   Sir,
It is your fault that I have loved Posthumus.   145
You bred him as my playfellow, and he is
A man worth any woman, over-buys me
Almost the sum he pays.

136 **senseless** insensible
136–7 **a touch . . . fears** Dowden glosses *a
  touch more rare* as 'a more exquisite pain',
  which other editors assume refers to her
  parting with Posthumus. But surely the
  'more exquisite pain' which defeats all
  other pains is death; compare 4.2.259–
  82, and, expressed more prosaically,
  5.3.251–64.
137–8 **Past grace . . . past grace** By *Past grace*
  Cymbeline means 'devoid of a sense of
  duty'; Innogen widens it to mean
  'beyond heavenly salvation': *despair*
  was taken to be a sin against the Holy
  Ghost (Matthew 12 : 31–2) and therefore
  unforgivable (i.e. *past grace*) by the medieval church, a view summarized by Thomas Aquinas (*Summa Theologica*, second
  part, 2, Q 14, Art. 1–4).
140 This may be one of several alexandrines
  (twelve-syllable, six-stress lines) in the
  play, or an eleven-syllable iambic line.
  The Folio's 'blessed' suggests the former,
  since it is usually consistent in distin-

guishing typographically between a past
tense or past participle ending which is
syllabic, and therefore pronounced (*-ed* in
F) and one which is not (*-'d* in F); but
there are exceptions (for example 1.6.7,
where F's 'blessed' certainly is a monosyllable), and this edition suggests that
'blessed' is a monosyllable here too
(hence the spelling) and the line iambic,
since then the stresses point the sense:
see the next note.
140 **might not** was not able to (playing on
  Cymbeline's *mightst* in the previous line)
140–1 **eagle . . . puttock** The *eagle* was supposed to be the king of birds, and the
  puttock (kite), a scavenger, a particularly
  ignoble one. Posthumus is associated
  with the eagle elsewhere: see note to
  1.4.11; and later Jupiter descends upon
  an eagle to promise him a happy future
  (5.3.186–207).
147–8 **over-buys . . . pays** the amount he
  suffers on my account is almost too high
  a price to pay for me

95

CYMBELINE   What, art thou mad?

INNOGEN

Almost sir, heaven restore me! Would I were
A neatherd's daughter, and my Leonatus   150
Our neighbour shepherd's son.

    Enter the Queen

CYMBELINE   Thou foolish thing.
(*To the Queen*) They were again together; you have done
Not after our command. Away with her,
And pen her up.

QUEEN   Beseech your patience. Peace,
Dear lady daughter, peace. Sweet sovereign,   155
Leave us to ourselves, and make yourself some comfort
Out of your best advice.

CYMBELINE   Nay, let her languish
A drop of blood a day, and being aged,
Die of this folly.   *Exit with Lords*

QUEEN   Fie, you must give way.

    Enter Pisanio

Here is your servant. How now, sir? What news?   160

PISANIO

My lord your son drew on my master.

QUEEN   Ha!
No harm I trust is done?

PISANIO   There might have been,
But that my master rather played than fought,
And had no help of anger; they were parted

---

159 *Exit with Lords*] *Exit.* | *Enter Pisanio.* F

---

150 **neatherd** cowherd. Innogen's longing
for a simple rural life free from the
pressures of the court anticipates her subsequent adventures in Wales.

153 **after** according to

154 **Beseech** shortened colloquial form of 'I
beseech' (implore)

157 **advice** Probably 'consideration' (*OED* 4
cites *Merchant* 4.2.6–7: 'Bassanio upon
more advice | Hath sent you here this
ring'); but perhaps the Queen means
advice given him by his councillors.

157–8 **languish . . . a day** *Languish* can be
used either transitively or intransitively;

so here it could mean either 'spend,
waste', as at 1.6.72, or, as Dowden
glosses it, 'languish [decline] at the rate
of a drop of blood a day'. The second
usage is rare.

159 **you . . . way** This could be called out
after the departing Cymbeline, to per-
suade Innogen that she is on her side, or
(less likely in view of the Queen's devious
methods) addressed to Innogen herself.

160 **How now** A common form of greeting
(an abbreviation of 'How is it now?').

161 **drew** i.e. drew his sword

164 **had no help of** was not motivated by

By gentlemen at hand.

QUEEN   I am very glad on 't.   165

INNOGEN

Your son's my father's friend, he takes his part
To draw upon an exile. O brave sir!
I would they were in Afric both together,
Myself by with a needle, that I might prick
The goer-back. (*To Pisanio*) Why came you from your
      master?   170

PISANIO

On his command. He would not suffer me
To bring him to the haven, left these notes
Of what commands I should be subject to
When't pleased you to employ me.

QUEEN   This hath been
Your faithful servant. I dare lay mine honour   175
He will remain so.

PISANIO I humbly thank your highness.

QUEEN Pray walk a while.

INNOGEN

About some half-hour hence, pray you speak with me.
You shall at least go see my lord aboard.   180
For this time leave me.

> *Exeunt the Queen and Innogen at one door,*
> *Pisanio at another*

I.2   *Enter Cloten and two Lords*

FIRST LORD Sir, I would advise you to shift a shirt. The
violence of action hath made you reek as a sacrifice.

181.1–2 *Exeunt . . . another*] *Exeunt.* F   I.2] *Scena Tertia.* F   0.1 *Cloten*] *Clotten* F

166 **takes his part** sides with Cymbeline
169 **needle** (pronounced as a monosyllable)
171 **suffer** allow
172 **haven** harbour
     notes instructions
175 **lay** wager
181.1–2 *at one door . . . at another*
     Standard terms for separate exits (though
     here editorial), derived from the two
     doors set into the back wall on either
     side of the Elizabethan and Jacobean
     stage.

1.2.0.1 *Cloten* For the spelling and pronun-
     ciation, see Appendix A.
     two Lords The first flatters Cloten, the
     second mocks him; but the laboured wit-
     ticisms of the First Lord may imply that
     he, too, mocks Cloten even as he appears
     to flatter him. Kenneth Tynan describes
     this pair at Stratford-upon-Avon in 1962
     interestingly: 'the courtiers treat Cloten
     with bored, habitual disdain: their com-
     pliments are a kind of poker-faced mock-
     ery' (*Observer*, 22 July 1962).

> Where air comes out, air comes in. There's none abroad
> so wholesome as that you vent.

CLOTEN If my shirt were bloody, then to shift it. Have I hurt   5
him?

SECOND LORD (*aside*) No, faith, not so much as his patience.

FIRST LORD Hurt him? His body's a passable carcass if he be
not hurt. It is a thoroughfare for steel if he be not hurt.

SECOND LORD (*aside*) His steel was in debt, it went o'th'   10
backside the town.

CLOTEN The villain would not stand me.

SECOND LORD (*aside*) No, but he fled forward still, toward
your face.

FIRST LORD Stand you? You have land enough of your own,   15
but he added to your having, gave you some ground.

SECOND LORD (*aside*) As many inches as you have oceans.
Puppies!

CLOTEN I would they had not come between us.

SECOND LORD (*aside*) So would I, till you had measured how   20
long a fool you were upon the ground.

---

9 thoroughfare] F3; through-fare F1   he] OXFORD (*conj.* H. F. Brooks *in* Nosworthy); it F

---

1 **shift** change

2 **reek** give off stinking vapours (hence the comparison to the smoke of a *sacrifice*)

3–4 **Where air . . . vent** Dowden glosses: 'he must take air in to supply what he loses, and the outer air is less wholesome than that of his own sweet body.'

3 **abroad** outside

4 **vent** literally 'let out breath' (from Latin *ventus*, wind)

5 **then to** then would be the time to

7 **faith** An abbreviation of 'in faith, by my faith' (a mild oath, used for emphasis).

8 **passable** An intensifying phrase, like 'veritable', with a pun on 'something that can be passed through (by sword thrusts)'.

10–11 **His steel . . . town** His sword was like a debtor, taking to the back-streets of a town to avoid arrest (i.e. it missed Posthumus). At *Errors* 4.2.37–8, in a context of arrest for debt, an Officer is described as 'A back-friend . . . that countermands |

The passages of alleys'. For *backside the town* meaning 'back-streets', compare an account of James I's visit to Cambridge cited by Dowden: Jesuits were 'carried over the back side of the town' to prison, not through the town centre.

12 **stand** stand his ground against. The implied 'ground' leads to the joke, such as it is, in the next speech.

13 **still** continually

16 **gave . . . ground** retreated

17 **inches . . . oceans** i.e. Posthumus yielded nothing, whereas Cloten retreated. An *inch* is a small island (contrasted with *oceans*) as well as a unit of measurement.

18 **Puppies** fools. The Second Lord seems to include the First Lord as well as Cloten in his contempt.

20–1 **measured . . . ground** i.e. fell down. Shakespeare also uses this expression at *Dream* 3.3.17 and *Tragedy of Lear* 1.4.89–90, *OED*'s earliest examples of this sense (*v*. 2f).

CLOTEN And that she should love this fellow and refuse me!

SECOND LORD (*aside*) If it be a sin to make a true election, she is damned.

FIRST LORD Sir, as I told you always, her beauty and her   25
brain go not together. She's a good sign, but I have seen
small reflection of her wit.

SECOND LORD (*aside*) She shines not upon fools lest the
reflection should hurt her.

CLOTEN Come, I'll to my chamber. Would there had been   30
some hurt done.

SECOND LORD (*aside*) I wish not so, unless it had been the fall
of an ass, which is no great hurt.

CLOTEN (*to Second Lord*) You'll go with us?

FIRST LORD I'll attend your lordship.   35

CLOTEN Nay, come, let's go together.

SECOND LORD Well, my lord.   *Exeunt*

I.3   *Enter Innogen and Pisanio*

INNOGEN

I would thou grew'st unto the shores o'th' haven
And questioned'st every sail. If he should write
And I not have it, 'twere a paper lost
As offered mercy is. What was the last
That he spake to thee?

PISANIO   It was his queen, his queen.   5

INNOGEN

Then waved his handkerchief?

PISANIO   And kissed it, madam.

1.3] *Scena Quarta.* F   2 questioned'st] F; question'st OXFORD

23 **election** choice (as at 1.1.53); but
the antithesis with *damned* (l. 24) suggests a play on the theological meaning,
i.e. that God chooses some people to be
saved, others to be damned (*OED* 3).

26 **go not together** do not correspond
She's . . . sign she has a good outward
appearance. *Sign* may also play on the
sense 'heavenly constellation' (*OED
sb.* 11) in view of *reflection* in the following lines.

27, 29 **reflection . . . reflection** The first *reflection* means 'indication' (literally 'radi-
ance'), the second something thrown
back from a reflecting surface.

27 **wit** intelligence

33 **ass** Perhaps there is a pun on 'arse',
hence *no great hurt*.

35 **attend** wait on, follow

1.3.1 **grew'st unto** remained at, until you
became a part of, like a plant

4 **offered mercy** Perhaps the mercy of God,
offered but rejected; more likely,
since the point of comparison is a
paper, a pardon for a reprieved criminal
that doesn't arrive in time; compare
All's Well 5.3.58–9: 'a remorseful
pardon slowly carried' that 'comes too
late'.

INNOGEN
    Senseless linen, happier therein than I!
    And that was all?
PISANIO   No madam, for so long
    As he could make me with this eye or ear
    Distinguish him from others he did keep   10
    The deck, with glove or hat or handkerchief
    Still waving, as the fits and stirs of's mind
    Could best express how slow his soul sailed on,
    How swift his ship.
INNOGEN   Thou shouldst have made him
    As little as a crow, or less, ere left   15
    To after-eye him.
PISANIO   Madam, so I did.
INNOGEN
    I would have broke mine eye-strings, cracked them, but
    To look upon him till the diminution
    Of space had pointed him sharp as my needle;
    Nay, followed him till he had melted from   20
    The smallness of a gnat to air, and then
    Have turned mine eye and wept. But good Pisanio,
    When shall we hear from him?
PISANIO Be assured madam,
    With his next vantage.   25
INNOGEN
    I did not take my leave of him, but had

9 this] THEOBALD (*conj.* Warburton); his F

7 **Senseless** lacking the capacity for feeling
10 **keep** stay on
12 **as** as if
   fits . . . mind mental turmoil. There is an interesting parallel between this description of Posthumus' mind and Belarius' of Cloten's at 4.2.133–4: 'his humour | Was nothing but mutation'. See Introduction, pp. 50–1.
13 **how . . . on** how reluctant his soul was to leave
14–22 **Thou shouldst . . . wept** In this remarkable passage, Innogen imagines the departure of Posthumus which she did not see. First he appears as small as a *crow* in the distance (l. 15), then the focus narrows down to the point of a *needle* (l. 19), thence to something so small as to be almost invisible, a *gnat* (l. 21), and finally to nothing but *air*.
14 **made** discerned, 'made (him) out'
15 **ere** before
16 **after-eye** look after (a nautical usage: *OED, after-* II)
17 **eye-strings** the muscles of the eye, thought to break at death or at the loss of sight
18 **diminution** contraction
19 **sharp . . . needle** This expresses, not just smallness, since Posthumus is now a mere dot on the horizon, but the sharp pain of straining the eye and of their parting.
25 **With . . . vantage** at his earliest opportunity

Most pretty things to say. Ere I could tell him
How I would think on him at certain hours,
Such thoughts and such, or I could make him swear
The shes of Italy should not betray   30
Mine interest and his honour, or have charged him
At the sixth hour of morn, at noon, at midnight
T'encounter me with orisons, for then
I am in heaven for him, or ere I could
Give him that parting kiss which I had set   35
Betwixt two charming words, comes in my father,
And like the tyrannous breathing of the north,
Shakes all our buds from growing.
          Enter a Lady
LADY   The Queen, madam,
Desires your highness' company.
INNOGEN (*to Pisanio*)
Those things I bid you do, get them dispatched.   40
I will attend the Queen.
PISANIO   Madam, I shall.
          Exeunt Innogen and Lady at one door,
          Pisanio at another

1.4   *Enter Philario, Giacomo, a Frenchman, a Dutchman,*
        and a Spaniard
GIACOMO Believe it, sir, I have seen him in Britain. He was
   then of a crescent note, expected to prove so worthy as

41.1–2 *Exeunt . . . another*] *Exeunt.* F
1.4] *Scena Quinta.* F

29 **Such . . . such** Innogen is intentionally
   vague about her most intimate feelings,
   even with the sympathetic Pisanio: she
   displays a similar reticence in her scene
   with Giacomo (1.6.26–8).
30 **shes** women
31 **interest** right
32 **sixth . . . midnight** These are three of
   the Church's seven canonical hours,
   fixed times for prayer.
33 **T'encounter . . . orisons** i.e. if we both say
   our prayers (*orisons*) at the same time, it
   will be as if we are meeting.
34 **I am . . . him** I am praying for him

35 **set** placed (perhaps like a precious stone
   in a ring)
36 **charming** having the power of a magic
   charm (against danger)
37 **north** north wind
38 **Shakes . . . growing** The north wind
   dashes the spring buds and so prevents
   them from developing (as the love of
   Innogen and Posthumus is prevented
   from maturing). Compare Sonnet 18.3:
   'Rough winds do shake the darling buds
   of May'.
1.4 The equivalent scene in the principal
   sources takes place during a meal, and

since he hath been allowed the name of. But I could then
have looked on him without the help of admiration,
though the catalogue of his endowments had been tabled   5
by his side and I to peruse him by items.

PHILARIO You speak of him when he was less furnished
than now he is with that which makes him both without
and within.

FRENCHMAN I have seen him in France. We had very many   10
there could behold the sun with as firm eyes as he.

GIACOMO This matter of marrying his king's daughter,
wherein he must be weighed rather by her value than
his own, words him, I doubt not, a great deal from the
matter.   15

FRENCHMAN And then his banishment.

at 5.4.155 Giacomo speaks of a 'feast',
though his retrospective account is not
strictly accurate (see Introduction, p. 58).
A table is sometimes used in performance
to focus an initially relaxed gathering
which becomes very tense. Perhaps that
relaxation explains why the scene is in
prose, though it is a prose sometimes so
elaborate and mannered that the sense is
in doubt. Lines 1–24 create a world of
cosmopolitan gossip, upon which Posthumus tries to impose his idealistic
views by attempting to force the prose
into verse or near-verse (ll. 61, 73, 83,
120); but later he readily adopts the
worldly tone of the others as he accepts
their values, and wagers on his wife's
fidelity.

0.1 *Philario* See note to 1.1.98.
   Giacomo This is the modern equivalent of
   F's 'Iachimo', pronounced 'Jacomo' and
   stressed on the first syllable. The name is
   discussed in Appendix A.

0.1–2 *Dutchman . . . Spaniard* The probable
   function of these mute characters is discussed in the Introduction, p. 34.

1 **him** Posthumus
2 **crescent note** growing reputation. Posthumus' star is rising, like the increasing,
   crescent-shaped moon.
   so as

3 **allowed . . . of** called
4 **without . . . admiration** without feeling
   any amazement. *Admiration* had a stronger sense in the seventeenth century

than it does now, though something of
the modern sense is also present:
Giacomo's grudging, irritated reaction
to Posthumus is established from the
start (see ll. 106–7). For the idiom *without the help of* compare 1.1.164.

5 **though** even if
   catalogue . . . endowments list of his
   qualities
   tabled formally set out, as in a list

6 **I to peruse** i.e. I had been required
   (another elliptical phrase characteristic
   of the play)
   by items point by point. Giacomo is
   mocking the literary habit of itemizing a
   person's qualities virtually like a shop-
   ping list, as in Lance's *catalogue* of his
   girlfriend's at *Two Gentlemen* 3.1.271–
   358.

7 **furnished** equipped
8 **makes** makes him what he is
8–9 **without and within** both in appearance and personality (as at 1.1.23)

11 **could . . . he** The ability to stare
   directly into the sun was thought to be
   the prerogative of the eagle, to which
   Posthumus has already been compared
   at 1.1.140; but the Frenchman implies
   that Posthumus is no more exceptional
   than many of his countrymen. The ideal
   image of Posthumus given at the start of
   the play is starting to be modified; the
   process accelerates during this scene.

13 **value** valuation
14–15 **words him . . . matter** amplifies his
   reputation beyond what it really is

GIACOMO Ay, and the approbation of those that weep this
lamentable divorce under her colours are wonderfully to
extend him, be it but to fortify her judgement, which else
an easy battery might lay flat for taking a beggar without   20
less quality. But how comes it he is to sojourn with you?
How creeps acquaintance?

PHILARIO His father and I were soldiers together, to whom I
have been often bound for no less than my life.

    Enter Posthumus

Here comes the Briton. Let him be so entertained   25
amongst you as suits with gentlemen of your knowing
to a stranger of his quality. I beseech you all, be better
known to this gentleman, whom I commend to you as
a noble friend of mine. How worthy he is I will leave
to appear hereafter, rather than story him in his own   30
hearing.

FRENCHMAN (*to Posthumus*) Sir, we have known together in
Orléans.

POSTHUMUS Since when I have been debtor to you for cour-
tesies which I will be ever to pay, and yet pay still.   35

---

25 Briton] F (Britaine *throughout the play*)

17 **Ay yes.** *OED* says that 'ay' appeared suddenly about 1575, of unknown origin. It
was usually spelt 'I' (as in the Folio text
here), which indicates the pronunciation. It survives in English dialects and
regional accents.

17–19 **the approbation . . . him** This difficult
sentence probably means: 'the approval
of those who take Innogen's side and
therefore lament her separation from
Posthumus has the effect of greatly inflat-
ing his reputation.'

17–18 **the approbation of those . . . are** Singular nouns with plural verbs, and vice
versa, are common in seventeenth-century English; but perhaps *are* was suggested by *those*.

18 **under her colours** on her side (a military
expression—*colours* means an army's
banner—continued in *fortify* (l. 19) and
battery (l. 20))

19 **extend him** exaggerate his worth
be it but if only

20 **an easy . . . flat** an easy assault might

destroy (i.e. Innogen might be criticized)

20–1 **without less quality** The sense seems to
require 'without *more* quality' (i.e. who
had no more rank), which Rowe reads.
The phrase is probably a double negative,
designed to emphasize Posthumus'
worthlessness.

22 **How creeps acquaintance** How have you
stolen into friendship (i.e. how do you
come to be acquainted)? The idiom
sounds sneering, and may be proverbial:
'Kindness (Love, Kind) will creep where it
cannot go' (Tilley K49).

26 **suits with** becomes
knowing experience of the world, *savoir
faire* (Maxwell)

30 **story** give an account of (implying 'sing
his praises')

32 **known together** met before

35 **which . . . still** for which I will always
be in your debt, though I continue to
repay for ever. Compare *All's Well*
3.7.16: 'which I will over-pay, and pay
again'.

FRENCHMAN Sir, you o'errate my poor kindness. I was glad
  I did atone my countryman and you ; it had been pity you
  should have been put together with so mortal a purpose
  as then each bore, upon importance of so slight and
  trivial a nature.   40
POSTHUMUS By your pardon sir, I was then a young travel-
  ler, rather shunned to go even with what I heard than in
  my every action to be guided by others' experiences ; but
  upon my mended judgement—if I offend not to say it is
  mended—my quarrel was not altogether slight.   45
FRENCHMAN Faith yes, to be put to the arbitrement of
  swords, and by such two that would by all likelihood
  have confounded one the other, or have fallen both.
GIACOMO Can we with manners ask what was the differ-
  ence ?   50
FRENCHMAN Safely, I think. 'Twas a contention in public,
  which may without contradiction suffer the report. It
  was much like an argument that fell out last night,
  where each of us fell in praise of our country mistresses,
  this gentleman at that time vouching—and upon war-   55
  rant of bloody affirmation—his to be more fair, virtuous,
  wise, chaste, constant, qualified, and less attemptable
  than any the rarest of our ladies in France.

44 not to] ROWE ; to F

37 **atone** reconcile
38 **put together** opposed in combat
39 **importance** prompting (i.e. importuning
    of a very mild kind)
42–3 **rather . . . experiences** The difficulty
    here is that both halves of the sentence,
    though apparently contrasted (*rather . . .
    than*), seem to mean substantially the
    same thing, to be assertions of indepen-
    dence : 'I avoided going along with what
    I heard rather than allowing myself to be
    guided by other people's experience.' Per-
    haps Furness's summary solves the diffi-
    culty : 'rather than appear to be guided
    by others' experience I avoided giving
    consent to what I heard.'
42 **rather shunned** one who rather avoided.
    (*Shunned* is an active verb, not a partici-
    ple.)
    go even agree
46 **Faith yes** indeed it was

46 **the arbitrement of** settlement by
48 **confounded** destroyed
49–50 **difference** cause of the argument
52 **without** i.e. without the risk of
    suffer the report bear recounting
54 **country mistresses** i.e. the ladies whom
    they loved in their respective countries
55–6 **warrant . . . affirmation** a pledge that
    he would affirm it with bloodshed
57 **constant** From Latin *constans, constant*
    basically means 'consistent, holding
    firm', but when Shakespeare uses it in
    contexts involving love, it also carries
    the implication 'true' or 'faithful', as at
    5.4.450, and Sonnet 105.5–6 : 'Kind is
    my love today, tomorrow kind, | Still
    constant in a wondrous excellence.'
    qualified endowed with good qualities,
    perfect (*OED* 1b)
    attemptable vulnerable to seduction
58 **any the** any of the

GIACOMO That lady is not now living, or this gentleman's
opinion by this worn out.   60

POSTHUMUS She holds her virtue still, and I my mind.

GIACOMO You must not so far prefer her 'fore ours of Italy.

POSTHUMUS Being so far provoked as I was in France I
would abate her nothing, though I profess myself her
adorer, not her friend.   65

GIACOMO As fair and as good—a kind of hand-in-hand
comparison—had been something too fair and too good
for any lady in Britain. If she went before others I have
seen, as that diamond of yours outlustres many I have
beheld, I could not but believe she excelled many; but I   70
have not seen the most precious diamond that is, nor you
the lady.

POSTHUMUS I praised her as I rated her; so do I my stone.

GIACOMO What do you esteem it at?

POSTHUMUS More than the world enjoys.   75

GIACOMO Either your unparagoned mistress is dead, or
she's outprized by a trifle.

68 Britain] JOHNSON; Britanie F   70 not but] MALONE; not F

60 **by this** by this time

61 This line has the rhythm of verse: Posthumus attempts to lend dignity to the
argument.

62 **prefer her** advance her claims
'fore before

64 **abate her nothing** not lessen her value at
all
profess declare

64–5 **her adorer, not her friend** her worship-
per, not her lover. Posthumus idealisti-
cally portrays Innogen as a goddess
rather than a sexual partner. *Friend* for
'lover' is a common Shakespearian
usage, as at *Measure* 1.4.29: 'He hath
got his friend with child.'

66 **As fair and as good** The emphasis falls on
each *as*, contrasted with '*too* fair and *too*
good' in l. 67, in order to stress the ordi-
nariness of Innogen, after Posthumus
has implied that she is a goddess. For
this use of *as* to stress a realistic assess-
ment of a lover, compare Sonnet 21.10–
12: 'my love is as fair | As any mother's
child, though not so bright | As those
gold candles fixed in heaven's air'. This
sonnet's concluding line provides a perspective on Posthumus' behaviour: 'I
will not praise that purpose not to sell.'

66–7 **a kind . . . comparison** *Hand-in-hand*
means equal, equally balanced; the
whole mocking phrase implies that the
most you could say of any British lady
was that she might equal, not surpass,
those of other countries.

67 **something** somewhat

68–70 **If . . . many** Giacomo continues to
deflate any idea that Innogen is special:
'Even if she excelled *some* women, that is
all she did' (i.e. she didn't excel them all);
or perhaps 'if she excelled others to the
same extent as your diamond'. Either
way, his parenthetical equation of her
to Posthumus' ring suggests that her
value is less divine than commercial.
This prepares for the wager, and focuses
attention on the ring that will be
wagered.

70 **could not but believe** F's 'could not
beleeue' does not convey the required
sense; another possible emendation is
'could but believe'.

75 **More . . . enjoys** more than all the wealth
of the world, beyond price
enjoys possesses (perhaps with sexual
overtone)

77 **outprized . . . trifle** her value is exceeded
by a trifle (the ring)

POSTHUMUS You are mistaken. The one may be sold or
　　given, or if there were wealth enough for the purchase
　　or merit for the gift. The other is not a thing for sale, and　　80
　　only the gift of the gods.

GIACOMO Which the gods have given you?

POSTHUMUS Which by their graces I will keep.

GIACOMO You may wear her in title yours; but you know,
　　strange fowl light upon neighbouring ponds. Your ring　　85
　　may be stolen too; so your brace of unprizable estima-
　　tions, the one is but frail, and the other casual. A cun-
　　ning thief or a that-way accomplished courtier would
　　hazard the winning both of first and last.

POSTHUMUS Your Italy contains none so accomplished a　　90
　　courtier to convince the honour of my mistress, if in the
　　holding or loss of that you term her frail. I do nothing
　　doubt you have store of thieves; notwithstanding, I fear
　　not my ring.

PHILARIO Let us leave here, gentlemen.　　95

POSTHUMUS Sir, with all my heart. This worthy signor, I
　　thank him, makes no stranger of me, we are familiar at
　　first.

79 purchase] ROWE ; purchases F

79 **or** either
83 **Which . . . keep** This can be regarded as
　　an octosyllabic verse line, Posthumus
　　answering Giacomo's ironic question by
　　reasserting his ideal view of Innogen.
84 **wear . . . yours** possess her as your legal
　　right (*OED, title, sb.* 7)
　　wear possess and enjoy as one's own
　　(*OED v.*[1] 8b). This seems to be a contrac-
　　tion of the proverbial phrase to 'win and
　　wear' someone as one's wife (Tilley
　　W408).
85 **strange . . . ponds** A flippant version of
　　Leontes' obsessive view of how men's
　　wives are seduced by their neighbours:
　　'many a man [has] his pond fished by . . .
　　Sir Smile, his neighbour' (*Winter's Tale*
　　1.2.193–7).
86–7 **your brace . . . estimations** the two
　　objects that you esteem beyond price
87–9 **the one . . . last** *the one* is Innogen (see
　　Posthumus' reaction, l. 92), *the other* the
　　ring; but in the next sentence, the *thief*
　　obviously refers to stealing the ring, the
　　courtier to seducing Innogen, so that *first*

is now the ring, *last* Innogen. But perhaps Giacomo is deliberately equating,
and confusing, the two.
87 **casual** subject to accident (compare mod-
　　ern 'casualty')
89 **hazard** venture
90–1 **none . . . courtier** no courtier so accom-
　　plished
91 **convince the honour** overcome the chas-
　　tity
93 **store of thieves** plenty of thieves. Posthu-
　　mus refers back to Giacomo's *cunning
　　thief* (ll. 87–8). This is the first insult;
　　the argument is hotting up, prompting
　　Philario to the first of his three interven-
　　tions (see ll. 115 and 142); and each
　　time it is Posthumus who has to be
　　calmed, not Giacomo.
95 **leave here** stop here. F's line makes sense,
　　but 'heere' may be a slip for 'her' (i.e.
　　'stop talking about Innogen'). A 'here/
　　her' confusion occurs at *Tempest* 4.1.74
　　(TLN 1732), where F has 'here [for
　　"her"] Peacocks flye amaine'.
97–8 **at first** from the start

GIACOMO With five times so much conversation I should
get ground of your fair mistress, make her go back even   100
to the yielding, had I admittance and opportunity to
friend.

POSTHUMUS No, no.

GIACOMO I dare thereupon pawn the moiety of my estate to
your ring, which in my opinion o'ervalues it something.   105
But I make my wager rather against your confidence
than her reputation; and to bar your offence herein
too, I durst attempt it against any lady in the world.

POSTHUMUS You are a great deal abused in too bold a persuasion, and I doubt not you sustain what you're worthy   110
of by your attempt.

GIACOMO What's that?

POSTHUMUS A repulse; though your attempt, as you call it,
deserve more: a punishment, too.

PHILARIO Gentlemen, enough of this. It came in too sud-   115
denly. Let it die as it was born, and I pray you be better
acquainted.

GIACOMO Would I had put my estate and my neighbour's
on th'approbation of what I have spoke.

POSTHUMUS What lady would you choose to assail?   120

GIACOMO Yours, whom in constancy you think stands so
safe. I will lay you ten thousand ducats to your ring, that

107–8 herein too] F; hereunto (ANON. *conj. cited in* Cambridge)   122 thousand] F3; thousands F1

99 **With . . . conversation** i.e. only five times as much conversation as we have had so far

100 **get ground of** Literally 'gain advantage of', a metaphor from fencing, continued in the next phrase, but with a sexual overtone, 'make progress with'.

100–1 **go back . . . yielding** More fencing terms, with more sexual innuendo.

101 **to** as a

103 **No, no** The simple monosyllables are capable of many different interpretations: offhand dismissal, furious denial, or the first relaxed and the second tense, as in Tim Pigott-Smith's performance at Stratford-upon-Avon in 1974.

104 **moiety** half

105 **something** somewhat

107 **bar your offence** prevent your feeling (personally) affronted

109 **abused** deceived

109–10 **persuasion** opinion

110 **you sustain** you will receive

113–14 **repulse . . . punishment** With these words, the gloves are off in the argument, and significantly it is Posthumus who explodes first, so Philario has to intervene again, to try to make peace. For a moment he seems to have succeeded: in ll. 118–19 Giacomo (perhaps) retreats to a more general position; if so, Posthumus brings him back to the specific argument in l. 120, and by l. 122 the terms of the wager have been proposed.

119 **approbation** proof

121 **whom** *OED* 11 gives various examples of *whom* 'used ungrammatically for the nominative WHO'.

122 **lay** bet
ten thousand ducats A *ducat* was a gold

commend me to the court where your lady is, with no
more advantage than the opportunity of a second conference, and I will bring from thence that honour of hers,   125
which you imagine so reserved.

POSTHUMUS I will wage against your gold, gold to it. My ring
I hold dear as my finger, 'tis part of it.

GIACOMO You are afraid, and therein the wiser. If you buy
ladies' flesh at a million a dram, you cannot preserve it   130
from tainting; but I see you have some religion in you,
that you fear.

POSTHUMUS This is but a custom in your tongue; you bear a
graver purpose, I hope.

GIACOMO I am the master of my speeches, and would   135
undergo what's spoken, I swear.

POSTHUMUS Will you? I shall but lend my diamond till your
return. Let there be covenants drawn between's. My
mistress exceeds in goodness the hugeness of your
unworthy thinking. I dare you to this match. Here's my   140
ring.

PHILARIO I will have it no lay.

---

129 afraid] THEOBALD; a Friend F

coin. It is notoriously difficult to
find modern equivalents for money of
the past; but in the late sixteenth century, the annual income of a well-off
Italian nobleman was roughly one thousand ducats (J. C. Davis, *A Venetian
Family and its Fortune, 1500–1900*
(Philadelphia, 1975), pp. 41, 56), so
Giacomo is setting the stakes of the
wager very high.

123 **commend me** i.e. give me a letter of
introduction
127 **wage** stake
gold to it i.e. a sum of gold to match it
129 **afraid** F has 'a Friend', which makes a
kind of sense—'You are her friend, her
lover, and know her, so you know she
will yield, and wisely won't accept the
wager'—but surely no audience would
pick all this up, whereas *afraid* is perfectly
calculated to exploit Posthumus' apparent evasion, and to provoke him further;
and Giacomo returns to *fear* at the end
of the speech, in a phrase which

suggests that he has already introduced
the idea.
130 **a million a dram** i.e. a large amount of
money for a very small amount of flesh (a
dram is a small unit of weight)
131–2 **you have . . . fear** You show some
signs of religious belief since you are
afraid (in the sense of showing awe of
God; compare Psalm 111: 10: 'The
beginning of wisdom is the fear of the
Lord'), but Giacomo implies ironically
that Posthumus' *religion* is to show a
wise doubt about his goddess, Innogen.
132 **that** since
133 **custom in your tongue** way of speaking
136 **undergo** carry out
138 **covenants** agreements
between's between us
138–40 **My mistress . . . thinking** The scale
of this hyperbole expresses Posthumus'
fury at Giacomo's proposal, and by the
end of the speech he has taken the initia-
tive in the wager: 'I dare *you*'.
142 **I will . . . no lay** I will not allow this
wager

GIACOMO By the gods, it is one. If I bring you no sufficient
testimony that I have enjoyed the dearest bodily part of
your mistress, my ten thousand ducats are yours, so is   145
your diamond too; if I come off and leave her in such
honour as you have trust in, she your jewel, this your
jewel, and my gold are yours, provided I have your
commendation for my more free entertainment.

POSTHUMUS I embrace these conditions; let us have articles   150
betwixt us. Only thus far you shall answer: if you make
your voyage upon her and give me directly to understand you have prevailed, I am no further your enemy;
she is not worth our debate. If she remain unseduced,
you not making it appear otherwise, for your ill opinion   155
and th'assault you have made to her chastity you shall
answer me with your sword.

GIACOMO Your hand, a covenant. We will have these
things set down by lawful counsel, and straight away
for Britain, lest the bargain should catch cold and starve.   160
I will fetch my gold and have our two wagers recorded.

POSTHUMUS Agreed.   [*Exit with Giacomo*]

FRENCHMAN Will this hold, think you?

PHILARIO Signor Giacomo will not from it. Pray let us
follow 'em.   *Exeunt*   165

I.5   *Enter the Queen, Ladies, and Cornelius*

QUEEN
Whiles yet the dew's on ground, gather those flowers.
Make haste. Who has the note of them?

A LADY   I, madam.

---

162 *Exit with Giacomo*] not in F
   I.5] *Scena Sexta.* F

143–9 **If ... entertainment** Giacomo twice
   describes the conditions under which
   Posthumus will win, rather than stating
   both sides of the wager, but, as Johnson
   says, 'One condition of a wager implies
   the other'.
149 **commendation** introduction
   free entertainment easy reception
150 **articles** an itemized agreement
151–2 **make ... upon** seduce
152 **directly** plainly

159 **straight away** immediately set out
160 **starve** die. This was the original
   meaning (from OE *steorfan*), from
   which the modern 'die of hunger'
   derives.
164 **from it** i.e. depart from it
I.5.1 **Whiles ... ground** while the dew is still
   on the ground. *Whiles* is an older form of
   'while' (Abbott §137).
   flowers There may be a deliberate contrast between the apparently innocent

QUEEN Dispatch.   *Exeunt Ladies*
    Now Master Doctor, have you brought those drugs?
CORNELIUS
    Pleaseth your highness, ay. Here they are, madam.   5
       He gives her a box
    But I beseech your grace, without offence—
    My conscience bids me ask—wherefore you have
    Commanded of me these most poisonous compounds,
    Which are the movers of a languishing death,
    But though slow, deadly.
QUEEN   I wonder, doctor,   10
    Thou ask'st me such a question. Have I not been
    Thy pupil long? Hast thou not learned me how
    To make perfumes, distil, preserve—yea, so
    That our great King himself doth woo me oft
    For my confections? Having thus far proceeded,   15
    Unless thou think'st me devilish, is't not meet
    That I did amplify my judgement in
    Other conclusions? I will try the forces
    Of these thy compounds on such creatures as
    We count not worth the hanging, but none human,   20
    To try the vigour of them, and apply
    Allayments to their act, and by them gather
    Their several virtues and effects.
CORNELIUS   Your highness

---

3 *Exeunt Ladies*] F2; *Exit Ladies*. F1   5.1 *He gives her a box*] not in F

lyricism of the flower-gathering and her sinister interest in poison, perhaps marked in the pause implied by the short line 3. The note to l. 82 suggests a transition in the opposite direction.

3 **Dispatch** be quick
5 **Pleaseth** if it pleases
6 **without offence** i.e. if I may do so without causing offence
7 **wherefore** why
8 **compounds** compounded drugs
9 **languishing** long-drawn-out
12 **learned** taught. This older usage (*OED*, *learn*, *v*. 4c) is still in use in some English regions.
13 **distil, preserve** extract the essence from the flowers, and preserve them
    yea yes (often used for emphasis, as here)
15 **confections** mixtures
17 **did amplify** extended
    judgement knowledge
18 **conclusions** experiments
21 **try . . . them** test how well the drugs work
22 **Allayments . . . act** antidotes to their action
23 **several** individual
    virtues powers

Shall from this practice but make hard your heart.
Besides, the seeing these effects will be   25
Both noisome and infectious.
QUEEN   O content thee.

Enter Pisanio

(*Aside*) Here comes a flattering rascal, upon him
Will I first work. He's factor for his master,
And enemy to my son.—How now, Pisanio?—
Doctor, your service for this time is ended.   30
Take your own way.
CORNELIUS (*aside*)   I do suspect you, madam,
But you shall do no harm.
QUEEN (*to Pisanio*)   Hark thee, a word.
CORNELIUS (*aside*)

I do not like her. She doth think she has
Strange ling'ring poisons. I do know her spirit,
And will not trust one of her malice with   35
A drug of such damned nature. Those she has
Will stupefy and dull the sense a while,
Which first, perchance, she'll prove on cats and dogs,
Then afterward up higher; but there is
No danger in what show of death it makes   40
More than the locking up the spirits a time,
To be more fresh, reviving. She is fooled
With a most false effect, and I the truer
So to be false with her.
QUEEN   No further service, doctor,
Until I send for thee.
CORNELIUS   I humbly take my leave.   *Exit*   45

28 factor for] HUDSON 1881 (*conj*. W. S. Walker); for F

24 **practice** activity
26 **noisome** disagreeable. In other Shakespearian examples, it is associated with
foul smells, so perhaps it means that the
after-effects of the drugs were foul-
smelling.
content thee set your mind at rest
28 **factor** agent. F reads 'Hee's for his Master', which makes sense; but Hudson's
conjecture 'factor for' provides a
balanced phrase to match *enemy to my*

son in the next line.
38 **prove** try
39 **higher** (in the scale of creation)
40 **what . . . makes** the appearance of death
the drug makes
42 **To be . . . reviving** The idea that an
extreme or deathlike experience leads to
new life is central to this play, as in Innogen's recovery in 4.2 and Jupiter's promise at 5.3.202.

QUEEN (*to Pisanio*)

    Weeps she still, sayst thou? Dost thou think in time
    She will not quench, and let instructions enter
    Where folly now possesses? Do thou work.
    When thou shalt bring me word she loves my son
    I'll tell thee on the instant thou art then   50
    As great as is thy master—greater, for
    His fortunes all lie speechless, and his name
    Is at last gasp. Return he cannot, nor
    Continue where he is. To shift his being
    Is to exchange one misery with another,   55
    And every day that comes comes to decay
    A day's work in him. What shalt thou expect
    To be depender on a thing that leans,
    Who cannot be new built nor has no friends
    So much as but to prop him?
        ⌈*She drops her box. He takes it up*⌉
                                  Thou tak'st up   60
    Thou know'st not what; but take it for thy labour.
    It is a thing I made which hath the King
    Five times redeemed from death. I do not know
    What is more cordial. Nay, I prithee take it.
    It is an earnest of a farther good   65
    That I mean to thee. Tell thy mistress how
    The case stands with her; do't as from thyself.
    Think what a chance thou changest on, but think

---

60 *She drops . . . up*] *not in* F   68 chance thou changest] F ; change thou chancest THEOBALD

47 **quench** *OED v.* 6c, citing this line, thinks this an obsolete use meaning 'cool down'—presumably implying 'cool her passion'.
    instructions good advice
52–3 **His fortunes . . . gasp** Posthumus' powerless state is expressed by personifying his *fortunes* and his *name* (reputation) as people at the point of death.
54 **being** place of abode
56–7 **every . . . him** Either 'every day that comes has the effect of destroying a day's work in him' (i.e. he simply wastes another day of his life) or 'on every day that comes, a day's work comes to decay' (i.e. is wasted).

58 **thing that leans** something that cannot even stand upright
59 **new built** restored (i.e. Posthumus' fortunes are hopeless)
60 **So much as but to** who can even
64 **cordial** restorative
    prithee A common colloquialism for 'pray you' (a polite phrase).
65 **earnest** foretaste (literally 'advance payment')
67 **as from thyself** as if it was your own idea
68 **Think . . . changest on** i.e. consider what an opportunity for advancement you have by changing sides. Theobald's emendation 'change thou chancest on', i.e. 'change of fortune, advancement, you have stumbled on' is very tempting.

Thou hast thy mistress still, to boot, my son,
Who shall take notice of thee. I'll move the King   70
To any shape of thy preferment, such
As thou'lt desire; and then myself, I chiefly,
That set thee on to this desert, am bound
To load thy merit richly. Call my women.   *Exit Pisanio*
Think on my words. A sly and constant knave,   75
Not to be shaked; the agent for his master,
And the remembrancer of her to hold
The hand-fast to her lord. I have given him that
Which if he take, shall quite unpeople her
Of liegers for her sweet, and which she after,   80
Except she bend her humour, shall be assured
To taste of too.
            Enter Pisanio and Ladies
                    So, so; well done, well done.
The violets, cowslips, and the primroses
Bear to my closet. Fare thee well, Pisanio.
Think on my words, Pisanio.
PISANIO   And shall do.   85
                    Exeunt Queen and Ladies

---

85 words, Pisanio] OXFORD (*conj.* Dowden); words F   85.1 *Exeunt*] *Exit Qu. and Ladies* F (*after* 'my words')

69 **to boot** to (your) advantage (*OED sb.*[1] 1)
70 **take notice of** bestow attention on
71–2 **any . . . desire** any kind of promotion that you would like
73 **That set . . . desert** who started you on the path to this reward
74 *Exit Pisanio* Some editors move this to after 'my words' in the next line; but presumably the Queen calls out after him as he goes.
75–8 **A sly . . . lord** Pisanio has remained completely silent during the Queen's blandishments, and she interprets his silence correctly.
77 **remembrancer of her** one who reminds her (a legal term, perhaps preparing for the next phrase)
77–8 **hold | The hand-fast** stay faithful to the betrothal or marriage contract
80 **liegers for her sweet** A *lieger* is a resident ambassador (*OED, ledger, sb.* 6), so the

phrase means 'representatives of her husband'.
81 **bend her humour** change her mind
82 This line is a good example of the sharp contrasts that operate in this play, a point nicely made by Joan Miller at Stratford-upon-Avon in 1957, modulating 'in a breath from her murderous hate of Pisanio to the innocent charm of her supervision of the posy-gatherers' (Nigel Townshend, *Leamington Spa Courier*, 5 July 1957).
84 **closet** private apartment
85 This line is metrically defective in F, and Dowden conjectured that the compositor misread a *Pisanio* ending the speech as a prefix for the next speech. To restore *Pisanio* makes the line regular, and the caressing repetition of the name from l. 84 is characteristic of the Queen's methods; it also intensifies the anticlimax of Pisanio's concluding couplet.

But when to my good lord I prove untrue,
I'll choke myself: there's all I'll do for you.   *Exit*

1.6   *Enter Innogen alone*
INNOGEN
A father cruel and a stepdame false,
A foolish suitor to a wedded lady
That hath her husband banished. O that husband,
My supreme crown of grief, and those repeated
Vexations of it! Had I been thief-stol'n,   5
As my two brothers, happy; but most miserable
Is the desire that's glorious. Blest be those,
How mean soe'er, that have their honest wills,
Which seasons comfort. Who may this be? Fie!
     Enter Pisanio and Giacomo
PISANIO
Madam, a noble gentleman of Rome   10

1.6] *Scena Septima.* F   7 desire] F2; desires F1

1.6.0.1 *Enter Innogen alone* F's stage direction emphasizes Innogen's isolation,
which the soliloquy then develops, and
her consequent vulnerability to Giacomo. It invites, and often receives, a
slow, pensive entry; the BBC television
version makes the point differently, with
the camera panning slowly along a gal-
lery towards her isolated, seated figure in
the distance.
3 **That . . . banished** whose husband has
been banished
4 **supreme** The stress is on the first syllable,
unlike modern prose usage.
   repeated renewed (i.e. Posthumus' banishment is the main cause of her grief, but
   her father's cruelty, the Queen's deceit,
   and Cloten's pestering keep renewing
   and intensifying it)
5–6 **Had . . . happy** 'If I had been stolen by
thieves like my brothers, I had been
happy.' This usefully reminds the audience about the stolen princes, first mentioned at the start of the play.
6–7 **most . . . glorious** Perhaps this means
'the desire for great things is doomed to
misery'; but more likely is 'the desire of

great people (like herself) is miserable',
since this contrasts both with the *thief-
stol'n* princes that precede it and the
humble people who can have what they
want (*their honest wills*) in the following
line.
7 The line is regular if *glorious* is two syllables and F's *blessed* is one; see the note to
1.1.140.
8 **How mean soe'er** however humble they
are
   wills desires
9 **Which seasons comfort** To *season* is to add
flavouring to food, so figuratively it
means 'gives a relish to comfort,
intensifies it'. But it is possible that
seasons comfort means 'the seasons
bring comfort' to poor people who
nevertheless have their desires, and
ripen them.
   Who . . . Fie Innogen exclaims in irrita-
   tion at being disturbed in her private
   apartments. Some editors move the
   entry of Pisanio and Giacomo to before
   this phrase, but she can as easily hear or
   see them approaching offstage (see
   1.1.69–70 and note).

Comes from my lord with letters.

GIACOMO   Change you, madam?
The worthy Leonatus is in safety,
And greets your highness dearly.

He gives her the letters

INNOGEN   Thanks good sir,
You're kindly welcome.

She reads the letters

GIACOMO (*aside*)
All of her that is out of door most rich!   15
If she be furnished with a mind so rare
She is alone th'Arabian bird, and I
Have lost the wager. Boldness be my friend;
Arm me audacity from head to foot,
Or like the Parthian I shall flying fight;   20
Rather, directly fly.

INNOGEN (*reads aloud*) 'He is one of the noblest note, to
whose kindnesses I am most infinitely tied. Reflect upon
him accordingly, as you value your trust.

                              Leonatus.'   25

(*To Giacomo*) So far I read aloud,

---

13 *He . . . letters*] not in F   14.1 *She . . . letters*] not in F   17 alone‸] F; alone, OXFORD (*conj.* Seymour)   22 *reads aloud*] *Imogen reads.* F (*centred*)   24 trust] F; truest HANMER

11 **Change you, madam** *Change* means 'change colour, blush': Innogen's face is flushed with excitement or anxiety. Giacomo assumes the latter, and assures her of her husband's safety.

14 This is an incomplete line; the pause is partly for Innogen to start reading her letters, but also for Giacomo to observe her.

15 **out of door** outside, external

16 **furnished** equipped
rare exceptional. See note to 1.1.47.

17 **She . . . Arabian bird** She only is the Phoenix, a mythical bird of which only one existed at any one time, and therefore an image of uniqueness. Some editors emphasize this by phrasing 'She is alone, th'Arabian bird'.

18 **Boldness be** may boldness be

19 **Arm me audacity** may audacity arm me

20–1 **Or . . . fly** If *boldness* and *audacity* cannot help him, he will have to adopt more devious methods, like the Parthians,

whose fighting method was to retreat, shooting arrows at their pursuers as they went—but probably not even something like that will work, so he will have to flee outright (*directly fly*).

22–5 Innogen has been reading the early part of the letter during Giacomo's soliloquy, and this is probably its conclusion, the introduction that Giacomo asked Posthumus to provide at 1.4.123.

22 **note** reputation

23 **Reflect** look (Schmidt)

24 **as . . . trust** as you observe your duty or loyalty as my wife (or perhaps 'as you value your faith in me'). Some editors feel that the letter should end more affectionately, and read 'Your truest Leonatus'; but the Folio suggests something different, and makes good sense.

26 **So far** so much. *So far* need not imply that what Innogen suppresses—see the next lines, and note—follows what she has read aloud.

But even the very middle of my heart
Is warmed by th' rest, and takes it thankfully.
You are as welcome, worthy sir, as I
Have words to bid you, and shall find it so   30
In all that I can do.

GIACOMO   Thanks, fairest lady.
What, are men mad? Hath nature given them eyes
To see this vaulted arch and the rich crop
Of sea and land, which can distinguish 'twixt
The fiery orbs above and the twinned stones   35
Upon th'unnumbered beach, and can we not
Partition make with spectacles so precious
'Twixt fair and foul?

INNOGEN   What makes your admiration?
GIACOMO
It cannot be i'th' eye—for apes and monkeys,

---

28 takes] POPE; take F   36 th'unnumbered] THEOBALD; the number'd F

27–8 **But even . . . thankfully** Innogen keeps
intimate details from Giacomo, as she
does from Pisanio at 1.3.29.

32–126 These speeches are the most
extreme examples of what James Sutherland calls 'a sort of impressionism'
(p. 147). The dramatic purpose is clear:
Giacomo uses a kind of verbal obscurity,
usually sexual, to bewilder Innogen and
catch her off guard. Both she and the
audience grasp the general, suggestive
drift, if not any paraphrasable detail. In
ll. 32–51 Giacomo delivers what Dowden
calls a 'feigned soliloquy': he appears to
be talking to the audience, but in fact it is
a soliloquy which, breaking the theatrical convention, he intends Innogen to
overhear.

33 **vaulted arch** i.e. the sky, imagined as the
archway of a large building, such as a
cathedral
crop surface (*OED sb.* 6, citing examples
of its use for the surface of both sea and
ground). Many editors interpret *crop* as
'harvest', and the whole phrase as
'what sea and land produce', but this
implies a god's-eye-view, whereas
Giacomo is talking about what *men* can
distinguish.

34–5 **distinguish . . . stones** distinguish one
orb from another, and stone from stone

35 **orbs** heavenly bodies
twinned identical. This phrase and *Timon*
4.3.3, 'Twinned brothers of one womb',
again in a context of heavenly spheres,
are *OED*'s earliest examples of this usage.

36 **unnumbered** innumerable. The Folio's
'number'd' has its defenders, glossing it
'numerous'; but Giacomo wants to convey a sense of wide expanses, looking up
to the heavenly spheres and then down
to the seashore, and this implication of
unnumbered is supported by *Tragedy of
Lear* 4.5.20–1: 'The murmuring surge |
That on th'unnumbered idle pebble
chafes'.

37 **Partition** separation, distinction
spectacles so precious eyes. For the transferred use of *spectacles* from something
that assists the eyes to mean the eyes
themselves, compare *Contention* (2
Henry VI) 3.2.111–12: '[I] bid mine
eyes be packing with my heart, | And
called them blind and dusky spectacles'.

38 **makes your admiration** causes your
amazement

39–46 **It cannot . . . feed** This speech, while
maintaining the balanced contrasts of
the previous one, widens the focus from
sight in the first speech to *judgement* and
then *appetite*. The style is discussed in the
Introduction, p. 22.

'Twixt two such shes, would chatter this way and   40
Contemn with mows the other; nor i'th' judgement,
For idiots in this case of favour would
Be wisely definite; nor i'th' appetite:
Sluttery, to such neat excellence opposed,
Should make desire vomit emptiness,   45
Not so allured to feed.

INNOGEN What is the matter, trow?

GIACOMO The cloyèd will,
That satiate yet unsatisfied desire, that tub
Both filled and running, ravening first the lamb,   50
Longs after for the garbage.

INNOGEN   What, dear sir,
Thus raps you? Are you well?

GIACOMO

Thanks madam, well. (*To Pisanio*) Beseech you sir,

---

39 **apes and monkeys** i.e. even gross creatures like this could make distinctions which, it is implied, Posthumus cannot.

40 **shes** women. At last Giacomo, though still obscurely, hints at what his contrast between *fair* and *foul* (l. 38) might be about.

40–1 **chatter ... other** chatter approvingly in this direction and scorn (*contemn*) with grimaces (*mows*) in the other.

40 **this way** i.e. in Innogen's direction

41 **the other** i.e. in the direction of some much uglier she

42 **case of favour** beauty contest

43 **Be wisely definite** make a wise decision
appetite implying both 'hunger' and 'sexual desire': the two senses are fused in ll. 45–51.

44 **Sluttery . . . neat excellence** The other woman and Innogen. What J. B. Leishman calls the 'dynamic abstractions' here (*Milton's Minor Poems* (1969), p. 243) are characteristic of Shakespeare's style; Leishman compares those in Sonnet 66, e.g. 'captive good attending captain ill' (l. 12).

45 **Should . . . emptiness** should make someone with a hungry appetite retch on an empty stomach, without actually vomiting

45 **desire** both 'appetite' and 'sexual desire'

46 **Not . . . feed** not enticed by the slut to feed (upon her, i.e. have intercourse with her)

47 **What . . . trow** What are you talking about? *Trow* is hardly more than an expletive, deriving from 'Trow you', 'do you believe'.

48 **cloyèd will** lust that is surfeited. Compare *Antony* 2.2.242–4: 'Other women cloy | The appetites they feed, but she makes hungry | Where most she satisfies', where the second idea is relevant to Giacomo's next lines.

49 **to that tub . . . running** The desire which is unsatisfied even after intercourse is emphasized by evoking both the classical legend of the leaky tub which the Danaïds were condemned to keep filling in Hades (Horace, *Odes* 3.11.23–6) and the more down-to-earth 'sweating tub' used to cure venereal diseases (perhaps anticipating the *boiled stuff* of l. 125).

50 **running** running out, emptying
ravening feeding ravenously on
lamb the symbol of innocent purity, i.e. the virtuous woman

51 **garbage** i.e. the slut

51–2 **What . . . well** Innogen wittily undercuts Giacomo's obscurities.

52 **raps** transports (*OED v.*³ 2b)

Desire my man's abode where I did leave him.
He's strange and peevish.

PISANIO   I was going, sir,   55
  To give him welcome.   *Exit*

INNOGEN   Continues well my lord?
  His health, beseech you?

GIACOMO   Well, madam.

INNOGEN
  Is he disposed to mirth? I hope he is.

GIACOMO
  Exceeding pleasant, none a stranger there
  So merry and so gamesome. He is called   60
  The Briton Reveller.

INNOGEN   When he was here
  He did incline to sadness, and oft-times
  Not knowing why.

GIACOMO   I never saw him sad.
  There is a Frenchman his companion, one
  An eminent monsieur, that it seems much loves   65
  A Gallian girl at home. He furnaces
  The thick sighs from him, whiles the jolly Briton—
  Your lord I mean—laughs from's free lungs, cries 'O,
  Can my sides hold, to think that man, who knows
  By history, report, or his own proof   70
  What woman is, yea what she cannot choose

---

54 **Desire . . . him** ask my servant to wait for me where I left him. This is obviously an excuse to get rid of Pisanio, which Giacomo realizes he must do if he is to make any headway with Innogen.

55 **strange** a foreigner
peevish temperamental

56 Pisanio's exit marks the end of the first stage of the scene, but Innogen's question about Posthumus shows that she has not missed the significance of Giacomo's obscure sexual innuendoes; this gives him the opportunity to slander Posthumus more openly.

57 This is a short line, perhaps indicating an awkward silence after Pisanio's exit, as they get the conversation going again.

59 **none a stranger** not a foreigner (an emphatic use: Abbott §53)

60 **gamesome** sportive. This is the first of a series of words that suggest both cheerfulness and licentiousness: others are *Reveller* (l. 61), *jolly* (67), *free, languish* (72).

62 **sadness** seriousness (or perhaps melancholy, as at *Merchant* 1.1.1: 'I know not why I am so sad', in view of the next phrase)

65 **monsieur** (a French courtesy title)

66 **Gallian** French

66–7 **furnaces . . . sighs** heaves sighs as if they were smoke from a furnace

67 **thick** close together

68 **from's free lungs** from his open lungs, i.e. without restriction (*OED, free, a.* 11); *free* has taken on sexual overtones by l. 72.

70 **proof** experience

But must be, will's free hours languish
For assurèd bondage?'
INNOGEN   Will my lord say so?
GIACOMO
Ay madam, with his eyes in flood with laughter.
It is a recreation to be by   75
And hear him mock the Frenchman. But heavens know
Some men are much to blame.
INNOGEN   Not he I hope.
GIACOMO
Not he; but yet heaven's bounty towards him might
Be used more thankfully. In himself 'tis much;
In you, which I account his, beyond all talents.   80
Whilst I am bound to wonder, I am bound
To pity too.
INNOGEN   What do you pity, sir?
GIACOMO
Two creatures heartily.
INNOGEN   Am I one, sir?
You look on me; what wreck discern you in me
Deserves your pity?
GIACOMO   Lamentable! What,   85
To hide me from the radiant sun, and solace
I'th' dungeon by a snuff?
INNOGEN   I pray you sir,

---

84 wreck] F (wrack)

72 **will's . . . languish** will waste his independent hours pining with love
73 **assurèd** Both 'certain' and 'married'.
79 **In himself 'tis much** i.e. Heaven has
   been generous in giving him personal
   qualities
80 **In you . . . talents** In giving you to him,
   Heaven has given him something far
   beyond his merits and beyond price.
   Talents plays on the meanings 'riches',
   derived from the monetary measure
   used, for example, throughout *Timon of
   Athens*, and 'natural endowments'. Both
   senses are also present in the biblical
   parable of the talents (Matthew 25 : 14–
   29), which argues that we should make
   the most of what we are given.

80 **account** reckon (leading naturally into
   the financial sense of *talents*; see previous
   note)
83 **Two creatures** Posthumus, for failing to
   value his wife, and Innogen, for being
   betrayed by him.
84 **wreck** ruin
85 **Lamentable** The stress falls on the first
   syllable.
86 **hide me** hide myself. He is of course referring not to himself but to Posthumus,
   hiding from the *sun* of Innogen and
   taking comfort (*solace*) with a prostitute
   in the dark.
87 **by a snuff** beside the burnt-out wick of a
   candle
87–9 Innogen begins to lose patience with

Deliver with more openness your answers
To my demands. Why do you pity me?

GIACOMO That others do—   90
    I was about to say enjoy your—but
    It is an office of the gods to venge it,
    Not mine to speak on't.

INNOGEN   You do seem to know
    Something of me, or what concerns me. Pray you,
    Since doubting things go ill often hurts more   95
    Than to be sure they do—for certainties
    Either are past remedies, or, timely knowing,
    The remedy then born—discover to me
    What both you spur and stop.

GIACOMO   Had I this cheek
    To bathe my lips upon; this hand whose touch,   100
    Whose every touch, would force the feeler's soul
    To th'oath of loyalty; this object which
    Takes prisoner the wild motion of mine eye,
    Firing it only here: should I, damned then,

---

101 every] F1; very F3   104 Firing] F1 (Fiering); Fixing F2

Giacomo's insinuations, and characteristically asks him to speak more plainly. She repeats this request more emphatically at ll. 94–9.

91 **enjoy your—** Presumably Giacomo is about to say 'your husband'; his sudden breaking-off makes the sexual connotation of *enjoy* virtually certain.

92 **office** function
    venge revenge

94–9 **Pray . . . stop** This speech is very characteristic of much of the play's style, and Innogen's in particular, in using a parenthesis (ll. 96–8) to define the meaning more precisely.

94 **Pray you** I pray you, I ask you

95 **doubting** suspecting

96–8 **for . . . born** for if you are certain that things go badly, either you realize that the situation is irredeemable, or, if you know in time, you can do something to save it

98 **discover** reveal, make known

99 **spur and stop** urge on and hold back. The expression is from horse-riding, spurring the horse on and suddenly pulling it back. Compare modern 'stop and start'.

99–112 **Had I . . . revolt** The general sense of

this convoluted speech is: 'If I had this creature to kiss, to hold, and to look at, how could I kiss, hold, and look at a prostitute? I should deserve every punishment of hell for such disloyalty.' As well as continuing his sexual allusiveness, Giacomo introduces the idea of having Innogen himself. The scene is intensifying, and in the next speech Innogen's faith in Posthumus wavers for the first time.

101–2 **force . . . loyalty** compel the person who is touching to be (or remain) loyal

102 **this object** Perhaps Innogen herself; perhaps her eye, introducing the next idea, and contrasting with the *base* eye of the prostitute in ll. 108–9.

103 **motion** Perhaps 'passion', as at *Twelfth Night* 2.4.17: 'Unstaid and skittish in all motions else'.

104 **Firing** setting it afire (i.e. Innogen, or her eye—see note to l. 102—sets his eyes aflame, makes them flash). But F2's 'Fixing' has much to be said for it: Innogen compels Giacomo's eye to be fixed only on her. This is probably easier to communicate in performance.
    damned then damned by so doing

Slaver with lips as common as the stairs   105
That mount the Capitol; join grips with hands
Made hard with hourly falsehood—falsehood as
With labour—then by-peeping in an eye
Base and illustrous as the smoky light
That's fed with stinking tallow: it were fit   110
That all the plagues of hell should at one time
Encounter such revolt.
INNOGEN   My lord, I fear,
Has forgot Britain.
GIACOMO   And himself. Not I
Inclined to this intelligence pronounce
The beggary of his change, but 'tis your graces   115
That from my mutest conscience to my tongue
Charms this report out.
INNOGEN   Let me hear no more.
GIACOMO
O dearest soul, your cause doth strike my heart
With pity that doth make me sick. A lady
So fair, and fastened to an empery   120
Would make the great'st king double, to be partnered
With tomboys hired with that self exhibition

---

109 illustrous] F (illustrious)

105–6 **Slaver . . . Capitol** kiss lips as much-used as are the hundred steps that ascend the Capitoline Hill to the temple of Jupiter in Rome
105 **Slaver** slobber
　as common . . . stairs For the idiom, compare *2 Henry IV* 2.2.159–60, about the prostitute Doll Tearsheet: 'as common as the way between Saint Albans and London'.
107 **Made . . . falsehood** i.e. made hard with clasping and fondling different men every hour (unlike the touch of Innogen's hand in ll. 100–2, which inspires loyalty)
107–8 **falsehood . . . labour** The prostitute's attentions are as deceitful as active.
108 **by-peeping** peeping sideways (seductively)
109 **illustrous** lack-lustre (i.e. not lustrous, not giving light)
110 **tallow** i.e. tallow candle (picking up from the *snuff* of l. 87)

112 **Encounter** confront
113–14 **Not . . . pronounce** it is not because I am disposed to give this information that I report
115 **beggary** contemptible nature
116 **conscience** inmost thought
117 **Charms** lures, as if by magic
120 I **empery . . . double** which would make the greatest king in the world twice as great (Innogen is heir-apparent to the British crown)
121 **partnered** equated
122 **tomboys** prostitutes. Dowden points out a relevant parallel in W. Warren's *Nursery of Names* (1581): 'Like tomboys such as lives in Rome | For every knave's delight.'
　self exhibition same allowance (of money). Compare *Two Gentlemen* 1.3.68–9: 'What maintenance he . . . receives, | Like exhibition thou shalt have from me.'

Which your own coffers yield; with diseased ventures
That play with all infirmities for gold,
Which rottenness can lend nature; such boiled stuff   125
As well might poison poison! Be revenged,
Or she that bore you was no queen, and you
Recoil from your great stock.

INNOGEN   Revenged?
How should I be revenged? If this be true—
As I have such a heart that both mine ears   130
Must not in haste abuse—if it be true,
How should I be revenged?

GIACOMO   Should he make me
Live like Diana's priest betwixt cold sheets
Whiles he is vaulting variable ramps,
In your despite, upon your purse—revenge it.   135
I dedicate myself to your sweet pleasure,
More noble than that runagate to your bed,
And will continue fast to your affection,
Still close as sure.

INNOGEN   What ho, Pisanio!

GIACOMO
Let me my service tender on your lips.   140

125 lend] F; lend to OXFORD   133 Live] F; Lie HUDSON 1881 (*conj.* W. S. Walker)

123 **ventures** i.e. people who venture, run
risks (in the prostitute's case, the diseases
which they risk in exchange for the
money they earn, as the next lines specify)
124 **play** gamble
125 **Which** i.e. the *infirmities* of l. 124
lend Oxford reads 'lend to' since 'F pro-
duces a highly anomalous string of
syllables' and their emendation 'a
normal hexameter' (*Textual Companion*,
p. 605); but F's line is neither unspeak-
able nor (for this play) notably irregular.
boiled stuff prostitutes who have been
treated for venereal disease by sweating
in tubs of steam from boiling water. Compare the *tub* of l. 49.
126 **poison poison** i.e. they are so diseased
that they would infect even poison itself.
Giacomo rises to a peak of revolting suggestiveness just before urging Innogen,
in the same line, to take revenge for
such behaviour.

128 **Recoil from** prove degenerate to
stock birth, ancestry
130–1 **I . . . abuse** what my ears have heard
(about Posthumus) must not easily
mislead my heart (away from my love
for him)
133 **Diana** goddess of chastity. She is evoked
elsewhere in the play, in each case, as
here, in an unchaste context (2.3.67;
2.4.82, 159; 5.4.180).
134 **vaulting** sexually straddling
variable ramps a variety of whores
135 **In your despite** in scorn of you
upon your purse i.e. you are not only
wronged, you are paying for it as well
136 **I . . . pleasure** This is the turning-point of
the scene. Giacomo must of course make
his move, but it is fatal: Innogen
instantly recoils.
137 **runagate** runaway, vagabond
138 **fast** constant (i.e. holding fast)
139 **Still . . . sure** always as secret as loyal
140 **tender** offer

INNOGEN

Away, I do condemn mine ears that have
So long attended thee. If thou wert honourable
Thou wouldst have told this tale for virtue, not
For such an end thou seek'st, as base as strange.
Thou wrong'st a gentleman who is as far   145
From thy report as thou from honour, and
Solicit'st here a lady that disdains
Thee and the devil alike. What ho, Pisanio!
The King my father shall be made acquainted
Of thy assault. If he shall think it fit   150
A saucy stranger in his court to mart
As in a Romish stew, and to expound
His beastly mind to us, he hath a court
He little cares for, and a daughter who
He not respects at all. What ho, Pisanio!   155

GIACOMO

O happy Leonatus I may say,
The credit that thy lady hath of thee
Deserves thy trust, and thy most perfect goodness
Her assured credit. Blessèd live you long,
A lady to the worthiest sir that ever   160
Country called his; and you his mistress, only
For the most worthiest fit. Give me your pardon.
I have spoke this to know if your affiance

141 **condemn** Stanley Wells suggests privately that this may be an error for *contemn*, scorn, but surely Innogen is condemning, not merely scorning, her guilty ears?

142 **thee** As she rejects him, Innogen switches from the polite *you* to the contemptuous *thee*; when Giacomo recants his slander, she reverts to *you* (l. 168).

151 **saucy** insolent (a stronger term then than now)
to mart should do business. The verb derives from the noun *mart*, marketplace.

152 **Romish** (not otherwise used by Shakespeare for 'Roman')
stew brothel. The origin of the word is obscure; *OED sb.*² 4 conjectures that it may derive from association with a

heated bath-house; though it occurs elsewhere in Shakespeare, it is an especially appropriate word for Innogen to choose in contemptuous reaction to Giacomo's allusions to sexual diseases and the sweating cures associated with them.

156 **O happy . . . say** F's punctuation, or lack of it, followed here, implies 'I may call you happy Leonatus', rather than a direct address to him.

157 **credit . . . thee** reputation she has from you

159 **Her assured credit** (deserves) her unwavering faith. The stress falls on the first syllable of *assured*, unlike modern prose usage.

161 **called his** called its own

163 **affiance** engagement promise, 'trothplight'

Were deeply rooted, and shall make your lord
That which he is new o'er; and he is one   165
The truest mannered, such a holy witch
That he enchants societies into him;
Half all men's hearts are his.

INNOGEN   You make amends.

GIACOMO

He sits 'mongst men like a descended god.
He hath a kind of honour sets him off   170
More than a mortal seeming. Be not angry,
Most mighty princess, that I have adventured
To try your taking of a false report, which hath
Honoured with confirmation your great judgement
In the election of a sir so rare   175
Which you know cannot err. The love I bear him
Made me to fan you thus, but the gods made you,
Unlike all others, chaffless. Pray, your pardon.

INNOGEN

All's well, sir. Take my power i'th' court for yours.

GIACOMO

My humble thanks. I had almost forgot   180
T'entreat your grace but in a small request,
And yet of moment too, for it concerns
Your lord; myself and other noble friends
Are partners in the business.

168 men's] F2; men F1   169 descended] F2; defended F1   182 concerns‸] F4; concernes: F1

165 **new o'er** over again
   one i.e. one who is. For the idiom, compare *All is True* (*Henry VIII*) 2.4.46–7: 'one | The wisest prince' (Abbott §18).
166 **The truest mannered** the most faithful
   holy witch enchanter, wizard who practises *holy* (white) magic, not black. *Witch* was applicable to enchanters of either sex.
167 **societies** groups of people
   into to
168 **Half ... his** i.e. every man has given him half his heart
169 **like a descended god** Perhaps an anticipation of the real *descended god* who will visit Posthumus himself at

5.3.186.1.
170 **sets him off** shows him to advantage
171 **More ... seeming** making him seem more than a mortal
173 **try your taking** test your reception
175 **election** choice
176 **Which** i.e. the *judgement* of l. 174.
177 **fan** blow upon in order to winnow (i.e. separate the chaff from the grain, or, figuratively, the good from the bad)
178 **chaffless** pure grain, uncontaminated with chaff (i.e. perfect)
180 **I ... forgot** Just as the scene appears to be over, Giacomo introduces his fall-back plan, the trunk.
181 **but** only
182 **moment** importance

INNOGEN   Pray what is't?

GIACOMO

   Some dozen Romans of us, and your lord—   185

   The best feather of our wing—have mingled sums

   To buy a present for the Emperor,

   Which I, the factor for the rest, have done

   In France : 'tis plate of rare device, and jewels

   Of rich and exquisite form, their values great,   190

   And I am something curious, being strange,

   To have them in safe stowage. May it please you

   To take them in protection?

INNOGEN   Willingly,

   And pawn mine honour for their safety ; since

   My lord hath interest in them, I will keep them   195

   In my bedchamber.

GIACOMO   They are in a trunk

   Attended by my men. I will make bold

   To send them to you, only for this night.

   I must aboard tomorrow.

INNOGEN   O no, no!

GIACOMO

   Yes I beseech, or I shall short my word   200

   By length'ning my return. From Gallia

   I crossed the seas on purpose and on promise

   To see your grace.

INNOGEN   I thank you for your pains ;

   But not away tomorrow!

GIACOMO   O I must, madam.

   Therefore I shall beseech you, if you please   205

   To greet your lord with writing, do't tonight.

   I have outstood my time, which is material

   To th' tender of our present.

---

188 **factor** agent

190 **their values** the value of each

191 **something** somewhat

   curious anxious

   strange a stranger

195 **interest** a stake

199 **O no, no** This simple phrase permits widely different interpretations, from Peggy Ashcroft's generous warmth to Judi Dench's icy politeness which did not conceal intense dislike of Giacomo and his methods.

200 **short** break

201 **Gallia** France (Gaul)

202 **on promise** having promised Posthumus to do so

207 **outstood** outstayed

   material crucial, relevant

208 **tender** offering

INNOGEN   I will write.
    Send your trunk to me, it shall safe be kept,
    And truly yielded you. You're very welcome.   210

                               Exeunt severally

2.1   *Enter Cloten and the two Lords*

CLOTEN   Was there ever man had such luck? When I kissed
    the jack upon an upcast, to be hit away! I had a hundred
    pound on't, and then a whoreson jackanapes must take
    me up for swearing, as if I borrowed mine oaths of him,
    and might not spend them at my pleasure.   5
FIRST LORD   What got he by that? You have broke his pate
    with your bowl.
SECOND LORD   (*aside*) If his wit had been like him that broke
    it, it would have run all out.
CLOTEN   When a gentleman is disposed to swear it is not for   10
    any standers-by to curtail his oaths, ha?
SECOND LORD   No my lord—(*aside*) nor crop the ears of them.
CLOTEN   Whoreson dog! I give him satisfaction? Would he
    had been one of my rank.

210.1 *severally*] *not in* F
   2.1.0 *Cloten*] Clotten F   13 give] F2 ; gaue F1

---

210 **truly yielded** faithfully given back
210.1 **severally** separately (a standard Eli-
    zabethan and Jacobean stage direction,
    though here editorial)
2.1.1–3 **Was . . . on't** Cloten has just lost a
    game of bowls.
1–2 **kissed the jack** In bowls, the *jack* is
    the target bowl, and to *kiss* it is to
    roll your own bowl close enough to
    touch it.
   2 **upon an upcast** *OED sb.* 1 glosses *upcast* as
    'accident'; but this may be a character-
    istically Shakespearian use of a verb as a
    noun (*OED v.* 3) and simply mean 'By my
    own throw'.
    hit away i.e. have my bowl knocked
    away by someone else's
    had i.e. had wagered
   3 **whoreson** A general term of abuse, lit-
    erally meaning 'son of a whore'.
    jackanapes upstart (literally 'jack-ape',
    'little monkey'). 'Jack' meaning 'knave'
    was often used to deride social aspiration,
    as at *Richard III* 1.3.72: 'every jack
    became a gentleman', hence compounds

like *jack-slave* (l. 19). Cloten certainly
views his opponents like this (ll. 13–14).
3–4 **take me up** 'rebuke me' or perhaps
    'challenge me' (*OED, take, v.* 93p) since
    he expects *satisfaction* (l. 13)
   6 **pate** head
8–9 **If . . . all out** If his wit had been like
    Cloten's, it would have run out, since
    Cloten's brains are so watery.
11 **curtail** cut short. F's spelling 'curtall' is a
    reminder that the word is associated with
    cropping the tail or ears of a dog or horse;
    these associations are picked up by the
    Second Lord in the next line and, perhaps
    unconsciously, by Cloten in l. 13.
13 **I give him satisfaction?** i.e. by accepting a
    challenge to a duel. F's 'gaue' may be
    correct, Cloten exclaiming 'Indeed I
    gave him satisfaction' (by breaking his
    head with the bowl, ll. 6–7). Seven-
    teenth-century printers often used ques-
    tion marks for exclamation marks.
14 **rank** Cloten uses this to mean 'social
    position'; in the next line, the Second
    Lord uses its other sense 'foul-smelling'.

SECOND LORD (*aside*) To have smelled like a fool.   15

CLOTEN I am not vexed more at anything in th'earth, a pox
    on't! I had rather not be so noble as I am; they dare not
    fight with me because of the Queen my mother. Every
    jack-slave hath his bellyful of fighting, and I must go up
    and down like a cock that nobody can match.   20

SECOND LORD (*aside*) You are cock and capon too, an you
    crow cock with your comb on.

CLOTEN Sayst thou?

SECOND LORD It is not fit your lordship should undertake
    every companion that you give offence to.   25

CLOTEN No, I know that, but it is fit I should commit offence
    to my inferiors.

SECOND LORD Ay, it is fit for your lordship only.

CLOTEN Why, so I say.

FIRST LORD Did you hear of a stranger that's come to court   30
    tonight?

CLOTEN A stranger, and I not know on't?

SECOND LORD (*aside*) He's a strange fellow himself and
    knows it not.

FIRST LORD There's an Italian come, and 'tis thought one of   35
    Leonatus' friends.

CLOTEN Leonatus? A banished rascal; and he's another,
    whatsoever he be. Who told you of this stranger?

FIRST LORD One of your lordship's pages.

CLOTEN Is it fit I went to look upon him? Is there no deroga-   40
    tion in't?

17 an] F (and)   24 your] F3; you F1   31 tonight] F2; night F1

19 **jack-slave** See note to *jackanapes*, l. 3.
20 **cock** leader, as in 'cock of the walk',
    derived from the cockerel asserting his
    rights over his hens against rivals, but
    with (unconscious?) phallic significance
    suggested by *up and down*
21 **capon** castrated cock. *Capon* thus came to
    mean 'fool', as at *Errors* 3.1.32: 'capon,
    coxcomb, idiot'; the idea is developed in
    the next phrase.
    an if
21-2 **you . . . on** you brag as if you were as
    proud as a cockerel in your red crest
    (with a play on fool's cap or 'cock's-
    comb')
23 **Sayst thou** 'What do you say?' (as if

Cloten half hears, and half suspects
    some criticism)
24 **undertake** take on, fight with
25 **companion** fellow (widely used in Shake-
    speare as a term of contempt)
26 **commit offence** Cloten means 'engage
    in combat', the Lord 'be offensive to'
28 **fit . . . only** i.e. only you would
    disgrace your social rank by attacking
    an inferior; Cloten misunderstands the
    force of *only* (taking it as 'exclusive') in
    his reply.
30 **stranger** foreigner
38 **whatsoever he be** whoever he is
40-1 **derogation** loss of dignity

SECOND LORD You cannot derogate, my lord.

CLOTEN Not easily, I think.

SECOND LORD (*aside*) You are a fool granted, therefore your
  issues, being foolish, do not derogate.   45

CLOTEN Come, I'll go see this Italian. What I have lost
  today at bowls I'll win tonight of him. Come, go.

SECOND LORD I'll attend your lordship.

                      Exeunt Cloten and First Lord

  That such a crafty devil as is his mother
  Should yield the world this ass: a woman that   50
  Bears all down with her brain, and this her son
  Cannot take two from twenty, for his heart,
  And leave eighteen. Alas poor princess,
  Thou divine Innogen, what thou endur'st,
  Betwixt a father by thy stepdame governed,   55
  A mother hourly coining plots, a wooer
  More hateful than the foul expulsion is
  Of thy dear husband, than that horrid act
  Of the divorce he'd make! The heavens hold firm
  The walls of thy dear honour, keep unshaked   60
  That temple, thy fair mind, that thou mayst stand
  T'enjoy thy banished lord and this great land!   *Exit*

2.2 *A trunk is put in position. A bed ⌈is put forth⌉*
     with Innogen in it, reading a book. Enter to
     her Helen, a lady

INNOGEN

  Who's there? My woman Helen?

HELEN   Please you, madam.

48.1 *Exeunt . . . Lord*] *Exit* F   58 husband, than] F3 ; Husband. Then F1   59 make! The]
THEOBALD (*subs.*) ; make the F   62 *Exit*] *Exeunt.* F
  2.2.0.1–3 *A trunk . . . lady*] OXFORD (*subs.*) ; *Enter Imogen, in her Bed, and a Lady.* F 1 HELEN]
La⟨dy⟩. F

42 **cannot derogate** (because of his great dignity, and because he in fact has no dignity to lose)

44 **granted** acknowledged

45 **issues** deeds, i.e. what issues from you,
   with a play on 'offspring'

49 **devil** (monosyllabic, as at *Twelfth
   Night* 2.3.141 : 'The dev'l a puritan that
   he is')

51 **Bears all down** carries all before her

52 **for his heart** 'to save his life'

55 **Betwixt** between

56 **coining** inventing

59 **divorce he'd make** Cloten wants to
   divorce Posthumus and Innogen.

2.2 For ways of staging this scene, and its
   theatrical impact, see Introduction,
   pp. 12–15.

0.1 *put forth* i.e. pushed out from the 'discovery space' or central, wide entry at

INNOGEN

  What hour is it?

HELEN   Almost midnight, madam.

INNOGEN

  I have read three hours then. Mine eyes are weak.

  Fold down the leaf where I have left. To bed.

  Take not away the taper, leave it burning;   5

  And if thou canst awake by four o'th' clock,

  I prithee call me. Sleep hath seized me wholly.

                      ⌈*Exit Helen*⌉

  To your protection I commend me, gods.

  From fairies and the tempters of the night

  Guard me beseech ye.   10

      She sleeps.

      Giacomo comes from the trunk

GIACOMO

  The crickets sing, and man's o'er-laboured sense

  Repairs itself by rest. Our Tarquin thus

  Did softly press the rushes ere he wakened

7.1 *Exit Helen*] *not in* F   10.1 *She*] *not in* F   10.2 *comes*] *not in* F

the back of the Jacobean stage. *Put forth* is a standard term in stage directions of the period (occurring, for example, in the Folio text of *Contention* (*2 Henry VI*) 3.2.146.2) though here editorial: it is implied by F's '*Enter Imogen, in her Bed*'. Oxford suggests that the trunk was simultaneously pushed up through the trap (*Textual Companion*, p. 605).

5 **taper** candle. This very localized source of light helps to focus the darkness, intimacy, and tension of the scene.

9 **fairies** In folklore fairies are sinister, malevolent spirits who harm mortals; at 4.2.218, Innogen, in another kind of bed, is only to be haunted by '*female* fairies', presumably the less dangerous kind.

  tempters . . . night evil spirits, perhaps devils, since this echoes the third Collect for Evening Prayer in *The Book of Common Prayer* (1559): 'defend us from all perils and dangers of this night'.

10.1 **She sleeps** There is usually a long silence in performance before the lid of

the trunk slowly opens, thus increasing the tension.

11 **The crickets sing** Both the aural and the visual aspects of the situation are evoked in Giacomo's exceptionally sensuous soliloquy.

  o'er-laboured exhausted from work

12 **Our Tarquin** Tarquin was a semi-legendary king of Rome, notorious for his rape of Lucrece, the subject of one of Shakespeare's two narrative poems. (The other, *Venus and Adonis*, is much echoed in this soliloquy, whose eroticism resembles that of the poem.) The force of *Our* is that Giacomo, like Tarquin, is Italian; by associating himself with a legendary rapist at the start of his speech, Giacomo raises the possibility of rape here too.

  thus i.e. *softly* (l. 13), gently, so as not to wake her

13 **rushes** (used as a floor-covering in the seventeenth century, including perhaps the stage floor, but also in Lucrece's Roman bedroom (*Lucrece* 318))

The chastity he wounded. Cytherea,
How bravely thou becom'st thy bed, fresh lily,   15
And whiter than the sheets! That I might touch,
But kiss, one kiss! Rubies unparagoned,
How dearly they do't! 'Tis her breathing that
Perfumes the chamber thus. The flame o'th' taper
Bows toward her, and would underpeep her lids   20
To see th'enclosèd lights, now canopied
Under these windows, white and azure-laced
With blue of heaven's own tinct. But my design—
To note the chamber. I will write all down.

    He writes in his tables

Such and such pictures, there the window, such   25
Th'adornment of her bed, the arras, figures,

---

20 lids$_\wedge$] CAMBRIDGE; lids. F   22 azure-laced] MAXWELL (*conj.* B. Nicholson, *cited in* Cambridge); Azure lac'd F   24.1 *He . . . tables*] *not in* F

---

14 **Cytherea** i.e. Venus, the goddess of love, so named because she rose from the sea near the island of Cythera. This is surely not an invocation of Venus, as has been suggested, but an address to Innogen herself, whom Giacomo sees as the goddess, and embodiment, of love.

15 **bravely** finely
lily In its whiteness, the lily was a traditional image of purity and chastity.

16 **whiter . . . sheets** Compare *Venus* 398: 'Teaching the sheets a whiter hue than white'.

17 **Rubies** i.e. her red lips
unparagoned matchless

18 **dearly** beautifully, exquisitely
do't i.e. kiss. He has presumably kissed her in the previous line, or does so here; it is dramatically important that he should be so overwhelmed by her beauty as to run the risk of waking her by kissing her; this leads naturally into his next phrase, about her breathing. Some editors interpret *do't* as the lips kissing each other, but this is surely strained and much less dramatically effective, despite the support of *Venus* 505: 'Long may [Adonis' lips] kiss each other'.

18–19 **'Tis her . . . thus** Compare *Venus* 443–4: 'For from the stillitory [still] of thy face excelling | Comes breath perfumed, that breedeth love by smelling.' So here Innogen's breath 'breeds love' in Giacomo.

21 **lights** eyes
canopied curtained, covered, as if by a canopy

22 **windows** eyelids (as often in Shakespeare, for example *Romeo* 4.1.100: 'thy eyes' windows fall'). The image here is of wooden shutters closed and curtains drawn which, as Nosworthy says, 'effectively conveys the *deepness* of [her] sleep'.
white and azure-laced white laced with blue. This might refer to the *windows*, in which case Shakespeare is visualizing latticed shutters and *azure-laced* refers to the veins in the eyelid (compare 4.2.223: 'The azured harebell, like thy veins'); or simply to her blue eyes.

23 **tinct** colour
design plan. Giacomo wrenches himself away from absorption in Innogen to gather details about the room.

24.1 *tables* notebook

25–7 **Such . . . story** Innogen's bed might have been *adorned* with hangings, and an *arras* might have covered the discovery space; but otherwise, even at the Blackfriars theatre (see Introduction, pp. 2–3), Giacomo is unlikely to be describing physical details visible on stage; the elaborate description of the room occurs in retrospect (2.4.66–91).

26 **arras** hangings of tapestry, often with scenes and *figures* woven into them

Why such and such; and the contents o'th' story.
Ah, but some natural notes about her body
Above ten thousand meaner movables
Would testify t'enrich mine inventory.   30
O sleep, thou ape of death, lie dull upon her,
And be her sense but as a monument
Thus in a chapel lying. Come off, come off;
As slippery as the Gordian knot was hard.
          He takes the bracelet from her arm
'Tis mine, and this will witness outwardly,   35
As strongly as the conscience does within,
To th' madding of her lord. On her left breast
A mole cinque-spotted, like the crimson drops
I'th' bottom of a cowslip. Here's a voucher
Stronger than ever law could make; this secret   40
Will force him think I have picked the lock and ta'en
The treasure of her honour. No more. To what end?
Why should I write this down that's riveted,
Screwed to my memory? She hath been reading late,
The tale of Tereus. Here the leaf's turned down   45
Where Philomel gave up. I have enough.

34.1 *He . . . arm*] *not in* F

27 **contents o'th' story** the narrative design
on the arras. We learn only subsequently
(2.4.69–70) that it was the first meeting
of Antony and Cleopatra.
28 **notes** distinguishing marks
29 **meaner** less important
   movables pieces of furniture (or more
   general items of property)
30 **inventory** (pronounced 'invent'ry', with
   stress on the first syllable)
31 **sleep . . . death** This is the first of two
   occasions where Innogen sleeps a deep
   sleep that resembles death; compare
   4.2.196–291. The phrase was proverbial: 'Sleep is the image of death' (Tilley
   S527).
   ape mimic (from the ability of monkeys to
   imitate human behaviour)
   dull heavy
32–3 **be . . . lying** let her have only as much
   feeling as if she were an effigy on a tomb.
   Compare *Lucrece* 391: 'like a virtuous
   monument she lies'.
34 **As slippery . . . hard** Since at *Antony*
   1.2.177 'Our slippery people' means

'tricky, devious', removing the bracelet
is presumably as tricky a problem as
the Gordian knot was before Alexander
literally cut through it (see the next
note).
   Gordian knot An intricate knot which
   Gordius, a Phrygian king, tied and chal-
   lenged anyone to untie; Alexander the
   Great cut through it with his sword.
36 **conscience** inward consciousness (rather
   than the specifically moral sense referred
   to by Innogen at 3.4.46)
37 **To th' madding** to contribute to the mad-
   dening
38 **cinque-spotted** having five spots
   drops spots of colour (like the mark or
   stain made by a drop; Giacomo refers to
   the mole itself as a *stain* at 2.4.139)
39 **voucher** piece of evidence (*OED sb.*[1] 2a)
45, 46 **Tereus, Philomel** Tereus was a
   legendary king of Athens who raped his
   sister-in-law Philomela and cut out her
   tongue so that she could not reveal
   what had happened. See Introduction,
   pp. 25–6.

To th' trunk again, and shut the spring of it.
Swift, swift, you dragons of the night, that dawning
May bare the raven's eye! I lodge in fear.
Though this a heavenly angel, hell is here.   50
    Clock strikes
One, two, three. Time, time!
    Exit into the trunk. ⌈*The bed and trunk are removed*⌉

2.3   *Enter Cloten and the two Lords*
FIRST LORD Your lordship is the most patient man in loss,
    the most coldest that ever turned up ace.
CLOTEN It would make any man cold to lose.
FIRST LORD But not every man patient after the noble tem-
    per of your lordship. You are most hot and furious when   5
    you win.
CLOTEN Winning will put any man into courage. If I could
    get this foolish Innogen, I should have gold enough. It's
    almost morning, is't not?
FIRST LORD Day, my lord.   10
CLOTEN I would this music would come. I am advised to
    give her music a-mornings, they say it will penetrate.
    Enter Musicians

49 bare] HANMER (*conj.* Theobald); beare F   51.1 *Exit...trunk*] Exit. F   *The...removed*]
OXFORD; *not in* F
    2.3.0.1 *Cloten*] Cloten F   *the two*] not in F   7 CLOTEN] F ('Clot' catchword; no speech-prefix in text)

47 **spring** locking mechanism
48 **dragons . . . night** Compare *Dream*
3.2.380: 'night's swift dragons cut the
clouds full fast'. Night seems to be imaged
as a dragon-drawn chariot, which may
have been suggested by that of the sorceress Medea (Ovid, *Metamorphoses* 7.217–
23), whose invocation of the night was
the model for Prospero's renunciation of
his magic at *Tempest* 5.1.33–57.
49 **bare . . . eye** cause the raven to wake.
They were supposed to sleep facing the
east.
50 **hell is here** danger is all around me (perhaps with the uneasy subliminal suggestion that *hell* is inside him for his plan to
slander Innogen. For the idea that we
carry our hells around with us, compare
Marlowe's *Dr Faustus*, A text, Revels edn.
(1993), 2.1.125–6: 'where we are is
hell, | And where hell is must we ever
be.')

50.1 *Clock strikes* Perhaps it struck at
other points in the scene, to indicate the
(condensed) passing of time from midnight (l. 2) to three (l. 51), as in the final
scene of *Dr Faustus*.
2.3.2 **most coldest** least passionate
    turned up ace When Cloten threw the
    dice, what lay upwards was the *ace*, the
    side of the die marked with only one
    point, the lowest score (*OED sb.* 1).
3 **cold** depressed
4 **after** according to
4–5 **temper** disposition, temperament
5 **furious** passionate
12 **a-mornings** in the morning. *OED prep.*[1]
    says that *a* here is a worn-down form of
    the OE preposition *an*, *on*, which
    absorbed the preposition *in*, giving the
    meaning 'on, in'; *a* was attached to OE
    adverbial genitives, giving *a nights*, *now-
    a-days*; *a-mornings* is formed on analogy
    with these.

Come on, tune. If you can penetrate her with your fingering, so; we'll try with tongue too. If none will do, let her remain; but I'll never give o'er. First, a very   15
excellent good-conceited thing; after, a wonderful sweet air with admirable rich words to it; and then let her consider.

⌈MUSICIAN⌉ (*sings*)

Hark, hark, the lark at heaven's gate sings,
    And Phoebus gins arise,   20
His steeds to water at those springs
    On chaliced flowers that lies,
And winking Mary-buds begin to ope their golden eyes;
With everything that pretty is, my lady sweet arise,
    Arise, arise!   25

---

19 MUSICIAN (*sings*)] SONG. F

12, 13 **penetrate** pierce, touch the heart (with sexual implication the second time)

14 **fingering ... with tongue** instrumental and vocal music (with sexual innuendoes)

so i.e. well and good

15 **give o'er** give up

16 **good conceited** ingeniously devised. This may imply that the song is preceded by an elaborate piece of instrumental music, in which case Cloten's 'aubade' or morning serenade is quite an extended performance. But perhaps the *good-conceited thing* is simply an elaborate flourish introducing the song, such as that found in the seventeenth-century setting provided in Appendix B.

17 **air** solo song

18 **consider** contemplate, think carefully

19 MUSICIAN There is no speech prefix in the Folio text here, only the heading 'SONG'; nor is there a prefix before Cloten's next speech, thus raising the possibility that Cloten himself sings the song, as in several modern productions. Although his mockery of an *unpaved eunuch* at l. 29 creates a difficulty (assuming that it refers to the performer of the song), there is otherwise no objection to the complex and often surprising character of Cloten (see notes to ll. 64–73 and 108–21) having learnt the accomplishments of a prince and so being able to perform the song, without gaining any appreciation of its beauty and value.

19–25 For a seventeenth-century setting, see Appendix B.

19 **the lark ... sings** Compare Sonnet 29.11–12: 'the lark at break of day ... sings hymns at heaven's gate'. This parallel supports F's '*Heauens*' rather than the 'heauen' of the manuscript setting discussed in Appendix B.

20 **Phoebus** Apollo, the sun-god
   gins begins to

21 **His ... water** to allow his horses to drink. Each dawn, Apollo was drawn in a jewelled chariot through the sky (Ovid, *Metamorphoses* 2.105–10). Giacomo refers to its jewels at 5.4.189–90.

21–2 **those ... lies** i.e. the dew that has collected on the petals of the flowers

22 **chaliced flowers** flowers with petals shaped like cups or chalices. *OED*, *chalice*, 4 notes that 'chalice-flower' was 'said to be an old name for the Daffodil' because the nectary was shaped like a chalice. The daffodil certainly provides an apt drinking vessel for these mythological horses; and daffodils and marigolds (see the next note) are associated in the contemporaneous *Winter's Tale* 4.4.105–18.

23 **winking ... eyes** marigolds with closed petals open them. *Winking* means 'sleeping'; for the sleeping marigold awaking, drenched in dew, in response to the sun, compare *Winter's Tale* 4.4.105–6: 'The marigold, that goes to bed wi'th' sun, | And with him rises, weeping.'

⌈CLOTEN⌉ So, get you gone. If this penetrate I will consider
your music the better; if it do not, it is a vice in her ears
which horse hairs and calves' guts nor the voice of
unpaved eunuch to boot can never amend.

Exeunt Musicians

Enter Cymbeline and the Queen

SECOND LORD Here comes the King.   30

CLOTEN I am glad I was up so late, for that's the reason I
was up so early. He cannot choose but take this service I
have done fatherly.—Good morrow to your majesty, and
to my gracious mother.

CYMBELINE
    Attend you here the door of our stern daughter?   35
    Will she not forth?

CLOTEN I have assailed her with musics, but she vouchsafes
no notice.

CYMBELINE
    The exile of her minion is too new.
    She hath not yet forgot him. Some more time   40
    Must wear the print of his remembrance out,
    And then she's yours.

QUEEN (*to Cloten*)   You are most bound to th' King,
    Who lets go by no vantages that may
    Prefer you to his daughter. Frame yourself

---

26 CLOTEN] *not in* F   27 vice] ROWE; voyce F   29 amend] F2; amed FI   29.1 *Exeunt Musicians*] *not in* F   41 out] F2 (ou't); on't FI

26 **consider** 'judge', or 'reward' (as at *Winter's Tale* 4.2.17: 'if I have not enough
considered'), or both
27 **vice** defect
28 **horse . . . guts** These were used for musical instruments, the *hairs* for the bow,
the *guts* for the strings.
29 **unpaved** without testicles or 'stones',
castrated. According to *OED*, this is
the only recorded use of *unpaved* in this
sense.
   to boot into the bargain
31–2 **I am glad . . . early** The joke, such as it
is, also occurs at *Twelfth Night* 2.3.7: 'To
be up after midnight and to go to bed then
is early'.
33 **fatherly** in a fatherly fashion
35 **Attend** wait at
37 **musics** This is not necessarily a clumsy
phrase of Cloten's (compare *All's Well*

3.7.40: 'musics of all sorts'), and in any
case it may refer to both instrumental
and vocal music.
37 **vouchsafes** bestows in a gracious or
condescending manner (*OED v.* 2). In
using this word (rather than 'takes'), Cloten may be polite to Innogen, or critical,
or a mixture of the two.
39 **minion** sexual favourite (almost always
used contemptuously in Shakespeare)
41 **wear . . . out** erase the memory of him.
For the idiom, compare 4.4.22–4: 'Many
years . . . not wore him | From my
remembrance.' F's 'on't' is almost certainly a slip for *out*; the same error probably occurs at *Twelfth Night* 3.4.198 and
Winter's Tale 4.4.160. (All three passages
were set by F's Compositor B.)
43 **vantages** opportunities
44 **Prefer** recommend

To orderly solicits, and be friended   45
With aptness of the season. Make denials
Increase your services; so seem as if
You were inspired to do those duties which
You tender to her; that you in all obey her,
Save when command to your dismission tends,   50
And therein you are senseless.

CLOTEN   Senseless? Not so.

Enter a Messenger

MESSENGER (*to Cymbeline*)
So like you, sir, ambassadors from Rome;
The one is Caius Lucius.

CYMBELINE   A worthy fellow,
Albeit he comes on angry purpose now;
But that's no fault of his. We must receive him   55
According to the honour of his sender,
And towards himself, his goodness forespent on us,
We must extend our notice. Our dear son,
When you have given good morning to your mistress,
Attend the Queen and us; we shall have need   60
T'employ you towards this Roman. Come, our queen.

Exeunt all but Cloten

---

45 solicits] F2 ; solicity F1 ; soliciting COLLIER   51.1 *Enter a Messenger*] not in F   61.1 *all but Cloten*] not in F

44–5 **Frame . . . solicits** prepare yourself for
properly regulated wooing
45 **solicits** F's 'solicity', not recorded
elsewhere, is probably not a Shakespearian coinage, but a compositor's slip,
influenced by the preceding *orderly*.
45–6 **friended | With** assisted by
46 **aptness . . . season** the appropriateness of
the time
47 **so seem** make it appear
49 **tender** offer
50 **command** i.e. her command
dismission dismissal (or more strongly,
'rejection'; *OED* 5 suggests that this is
the earliest example of a more specific
sense 'repudiation of a partner')
51 **senseless** insensible (i.e. he should pretend not to understand her; but Cloten
misunderstands it as 'stupid')
52 **So like . . . Rome** Just as the wager story
approaches its climax in the next

scene, Shakespeare begins to set up the
story of the dispute between Britain and
Rome.
52 **So like you** if it may please you (a defer-
ential address to a person of high rank)
53 **one** i.e. principal one, leader
54 **Albeit** although
56 **his sender** i.e. Augustus Caesar (the Octavius who appears in *Julius Caesar* and
Antony and Cleopatra)
57 **his goodness . . . us** (because of) his virtue
in previous dealings with us. This indication of an existing friendship with Caius
Lucius emphasizes that Cymbeline was
brought up in Rome (see 3.1.68–9),
and prepares for the tone of friendly courtesy beneath the political negotiations in
3.1 and 3.5.
forespent spent previously
58 **extend our notice** grant our attention

CLOTEN
   If she be up, I'll speak with her; if not,
   Let her lie still and dream. ⌈*He knocks*⌉ By your leave,
      ho!—
   I know her women are about her; what
   If I do line one of their hands? 'Tis gold   65
   Which buys admittance—oft it doth—yea, and makes
   Diana's rangers false themselves, yield up
   Their deer to th' stand o'th' stealer; and 'tis gold
   Which makes the true man killed and saves the thief,
   Nay, sometime hangs both thief and true man. What   70
   Can it not do and undo? I will make
   One of her women lawyer to me, for
   I yet not understand the case myself.—
   By your leave.
      Knocks. Enter a Lady
LADY
   Who's there that knocks?
CLOTEN   A gentleman.
LADY   No more?   75

---

63 *He knocks] not in* F

64–73 **I know . . . myself** This complex
   speech (see the next note) is the first
   indication that Cloten is not altogether
   cretinous. He has a limited capacity for
   thought, and even, later in the play, a
   kind of imagination and weird logic (as
   at 3.5.130–44). His problem is that this
   capacity comes and goes, and *I . . . not
   understand* at the end of this speech may
   show it petering out.
64–8 **what . . . stealer** Cloten compares
   Innogen's ladies-in-waiting to those of
   Diana, goddess of chastity, but also of
   hunting; Diana's ladies are then represented as *rangers* (foresters, or game-
   keepers) who can be bribed into
   allowing poachers (*stealers*) to shoot the
   deer they are supposed to protect. But
   deer probably also refers to Diana herself,
   betrayed by her ladies to an onlooker;
   there may be an allusion to the story of
   the huntsman Actaeon who saw Diana
   bathing naked (Ovid, *Metamorphoses*
   3.138–252)—in which case Cloten
   embroiders the legend by implying that

Actaeon bribed one of the ladies to betray
Diana, as he hopes one of Innogen's will
betray her.
65 **line** fill, cram, with gold (as if lining a
   garment)
67 **false themselves** betray, corrupt
   themselves. But *false* may be an adjective,
   i.e. gold makes them false. Either
   way, the meaning is the same:
   Diana's ladies fail in their loyalty to
   their mistress.
68 **stand . . . stealer** hiding place where the
   poacher waits to shoot (with sexual
   innuendo 'erection of the concealed
   onlooker')
69 **true** honest
72 **lawyer** (because paid to plead for him)
73 **I . . . myself** I do not understand how to
   plead my suit yet
   not understand 'Do' is often omitted
   before *not* in Elizabethan usage (Abbott
   §305).
   case suit (i.e. his love-suit to Innogen, but
   playing on the legal sense, developed
   from *lawyer* in l. 72)

CLOTEN

Yes, and a gentlewoman's son.

LADY   That's more

Than some whose tailors are as dear as yours

Can justly boast of. What's your lordship's pleasure?

CLOTEN

Your lady's person, is she ready?

LADY   Ay.

To keep her chamber.

CLOTEN   There is gold for you.   80

Sell me your good report.

LADY

How, my good name? Or to report of you

What I shall think is good? The Princess.   [*Exit*]

  Enter Innogen

CLOTEN

Good morrow fairest sister, your sweet hand.

INNOGEN

Good morrow sir, you lay out too much pains   85

For purchasing but trouble. The thanks I give

Is telling you that I am poor of thanks,

And scarce can spare them.

CLOTEN   Still I swear I love you.

INNOGEN

If you but said so, 'twere as deep with me.

If you swear still, your recompense is still   90

---

83 *Exit*] *not in* F 84 fairest sister] CAPELL; fairest, Sister F

76–8 **That's . . . boast of** Perhaps these lines, and the Lady's *To keep her chamber* (l. 80) are asides; but they may equally well be wit-skirmishes, anticipating in a minor key the dispute between Cloten and Innogen that follows. The Lady means that a gentleman's rich clothes do not necessarily reveal a gentleman.

79 **ready** i.e. dressed ready to come out

80 **keep** remain inside

84 **fairest sister** The Folio punctuation (see collation) makes sense, but Capell's makes a more natural, flowing line.

 your (give me) your

85–108 Innogen's speeches are a mixture of courtesy and an exasperation which she manages to keep under control until provoked beyond endurance by Cloten's attack on Posthumus.

85 **lay out** expend (compare modern 'outlay')

86 **but** only

87 **I . . . thanks** i.e. I have very few thanks to give

88 **scarce** hardly

89 **but said** i.e. said without swearing

 deep solemn, weighty (often associated with swearing in Shakespeare, as at Sonnet 152.9: 'I have sworn deep oaths')

90 **still** continually

That I regard it not.
CLOTEN   This is no answer.
INNOGEN
But that you shall not say I yield being silent,
I would not speak. I pray you spare me. Faith,
I shall unfold equal discourtesy
To your best kindness. One of your great knowing   95
Should learn, being taught, forbearance.
CLOTEN
To leave you in your madness, 'twere my sin.
I will not.
INNOGEN   Fools cure not mad folks.
CLOTEN
Do you call me fool?
INNOGEN   As I am mad I do.
If you'll be patient, I'll no more be mad.   100
That cures us both. I am much sorry, sir,
You put me to forget a lady's manners
By being so verbal; and learn now for all
That I, which know my heart, do here pronounce
By th' very truth of it, I care not for you,   105
And am so near the lack of charity

98 cure] THEOBALD (*conj*. Warburton); are F

92 **But that** except to ensure that
    I yield being silent Proverbial: 'Silence
    gives consent' (Tilley S446).
93 **spare me** leave me alone
94 **unfold** display
94–5 **equal . . .** To as great as
95 **knowing** knowledge. Is she trying to be
    polite, or is the sarcasm breaking
    through?
96 **forbearance** restraint. But in view of his
    reply, perhaps Cloten takes it in the sense
    'withdrawal', as the First Lord uses it at
    1.1.69, and thinks that she is dismissing
    him (as in a way she is).
98 **Fools cure not mad folks** F's 'Fooles are
    not mad Folkes' yields some sense.
    Dowden proposes that Innogen self-
    deprecatingly means 'I am not mad, I
    am only a fool, and so you may safely
    leave me to my folly', which Cloten then
    takes as an obscure insult. Perhaps it is
    too obscure, even for him, and the emen-
    dation adopted here suggests that Inno-

gen is losing patience: it certainly gives
her more to apologize for in her next
speech (ll. 101–3), and prepares for the
heatedness only just kept in check under
the formal politeness of that speech. *Cures*
in l. 101 may be a development of the
idea
101 **much** very
102 **put** cause
103 **verbal** talkative. She is almost certainly
    referring to herself, especially if the
    emendation in l. 98 is correct. She
    would rather be *silent* (l. 92). But she
    could be referring to Cloten's persistence
    in his love-suit.
    for all once and for all
106–7 **am . . . hate you** [I] am so near to
    lacking Christian charity that I can
    charge myself with hating you. Christian
    charity teaches us to love one another;
    Innogen feels that she lacks *charity* not
    only in hating Cloten, but in bringing an
    accusation against herself.

To accuse myself I hate you, which I had rather
You felt than make't my boast.
CLOTEN   You sin against
Obedience which you owe your father. For
The contract you pretend with that base wretch,   110
One bred of alms and fostered with cold dishes,
With scraps o'th' court, it is no contract, none;
And though it be allowed in meaner parties—
Yet who than he more mean?—to knit their souls,
On whom there is no more dependency   115
But brats and beggary, in self-figured knot,
Yet you are curbed from that enlargement by
The consequence o'th' crown, and must not foil
The precious note of it with a base slave,
A hilding for a livery, a squire's cloth,   120
A pantler—not so eminent.
INNOGEN   Profane fellow,

108 **boast** overt declaration
108–21 **You sin . . . eminent** This speech is
   another indication (see note to ll. 64–73)
   that Cloten is something more than a
   fool. However insultingly he puts it, he
   is right in pointing out that Innogen has
   disregarded her responsibilities as heir to
   the throne in her secret marriage to a
   commoner. A realization that he (infuri-
   atingly) has a point no doubt intensifies
   the ferocity of her reply.
109 **For** as for
110 **you pretend** which you profess to have
111 **bred of alms** brought up on charitable
   relief (the King's)
111–12 **cold . . . court** food that has gone
   cold, leftovers from royal feasts
113–16 **though . . . knot** The main line of
   thought is 'though commoners may be
   allowed to form a betrothal contract simply by making a mutual declaration
   (princesses may not)'.
113 **meaner** socially inferior
115 **dependency** i.e. people or circumstances
   who depend. A contrast is being drawn
   between the results of the marriage of
   poor people and the *consequence* of a
   royal marriage (l. 118).
116 **But brats and beggary** than children
   (contemptuously expressed) and extreme
   poverty
   self-figured knot bond created by your-
   selves. Hudson glosses: 'marrying to suit

themselves; whereas the expectant of a
throne must marry to serve the interests
of his or her position' (1886 edn., p. 50).
Cloten may be suggesting that Posthumus and Innogen have only undertaken
a betrothal or common-law marriage
unsanctified by a religious ceremony
(implying it could more easily be
annulled); but Jupiter is explicit that 'in
| Our temple was [Posthumus] married'
(5.3.199–200).
117 **curbed . . . enlargement** restrained from
   that freedom
118 **consequence o'th' crown** the importance of the crown, and the fact that you
   will inherit it
   foil defile
119 **note** renown
120 **hilding** 'good-for-nothing'
   for a livery fit for a livery (i.e. only fit to be
   a servant, wearing the distinctive livery
   of his master's employees)
   squire's cloth servant's outfit
121 **pantler** the controller of the bread in a
   large household, who was in charge of
   the pantry
   Profane one who blasphemes, takes
   the name of God in vain. This connects
   with ll. 129–30, and leads naturally
   into the first of the play's many
   references to Jupiter, King of the
   Roman gods, who will materialize
   in 5.3.

Wert thou the son of Jupiter, and no more
But what thou art besides, thou wert too base
To be his groom. Thou wert dignified enough,
Even to the point of envy, if 'twere made   125
Comparative for your virtues to be styled
The under-hangman of his kingdom, and hated
For being preferred so well.

CLOTEN   The south-fog rot him!

INNOGEN

He never can meet more mischance than come
To be but named of thee. His meanest garment   130
That ever hath but clipped his body is dearer
In my respect than all the hairs above thee,
Were they all made such men. How now, Pisanio!

     Enter Pisanio

CLOTEN

His garment? Now the devil—

INNOGEN (*to Pisanio*)

To Dorothy my woman hie thee presently.   135

CLOTEN

His garment?

INNOGEN (*to Pisanio*) I am sprited with a fool,

---

130 meanest] F2; mean'st F1   134 garment] F2; Garments F1

---

124 **dignified** raised in status
125 **of envy** where people envied you
125–6 **if . . . virtues** if a comparison were to
    be made between your (i.e. Cloten's and
    Posthumus') virtues
126 **to be styled** for you to be given the title of
127 **under-hangman** assistant hangman (a
    job that was generally despised)
    his Posthumus'
128 **preferred so well** promoted even that far
    south-fog damp fog brought by the south
    wind. Compare 'the spongy south'
    (4.2.350). It was thought to breed illness,
    as at *Tempest* 1.2.325–6: 'A southwest
    blow on ye, | And blister you all o'er!'
130 **of** by
130–3 **His meanest . . . such men** Post-
    humus' *meanest garment* is presumably
    his underwear, chosen by the now
    enraged Innogen because the point at
    which it *clipped* (encircled) Posthumus'
    body will be particularly provocative
    and humiliating to Cloten. This insult,

and Cloten's repetitions of it, prepare for
his subsequent dressing in Posthumus'
clothes and so for the central crisis of the
play when Innogen wakes by his headless
body. In this respect, Innogen brings that
appalling nightmare upon herself.
130, 153 **meanest garment** *Meanest* is F2's
    correction of F1's 'mean'st', to regularize
    the metre; and it probably establishes the
    insult, and Cloten's obsessive repetitions
    of it, more effectively.
132 **respect** regard
    hairs above thee hairs on his head (or
    more generally, all the hairs on the sur-
    face of his body)
135 **hie thee presently** make haste immedi-
    ately
136 **sprited with** haunted by, as if by a spirit.
    This may be a stronger expression than it
    seems, since *spirit* could also mean 'devil'
    in Elizabethan English; perhaps Innogen
    is exasperatedly picking up Cloten's
    exclamation *Now the devil* in l. 134.

Frighted, and angered worse. Go bid my woman
Search for a jewel that too casually
Hath left mine arm; it was thy master's. 'Shrew me
If I would lose it for a revenue   140
Of any king's in Europe! I do think
I saw't this morning; confident I am
Last night 'twas on mine arm; I kissed it.
I hope it be not gone to tell my lord
That I kiss aught but he.
PISANIO   'Twill not be lost.   145
INNOGEN
I hope so. Go and search.   *Exit Pisanio*
CLOTEN   You have abused me.
'His meanest garment'?
INNOGEN   Ay, I said so sir.
If you will make't an action, call witness to't.
CLOTEN
I will inform your father.
INNOGEN   Your mother too.
She's my good lady, and will conceive, I hope,   150
But the worst of me. So I leave you, sir,
To th' worst of discontent.   *Exit*
CLOTEN   I'll be revenged.
'His meanest garment'? Well.   *Exit*

2.4   *Enter Posthumus and Philario*
POSTHUMUS
Fear it not, sir. I would I were so sure
To win the King as I am bold her honour
Will remain hers.
PHILARIO   What means do you make to him?

---

142 am] F4 (am,); am. F   146 *Exit Pisanio] not in* F   151 you] F3; your F1

---

138 **casually** accidentally
139 **'Shrew me** An emphatic assertion, an
 aphetic form of 'beshrew me', 'may the
 devil take me'.
145 **aught** anything
146 **I hope so** The modern idiom would be 'I
 hope not'.
148 **action** law-suit

150 **good lady** my good benefactress
 (ironical)
 conceive think
 hope expect
2.4.1–2 **sure . . . win** certain of winning
 over
 2 **bold** confident
 3 **means** approaches

POSTHUMUS

Not any; but abide the change of time,
Quake in the present winter's state, and wish   5
That warmer days would come. In these seared hopes
I barely gratify your love; they failing,
I must die much your debtor.

PHILARIO

Your very goodness and your company
O'erpays all I can do. By this, your king   10
Hath heard of great Augustus. Caius Lucius
Will do's commission throughly. And I think
He'll grant the tribute, send th'arrearages,
Or look upon our Romans, whose remembrance
Is yet fresh in their grief.

POSTHUMUS   I do believe,   15
Statist though I am none, nor like to be,
That this will prove a war; and you shall hear
The legions now in Gallia sooner landed
In our not-fearing Britain than have tidings
Of any penny tribute paid. Our countrymen   20
Are men more ordered than when Julius Caesar
Smiled at their lack of skill, but found their courage

2.4.6 seared] KNIGHT (*conj.* Tyrwhitt); fear'd F   hopes] F2; hope F1
18 legions] THEOBALD; Legion F

---

6 **seared** withered. F's 'fear'd' may be correct, meaning 'mixed with fear'
(Schmidt). But *seared*, following *winter's
state* in l. 5, is supported by *Macbeth*
5.3.24–5: 'My way of life | Is fall'n into
the sere [F: Seare], the yellow leaf'.
7 **gratify** repay
10–26 **By . . . world** Just before the wager
plot reaches its crisis, the audience is
given more information about the next
strand in the narrative, the coming war
between Britain and Rome, in preparation for the first scene devoted to it, 3.1.
10 **this** this time
12 **throughly** thoroughly
13 **He** Cymbeline
arrearages arrears, the overdue payments of tribute
14 **Or** Oxford interprets this as an obsolete
form of 'ere', meaning 'rather than'; but
the normal modern sense of 'or' is per-

fectly satisfactory: pay the tribute or face
the Roman armies.
14 **look upon** face
whose remembrance the memory of
whom
15 **their grief** i.e. the harm which the
Romans have previously inflicted on the
Britons (or perhaps the grief that the Britons have experienced in the past)
16 **Statist** politician, statesman (a common
seventeenth-century usage, as *OED*'s
examples testify, though Shakespeare
uses it only here and at *Hamlet* 5.2.34)
18 **The legions . . . Gallia** F's single legion
seems hardly adequate to the task; compare *the legions now in Gallia* at 3.7.4.
Substitution of singular for plural and
vice versa is a characteristic error of the
Folio's Compositor E.
19 **not-fearing** fearless
21 **more ordered** better organized

Worthy his frowning at. Their discipline,
Now wing-led with their courages, will make known
To their approvers they are people such   25
That mend upon the world.

    Enter Giacomo

PHILARIO   See Giacomo.

POSTHUMUS
The swiftest harts have posted you by land,
And winds of all the corners kissed your sails
To make your vessel nimble.

PHILARIO   Welcome sir.

POSTHUMUS
I hope the briefness of your answer made   30
The speediness of your return.

GIACOMO   Your lady is
One of the fair'st that I have looked upon.

POSTHUMUS
And therewithal the best, or let her beauty
Look through a casement to allure false hearts,
And be false with them.

---

24 wing-led] F1; mingled F2; wingèd CARTWRIGHT *conj.* courages] F; courage DYCE
32 One of the] F1; of the POPE; one the STEEVENS–REED 1793   34 through] ROWE;
thorough F

21–3 **Julius . . . at** See note to 3.1.2–5.
24 **wing-led . . . courages** *Wing-led* caused
trouble as early as F2, which substituted
'mingled'. This makes sense: whereas
the Britons previously *lacked skill*, they
now possess a mixture of courage and
discipline. But it is unusual for a scribe
or compositor to substitute such an
uncommon word for a simple one.
Wing-led may mean 'led in disciplined
formation' (*wings*, which occurs at
5.3.5), as Dowden suggests. If so,
courages may mean 'gallant spirits, i.e.
their commanders' (*OED sb.* 1c). Compare *Hamlet* 1.3.65, where Q1 and Q2
read 'each new-hatched unfledged courage' (F: comrade); the association in
both passages of feathers ('unfledged'
and *wing*) with 'courage(s)' is notable.
25 **their approvers** i.e. those who seek to test
them

26 **That mend upon** who improve in the
estimation of
27 **harts** deer
    posted conveyed swiftly (derived from the
carrying of letters by a relay of post-
horses). Compare *2 Henry IV* Induction
4: 'Making the wind my post-horse'.
28 **corners** (of a map, with puffing faces
personifying the winds, their lips looking
as if they are kissing)
30 **your answer** the answer you received
33 **therewithal** in addition
34 **Look . . . casement** look out through a
window (like a prostitute attracting customers). Compare *Timon* 4.3.116–17:
'those milk paps | That through the win-
dow-bars bore at men's eyes'. It is
interesting that the first association of
Innogen with *false* behaviour should
come from Posthumus rather than Giacomo, perhaps hinting at a greater

GIACOMO   Here are letters for you.   35
POSTHUMUS
  Their tenor good, I trust.
GIACOMO   'Tis very like.
   Posthumus reads the letters
⌈PHILARIO⌉
  Was Caius Lucius in the Briton court
  When you were there?
GIACOMO   He was expected then,
  But not approached.
POSTHUMUS   All is well yet.
  Sparkles this stone as it was wont, or is't not   40
  Too dull for your good wearing?
GIACOMO   If I had lost it
  I should have lost the worth of it in gold.
  I'll make a journey twice as far t'enjoy
  A second night of such sweet shortness which
  Was mine in Britain, for the ring is won.   45
POSTHUMUS
  The stone's too hard to come by.
GIACOMO   Not a whit,
  Your lady being so easy.
POSTHUMUS   Make not, sir,
  Your loss your sport. I hope you know that we
  Must not continue friends.
GIACOMO   Good sir, we must,
  If you keep covenant. Had I not brought   50
  The knowledge of your mistress home, I grant
  We were to question farther; but I now

36.1 *Posthumus reads the letters*] *not in* F   37 PHILARIO] CAPELL; *Post⟨humus⟩.* F   41 had]
SINGER 1856; haue F   43 I'll] F; I'ld NOSWORTHY *conj.*   47 not] F2; note F1

anxiety than he admits to Philario at ll.
1–3. If so, Giacomo does not rise to it,
but simply hands him his letters.

35 **letters** One is from Innogen, as ll. 105–6
  make clear.
36 **tenor** drift, content
37–8 **Was . . . there** F gives this speech to
  Posthumus, but an interest in the
  Roman ambassador comes more naturally from Philario, and Posthumus

needs time at least to glance through his
letters.
39 **not approached** had not arrived. This line
is two syllables short, suggesting a pause
before Posthumus turns the conversation
to what most interests (and disturbs?)
him.
50 **keep covenant** adhere to the agreement
51 **knowledge** i.e. carnal knowledge
52 **question** dispute (by fighting a duel)

Profess myself the winner of her honour,
Together with your ring; and not the wronger
Of her or you, having proceeded but   55
By both your wills.

POSTHUMUS   If you can make't apparent
That you have tasted her in bed, my hand
And ring is yours. If not, the foul opinion
You had of her pure honour gains or loses
Your sword or mine, or masterless leaves both   60
To who shall find them.

GIACOMO   Sir, my circumstances,
Being so near the truth as I will make them,
Must first induce you to believe; whose strength
I will confirm with oath, which I doubt not
You'll give me leave to spare when you shall find   65
You need it not.

POSTHUMUS   Proceed.

GIACOMO   First, her bedchamber—
Where I confess I slept not, but profess
Had that was well worth watching—it was hanged
With tapestry of silk and silver; the story
Proud Cleopatra when she met her Roman,   70
And Cydnus swelled above the banks, or for
The press of boats or pride: a piece of work

---

57 you] F2; yon F1   60 leaves] ROWE; leaue F

53 **Profess** declare
57 **tasted** had intercourse with, 'enjoyed'.
Compare the Bawd's promise to Marina at *Pericles* Sc. 16.75–6 that she will 'taste gentlemen of all fashions'. As at l. 34, Posthumus is slipping into sexually loaded expressions very early in the scene, before any evidence has been supplied.
59–60 **gains . . . both** i.e. means that one or other of us will win the duel, or that both of us will be killed in it
61 **my circumstances** details of my evidence
65 **spare** omit
68 **watching** staying awake for
69 **silk and silver** This is explained by the theatrical impresario Philip Henslowe's reference to 'panes of silk laid [interwoven] with silver lace' in his 'diary' entry for 1 February 1599 (*Henslowe's Diary*, p. 104). The phrase, which also occurs in Middleton's *Michaelmas Term* (*c.* 1605), Induction 34, and *The Revenger's Tragedy* (*c.* 1605–6), 1.1.52, seems to have been a standard description or trade name.
70 **her Roman** i.e. Mark Antony. Their meeting on the river Cydnus (see next line) is described at *Antony* 2.2.198–225. Giacomo implies a comparison between Cleopatra's *Roman* and Innogen's—himself.
71–2 **or . . . pride** either because of the crowd of boats or pride at carrying Antony and Cleopatra

So bravely done, so rich, that it did strive
In workmanship and value; which I wondered
Could be so rarely and exactly wrought,   75
Such the true life on't was.

POSTHUMUS   This is true.
And this you might have heard of here, by me
Or by some other.

GIACOMO   More particulars
Must justify my knowledge.

POSTHUMUS   So they must,
Or do your honour injury.

GIACOMO   The chimney   80
Is south the chamber, and the chimney-piece
Chaste Dian bathing. Never saw I figures
So likely to report themselves; the cutter
Was as another nature, dumb, outwent her,
Motion and breath left out.

POSTHUMUS   This is a thing   85
Which you might from relation likewise reap,
Being, as it is, much spoke of.

GIACOMO   The roof o'th' chamber
With golden cherubins is fretted. Her andirons—
I had forgot them—were two winking Cupids

76 Such] SINGER 1856 (*conj.* Mason); Since F   on't was.] HANMER; on't was—F; was out on't. MAXWELL (*anon. conj., cited in* Cambridge)

73 **bravely** excellently, exquisitely
73–4 **it . . . value** craftsmanship and intrinsic worth competed for pre-eminence
75 **exactly wrought** perfectly made
76 **Such . . . was.** To read *Such* for F's 'Since' assumes that the speech is finished: 'it was so lifelike.' F's dash after *was* may imply that Posthumus, impatient at details which do not prove anything, interrupts; but there is a similar dash after *Jove* (l. 98), where there is no question of an interruption.
79 **justify** corroborate
80 **chimney** fireplace
81 **south** on the south wall of
chimney-piece sculpture or wood-carving over and/or around the fireplace (*OED*'s earliest citation of the phrase)
82 **Chaste Dian bathing** Since the goddess of chastity is represented *bathing*, this may

suggest the story of Diana and Actaeon (see note to 2.3.64–8).
83 **likely . . . themselves** apt to give an account of themselves
cutter sculptor (if the chimney-piece is stone) or carver (if wood)
84–5 **as another . . . out** like a second nature, though a dumb one, who surpassed nature except that he could not provide movement or breathing
86 **relation** report
88 **cherubins** angels
fretted adorned with carvings, 'fretwork'
andirons 'fire-dogs', a pair of ornamented supports for the iron bars which support the burning wood in a fireplace (a corruption of Old French *andier*)
89 **winking** with eyes closed. Cupid, the god of love, was usually portrayed as blind or blindfolded.

Of silver, each on one foot standing, nicely   90
Depending on their brands.
POSTHUMUS   This is her honour!
Let it be granted you have seen all this—and praise
Be given to your remembrance—the description
Of what is in her chamber nothing saves
The wager you have laid.
GIACOMO   Then if you can   95
Be pale, I beg but leave to air this jewel: see,
        He shows the bracelet
And now 'tis up again; it must be married
To that your diamond, I'll keep them.
POSTHUMUS   Jove!
Once more let me behold it. Is it that
Which I left with her?
GIACOMO   Sir, I thank her, that.   100
She stripped it from her arm. I see her yet.
Her pretty action did outsell her gift,
And yet enriched it too. She gave it me,
And said she prized it once.
POSTHUMUS   Maybe she plucked it off
To send it me.
GIACOMO   She writes so to you, doth she?   105
POSTHUMUS
O no, no, no, 'tis true. Here, take this too.
        He gives Giacomo his ring

---

95 6 can‸ | Be pale] rɜ can, | Be pale CAPELL   96.1 *He shows the bracelet*] *not in* F
106.1 *He . . . ring*] *not in* F

90 **nicely** ingeniously
91 **Depending . . . brands** leaning on their
    flaming torches
94 **nothing saves** by no means wins
95-6 **if . . . pale** if you are able to turn pale
    (i.e. if you are capable of reacting to
    evidence that I've won the wager).
    Capell's punctuation (see collation)
    makes essentially the same point:
    Giacomo is becoming irritated at
    Posthumus' failure to react to his
    'proofs'.
96 **air** show
97 **up** put up, hidden
98 **Jove** Jupiter. See ll. 121-2 and note. Here

Jove is an exclamation, there *By Jupiter* is
a solemn oath.
99-100 **Is it that . . . that** Posthumus gives
    Giacomo a piece of information he could
    not have known, but which he is quick to
    seize upon and amplify in ll. 101-4.
102 **outsell** exceed in value
105-6 **She writes . . . true** Giacomo's
    mockingly understated question usually
    releases a furious outburst from Post-
    humus in his repetitions of *no*; but
    Michael Pennington in the BBC television
    version uses them to check slowly
    through the letter, each *no* increasing in
    certainty and intensity.

It is a basilisk unto mine eye,
Kills me to look on't. Let there be no honour
Where there is beauty, truth where semblance, love
Where there's another man. The vows of women   110
Of no more bondage be to where they are made
Than they are to their virtues, which is nothing.
O, above measure false!

PHILARIO   Have patience sir,
And take your ring again, 'tis not yet won.
It may be probable she lost it, or   115
Who knows if one her woman, being corrupted,
Hath stol'n it from her?

POSTHUMUS   Very true,
And so I hope he came by't. Back my ring.

    He takes his ring again

Render to me some corporal sign about her
More evident than this; for this was stol'n.   120

GIACOMO

By Jupiter, I had it from her arm.

POSTHUMUS

Hark you, he swears, by Jupiter he swears.
'Tis true, nay keep the ring, 'tis true. I am sure
She would not lose it. Her attendants are
All sworn and honourable. They induced to steal it?   125
And by a stranger? No, he hath enjoyed her.
The cognizance of her incontinency

116 her woman] COLLIER; her women F1; of her women F2   118.1 *He...again*] *not in* F

107–13 **It is . . . false** Once Posthumus' jealousy is released, it takes hold very
  quickly, on evidence that is still only circumstantial, as Philario's following,
  moderating speech emphasizes.
107 **basilisk** A mythical serpent that killed
  anyone who looked at it with its glance.
109 **semblance** appearance, outward seeming
110–12 **The vows . . . nothing** women's
  vows no more bind them to those to
  whom they were made than women
  themselves are bound to their own virtues, which is not at all (or *be* may mean
  let be: i.e. 'let women's vows', etc.)
115 **probable** capable of proof (*OED a.* 1)
116 **one her woman** one of her women. For
  the idiom, compare 1.6.165–6.

116 **corrupted** bribed
117 This is another short, octosyllabic line
  (compare l. 39); perhaps there is a pause
  as Posthumus temporarily recovers himself.
118 **Back** i.e. give back
120 **evident** conclusive
121–2 **By Jupiter . . . he swears** Jupiter was
  the King of the Roman gods, so that to
  swear by him was a solemn oath, as Posthumus' reply emphasizes. Giacomo is
  saved from perjury by the technicality
  that he *had it from her arm*.
125 **sworn** bound by oath
127 **cognizance** token. This was originally
  a heraldic term, meaning the badge
  worn by servants of a noble house
  (*OED* 5).

Is this : she hath bought the name of whore thus dearly.
        He gives Giacomo his ring
There, take thy hire, and all the fiends of hell
Divide themselves between you !
PHILARIO   Sir, be patient.   130
This is not strong enough to be believed
Of one persuaded well of.
POSTHUMUS   Never talk on't.
She hath been colted by him.
GIACOMO   If you seek
For further satisfying, under her breast—
Worthy the pressing—lies a mole, right proud   135
Of that most delicate lodging. By my life,
I kissed it, and it gave me present hunger
To feed again, though full. You do remember
This stain upon her?
POSTHUMUS   Ay, and it doth confirm
Another stain as big as hell can hold,   140
Were there no more but it.
GIACOMO   Will you hear more?
POSTHUMUS
Spare your arithmetic, never count the turns.
Once, and a million !
GIACOMO   I'll be sworn.
POSTHUMUS   No swearing.
If you will swear you have not done't, you lie,

128.1 *He...ring*] *not in* F   135 the] ROWE; her F

---

128 **Is this** i.e. the ring is the token of her
    infidelity
    thus dearly i.e. by giving the precious
    ring
129 **hire** fee
130 **you** i.e. Giacomo and Innogen
131 **This . . . believed** Again, Philario pro-
    vides a sane perspective on Posthumus'
    rushing to believe *before* the crucial
    piece of evidence, the mole, is even
    mentioned.
132 **Of . . . of** about one who is thought well
    of
133 **been colted by** had intercourse with.
    OED gives no other example of *colted* in

this sense, but colts are described as
'wanton' at *Merchant* 5.1.71–2, so this
is perhaps the start of Posthumus'
expressing Innogen's sexuality in terms
of animals, culminating in the German
boar at l. 168.
137 **present** immediate
138 **feed** Sexual desire is expressed in terms
    of eating as at 1.6. 46.
139–40 **stain . . . stain** 'mark', which is then
    turned into 'blot, moral disgrace'
142 **turns** Compare *Antony* 2.5.59 : 'the best
    turn i'th' bed'.
144–6 **If you . . . cuckold** In the grip of his
    obsession, Posthumus does not want to

And I will kill thee if thou dost deny   145
Thou'st made me cuckold.

GIACOMO   I'll deny nothing.

POSTHUMUS
O that I had her here to tear her limb-meal!
I will go there and do't, i'th' court, before
Her father. I'll do something.   *Exit*

PHILARIO   Quite besides
The government of patience! You have won.   150
Let's follow him and pervert the present wrath
He hath against himself.

GIACOMO   With all my heart.   *Exeunt*

        Enter Posthumus

POSTHUMUS
Is there no way for men to be, but women
Must be half-workers? We are all bastards,
And that most venerable man which I   155
Did call my father was I know not where
When I was stamped. Some coiner with his tools

---

154 all bastards] F; bastards all POPE

be disabused, and the shift from the polite
you to the abusive *thee* underlines his
fury.
147 **limb-meal** limb from limb. Compare
Tempest 2.2.3: 'By inch-meal' (i.e. inch
by inch), and modern 'piecemeal'.
148–9 **I will go . . . something** His frenzy
increases, phrase by phrase, until the
final *I'll do something*, which is almost
incoherent. His urge to do Innogen violence in front of her father is interestingly
close to Cloten's at 4.1.17–18. See Introduction, pp. 50–1.
150 **government** control
151 **pervert** turn aside
152.1 *Enter Posthumus* Most editors
follow Pope in beginning a new scene
here, but in the Folio the action is continuous. Presumably Posthumus left at l.
149 through one of the two doors at the
back of the Jacobean stage, followed after
their short dialogue by Philario and Giacomo, and then re-entered through the
other door as they left. This has the great
advantage of emphasizing that the soliloquy develops out of the scene, is indeed
the climax of it. And Posthumus' rapid
exit and reappearance prepare for the

turbulence and volatile changes of mood
in the speech itself, which alternates
between specific analysis of his own
situation and Innogen's (ll. 155–71)
and a general attack on women
(ll. 153–4, 171–87). For further discussion of this speech, see Introduction,
pp. 30–3.
153 **be** exist
154 **half-workers** co-workers
all bastards Oxford follows Pope in reading 'bastards all' since 'F has the commoner, and less metrical, word-order'
(*Textual Companion*, p. 606). Pope's line
certainly flows more smoothly, but perhaps F's less fluent one is more appropriate to Posthumus' agitation, in a speech
where the verse structure breaks down at
l. 181, and where the apparent final
couplet is undercut by an anticlimactic
single line.
155 **venerable** old and worthy of respect
157 **stamped** conceived. Posthumus
expresses his apparently illegitimate
conception in terms of the making of
(counterfeit) coins, an expression developed in *coiner*, *tools*, and *counterfeit*.
coiner maker of counterfeit coins

Made me a counterfeit; yet my mother seemed
The Dian of that time: so doth my wife
The nonpareil of this. O vengeance, vengeance!   160
Me of my lawful pleasure she restrained,
And prayed me oft forbearance, did it with
A pudency so rosy the sweet view on't
Might well have warmed old Saturn, that I thought her
As chaste as unsunned snow. O all the devils!   165
This yellow Giacomo in an hour—was't not?—
Or less—at first? Perchance he spoke not, but
Like a full-acorned boar, a German one,
Cried 'O!' and mounted; found no opposition
But what he looked for should oppose, and she   170
Should from encounter guard. Could I find out
The woman's part in me—for there's no motion

---

168 German one] F (Iarmen on)

tools i.e. of his trade, but also with the sexual sense of 'genitals'; a phrase from Becon's *Reliques of Rome* (1553) cited at *OED sb.* 2b pins down this sense: 'All his tools that appertain unto the court of Venus.'

158 **a counterfeit** illegitimate
159 **Dian** i.e. the goddess Diana, embodiment of chastity
160 **nonpareil** one without equal
162 **forbearance** restraint, moderation
163 **pudency** modesty. This is *OED*'s earliest example of the word.
   rosy This presumably implies blushing cheeks. In Ovid's account of how the goddess Diana was seen naked (*Metamorphoses* 3.183–5), a story that seems to recur in this part of the play (see 2.3.66–8, 2.4.82 and notes), 'red as the rosy dawn were the cheeks of Diana' (Loeb translation, p. 137).
   on't of it
164 **Saturn** A god who was associated with coldness and melancholy; compare *The Two Noble Kinsmen* 5.6.62: 'Cold as old Saturn'.
165 **unsunned snow** i.e. snow before the sun warmed and melted it
166 **yellow** sallow (in complexion)
166–7 **in an . . . not** Posthumus decreases the time it took Giacomo to seduce Innogen: an hour, less than that, immedi-

ately on meeting, without even speaking. This culminates in the gross image of the German boar (l. 168).
168 **full-acorned** fed full of acorns. Pigs feed on acorns and 'mast' from oak trees.
   German Rowe's modernization of F's 'Iarmen'. In the Quarto text of *2 Henry IV* 2.1.147 (1600), 'Iarman' is an alternative spelling for 'German', as comparison with the Folio text makes clear. In Topsell's *History of Four-footed Beasts* (1607), the swine of Lower Germany are said to be 'fierce, strong, and very fat' (p. 514). The phrase suggests the gross animalism of Giacomo's intercourse with Innogen.
169–71 **found . . . guard** The implications of these lines are discussed in the Introduction, pp. 32–3.
170 **looked for** anticipated
171 **encounter** Compare 'vile encounters' at *Much Ado* 4.1.94, a scene in which the hero denounces the slandered heroine in terms very close to those of Posthumus: 'Out on thee, seeming! I will write against it. | You seem to me as Dian in her orb . . . | But you are more intemperate . . . | Than . . . those pampered animals | That rage in savage sensuality' (4.1.56–61).
172 **motion** impulse

That tends to vice in man but I affirm
It is the woman's part; be it lying, note it,
The woman's; flattering, hers; deceiving, hers;   175
Lust and rank thoughts, hers, hers; revenges, hers;
Ambitions, covetings, change of prides, disdain,
Nice longing, slanders, mutability,
All faults that man can name, nay, that hell knows,
Why hers, in part or all, but rather all—   180
For even to vice
They are not constant, but are changing still
One vice but of a minute old for one
Not half so old as that. I'll write against them,
Detest them, curse them, yet 'tis greater skill   185
In a true hate to pray they have their will.
The very devils cannot plague them better.   *Exit*

3.1   *Flourish. Enter in state Cymbeline, the Queen,*
           Cloten, and Lords at one door, and at another,
           Caius Lucius and attendants

CYMBELINE
Now say, what would Augustus Caesar with us?

---

179 man can name] OXFORD (*conj.* W. S. Walker); name F1; may be named F2; man may
name CRAIG (*conj.* W. S. Walker); earth can name OXFORD *conj.*
     3.1.0.1 *Flourish*] *not in* F   0.2 *Cloten*] Clotten F

---

176 **rank** lascivious
177 **change of prides** variety of excesses. Or
     perhaps, since *pride* could mean 'sexual
     desire' (*OED sb.*[1] 11), as at Sonnet
     144.8: 'Wooing his purity with her foul
     pride', Posthumus means 'variety of sex-
     ual choices'.
178 **Nice longing** wanton appetite
     mutability fickleness, inconstancy
181 Capell's re-distribution of an overlong
     line in F (see Appendix C), followed here,
     creates a very short line at this point. If
     correct, it indicates a long pause for
     emphasis, and perhaps also underlines
     the turbulence, even incoherence, of
     Posthumus' outburst against women.
182 **still** continuously
185 **skill** wisdom (or perhaps merely 'clever-
     ness')
3.1.0.1, 84 *Flourish* A musical fanfare

usually accompanied formal royal
entrances and exits (but not necessarily
a king's surprise entry, as at 1.1.125, the
suddenness of which may actually be
emphasized by the absence of a *flourish*,
or his entry in a private scene, as at
2.3.29.2). The absence of such cues in
the Folio text is discussed in the Introduction, p. 73.
0.1 *in state* with great pomp and ceremony.
     This is an international political confer-
     ence. So far, the play has been
     almost wholly concerned with the
     wager story, which reached a crisis
     point in the previous scene; now the
     action broadens out from the private to
     the public world as the story of the con-
     flict between Britain and Rome gets
     under way.
1 **Augustus Caesar** See the note to 2.3.56.

LUCIUS

　　When Julius Caesar—whose remembrance yet
　　Lives in men's eyes, and will to ears and tongues
　　Be theme and hearing ever—was in this Britain
　　And conquered it, Cassibelan thine uncle—　　　　　　　　5
　　Famous in Caesar's praises no whit less
　　Than in his feats deserving it—for him
　　And his succession granted Rome a tribute,
　　Yearly three thousand pounds, which by thee lately
　　Is left untendered.

QUEEN　　　　　　　　And to kill the marvel,　　　　　　　10
　　Shall be so ever.

CLOTEN　　　　　　　There be many Caesars
　　Ere such another Julius. Britain's a world
　　By itself, and we will nothing pay
　　For wearing our own noses.

QUEEN　　　　　　　　　　　That opportunity
　　Which then they had to take from's, to resume　　　　　15
　　We have again. Remember sir, my liege,
　　The kings your ancestors, together with

---

11 There] F; There will OXFORD

2–5 **When Julius . . . it** Julius Caesar's invasion of Britain took place in 55 and 54 BC. Caesar himself describes it in his *De Bello Gallico* and so do Plutarch in his Life of Caesar (*Lives*, p. 44) and Holinshed in his *Chronicles* (see Introduction, pp. 37–8).

2 **remembrance** memory

3 **eyes** Presumably this means 'mind's eyes', as at *Hamlet* 1.2.184: 'In my mind's eye, Horatio.'

5 **Cassibelan** See the note to 1.1.29–31.

6–7 **Famous . . . deserving it** i.e. he fully deserved all the praise he received from Caesar

8 **succession** successors

9 **pounds** i.e. pounds weight of gold or silver

10 **untendered** unpaid
　　to kill the marvel to put a stop to the amazement (because the non-payment will become the rule, not the exception). The Queen's extended interruption of the formal discussion between Cymbeline

and Caius Lucius, and to a lesser extent Cloten's, at ll. 10–44, makes it clear that it is under their influence that Cymbeline defies Rome; he himself makes the point at 5.4.463–4. Cloten and the Queen advocate a narrow isolationism, whereas Cymbeline, despite his defiance, is half-drawn to Rome at ll. 68–9, and also at 2.3.53–8.

11 **be** This has the force of 'will be' (i.e. many Caesars will have to appear before we see the like of Julius again), to which Oxford emends it. But this creates an unwanted extra syllable and so weakens the impact of Cloten's jibe, which is surely clear as it stands.

12–13 **Britain . . . itself** Cloten's nationalism contrasts with the wider view expressed by Innogen at 3.4.137–41.

15–16 **to resume . . . again** we now have to take back

16 **liege** lord (a formal mode of address to a superior, here used by the Queen as a courtesy title)

The natural bravery of your isle, which stands
As Neptune's park, ribbed and paled in
With oaks unscalable and roaring waters,   20
With sands that will not bear your enemies' boats,
But suck them up to th' topmast. A kind of conquest
Caesar made here, but made not here his brag
Of 'came and saw and overcame'. With shame—
The first that ever touched him—he was carried   25
From off our coast, twice beaten; and his shipping,
Poor ignorant baubles, on our terrible seas
Like eggshells moved upon their surges, cracked
As easily 'gainst our rocks; for joy whereof
The famed Cassibelan, who was once at point—   30
O giglot fortune!—to master Caesar's sword,
Made Lud's town with rejoicing fires bright,
And Britons strut with courage.

20 oaks] F; banks OXFORD; rocks HANMER

18 **bravery** This may mean 'excellence, quality', in the sense of 'bravely' at 2.2.15 and 2.4.73, or 'threatening appearance', as at *Julius Caesar* 5.1.9–10: 'come down | With fearful [frightening] bravery'. The latter is perhaps more likely in this context. The modern sense 'valour' does not appear in Shakespearian examples (Onions).

19 **Neptune's park** The island of Britain is visualized as a park in which the god of the sea might relax.
ribbed enclosed, like a body by its ribs (*OED, rib, v.*¹ 1a)
paled in fenced with pales, or vertical stakes

20 **oaks** Although usually emended, *oaks* makes good sense. Britain is imaged as a deer-park, where the protective pales (see the previous note) are living trees, as if the entire coastline is surrounded by a solid fence of huge *oaks* that are *unscalable* because they are too high to climb over, even if the invader manages to survive the *roaring waters* outside. This is a perfect image of an enclosed, self-sufficient world, appropriate to the Queen's narrow patriotism. Stanley Wells prefers 'banks' because it suggests both 'sea-coast' (*OED sb.*¹ 9, citing *Contention* (*2 Henry VI*)

3.2.83–4, where Queen Margaret's ship is 'from England's bank | Drove back again') and 'an artificial earthwork, an embankment, *esp.* for military use' (*OED sb.*¹ 3) (*Textual Companion*, p. 606).

21–2 **sands . . . topmast** Instead of supporting the enemy fleet, the quicksands will swallow them until even the highest point of the ship, the *topmast*, disappears.

24 **came . . . overcame** Julius Caesar reported his victory at the battle of Zela with the laconic phrase *Veni, vidi, vici* (Plutarch's *Lives*, p. 71), which became proverbial (Tilley C540).

27 **ignorant** i.e. of the dangerous seas
baubles toys

30 **at point** ready

31 **giglot** whore. Fortune is often so presented, because she is fickle; compare *Hamlet* 2.2.496: 'thou strumpet Fortune!'
master overcome. Holinshed tells how Cassibelan's brother Nenius 'in fight happened to get Caesar's sword fastened to his shield by a blow which Caesar struck at him' (Bullough, p. 42).

32 **Lud's town** London. *Lud's town* is a false etymology, derived from the name Lud, another mythological British king, Cymbeline's grandfather.

CLOTEN Come, there's no more tribute to be paid. Our king-
　　dom is stronger than it was at that time, and, as I said,　　　35
　　there is no more such Caesars. Other of them may have
　　crooked noses, but to owe such straight arms, none.
CYMBELINE Son, let your mother end.
CLOTEN We have yet many among us can grip as hard as
　　Cassibelan. I do not say I am one, but I have a hand. Why　　40
　　tribute? Why should we pay tribute? If Caesar can hide
　　the sun from us with a blanket, or put the moon in his
　　pocket, we will pay him tribute for light; else, sir, no
　　more tribute, pray you now.
CYMBELINE (*to Lucius*) You must know,　　　　　　　　　45
　　Till the injurious Romans did extort
　　This tribute from us we were free. Caesar's ambition,
　　Which swelled so much that it did almost stretch
　　The sides o'th' world, against all colour here
　　Did put the yoke upon's, which to shake off　　　　　　50
　　Becomes a warlike people, whom we reckon
　　Ourselves to be. We do say then to Caesar
　　Our ancestor was that Mulmutius which
　　Ordained our laws, whose use the sword of Caesar

---

36 more] F (mo)　52 be. We do say] MALONE; be, we do. Say F; be. | *Clo⟨ten⟩ and Lords.* We
do. | *Cym⟨beline⟩.* Say GLOBE

34–44 **Come . . . now** The diplomatically
　　formal verse of the opening speeches is
　　disrupted first by the Queen's mockery,
　　still in verse, and further by Cloten's des-
　　cent to personal abuse, in vigorous prose.
　　When verse resumes at l. 45, the short
　　line may imply an embarrassed pause as
　　Cymbeline tries to recover the necessary
　　formal tone to get the negotiations back
　　to the agenda.
37 **crooked noses** i.e. the distinctive, curved
　　'Roman' nose
　　owe own
　　straight strong, forceful
43 **else** otherwise
46 **injurious** 'prejudicial to the rights of
　　another' (*OED a.* 1), rather than 'insult-
　　ing', as at 4.2.88 (*OED a.* 2), in view of
　　what follows.
48–9 **swelled . . . th' world** The idea seems to
　　be that Caesar's ambition was so great
　　that it pushed back the frontiers of the
　　world in order to satisfy his urge to con-

quer. Perhaps it was suggested by a
phrase of Plutarch's, specifically referring to Caesar's invasion of Britain,
that he 'enlarged the Roman empire
beyond the earth inhabitable' (*Lives*,
p. 44).
49 **against all colour** without any show of
reason (*OED, colour, sb.*[1] 12a)
52 **We do** The Folio text tacks these words on
to the previous sentence; this has been
defended as an emphatic phrase (see Furness, pp. 176–7), but has usually been
emended (see collation). The simplest
emendation assumes that the scribe or
compositor broke the sentence in the
wrong place.
53 **Mulmutius** Another mythological British
king who, according to Holinshed, was
the son of Cloten, King of Cornwall; the
details about his laws and self-crowning
come direct from Holinshed (Bullough,
pp. 40–1).
54 **use** practice (of the *laws*)

Hath too much mangled, whose repair and franchise   55
Shall by the power we hold be our good deed,
Though Rome be therefore angry. Mulmutius made
 our laws,
Who was the first of Britain which did put
His brows within a golden crown and called
Himself a king.

LUCIUS   I am sorry, Cymbeline,   60
That I am to pronounce Augustus Caesar—
Caesar, that hath more kings his servants than
Thyself domestic officers—thine enemy.
Receive it from me then. War and confusion
In Caesar's name pronounce I 'gainst thee. Look   65
For fury not to be resisted. Thus defied,
I thank thee for myself.

CYMBELINE   Thou art welcome, Caius.
Thy Caesar knighted me; my youth I spent
Much under him; of him I gathered honour,
Which he to seek of me again perforce   70
Behoves me keep at utterance. I am perfect
That the Pannonians and Dalmatians for
Their liberties are now in arms, a precedent
Which not to read would show the Britons cold;
So Caesar shall not find them.

62 more] F (moe)

55 **repair** restoration
 franchise enfranchisement (with the
 implication that the laws will be freely
 exercised after the Romans *mangled*
 them)
64 **confusion** destruction
66 **Thus defied** i.e. now that war has been
 declared on you
67 **I thank . . . Caius** This moment of
 friendly courtesy emphasizes that Caius
 Lucius is characterized more fully than a
 mere ambassador needs to be, as a figure
 of humanity who brings out Cymbeline's
 better nature beneath his defiance, and
 who will later offer support and comfort
 to Innogen in her moment of greatest
 crisis (4.2.361–403).
68 **knighted me** This detail, from
 Holinshed, combines the world of

medieval chivalry with that of imperial
Rome.
70 **he . . . perforce** the fact that he demands it
 back from me, of necessity
71 **Behoves . . . utterance** necessitates my
 preserving at any cost, to the uttermost
 perfect well aware
72 **Pannonians and Dalmatians** inhabitants of the present-day Balkans.
 Shakespeare places their rebellion
 against Rome, which distracted Augustus Caesar from invading Britain, in
 Cymbeline's rather than his predeces-
 sor's reign (as in Holinshed) so that
 Cymbeline can indicate that he
 knows that all is not well in the Roman
 empire.
74 **read** interpret
 cold lacking in spirit

LUCIUS   Let proof speak.   75
CLOTEN His majesty bids you welcome. Make pastime with
    us a day or two or longer. If you seek us afterwards in
    other terms, you shall find us in our salt-water girdle. If
    you beat us out of it, it is yours ; if you fall in the adven-
    ture, our crows shall fare the better for you, and there's   80
    an end.
LUCIUS So, sir.
CYMBELINE
    I know your master's pleasure, and he mine.
    All the remain is 'Welcome'.   *Flourish. Exeunt*

3.2   *Enter Pisanio, reading of a letter*
PISANIO
    How ? Of adultery ? Wherefore write you not
    What monster's her accuser ? Leonatus,
    O master, what a strange infection
    Is fall'n into thy ear ! What false Italian,
    As poisonous tongued as handed, hath prevailed   5
    On thy too ready hearing ? Disloyal ? No.
    She's punished for her truth, and undergoes,
    More goddess-like than wife-like, such assaults
    As would take in some virtue. O my master,
    Thy mind to hers is now as low as were   10

84 *Flourish*] *not in* F
    3.2.2 accuser] CAPELL; accuse F   10 hers] HANMER; her F

75, 82 Caius Lucius' clipped monosyllables
    as he refuses to be provoked either by
    Cymbeline's bravado or Cloten's
    rudeness emphasize that he behaves
    with the restraint of the true statesman,
    as his opponents fail to do.
75 **proof** the result. The thought, and the
    cryptic phrasing, recall Prince Hal's 'Let
    the end try the man' (*2 Henry IV* 2.2.40).
    The expression was proverbial (Tilley
    E116).
79–80 **adventure** attempt
82 **So** i.e. so be it
84 **All the remain** all that remains (to be
    said)
3.2.1 **How?** Elliptical for 'How is it ?', 'How
    can this be ?', and so equivalent to
    'What?' (*OED adv.* 4a)
1–2 **Wherefore . . . accuser** Why don't you
    name her accuser ?

2 **monster's her accuser** F's 'Monsters her
    accuse' makes sense ; but elsewhere Pisa-
    nio speaks of only one accuser, and F's
    line limps metrically. F's 'accuse' is prob-
    ably an error, the compositor taking
    'Monsters' as a plural.
5 **As poisonous . . . handed** who is as skilled
    in verbal poison (slander) as in concoct-
    ing physical poison. Italians were notor-
    ious as poisoners.
7, 12 **truth** loyalty
7 **undergoes** endures
9 **take in** overcome
    some virtue the virtue of some people
10 **to hers** compared to hers. F reads 'to her' ;
    but Oxford notes that ' "hers" produces
    better symmetry, not only with "Thy
    mind" but with "Thy Fortunes" (which
    are "as lowe", by comparison with
    "hers")' (*Textual Companion*, p. 606).

Thy fortunes. How? That I should murder her,
Upon the love and truth and vows which I
Have made to thy command? I her? Her blood?
If it be so to do good service, never
Let me be counted serviceable. How look I,   15
That I should seem to lack humanity
So much as this fact comes to? (*Reads*) 'Do't. The letter
That I have sent her, by her own command
Shall give thee opportunity.' O damned paper,
Black as the ink that's on thee! Senseless bauble,   20
Art thou a fedary for this act, and look'st
So virgin-like without? Lo, here she comes.
   Enter Innogen
I am ignorant in what I am commanded.
INNOGEN How now, Pisanio?
PISANIO
Madam, here is a letter from my lord.   25
INNOGEN
Who, thy lord? That is my lord, Leonatus!
O learn'd indeed were that astronomer
That knew the stars as I his characters—
He'd lay the future open. You good gods,
Let what is here contained relish of love,   30
Of my lord's health, of his content—yet not

---

17 *Reads*] *not in* F 'Do't. The letter] *not italicized, as the letter is, in* F 21 fedary] F
(Foedarie)

12 **Upon** as a consequence of
13 **Her blood?** Should I shed her blood?
17 **fact** (evil) deed (the usual meaning in the
  sixteenth and seventeenth centuries
  (*OED* 1c))
  comes amounts
17–19 **Do't . . . opportunity** F does not
  print the words 'Do't. The letter' as
  part of the letter, though they surely
  must be. This extract from Posthumus'
  letter does not correspond to the letter as
  read out at 3.4.21–31, but such 'incon-
  sistencies' pass unnoticed in performance.
18 **by . . . command** by what she instructs
  you to do
20 **Senseless bauble** a trifle (i.e. the letter)
  without feeling (and also perhaps 'without making sense')
21 **fedary for** accomplice in. *OED* says that

this usage comes from an 'erroneous
association with Latin *foedus*' (covenant).
23 **am ignorant in** must pretend to be ignorant of
26 **thy lord . . . my lord** Innogen distin-
  guishes between Posthumus' status as
  Pisanio's master and as her husband.
  She makes a similar distinction at ll. 53–
  5.
27 **astronomer** astrologer
28 **characters** handwriting (with perhaps, in
  view of *astronomer* in the previous line, a
  pun on astrological symbols)
30 **relish** taste
31 **not** i.e. not content. Innogen's speeches
  in this scene are typical of her style (and
  of the play as a whole) in the use of
  elaborate parentheses to define precisely
  what she means, in this case exactly how
  she wants Posthumus to be *content*.

That we two are asunder, let that grieve him;
Some griefs are med'cinable, that is one of them,
For it doth physic love—of his content
All but in that. Good wax, thy leave. Blest be   35
You bees that make these locks of counsel! Lovers
And men in dangerous bonds pray not alike;
Though forfeiters you cast in prison, yet
You clasp young Cupid's tables. Good news, gods!

She opens and reads the letter

'Justice and your father's wrath, should he take me in his   40
dominion, could not be so cruel to me as you, O the
dearest of creatures, would even renew me with your
eyes. Take notice that I am in Cambria, at Milford Haven.
What your own love will out of this advise you, follow. So
he wishes you all happiness, that remains loyal to his   45
vow, and your increasing in love,

                    Leonatus Posthumus.'

O for a horse with wings! Hear'st thou, Pisanio?
He is at Milford Haven. Read, and tell me

39.1 *She ... letter*] *not in* F

33 **med'cinable** able to heal
34 **it . . . love** i.e. absence keeps love in good health. 'Absence sharpens love' was proverbial (Tilley A10); compare the modern 'absence makes the heart grow fonder', and Sonnet 56, which argues that lovers' absence intensifies the pleasures of their reunion.
35 **All but in that** in every way except that we are apart
   Good . . . leave Innogen echoes the mannered phrase of Malvolio at *Twelfth Night* 2.5.90–1 as she goes to break the wax that seals the letter; and she lingers even longer than Malvolio before breaking it, with an elaborate comparison between the ways that lovers and prisoners react to sealed documents (ll. 36–9). Actresses, notably Judi Dench at Stratford-upon-Avon in 1979, have rightly treated this mannered comparison, especially the verbal quibble 'be | You bees' (ll. 35–6), with self-mockery, Innogen's recognition of the silly things that people say when they are in love.
36 **locks of counsel** seals of secrecy

37 **in dangerous bonds** bound by risky contracts (which, like letters, were sealed with wax—hence the comparison, and contrast, with lovers' reactions)
38 **forfeiters** defaulters
   you i.e. the bees (or the wax)
   cast in prison (because the sealed bond indicted them)
39 **clasp** fasten (in an embrace, whereas you *cast* debtors *in prison*)
   young Cupid's tables i.e. love letters
   tables writing tablets
41 **as** but that
42 **even** This is probably used for emphasis, perhaps implying 'completely' (*OED adv.* 8b).
42–3 **with your eyes** i.e. by looking at me
43 **Cambria** Wales (Latin)
   Milford Haven a port in South Wales. Its resonance for a seventeenth-century audience is discussed in the Introduction, pp. 62–4.
44 **advise you** i.e. advise you to do
46 **and your** i.e. and remains your
48–82 **O . . . way** Innogen's speeches to the end of the scene give a rapturous, even feverish sense of excitement and speed, as

How far 'tis thither. If one of mean affairs   50
May plod it in a week, why may not I
Glide thither in a day? Then true Pisanio,
Who long'st like me to see thy lord, who long'st—
O let me bate—but not like me—yet long'st
But in a fainter kind—O not like me,   55
For mine's beyond beyond; say, and speak thick—
Love's counsellor should fill the bores of hearing,
To th' smothering of the sense—how far it is
To this same blessèd Milford. And by th' way
Tell me how Wales was made so happy as   60
T'inherit such a haven. But first of all,
How we may steal from hence; and for the gap
That we shall make in time from our hence-going
And our return, to excuse; but first, how get hence.
Why should excuse be born or ere begot?   65
We'll talk of that hereafter. Prithee speak,
How many score of miles may we well ride
'Twixt hour and hour?

PISANIO   One score 'twixt sun and sun
Madam's enough for you, and too much too.

67 score] F2; store F1   ride] F2; rid F1

one idea tumbles out after another, often
to be corrected (ll. 53–5, 64–6). Sometimes she is precise and practical (ll. 74–
7); sometimes her language is impressionistic, even vague (ll. 56, 78–80). Her
own speeches are good examples of what
she calls *speaking thick*. See l. 56 and note.
48 **O . . . wings** This may allude to the classical winged horse Pegasus, but swift
horses reappear, without wings, at ll.
71–3.

50 **mean affairs** unimportant business
54 **bate** An aphetic form of 'abate', lessen,
i.e. speak more moderately.
55 **fainter kind** less extreme fashion
56 **beyond beyond** Perhaps 'surpassing
everything' (Onions), but it is impossible
to pin down a phrase whose point seems
to be the impossibility of exact expression: Innogen uses the vagueness to suggest that her love can't be defined, try
though she has done in the previous
lines to define it.

56 **thick** quickly. Cotgrave's *Dictionary
of the French and English Tongues*
(1611) glosses *bretonner*: 'To speak
thick and short; or, as we say, nine
words at once'.
57–8 **Love's . . . sense** An adviser to a lover
should fill the cavities of the ears (*bores of
hearing*) until the *sense* (of hearing) is
overwhelmed.
59 **by th' way** on the journey
62–4 **for the gap . . . excuse** how to account
for the elapsed time between our departure and return
65 **or ere begot** even before the necessity for
it. The combination *or ere* is used for
emphasis (Abbott §131).
67 **ride** F's 'rid' makes sense, 'cover ground'
(*OED v.* 8); but the context surely justifies
F2's 'ride'.
68 **'Twixt . . . hour** between one hour and
the next
   'twixt . . . sun between sunrise and
sunset

INNOGEN

Why, one that rode to's execution, man,　　　　　　　70
Could never go so slow. I have heard of riding wagers
Where horses have been nimbler than the sands
That run i'th' clock's behalf. But this is fool'ry.
Go bid my woman feign a sickness, say
She'll home to her father; and provide me presently　　75
A riding-suit no costlier than would fit
A franklin's housewife.

PISANIO　　　　　　　　Madam, you're best consider.

INNOGEN

I see before me, man. Nor here, nor here,
Nor what ensues, but have a fog in them
That I cannot look through. Away, I prithee,　　　　80
Do as I bid thee. There's no more to say:
Accessible is none but Milford way.　　　　　　*Exeunt*

3.3　*Enter Belarius, Guiderius and Arviragus, from a cave*

BELARIUS

A goodly day not to keep house with such

---

78 nor here, nor] F2; nor heere, not F1
3.3.0.1 *from a cave*] *not in* F

---

70 **one . . . execution** (as she may unknowingly be doing)
71 **riding wagers** horse races with bets on them
72-3 **nimbler . . . behalf** quicker than the sands running through an hourglass
75 **presently** immediately
77 **franklin** a freeholder, below the rank of a gentleman
　you're best you had better (Abbott §230)
78-80 **Nor . . . through** This probably means: 'On one side of me and on the other, as well as behind me (*what ensues*), there is a fog that I cannot see through', implying that the only thing that is clear to her is *Milford way* (l. 82). But it could also mean, less probably: 'there is an impenetrable fog on all sides and also over what is to happen in the future (*what ensues*)', so that the journey to Milford, though vital, is also filled with the unknown—which would reinforce the irony of l. 70. Either way, the phrase is

another example of that impressionism which characterizes Innogen's language and the play's.
3.3 Acts 1 and 2 are primarily concerned with the wager story; 3.1 establishes the story of the conflict between Britain and Rome; this scene introduces the third major narrative strand, the story of the stolen princes, mentioned briefly at 1.1.57-68 and at 1.6.5-6.
0.1 *Guiderius, Arviragus* The names of Cymbeline's sons, as well as slightly different forms of their assumed names, occur in Holinshed.
　from a cave Entrances to and from the cave are not specified in a Folio stage direction until the start of 4.2, but are clearly implied by the dialogue. The cave may have been represented by a large property like a rock (see l. 8 and 4.2.164) such as that mentioned by the theatrical impresario Philip Henslowe in his inventory of properties belonging to the Lord Admiral's Men, 10 March 1598

Whose roof's as low as ours. Stoop, boys; this gate
Instructs you how t'adore the heavens, and bows you
To a morning's holy office. The gates of monarchs
Are arched so high that giants may jet through   5
And keep their impious turbans on without
Good morrow to the sun. Hail, thou fair heaven!
We house i'th' rock, yet use thee not so hardly
As prouder livers do.

GUIDERIUS   Hail, heaven!

ARVIRAGUS   Hail, heaven!

BELARIUS

Now for our mountain sport. Up to yon hill,   10
Your legs are young; I'll tread these flats. Consider,
When you above perceive me like a crow,
That it is place which lessens and sets off,
And you may then revolve what tales I have told you
Of courts, of princes, of the tricks in war.   15

---

2 Stoop] HANMER ; Sleepe F

(*Henslowe's Diary*, p. 319), or it may simply have been suggested by hangings
over the discovery-space at the back of
the stage, as on the mock-Elizabethan
stage at Stratford, Ontario in 1970.
Oxford adds '*in the woods*', on the
grounds that Simon Forman's account
of a performance in 1611 (see Introduction, p. 4) mentions woods twice.
Property trees were certainly used in
Shakespeare's theatre (Henslowe mentions several), and Forman may refer to
these; but the dialogue implies an open
mountainside from which the princes
can see Belarius *like a crow* (l. 12) from
far away, and woods are in fact only
mentioned once in these rural scenes
(4.2.391), so to specify them here seems
unduly prescriptive.

1–2 **A goodly . . . ours** i.e. people who live in
such cramped conditions as we do should
not waste such a beautiful day by staying
indoors.

2 **gate** entrance

3 **Instructs you** (because it makes you bend
to go under it)
bows you causes you to bow down (as if
in worship)

4 **holy office** religious service

5–6 **giants . . . turbans** 'The idea of a *giant*
was, among the readers of romances, . . .
always confounded with that of a
Saracen' (Johnson).

5 **jet** swagger, strut. Compare Malvolio at
Twelfth Night 2.5.30: 'how he jets under
his advanced plumes'.

6 **impious** (to   seventeenth-century
audiences, because their *turbans* are a
sign that they are Muslims, not
Christians)
without i.e. without saying

8 **hardly** badly

9 **prouder livers** those who live more splen-
didly

11 **these flats** this plain

12 **like a crow** Compare 1.3.15, where a
great distance makes a man look as
small as a crow.

13 **place** position (both literally, on the hill-
side, and in the metaphorical sense
'rank')
lessens and sets off diminishes and
enhances

14 **revolve** consider

15 **tricks** freaks, accidents (which can have
the result of giving a perhaps undeserved
promotion or *place* (l. 13))

This service is not service, so being done,
But being so allowed. To apprehend thus
Draws us a profit from all things we see,
And often to our comfort shall we find
The sharded beetle in a safer hold   20
Than is the full-winged eagle. O, this life
Is nobler than attending for a check,
Richer than doing nothing for a bauble,
Prouder than rustling in unpaid-for silk;
Such gain the cap of him that makes 'em fine,   25
Yet keeps his book uncrossed: no life to ours.

GUIDERIUS

Out of your proof you speak. We poor unfledged
Have never winged from view o'th' nest, nor know not
What air's from home. Haply this life is best,
If quiet life be best; sweeter to you   30
That have a sharper known, well corresponding
With your stiff age; but unto us it is
A cell of ignorance, travelling abed,

16 This] F; That POPE   23 bauble] ROWE; Babe F; Bribe HANMER; robe NOSWORTHY (*conj.*
Bulloch)   25 'em] CAPELL; him F   28 know] F2; knowes F1   33 travelling] F (trauailing)

16 **This . . . done** i.e. service which is done
simply because it is expected at a court or
by a prince, or which is a mere accident
in war, is not true service (which, it is
implied, should be done voluntarily, for
its own sake)
17 **But . . . allowed** merely deemed to be
(service), i.e. it isn't service at all (*OED*,
allow, *v.* 5)
To apprehend thus to look at things in
this way (i.e. by making distinctions
between true and false)
20 **sharded** having scaly wing-cases. See
*OED sb.*¹ 5, and *Macbeth* 3.2.43: 'The
shard-borne beetle'. *OED* (*shard*, *sb.*⁴
and *sharded*, *ppl. a.*²) argues that this
gloss is a misunderstanding, and that
sharded means 'living in dung' ('born in
dung' in *Macbeth*—i.e. 'shard-born'); but
any 'misunderstanding' seems to be Shakespeare's, since there is an obvious contrast between the wings of the *beetle* and
those of the *eagle* (l. 21). Dung seems to
have nothing to do with it.
hold shelter, refuge
22 **attending . . . check** waiting on a lord
only to be rebuked

23 **bauble** worthless reward. Rowe's emendation of F's 'Babe' is much the most
convincing. *Bauble,* contemptuously
used, occurs in both the previous scenes
(3.1.27, 3.2.20). Of other proposed
emendations, 'bribe' is attractive because
it exchanges one monosyllable for
another, but has the drawback of shifting
the focus from the *attending* courtier in ll.
22 and 24 to the lord who does nothing
for the bribe he is given.
25 **gain . . . fine** win the respect (shown by
removing the hat) of the tailor who is the
source of their grandeur
26 **keeps . . . uncrossed** continue to have
their debts uncancelled in the tailor's
account book
to compared to, like
27 **proof** experience
29 **What . . . home** what the air is like away
from home (i.e. what other places are
like)
Haply perhaps
33 **abed** in bed (i.e. only in imagination).
Compare Sonnet 27.1–3: 'Weary with
toil I haste me to my bed . . . | But then
begins a journey in my head'.

A prison for a debtor, that not dares
To stride a limit.

ARVIRAGUS   What should we speak of   35
When we are old as you? When we shall hear
The rain and wind beat dark December, how,
In this our pinching cave, shall we discourse
The freezing hours away? We have seen nothing.
We are beastly: subtle as the fox for prey,   40
Like warlike as the wolf for what we eat.
Our valour is to chase what flies; our cage
We make a choir, as doth the prisoned bird,
And sing our bondage freely.

BELARIUS   How you speak!
Did you but know the city's usuries,   45
And felt them knowingly; the art o'th' court,
As hard to leave as keep, whose top to climb
Is certain falling, or so slipp'ry that
The fear's as bad as falling; the toil o'th' war,
A pain that only seems to seek out danger   50
I'th' name of fame and honour, which dies i'th' search
And hath as oft a sland'rous epitaph
As record of fair act; nay, many times
Doth ill deserve by doing well; what's worse,
Must curtsy at the censure. O boys, this story   55
The world may read in me. My body's marked
With Roman swords, and my report was once

34 for] POPE; or F

35 **stride a limit** step over the threshold (of
   the *prison* in l. 34)
35–44 **What . . . freely** This speech is discussed in the Introduction, p. 43.
37 The power of this line to evoke the dreari-
   ness of winter depends in part on its
   rhythm, especially the monosyllables. In
   particular, *beat* gives a powerful sense of
   the winter *rain and wind* pounding on the
   cave; but since it actually says *beat dark
   December*, it is possible that *beat* here is
   another example of the rare usage found
   at *Hamlet* 1.1.37, 'The bell then beating
   [i.e. striking] one', and that it implies that
   the rain and wind mark, indicate, the fact
   that it is December.
38 **pinching** nippingly cold

40 **beastly** beast-like
41 **Like** as
44 **freely** Is this simply ironical, as Maxwell
   claims—'that is the only sort of freedom
   they have'—or does it suggest a hint of
   compensation for their privations?
45 **usuries** financial practices, particularly
   lending money at interest
46 **felt** experienced
   knowingly with (that) knowledge
   art artificial behaviour
47 **keep** stay in
50 **pain** labour
54 **deserve** earn
55 **curtsy . . . censure** do reverence on being
   censured
57 **report** reputation

First with the best of note. Cymbeline loved me,
And when a soldier was the theme my name
Was not far off. Then was I as a tree   60
Whose boughs did bend with fruit; but in one night
A storm or robbery, call it what you will,
Shook down my mellow hangings, nay my leaves,
And left me bare to weather.
GUIDERIUS   Uncertain favour!
BELARIUS

My fault being nothing, as I have told you oft,   65
But that two villains, whose false oaths prevailed
Before my perfect honour, swore to Cymbeline
I was confederate with the Romans. So
Followed my banishment, and this twenty years
This rock and these domains have been my world,   70
Where I have lived at honest freedom, paid
More pious debts to heaven than in all
The fore-end of my time. But up to th' mountains!
This is not hunter's language. He that strikes
The venison first shall be the lord o'th' feast,   75
To him the other two shall minister,
And we will fear no poison which attends
In place of greater state. I'll meet you in the valleys.
                                Exeunt Guiderius and Arviragus
How hard it is to hide the sparks of nature!

---

70 domains] F (Demesnes)   78.1 *Exeunt... Arviragus*] Exeunt. F

58 **best of note** most renowned
61–4 **but in . . . weather** There is a striking
    parallel at *Timon* 4.3.265–7, where
    Timon's false friends are compared to
    leaves that 'with one winter's brush |
    Fell from their boughs, and left me open,
    bare | For every storm that blows'.
63 **hangings** i.e. the fruit. Compare
    5.4.263–4: 'Hang there like fruit, my
    soul, | Till the tree die.'
    nay and even
64 **weather** Perhaps specifically 'bad
    weather, storms' (Schmidt). See the
    note to ll. 61–4.
67 **perfect** (implying that his honour was not
    violated by treachery or falsehood, in
    contrast to the *false oaths* of the sland-
    erers in the previous line)

70 **domains** F's 'Demesnes' means 'estates
    belonging to a lord'; but *OED* says that
    'demesne' is 'a differentiated spelling of
    the word DOMAIN', and that while
    'demesne' 'has been traditionally
    retained in the legal use', 'the two forms
    overlap' (*OED*, *domain*). Of these,
    'domains' seems to be the more intellig-
    ible to a modern audience.
71 **at** in
73 **fore-end . . . time** early part of my life
75 **venison** (living) deer
76 **minister** be servants
77 **attends** is ever-present
78 **place . . . state** a world where there is
    greater ceremony
79–107 **How hard . . . up** Johnson criticized
    this speech because there is 'no

These boys know little they are sons to th' King,   80
Nor Cymbeline dreams that they are alive.
They think they are mine, and though trained up thus
        meanly
I'th' cave wherein they bow, their thoughts do hit
The roofs of palaces, and nature prompts them
In simple and low things to prince it much   85
Beyond the trick of others. This Polydore,
The heir of Cymbeline and Britain, who
The King his father called Guiderius—Jove,
When on my three-foot stool I sit and tell
The warlike feats I have done, his spirits fly out   90
Into my story: say 'Thus mine enemy fell,
And thus I set my foot on's neck', even then
The princely blood flows in his cheek, he sweats,
Strains his young nerves, and puts himself in posture
That acts my words. The younger brother, Cadwal,   95
Once Arviragus, in as like a figure
Strikes life into my speech, and shows much more
His own conceiving.
        ⌈*A hunting-horn sounds*⌉
                                Hark, the game is roused!
O Cymbeline, heaven and my conscience knows
Thou didst unjustly banish me, whereon   100
At three and two years old I stole these babes,
Thinking to bar thee of succession as

83 wherein   they   bow,] WARBURTON; whereon   the   Bowe‸   F   86 Polydore] ROWE
(Polydor);   *Paladour* F   98, 107 *A hunting-horn sounds*] *not in* F

particular reason why Belarius should
now tell to himself what he could not
know better by telling it'. But he is telling
the audience, not himself. Soliloquy is the
art of communicating directly with the
audience, and this one works perfectly
well in performance.

82 **trained up** brought up
   meanly humbly
83 **wherein they bow** Warburton's emendation of F's 'whereon the Bowe' is needed
   for sense. The princes *bow* to avoid
   knocking their heads against the low
   roof of the cave, whereas their *thoughts*
   actually *hit* | *The roofs of palaces*.
85 **prince it** behave like princes

86 **trick** aptitude, skill
89 **three-foot** having three legs
91 **say** i.e. when I say
94 **nerves** sinews (as frequently in Shakespeare)
96 **in . . . figure** likewise acting a part
97–8 **shows . . . conceiving** reveals his own
   imagination (rather than merely acting
   out what I say). Arviragus' imagination
   emerges   in   the   exceptionally   vivid
   language he is given (e.g. ll. 35–44, and
   4.2.219–30).
98 **roused** startled
101 **two years** This is at variance with
   1.1.59, where Arviragus is said to have
   been a baby in swaddling clothes.

Thou reft'st me of my lands. Euriphile,
Thou wast their nurse; they took thee for their mother,
And every day do honour to her grave.   105
Myself, Belarius, that am Morgan called,
They take for natural father.
        ⌈*A hunting-horn sounds*⌉
                        The game is up.   *Exit*

3.4   *Enter Pisanio, and Innogen in a riding-suit*
INNOGEN
Thou told'st me when we came from horse the place
Was near at hand. Ne'er longed my mother so
To see me first as I have now. Pisanio, man,
Where is Posthumus? What is in thy mind
That makes thee stare thus? Wherefore breaks that sigh   5
From th'inward of thee? One but painted thus
Would be interpreted a thing perplexed
Beyond self-explication. Put thyself
Into a haviour of less fear, ere wildness
Vanquish my staider senses. What's the matter?   10
        Pisanio gives her a letter
Why tender'st thou that paper to me with

---

106 Morgan] F2; *Mergan* F1
    3.4.0.1 *in a riding-suit*] *not in* F   10.1 *Pisanio . . . letter*] *not in* F

103 **reft'st** robbed (past tense of 'reave')
    Euriphile (pronounced 'U-ri-fill-ee')
107 **up** flushed from cover
3.4 This is a long and difficult scene, with
    speeches that are convoluted, even gar-
    rulous, with apparent digressions (e.g. ll.
    33–9, 54–64, 155–66), and it is often
    severely cut in performance. When
    played complete, however, the function
    of its length becomes clear. This is the
    first great crisis for Innogen, as she thinks
    her husband has betrayed her (the sec-
    ond is the scene with 'his' headless body,
    4.2.292–333): she needs time to move
    from shock to recovery to the decision to
    start a new life as the page Fidele; and
    Pisanio, her sympathetic guide on her
    psychological journey, needs to give her
    that time (hence some of his digressions),
    and to prompt her gently to the next
    stage—for instance, in suggesting the

page's disguise.
0.1 **a riding-suit** This is specified at 3.2.76.
1 **came from horse** dismounted
3 **have** do (i.e. *have* longing to see Posthu-
    mus)
6 **but painted thus** only represented like
    that in a painting (let alone in reality)
7 **perplexed** distressed (a stronger term in
    seventeenth-century usage than now, as
    when Othello, having killed his wife and
    about to kill himself, says that he is 'Per-
    plexed in the extreme' (5.2.355))
8 **self-explication** being able to explain it
    even to oneself
9 **haviour . . . fear** less frightening appear-
    ance
    wildness madness, panic
10 **staider senses** more balanced feelings
11 **tender'st thou** do you offer (with a pun on
    the modern sense of *tender* in the next
    line)

A look untender? If't be summer news,
Smile to't before; if winterly, thou need'st
But keep that count'nance still. My husband's hand?
That drug-damned Italy hath out-craftied him,   15
And he's at some hard point. Speak, man. Thy tongue
May take off some extremity which to read
Would be even mortal to me.

PISANIO   Please you read,
And you shall find me, wretched man, a thing
The most disdained of fortune.   20

INNOGEN (*reads*) 'Thy mistress, Pisanio, hath played the
strumpet in my bed, the testimonies whereof lies bleeding
in me. I speak not out of weak surmises but from proof as
strong as my grief and as certain as I expect my revenge.
That part thou, Pisanio, must act for me, if thy faith be   25
not tainted with the breach of hers. Let thine own hands
take away her life. I shall give thee opportunity at Milford
Haven—she hath my letter for the purpose—where if
thou fear to strike and to make me certain it is done,
thou art the pander to her dishonour and equally to me   30
disloyal.'

PISANIO (*aside*)
What shall I need to draw my sword? The paper
Hath cut her throat already. No, 'tis slander,
Whose edge is sharper than the sword, whose tongue
Outvenoms all the worms of Nile, whose breath   35

12 **summer** i.e. joyful. Compare Sonnet
98.7: 'any summer's story'.
13 **to't** at it
winterly i.e. harsh. Compare Sonnet
56.13: 'call it winter...being full of care'.
14 **But** only
15 **drug-damned** cursed for its use of poisons
(Renaissance Italy was notorious for
ingenious poisonings). The phrase is a
Shakespearian coinage.
out-craftied deviously outwitted (another
Shakespearian coinage)
16 **at ... point** in some dangerous crisis
17 **take ... extremity** reduce the extreme
pain
17–18 **which ... me** which, if I read it,
would kill me
22 **testimonies ... lies** See note to 1.4.17–
18.

24 **grief** injury
32 **What** why, i.e. 'for what reason' (Abbott
§253)
33–9 **'tis slander ... enters** This apparent
digression is needed to give Innogen time
for the terrible news to sink in, a point
vividly made by Geraldine James at the
National Theatre in 1988: during this
speech, she stood rooted to the spot in
shock, the paper fluttering from her
nerveless hands.
33–4 **slander ... sword** An almost identical
phrase occurs at *Winter's Tale* 2.3.86–7,
'slander, | Whose sting is sharper
than the sword's', where 'sting' seems
to carry the association of the serpent's
tongue in l. 35 here (see the following
notes).
35 **Outvenoms** is more poisonous than

Rides on the posting winds and doth belie
All corners of the world. Kings, queens, and states,
Maids, matrons, nay the secrets of the grave
This viperous slander enters. (*To Innogen*) What cheer,
   madam?

INNOGEN

False to his bed? What is it to be false? 40
To lie in watch there and to think on him?
To weep 'twixt clock and clock? If sleep charge nature,
To break it with a fearful dream of him
And cry myself awake? That's false to's bed, is it?

PISANIO Alas, good lady. 45

INNOGEN

I false? Thy conscience witness. Giacomo,
Thou didst accuse him of incontinency.
Thou then looked'st like a villain; now methinks
Thy favour's good enough. Some jay of Italy,
Whose mother was her painting, hath betrayed him. 50
Poor I am stale, a garment out of fashion,

---

46 witness.] F (witnesse:); witness, ROWE

---

35 **worms** serpents (as at *Antony* 5.2.238–
9: 'the pretty worm | Of Nilus . . . that
kills and pains not')

36 **posting** speeding; see note to 2.4.27.
belie deceive, fill with lies

37 **states** people of high rank

41 **in watch** awake. For the idea of a lover
staying awake like a watchman, compare Sonnet 57.6: 'Whilst I, my sovereign, watch the clock for you'.
on of. 'On' and 'of' could be used inter-
changeably in seventeenth-century English (Abbott §175).

42 **'twixt clock and clock** from hour to hour,
continually
charge nature weigh down the vital
powers (i.e. if I ever manage to get to
sleep)

43 **fearful . . . him** terrifying nightmare about
him

46 **Thy conscience witness**. The obvious
sense of the Folio punctuation, substantially followed here, is that Innogen
addresses Pisanio, calling on him to
bear *witness* to her fidelity. She might be

asking Posthumus to search his *conscience* for any sign from his knowledge
of her that she could be false. She surely
cannot be addressing Giacomo, as
Rowe's punctuation implies (see collation), since that would make sense
only if she went on to say 'that I rejected
your advances', or similar; but she seems
to have a flash of intuition that somehow
Giacomo is involved in all this.

47 **incontinency** infidelity

49 **favour** outward appearance
jay Since this bird has strikingly showy
plumage, it was associated with whores,
ostentatiously dressed in the latest fashion. Innogen contrasts the whore's dress
with herself, *a garment out of fashion*, in l.
51.

50 **Whose . . . painting** who was created by
cosmetics, rather than by a natural
mother

51 **stale** The chief meaning is the modern
one, 'no longer fresh'; but it may also
carry the association of the noun 'stale',
meaning 'a lover or mistress whose
devotion is turned into ridicule for the

And for I am richer than to hang by th' walls
I must be ripped. To pieces with me! O,
Men's vows are women's traitors. All good seeming,
By thy revolt, O husband, shall be thought   55
Put on for villainy; not born where't grows,
But worn a bait for ladies.

PISANIO   Good madam, hear me.

INNOGEN

True honest men being heard like false Aeneas
Were in his time thought false, and Sinon's weeping
Did scandal many a holy tear, took pity   60
From most true wretchedness. So thou, Posthumus,
Wilt lay the leaven on all proper men:
Goodly and gallant shall be false and perjured
From thy great fail. (To Pisanio) Come fellow, be thou
       honest,
Do thou thy master's bidding. When thou seest him,   65
A little witness my obedience. Look,
I draw the sword myself; take it, and hit
The innocent mansion of my love, my heart.

---

amusement of a rival' (*OED sb.*[3] 6), as
when Adriana in *Errors* complains of
her husband, in a phrase almost identical
to Innogen's, 'Poor I am but his stale'
(2.1.100).

52 **for . . . walls** because I am too valuable
simply to be discarded (by being hung up
like an old coat)

53 **ripped** torn up (so that the material can
be used again)

53–64 **O . . . great fail** In her state of shock,
Innogen generalizes about men's treachery, as Posthumus generalized about
women's frailty in his (2.4.153–87).

54 **seeming** appearance

55 **revolt** betrayal

56 **Put on** worn as a cover
not . . . grows not natural but assumed

57 **bait** lure, temptation

58 **heard** listened to

58–9 **Aeneas . . . Sinon** Both are types of
male treachery. Although Aeneas is the
heroic founder of Rome in Virgil's *Aeneid*,
he betrayed Queen Dido of Carthage in
the process, which is probably what
Innogen is referring to, though there
was also a medieval tradition that

Aeneas was a traitor to his native Troy.
Sinon was the creator of the Trojan horse
in which the Greek army was concealed;
found *weeping* outside Troy, he persuaded
the Trojans to bring the horse into the
city, and then let the Greeks out to
destroy it.

60 **scandal** discredit

60–1 **took pity . . . wretchedness** robbed genuine misery of sympathy (because his
tears were faked)

62 **lay . . . men** *Leaven* is fermenting dough,
also known as 'sour-dough' (*OED sb.* 1),
used here to convey Posthumus' souring,
discrediting, honest (*proper*) men.

63 **Goodly** admirable
gallant chivalrous

64 **From . . . fail** The hammered monosyllables emphasize Innogen's disillusion with
Posthumus, and also conclude her gen-
eralization about male treachery, before
she begins the next phase of the scene (ll.
64–100), her attempt at death.
fail failure

66 **A little witness** testify somewhat to

68 **mansion . . . heart** Her heart is imagined
as a house in which her love lives.

Fear not, 'tis empty of all things but grief.
Thy master is not there, who was indeed   70
The riches of it. Do his bidding, strike.
Thou mayst be valiant in a better cause,
But now thou seem'st a coward.
PISANIO   Hence vile instrument,
Thou shalt not damn my hand!
INNOGEN   Why, I must die,
And if I do not by thy hand thou art   75
No servant of thy master's. Against self-slaughter
There is a prohibition so divine
That cravens my weak hand. Come, here's my heart.
Something's afore't. Soft, soft, we'll no defence,
Obedient as the scabbard. What is here?   80
        She takes letters from her bosom
The scriptures of the loyal Leonatus,
All turned to heresy? Away, away,
Corrupters of my faith, you shall no more
Be stomachers to my heart. Thus may poor fools
Believe false teachers. Though those that are betrayed   85
Do feel the treason sharply, yet the traitor
Stands in worse case of woe. And thou, Posthumus,
That didst set up my disobedience 'gainst the King
My father, and make me put into contempt the suits
Of princely fellows, shalt hereafter find   90

---

79 afore't] ROWE; a-foot F   80.1 *She ... bosom*] *not in* F   89 make] MALONE; makes F

77 **prohibition so divine** Compare *Hamlet* 1.2.131–2: 'that the Everlasting had not fixed | His canon 'gainst self-slaughter!' Suicide was not explicitly forbidden in the Bible, except under the general prohibition 'Thou shalt not kill', but by the early Church.

78 **cravens** makes cowardly

79 **afore't** in front of it
Soft, soft not so fast (an exclamation)

80 **Obedient . . . scabbard** i.e. her heart is as ready to receive the sword as the sword's own *scabbard*, or sheath, would be

81 **scriptures** letters, playing on the meaning 'sacred texts', which leads naturally into

the *heresy* of l. 82 : the letters which were an expression of the *loyal*, faithful, Leonatus have now become denials of his love, as heretical writings deny Christian orthodoxy, and hence are *Corrupters of my faith* (l. 83).

84 **stomacher** an ornamented panel at the front of a dress (so called because it covers the stomach)

85 **false teachers** This presumably refers back to the *heresy* of l. 82.

87 **Stands . . . woe** is worse off (presumably because treachery is contemptible)

88 **set up** instigate, was the cause of

90 **princely fellows** equals in royal rank

It is no act of common passage but
A strain of rareness; and I grieve myself
To think, when thou shalt be disedged by her
That now thou tirest on, how thy memory
Will then be panged by me. (*To Pisanio*) Prithee dispatch.   95
The lamb entreats the butcher. Where's thy knife?
Thou art too slow to do thy master's bidding
When I desire it too.

PISANIO   O gracious lady,
Since I received command to do this business
I have not slept one wink.

INNOGEN   Do't, and to bed then.   100

PISANIO
I'll wake mine eyeballs out first.

INNOGEN   Wherefore then
Didst undertake it? Why hast thou abused
So many miles with a pretence? This place,
Mine action, and thine own? Our horses' labour?
The time inviting thee? The perturbed court,   105
For my being absent, whereunto I never
Purpose return? Why hast thou gone so far
To be unbent when thou hast ta'en thy stand,

---

101 out] INGLEBY (*conj.* Johnson); *not in* F

91–2 **It . . . rareness** it (presumably her defiance of the King) is no commonplace
action, but arises from exceptional
qualities. Innogen is uncharacteristically
driven by the extremity of the situation to
praise herself, in contrast to the woman
who she thinks has superseded her
(ll. 93–4).
93 **be disedged** have your edge taken off (i.e.
when your sexual desires are satisfied).
Compare *Hamlet* 3.2.237: 'It would cost
you a groaning to take off mine edge.'
94 **tirest** feedest (in the violent manner of a
bird of prey). For the sexual connotation,
compare the description of Venus kissing
Adonis 'as an empty eagle, sharp by fast,
| Tires with her beak on feathers, flesh,
and bone' (*Venus* 55–6).
95 **panged** caused pain (pangs), tortured
dispatch do it quickly
100 **Do't . . . bed then** There is some helpful
ironic humour in this intense but varied

scene; here Innogen uses it to puncture
Pisanio's self-pity.
101 **wake . . . out** stay awake until my
eyes drop out. Compare Middleton
and Dekker, *The Roaring Girl*
(1611), 4.2.186: 'I'll . . . watch out
mine eyes'.
101–9 **Wherefore . . . thee** This torrent of
questions is often cut in performance;
but surely the point is that Innogen is
taking out on Pisanio her pent-up indignation against Posthumus; and in that
her aggression is directed at someone else
rather than suicidally upon herself, this
speech represents a first stage in her
recovery.
105 **The . . . thee** i.e. when you have such a
good opportunity
106 **whereunto** to which
107 **Purpose** intend to
108 **be unbent** i.e. not to have bent the bow
to shoot the arrow

Th'elected deer before thee?

PISANIO   But to win time

To lose so bad employment, in the which   110

I have considered of a course. Good lady,

Hear me with patience.

INNOGEN   Talk thy tongue weary, speak.

I have heard I am a strumpet, and mine ear,

Therein false struck, can take no greater wound,

Nor tent to bottom that. But speak.

PISANIO   Then madam,   115

I thought you would not back again.

INNOGEN   Most like,

Bringing me here to kill me.

PISANIO   Not so neither.

But if I were as wise as honest, then

My purpose would prove well. It cannot be

But that my master is abused. Some villain,   120

Ay, and singular in his art, hath done you both

This cursèd injury.

INNOGEN Some Roman courtesan.

PISANIO No, on my life.

I'll give but notice you are dead, and send him   125

Some bloody sign of it, for 'tis commanded

I should do so. You shall be missed at court,

And that will well confirm it.

INNOGEN   Why good fellow,

What shall I do the while, where bide, how live,

---

108 **stand** position (either a specially set-up platform or a cover of bushes) from which to shoot deer

109 **elected** chosen

113 **strumpet** prostitute

114 **false struck** abused with slander
take receive

115 **tent** This means either a surgical probe to explore the depths of the wound (in order to cure it) or a roll of lint to search and clean it (*OED*, *tent*, *sb.*³ 1, 2). Either implies that nothing could relieve the pain of the *wound* in l. 114.
bottom probe the depths

116 **back** return

117 **neither** Often used, as here, to intensify a negative.

119 **purpose would prove** my plan would turn out. Presumably his *purpose* is that she should adopt a boy's disguise, though he doesn't propose this until l. 155, when he is sure that she will be receptive.

120 **abused** deceived

121 **singular** pre-eminent

123 **courtesan** *OED* says that this is a more elegant term for a prostitute, citing Edward Sharpham's *The Fleire* (1607): 'your courtesan is for your courtier', though the one in *The Comedy of Errors* is patronized by the middle-class Antipholus of Ephesus.

129, 136 **bide** Apheptic form of 'abide'.

Or in my life what comfort when I am   130
Dead to my husband?
PISANIO   If you'll back to th' court—
INNOGEN
No court, no father, nor no more ado
With that harsh, noble, simple nothing,
That Cloten, whose love suit hath been to me
As fearful as a siege.
PISANIO   If not at court,   135
Then not in Britain must you bide.
INNOGEN   Where then?
Hath Britain all the sun that shines? Day, night,
Are they not but in Britain? I'th' world's volume
Our Britain seems as of it but not in't,
In a great pool a swan's nest. Prithee think   140
There's livers out of Britain.
PISANIO   I am most glad
You think of other place. Th'ambassador,
Lucius the Roman, comes to Milford Haven
Tomorrow. Now if you could wear a mind
Dark as your fortune is, and but disguise   145
That which t'appear itself must not yet be
But by self-danger, you should tread a course
Pretty and full of view; yea, haply near
The residence of Posthumus; so nigh, at least,

---

133 noble] F; churlish, noble OXFORD; feeble, noble MAXWELL   134 Cloten] *Clotten* F
148 haply] F (*happily*)

---

133 This line is irregular, and many emendations have been proposed (see collation), but perhaps the irregularity is deliberate, Innogen becoming incoherent in her dislike of Cloten.

138 **Are . . . but** do they not yet except

138–40 **I'th' . . . nest** This is an important moment in the play: the Princess of Britain expresses a more international view than the Queen's narrow isolationism (3.1.14–33), regarding Britain as remote from the rest of the world but still a part of it, as the play itself is about to broaden out to deal with the relations, and ultimately the peace, between Britain and Rome.

138–9 **I'th' . . . in't** 'Britain is a page of the world's great volume, but, as it were, a page torn from it' (Dowden).

141 **livers** people who live

145 **Dark** (a) secret (referring to her mind—i.e. she mustn't reveal who she is); (b) dismal (like her *fortune*)

146 **That** i.e. her appearance (as a woman)
t'appear itself if it reveals what it is

146–7 **must . . . self-danger** may not yet do so without putting itself into danger

148 **Pretty . . . view** desirable, with good prospects
haply perhaps

149 **nigh** near

That though his actions were not visible, yet   150
Report should render him hourly to your ear
As truly as he moves.
INNOGEN   O for such means,
Though peril to my modesty, not death on't,
I would adventure.
PISANIO   Well then, here's the point.
You must forget to be a woman : change   155
Command into obedience, fear and niceness—
The handmaids of all women, or more truly
Woman it pretty self—into a waggish courage,
Ready in gibes, quick-answered, saucy and
As quarrelous as the weasel. Nay, you must   160
Forget that rarest treasure of your cheek,
Exposing it—but O the harder heart!
Alack, no remedy—to the greedy touch
Of common-kissing Titan, and forget
Your laboursome and dainty trims wherein   165

---

151 **render** describe
152 **As . . . moves** i.e. an accurate account of his actions
153 **Though . . . on't** though the disguise involved a risk to her chastity, but not the certain loss of it
154 **adventure** take the risk
156 **Command** authority. She will lose the power that she has as a princess and prepare herself for the *obedience* of a page-boy.
niceness fastidiousness (or perhaps shyness)
157 **handmaids** attendants
158 **Woman . . . self** i.e. the *fear* and *niceness* (l. 156) are not simply women's *handmaids* (l. 157) but constitute woman herself
it This early form of the genitive 'its' is often used in Shakespearian contexts involving children (for example in Hermione's reference to her baby, 'The innocent milk in it most innocent mouth' (*Winter's Tale* 3.2.99)); this is relevant to the deliberately awkward style of Pisanio's entire speech, especially in parentheses like this. He is almost 'talking down' to a child: he has the tricky task of persuading Innogen to adopt the boy's disguise, and is feeling his way, hence the rather over-written

stereotypes he provides of women and of precocious page-boys.
158 **waggish** mischievous (like a saucy boy)
159 **quick-answered** ready with clever replies
160 **quarrelous** quarrelsome. This belief about the weasel derives from folk superstition (where it is associated with witchcraft) rather than from natural history.
161 **Forget** neglect (*OED v.* 4)
that . . . cheek i.e. your most beautiful complexion. In Shakespeare's day a pale complexion was a mark of aristocratic beauty and was protected from the sun ; a tanned complexion was the mark of those who laboured in the sun, as Innogen will have to do if she ceases to be an aristocrat.
162–3 **but . . . remedy** Another clumsy parenthesis (see the note to *it*, l. 158).
162 **the harder heart** Commentators have suggested that this refers to Posthumus' cruelty, or to Innogen's need as a man to be tough, or even to Pisanio himself. But isn't it simply an exclamation like Othello's 'O . . . the pity of it' (4.1.192)?
164 **common-kissing Titan** Titan (the sun) kisses (shines on) everyone indiscriminately.
165 **laboursome** requiring much effort
dainty trims attractive adornments

You made great Juno angry.
INNOGEN   Nay, be brief.
I see into thy end, and am almost
A man already.
PISANIO   First make yourself but like one,
Forethinking this, I have already fit—
'Tis in my cloak-bag—doublet, hat, hose, all   170
That answer to them. Would you in their serving,
And with what imitation you can borrow
From youth of such a season, 'fore noble Lucius
Present yourself, desire his service, tell him
Wherein you're happy—which will make him know   175
If that his head have ear in music; doubtless
With joy he will embrace you, for he's honourable,
And, doubling that, most holy. Your means abroad—
You have me rich, and I will never fail
Beginning nor supplement.
INNOGEN   Thou art all the comfort   180

166 **You made . . . angry** i.e. aroused her
jealousy, perhaps because Innogen in
her *dainty trims* might have attracted
Juno's husband Jupiter, who was notorious for his affairs with mortals. Anne
Barton thinks the reference more specific: as goddess of marriage, Juno was
angry because Innogen and Posthumus
were married in Jupiter's temple
(5.3.199–200), not in hers, and because
Innogen's hair was bound up with *dainty
trims* rather than flowing loose as a
bride's should (*Essays, Mainly Shakespearean* (Cambridge, 1994), pp. 24–5).
This certainly gives more point to a garrulous passage, though another explanation for its long-windedness is suggested
in the note on *it*, l. 158.
166–8 **Nay . . . already** Innogen, quick-
witted and impulsive as ever, cuts off
Pisanio's careful circumlocutions, and
enables him to spell out his plan in
much more practical terms; she also
demonstrates that she has virtually
recovered from her state of shock, and
embraces her new life with characteristic
positiveness.
167 **see . . . end** understand where you are
going
168 **but** only (i.e. it would help if only you
started to look like a man)

169 **Forethinking** anticipating
  fit prepared
170 **cloak-bag** a bag or case big enough to
  take cloaks or other clothes
  doublet close-fitting jacket (standard
  wear for Jacobean men)
  hose stockings
171 **answer** to correspond to, go with
  in their serving served by them, with
  their help
173 **season** age
  'fore before
174 **his service** i.e. to be in his service, serve
  him
175 **Wherein you're happy** in what you are
  accomplished
  make him know convince him
176 **If . . . music** if he is at all responsive to
  music (presumably to the musical way in
  which Innogen will speak rather than to
  any demonstration of her singing ability,
  although this is mentioned at 4.2.49)
177 **embrace** accept (in his service)
178 **holy** virtuous
  Your means abroad (as for) your
  subsistence
179 **You . . . rich** you have me to provide
  them, and I am rich in them
180 **Beginning nor supplement** in providing
  the original amount nor in continuing
  the supply

The gods will diet me with. Prithee away.
There's more to be considered, but we'll even
All that good time will give us. This attempt
I am soldier to, and will abide it with
A prince's courage. Away, I prithee.   185

PISANIO
Well madam, we must take a short farewell
Lest being missed, I be suspected of
Your carriage from the court. My noble mistress,
Here is a box, I had it from the Queen,
What's in't is precious. If you are sick at sea   190
Or stomach-qualmed at land, a dram of this
Will drive away distemper. To some shade,
And fit you to your manhood. May the gods
Direct you to the best.

INNOGEN   Amen. I thank thee.

Exeunt severally

3.5   [*Flourish.*] *Enter Cymbeline, the Queen, Cloten,*
       Lucius, and Lords

CYMBELINE (*to Lucius*)
Thus far, and so farewell.

LUCIUS   Thanks, royal sir.
My emperor hath wrote I must from hence,

194.1   *severally*] *not in* F
3.5.0.1   *Flourish*] *not in* F

180   **all the** the entire

181   **diet** feed
182   **even** keep pace with (Schmidt)
184   **soldier to** courageously prepared for
         abide endure
186   **short** hasty
188   **Your carriage** conveying you
189   **Here . . . box** Just as the scene seems
         to be over, Innogen is given the
         theatrical property which will lead to
         an even greater crisis for her in 4.2;
         compare   Giacomo's   last-minute
         introduction of the trunk at 1.6.180–
         99.
190–1   **are . . . stomach-qualmed** feel ill
192   **distemper** illness
         shade cover

193   **fit** adapt
194   **Amen** The standard answer to a prayer,
         here Pisanio's *May the gods* in l. 193.
3.5   This scene falls into three sections. In the
         first (ll. 1–17), Caius Lucius' departure
         brings war a step nearer; the middle sec-
         tion (ll. 18–69) moves to the discovery of
         Innogen's flight and the audience's last
         sight of the Queen, who after this scene
         succumbs to the fate she wishes on Inno-
         gen; and the final section deals with Clo-
         ten's plan to rape Innogen wearing
         Posthumus'   clothes,   another   step
         towards the central crisis of the play in
         4.2.
2, 21   **wrote** Onions points out that *wrote*
         for 'written' is rare in Shakespeare,
         whose preferred form is 'writ'.

And am right sorry that I must report ye
My master's enemy.

CYMBELINE   Our subjects, sir,
Will not endure his yoke, and for ourself   5
To show less sovereignty than they must needs
Appear unkinglike.

LUCIUS   So, sir. I desire of you
A conduct over land to Milford Haven.
(*To the Queen*) Madam, all joy befall your grace, ⌈*to*
    Cloten⌉ and you.

CYMBELINE
My lords, you are appointed for that office.   10
The due of honour in no point omit.
So farewell, noble Lucius.

LUCIUS   Your hand, my lord.

CLOTEN
Receive it friendly, but from this time forth
I wear it as your enemy.

LUCIUS   Sir, the event
Is yet to name the winner. Fare you well.   15

CYMBELINE
Leave not the worthy Lucius, good my lords,
Till he have crossed the Severn. Happiness.

                    Exeunt Lucius and Lords

QUEEN
He goes hence frowning, but it honours us
That we have given him cause.

CLOTEN   'Tis all the better.
Your valiant Britons have their wishes in it.   20

7 So, sir.] F (So Sir :); So, sir, CAPELL   17.1 *and Lords*] *&c* F

3 **am** I am
6 **sovereignty** royal dignity
  must needs would necessarily
7 **So** very good (a polite way, as Maxwell notes, of declining to discuss what Cymbeline has just said ; Lucius uses the same diplomatic expression at 3.1.82). Capell's reading, adopted by Oxford, 'So, sir, I desire' (i.e. 'since I have been recalled to Rome, I desire') creates a more flowing line at the expense of a nice dramatic detail.

8 **conduct** military escort to ensure safe passage
9 **and you** This probably refers to Cloten rather than Cymbeline, as has been suggested. Lucius bids Cloten a brusque farewell, but is snubbed ; having put up with enough rudeness in 3.1, Lucius then presses him at l. 12 : *Your hand, my lord.*
10 **office** function
14 **event** outcome
18 **honours us** does us credit (because we are patriotic)

CYMBELINE

    Lucius hath wrote already to the Emperor
    How it goes here. It fits us therefore ripely
    Our chariots and our horsemen be in readiness.
    The powers that he already hath in Gallia
    Will soon be drawn to head, from whence he moves   25
    His war for Britain.
QUEEN   'Tis not sleepy business,
    But must be looked to speedily and strongly.
CYMBELINE

    Our expectation that it would be thus
    Hath made us forward. But my gentle queen,
    Where is our daughter? She hath not appeared   30
    Before the Roman, nor to us hath tendered
    The duty of the day. She looks us like
    A thing more made of malice than of duty.
    We have noted it. Call her before us, for
    We have been too slight in sufferance.

Exit one or more

QUEEN   Royal sir,   35
    Since the exile of Posthumus most retired
    Hath her life been, the cure whereof, my lord,
    'Tis time must do. Beseech your majesty
    Forbear sharp speeches to her. She's a lady
    So tender of rebukes that words are strokes,   40
    And strokes death to her.

Enter a Messenger

CYMBELINE   Where is she, sir? How
    Can her contempt be answered?
MESSENGER   Please you sir,

---

32 looks us] JOHNSON; looke vs F1; lookes as F2   35 *Exit one or more*] *not in* F

22 **fits** is befitting to
    ripely immediately (since the time is ripe)
24 **Gallia** France (Gaul)
25 **drawn to head** brought to their full strength, mobilized
29 **forward** prepared
32 **The . . . day** the morning greeting (that she should give her king and father).

Compare l. 49.
32 **looks us** appears to us (or perhaps 'views us')
35 **slight in sufferance** weak in tolerance
36 **retired** withdrawn, unsocial
38 **Beseech** See note to 1.1.154.
39 **Forbear** avoid
40 **tender of** sensitive to
42 **answered** justified

179

Her chambers are all locked, and there's no answer
That will be given to th' loud'st of noise we make.

QUEEN

My lord, when last I went to visit her   45
She prayed me to excuse her keeping close,
Whereto constrained by her infirmity
She should that duty leave unpaid to you
Which daily she was bound to proffer. This
She wished me to make known, but our great court   50
Made me to blame in memory.

CYMBELINE   Her doors locked?
Not seen of late? Grant heavens that which I
Fear prove false.   *Exit with Messenger and Lords*

QUEEN   Son, I say, follow the King.

CLOTEN

That man of hers, Pisanio, her old servant,
I have not seen these two days.

QUEEN   Go, look after.   55

                                        Exit Cloten

Pisanio, thou that stand'st so for Posthumus!
He hath a drug of mine. I pray his absence
Proceed by swallowing that, for he believes
It is a thing most precious. But for her,
Where is she gone? Haply despair hath seized her,   60
Or winged with fervour of her love, she's flown
To her desired Posthumus. Gone she is
To death or to dishonour, and my end

44 loud'st of] CAPELL; lowd of F; loudest ROWE   53 *with … Lords*] *not in* F   55.1 *Exit Cloten*] *Exit*. F (*after* 'days')

44 **loud'st** Capell's emendation of F's 'lowd' is supported by *Winter's Tale* 2.2.42, 'Her advocate to th' loud'st'; only one seventeenth-century example of 'loud' as a noun has been found (see Furness, pp. 251–2), though Shakespeare often uses adjectives as nouns (Abbott §5).
46 **excuse** offer an excuse (to the King) for
   close private
47 **constrained** compelled
   infirmity illness
49 **bound** obliged
50 **great court** elaborate court occasion (i.e. the reception of the Roman embassy)
51 **to … memory** reprehensibly forgetful

52–3 **that which I | Fear** (either that she is dead or has fled)
56 **stand'st so for** so much take the part of
58 **Proceed by** results from
60 **Haply** perhaps. But since 'the form *happely* connects this with HAPPILY' (*OED*, *haply, adv.*), there may be the overtone 'fortunately', as the Queen would like to see the back of Innogen.
61–2 **winged … Posthumus** This is an echo of Innogen's cry 'O for a horse with wings!' (3.2.48) as she speeds, so she thinks, to *her desired Posthumus*.
63 **end** aim

Can make good use of either. She being down,
I have the placing of the British crown.   65
> *Enter Cloten*

How now, my son?
CLOTEN   'Tis certain she is fled.
Go in and cheer the King; he rages, none
Dare come about him.
QUEEN   All the better; may
This night forestall him of the coming day.   *Exit*
CLOTEN

I love and hate her. For she's fair and royal,   70
And that she hath all courtly parts more exquisite
Than lady, ladies, woman—from every one
The best she hath, and she, of all compounded,
Outsells them all—I love her therefore; but
Disdaining me, and throwing favours on   75
The low Posthumus, slanders so her judgement
That what's else rare is choked; and in that point
I will conclude to hate her, nay indeed,
To be revenged upon her. For when fools shall—
> *Enter Pisanio*

Who is here? What, are you packing, sirrah?   80

---

69 **forestall** deprive

70 **I love and hate her** Cloten's double-edged attitude to Innogen closely resembles that of Posthumus, and there are further parallels (see ll. 142–3 and note, and Introduction, pp. 50–1). The phrase itself is a translation of Catullus' 'Odi et amo' (*Carmina* 85). In this speech, and in the following exchange with Pisanio, Cloten shows further signs of being more than a mere fool: a capacity for thought, even argument, however hesitant; an imagination, however bizarre; a strange kind of courage (ll. 101–2); and even an anxiety that Pisanio be as faithful to him as to Posthumus (ll. 109–23, 154).

70–4 **For . . . therefore** The punctuation here follows Maxwell's, which brings out the construction (i.e. 'Because she's fair . . . and because she has all courtly parts . . . I love her for those reasons').

71 **parts** qualities

72 **Than . . . woman** Johnson's gloss 'than any *lady*, than all *ladies*, than all *womankind*' is supported by the parallel idiom at *All's Well* 2.3.194: 'To any count, to all counts, to what is man'.

72–3 **from . . . hath** Compare *As You Like It* 3.2.138–49, especially 'Rosalind . . . was devised | Of many faces, eyes, and hearts', and *Winter's Tale* 5.1.14–15: 'from the all that are took something good | To make a perfect woman'. The inspiration for all three passages is probably Pliny's *Natural History* 35.9 in which Zeuxis painted a picture based on 'all the lovely parts of . . . five [women], to make one body of incomparable beauty' (Philemon Holland's translation (1601), p. 534).

73 **compounded** made up

74 **Outsells** exceeds in value

76 **slanders** discredits

77 **what's else rare** her otherwise exceptional qualities
choked smothered

79 **For . . . shall** See note to ll. 159–60.

80 **packing** scheming, deceiving
sirrah fellow (a form of address to an inferior)

Come hither. Ah you precious pander, villain,
Where is thy lady? In a word, or else
Thou art straightway with the fiends.

PISANIO   O good my lord!

CLOTEN
Where is thy lady?—or by Jupiter,
I will not ask again. Close villain,   85
I'll have this secret from thy heart or rip
Thy heart to find it. Is she with Posthumus,
From whose so many weights of baseness cannot
A dram of worth be drawn?

PISANIO   Alas, my lord,
How can she be with him? When was she missed?   90
He is in Rome.

CLOTEN   Where is she, sir? Come nearer.
No farther halting. Satisfy me home
What is become of her.

PISANIO   O my all-worthy lord!

CLOTEN   All-worthy villain,   95
Discover where thy mistress is at once,
At the next word; no more of 'worthy lord'.
Speak, or thy silence on the instant is
Thy condemnation and thy death.

PISANIO   Then sir,
This paper is the history of my knowledge   100
Touching her flight.

---

81 **pander** go-between for Innogen and Posthumus (if not simply abusive)

85 **Close** secretive, uncommunicative

86–7 **heart . . . heart** Suspicious of this repetition, Oxford emends the first *heart* to 'tongue', citing, for example, the antithesis at *Shrew* 4.3.77: 'My tongue will tell the anger of my heart' (*Textual Companion*, p. 607). But the first *heart* implies this idea anyway ('if you do not tell me the secret of your heart'), so that emendation is unnecessary, and the repetition of *heart*, with the intensification of the idea of ripping it open, is surely dramatically effective.

88–9 **From . . . drawn** Posthumus' characteristics are represented as *weights* or

measures; a *dram* is a very tiny measure. Cloten argues that Posthumus is so composed of *baseness* that not even a tiny quantity of worth could be extracted (*drawn*) from him.

91 **Come nearer** Editors say that this means 'be more precise'; but Pisanio may simply be reluctant to approach the dangerous Cloten.

92 **halting** hesitation (literally 'limping in speech')
     home completely

96 **Discover** reveal

100 **This paper** (presumably Posthumus' letter to Innogen from 3.2.25)

101 **Touching** concerning

He gives Cloten a letter

CLOTEN   Let's see't. I will pursue her
Even to Augustus' throne.

PISANIO (*aside*)   Or this or perish.
She's far enough, and what he learns by this
May prove his travel, not her danger.

CLOTEN   Hum!

PISANIO (*aside*)
I'll write to my lord she's dead. O Innogen,   105
Safe mayst thou wander, safe return again!

CLOTEN
Sirrah, is this letter true?

PISANIO   Sir, as I think.

CLOTEN It is Posthumus' hand, I know't. Sirrah, if thou
wouldst not be a villain but do me true service, undergo
those employments wherein I should have cause to use   110
thee with a serious industry—that is, what villainy
soe'er I bid thee do, to perform it directly and truly—I
would think thee an honest man. Thou shouldst neither
want my means for thy relief nor my voice for thy preferment.   115

PISANIO Well, my good lord.

CLOTEN Wilt thou serve me? For since patiently and constantly thou hast stuck to the bare fortune of that beggar
Posthumus, thou canst not in the course of gratitude but
be a diligent follower of mine. Wilt thou serve me?   120

PISANIO Sir, I will.

CLOTEN Give me thy hand, here's my purse. Hast any of thy
late master's garments in thy possession?

PISANIO I have, my lord, at my lodging the same suit he
wore when he took leave of my lady and mistress.   125

101 *He ... letter*] *not in* F

102 **Or this or perish** (i.e. it was a matter
    either of showing him this letter or
    being killed)
104 **prove his travel** turn out to be a long
    journey for him
108–13 **if ... man** This speech is an excellent
    example of Cloten's capacity to work
    out an argument slowly, with a kind of
    weird logic, as he demonstrates how
    thoroughgoing villainy can make

someone an *honest man.*
109 **undergo** undertake
110 **employments** tasks
111 **industry** application
111–12 **what ... soe'er** whatever villainy
114 **relief** assistance
    voice support, vote
114–15 **preferment** promotion
119 **thou canst not ... but** you cannot avoid
    being

CLOTEN The first service thou dost me, fetch that suit hither.
Let it be thy first service, go.
PISANIO I shall, my lord.   *Exit*
CLOTEN Meet thee at Milford Haven.—I forgot to ask him
one thing, I'll remember't anon.—Even there, thou vil-   130
lain Posthumus, will I kill thee. I would these garments
were come. She said upon a time—the bitterness of it I
now belch from my heart—that she held the very garment of Posthumus in more respect than my noble and
natural person, together with the adornment of my   135
qualities. With that suit upon my back will I ravish
her: first kill him, and in her eyes; there shall she see
my valour, which will then be a torment to her contempt. He on the ground, my speech of insultment
ended on his dead body, and when my lust hath   140
dined—which, as I say, to vex her I will execute in the
clothes that she so praised—to the court I'll knock her
back, foot her home again. She hath despised me rejoi-
cingly, and I'll be merry in my revenge.
Enter Pisanio with Posthumus' clothes
Be those the garments?   145
PISANIO Ay, my noble lord.
CLOTEN How long is't since she went to Milford Haven?
PISANIO She can scarce be there yet.
CLOTEN Bring this apparel to my chamber. That is the
second thing that I have commanded thee. The third is   150

144.1 *with Posthumus' clothes*] not in F

129 **Meet . . . Haven** He is summarizing the
contents of the letter.
130 **one thing** something. This may have
been the question he ultimately asks at
l. 147, but it is probably, as Maxwell
says, 'a characterizing touch': after his
efforts to think logically at ll. 108–13,
and just as his imagination is about to
take flight in the rest of the speech, Cloten
becomes suddenly forgetful, reminding
us that his mental capacity comes and
goes.
132–5 **She said . . . person** This reminds us
that in one sense Innogen brings the
nightmare of the headless body (4.2)
upon herself.

134 **more respect** higher regard
134–5 **noble and natural** noble by nature
135–6 **with . . . qualities** with my talents
enhancing it
139 **insultment** contemptuous triumph
141–2 **which . . . praised** This parenthesis is
typical both of the play and of Cloten's
habit of spelling out his plans.
142–3 **to . . . again** This threat to humiliate
Innogen violently and publicly is characteristic of Cloten. It is also characteristic
of Posthumus (see 2.4.147–9, and the
Introduction, pp. 50–1).
142 **knock** beat
143 **foot** kick
148 **scarce** hardly

that thou wilt be a voluntary mute to my design. Be but
duteous, and true preferment shall tender itself to thee.
My revenge is now at Milford, would I had wings to
follow it. Come, and be true.   *Exit*

PISANIO

Thou bidd'st me to my loss, for true to thee   155
Were to prove false, which I will never be
To him that is most true. To Milford go,
And find not her whom thou pursu'st. Flow, flow,
You heavenly blessings, on her. This fool's speed
Be crossed with slowness; labour be his meed.   *Exit* 160

3.6   *Enter Innogen alone, in boy's clothes, before the cave*

INNOGEN

I see a man's life is a tedious one.
I have tired myself, and for two nights together
Have made the ground my bed. I should be sick,
But that my resolution helps me. Milford,
When from the mountain-top Pisanio showed thee,   5
Thou wast within a ken. O Jove, I think

3.6.0.1 *in . . . cave*] *not in* F

---

151 **be . . . to** be willing to keep quiet about
(as if speechless). *Mutes* were attendants
in harems, whose tongues were cut out
so that they could not reveal secrets;
Pisanio, however, is to be a *mute* by
choice.

152 **true preferment** (as opposed to any preferment that Posthumus could offer)
tender offer

153–4 **would . . . it** This echoes, and parod-
ies, Innogen's 'O for a horse with wings!'
(3.2.48): Cloten has some of her impulsive rashness.

155 **to my loss** to lose my honour

157 **him** i.e. Posthumus. This represents
Pisanio's basic view of him, rather than
his recent behaviour.

158 **Flow, flow** come as if in a flood-tide

159–60 **fool's . . . slowness** Proverbial:
'Fool's haste is no speed' (Tilley F518).
E. A. Thistleton thinks that Cloten may
have been about to use this proverb at l.
79, presumably as a comment on the
marriage of Posthumus and Innogen

(*Textual Notes on 'Cymbeline'* (1902),
cited in Furness, p. 255).

160 **crossed with** thwarted by
labour . . . meed Proverbial: 'He has his
labour for his pains' (Tilley L1).
meed reward

3.6.0.1 **in boy's clothes** For the rest of the
play, Innogen is disguised as a page-boy.

1 The soliloquy opens with a one-liner
which enables the actress of Innogen to
re-establish contact with the audience
immediately, as she needs to do in order
to take them with her through her coming ordeal in 4.2. Most actresses get a
sympathetic laugh on this line; the
humour in the soliloquy (e.g. ll. 7–9,
25–7) helps to involve the audience in
her situation.

2 **tired** Though the obvious sense is
'exhausted', some detect a pun on
'attired', dressed (as a man).

6 **a ken** sight (originally a nautical term for
the distance from which land was visible
(*OED sb.*[1] 1))

Foundations fly the wretched—such I mean,
Where they should be relieved. Two beggars told me
I could not miss my way. Will poor folks lie,
That have afflictions on them, knowing 'tis   10
A punishment or trial? Yes; no wonder,
When rich ones scarce tell true. To lapse in fullness
Is sorer than to lie for need, and falsehood
Is worse in kings than beggars. My dear lord,
Thou art one o'th' false ones. Now I think on thee   15
My hunger's gone, but even before I was
At point to sink for food. But what is this?
Here is a path to't. 'Tis some savage hold.
I were best not call; I dare not call; yet famine,
Ere clean it o'erthrow nature, makes it valiant.   20
Plenty and peace breeds cowards, hardness ever
Of hardiness is mother. Ho! Who's here?
If anything that's civil, speak; if savage,
Take or lend. Ho! No answer? Then I'll enter.
Best draw my sword; and if mine enemy   25
But fear the sword like me, he'll scarcely look on't.
Such a foe, good heavens!   *Exit into the cave*
            Enter Belarius, Guiderius, and Arviragus

BELARIUS
  You, Polydore, have proved best woodman and

---

27 *into the cave*] *not in* F   27.1 *Enter*] *Scena Septima.* | *Enter* F

---

7 **Foundations** This at first means the *foun-*
  dations of Milford, seen in the distance,
  which *fly* almost like a mirage—but in
  the next phrase, Innogen wittily uses
  the other meaning of *foundations*: charitable institutions that should relieve the
  poor, but which *fly* because they are
  never at hand when people most need
  them.
11 **trial** test (of their virtue; they shouldn't
  lie)
12 **scarce** hardly
  lapse in fullness do wrong when prosper-
  ous
13 **sorer** worse
  for need out of necessity
16 **even before** only a moment ago
17 **At point** about
  for i.e. for lack of

18 **hold** lair
19 **were best** had better
20 **clean** completely
21 **hardness** hardship
22 **hardiness** endurance
23 **civil** civilized
24 **Take or lend** take (life or money) or give
  (food or blows). Perhaps the casual
  phrase, like modern 'take it or leave it',
  expresses Innogen's faintness from
  exhaustion and hunger.
25–6 **if . . . But** if only
27 **Such a foe** i.e. let him be as great a coward as I am
27.1 *Enter . . . Arviragus* As at 1.1.71, the
  Folio text marks a new scene here,
  although the action is obviously continuous.
28 **woodman** hunter

Are master of the feast. Cadwal and I
Will play the cook and servant; 'tis our match.   30
The sweat of industry would dry and die
But for the end it works to. Come, our stomachs
Will make what's homely savoury. Weariness
Can snore upon the flint when resty sloth
Finds the down pillow hard. Now peace be here,   35
Poor house, that keep'st thyself.
GUIDERIUS   I am throughly weary.
ARVIRAGUS
I am weak with toil yet strong in appetite.
GUIDERIUS
There is cold meat i'th' cave. We'll browse on that
Whilst what we have killed be cooked.
BELARIUS (*looking into the cave*)   Stay, come not in.
But that it eats our victuals I should think   40
Here were a fairy.
GUIDERIUS   What's the matter, sir?
BELARIUS
By Jupiter, an angel—or if not,
An earthly paragon. Behold divineness
No elder than a boy.
            Enter Innogen from the cave
INNOGEN   Good masters, harm me not.
Before I entered here I called, and thought   45
To have begged or bought what I have took. Good truth,

---

39 *looking into the cave*] *not in* F   44 *from the cave*] *not in* F   46 truth] F (troth)

---

30 **match** agreement
31 **The sweat . . . die** 'i.e. men would no longer labour' (Maxwell, taking *sweat* in 'the common figurative use of toil', *OED sb.* 2b), or perhaps 'our labour would go for nothing'. Belarius means that it is the promise of their feast which makes the labour of hunting worthwhile.
33 **homely** plain
34 **flint** i.e. floor, made of flint-stones
    resty A variant of 'restive', this may either mean 'restless' (*OED a.*¹ 1a), or 'stiff with too much rest' (Schmidt). Either way, the contrast in ll. 33–5 is between those who can sleep anywhere because so tired, and those who

can't sleep because they have been so inactive.
36 **keep'st thyself** i.e. the cave looks after itself, is unoccupied
    throughly thoroughly
38 **browse** nibble. It literally refers to animals cropping scanty vegetation. Compare *Winter's Tale* 3.3.66–7, where the Old Shepherd's sheep are 'browsing of ivy'. Like him, the princes speak in terms of their rural surroundings (as also at l. 91).
40 **victuals** food. *OED* notes that the pronunciation, *vittles*, reflects the word's Old French origin.
46 **Good truth** An abbreviation of 'In good truth', an emphatic assertion.

I have stol'n naught, nor would not, though I had found
Gold strewed i'th' floor. Here's money for my meat.
I would have left it on the board so soon
As I had made my meal, and parted   50
With prayers for the provider.

GUIDERIUS   Money, youth?

ARVIRAGUS

All gold and silver rather turn to dirt,
As 'tis no better reckoned but of those
Who worship dirty gods.

INNOGEN   I see you're angry.

Know, if you kill me for my fault, I should   55
Have died had I not made it.

BELARIUS   Whither bound?

INNOGEN

To Milford Haven.

BELARIUS   What's your name?

INNOGEN

Fidele, sir. I have a kinsman who
Is bound for Italy; he embarked at Milford,
To whom being going, almost spent with hunger,   60
I am fall'n in this offence.

BELARIUS   Prithee, fair youth,

Think us no churls, nor measure our good minds
By this rude place we live in. Well encountered.
'Tis almost night. You shall have better cheer
Ere you depart, and thanks to stay and eat it.   65
Boys, bid him welcome.

---

48 **i'** This abbreviation of 'in' probably
means 'on', though it might refer to
gold *strewed* among the rushes or earth
of the cave floor.
49 **board** table
   so as
50 **made** finished
   parted departed
53 **of** by
57 **To . . . name** This line is two
syllables short, perhaps marking a
pause as Innogen searches for a new
name.
58 **Fidele** the faithful one (from Latin *fidelis*
or Italian *fidele*). Innogen chooses a sym-

bolic name: see Appendix A. The final 'e'
is pronounced.
59 **embarked** E. A. Thistleton interpreted
'about to embark' (cited in Furness,
p. 269), another probable example of
the play's impressionism—and maybe of
Innogen improvising her story. So too,
perhaps, is *being going* ('on the way') in
the next line.
60 **spent** exhausted
61 **in** into
62 **churls** peasants (contemptuous)
63 **rude** uncivilized
64 **cheer** food
65 **thanks** our approval

GUIDERIUS   Were you a woman, youth,
I should woo hard but be your groom in honesty,
Ay, bid for you as I'd buy.
ARVIRAGUS   I'll make't my comfort
He is a man, I'll love him as my brother.
(*To Innogen*) And such a welcome as I'd give to him   70
After long absence, such is yours. Most welcome.
Be sprightly, for you fall 'mongst friends.
INNOGEN   'Mongst friends
If brothers. (*Aside*) Would it had been so that they
Had been my father's sons, then had my price
Been less, and so more equal ballasting   75
To thee, Posthumus.
          The three men speak apart
BELARIUS   He wrings at some distress.
GUIDERIUS
Would I could free't.
ARVIRAGUS   Or I, whate'er it be,
What pain it cost, what danger. Gods!

68 Ay,] F (I)   I'd] JOHNSON (*conj.* Tyrwhitt); I do F   74 price] F (prize)   76 *The . . . apart*] *not in* F

67 **hard** vigorously
   but be if I would not otherwise become
   groom bridegroom
   in honesty honourably
68 **Ay . . . buy** 'yes, make an offer as if I were
   going to buy you'. This edition follows
   Oxford's modernization and emendation
   of the Folio's 'I bid for you, as I do buy'
   (where 'I do' is probably a misreading of
   'Ide'; see collation), which improves F's
   metre, but changes its sense ('I am bidding for you as honestly as I do in all my
   financial dealings').
68–9 **I'll . . . brother** 'I shall console myself
   for his being a man by loving him as my
   brother.' The talk of wooing Fidele and
   then needing consolation for 'his' being a
   man conveys the immediacy and intensity of their response to him/her; they are
   of course unconsciously drawn to their
   sister, but there is a sexual impulse as
   well. See note to ll. 72–3.
72 **sprightly** cheerful
72–3 **'Mongst . . . brothers** 'They must
   indeed be friends if they call me their
   brother.' This leads to the thought of

her own lost brothers, and perhaps also
implies that she would feel safer if loved
as a brother. The sexual overtone of ll.
66–9 is a potential threat to her disguise.
74 **price** worth. The words *price* and 'prize'
   (as in the Folio) 'were not distinguished
   in Shakespeare's day, though "price" seems
   the primary sense, though there is a pun
   on "prize" (as though a merchant ship,
   seized as booty)' (*Textual Companion*,
   p. 607). The second meaning is extended
   in *ballasting* (l. 75); she is also a 'prize'
   because she is heir to the throne.
75 **less** (because she would not then be heir
   to the throne)
   more equal ballasting of more equal
   weight (i.e. in rank). *Ballast* was any
   heavy material 'placed in the hold of a
   ship . . . to prevent her from capsizing'
   (*OED, ballast, sb.* 1a).
76 **wrings at** writhes in (suffers acutely)
77 **free** remove
78 The exclamation *Gods!* doesn't seem to
   have much point. Perhaps Arviragus is
   addressing his whole speech to the gods,
   almost as a vow.

BELARIUS   Hark, boys.
They whisper
INNOGEN (*aside*) Great men
    That had a court no bigger than this cave,   80
    That did attend themselves and had the virtue
    Which their own conscience sealed them, laying by
    That nothing-gift of differing multitudes,
    Could not outpeer these twain. Pardon me, gods,
    I'd change my sex to be companion with them,   85
    Since Leonatus' false.
BELARIUS   It shall be so.
    Boys, we'll go dress our hunt. Fair youth, come in.
    Discourse is heavy, fasting. When we have supped
    We'll mannerly demand thee of thy story,
    So far as thou wilt speak it.
GUIDERIUS   Pray draw near.   90
ARVIRAGUS
    The night to th' owl and morn to th' lark less welcome.
INNOGEN Thanks, sir.
ARVIRAGUS I pray draw near.   *Exeunt into the cave*

3.7   *Enter two Roman Senators, and Tribunes*
FIRST SENATOR
    This is the tenor of the Emperor's writ:
    That since the common men are now in action
    'Gainst the Pannonians and Dalmatians,
    And that the legions now in Gallia are

78.1 *They whisper*] not in F   93 *into the cave*] not in F
3.7] *Scena Octaua.* F

81 **attend themselves** i.e. who had no ser-   89 **demand** ask
   vants to wait on (*attend*) them   3.7 This scene is usually cut in modern per-
82 **sealed them** confirmed in them   formances, without much loss; it simply
   laying by setting aside   serves to keep the Roman invasion in
83 **nothing-gift** gift of no value (e.g. flattery)   mind, and perhaps, in its reference to
   differing multitudes fickle crowds   the mobilization of Roman gentlemen
84 **outpeer** surpass   (ll. 6–7), to prepare for Giacomo's return
86 **Leonatus'** Leonatus is   to Britain.
87 **dress our hunt** prepare our game for   1 **tenor** drift
   cooking   **writ** written command
88 **heavy, fasting** burdensome when we   2 **men** i.e. soldiers
   have not eaten   3 **Pannonians and Dalmatians** See the note
89 **mannerly** politely   to 3.1.72.

Full weak to undertake our wars against   5
The fall'n-off Britons, that we do incite
The gentry to this business. He creates
Lucius pro-consul, and to you the tribunes,
For this immediate levy, he commends
His absolute commission. Long live Caesar!   10
A TRIBUNE
    Is Lucius general of the forces?
SECOND SENATOR   Ay.
A TRIBUNE
    Remaining now in Gallia?
FIRST SENATOR   With those legions
Which I have spoke of, whereunto your levy
Must be supplyant. The words of your commission
Will tie you to the numbers and the time   15
Of their dispatch.
A TRIBUNE   We will discharge our duty.   *Exeunt*

4.1   *Enter Cloten alone, in Posthumus' clothes*
CLOTEN I am near to th' place where they should meet, if
    Pisanio have mapped it truly. How fit his garments serve
    me! Why should his mistress, who was made by him
    that made the tailor, not be fit too? The rather—saving
    reverence of the word—for 'tis said a woman's fitness   5

---

9 commends] F (commands)
    4.1.0.1 *Cloten*] *Clotten* F   *in Posthumus' clothes*] *not in* F

5 **Full** very
6 **fall'n-off** defaulting
   incite summon
9 **commends** entrusts
10 **absolute commission** complete authority
14 **supplyant** ready to supply (soldiers)
15 **tie you to** specify to you
4.1 Cloten's soliloquy as he arrives disguised
   in Wales echoes, and is perhaps a prose
   parody of, Innogen's as she arrives disguised in 3.6. Both comment on disguise
   and its consequences; both employ
   humour of different kinds (3.6.1, 7–9,
   25–7; 4.1.5–6, 18–19); both are much
   concerned with Posthumus.
2 **fit** well, becomingly. This initial sense
   then gives way to a series of puns on
   other senses of *fit*: sexually compatible
   (l. 4); sexual inclination (*fitness*, l. 5);

and finally 'fits and starts' (l. 6). The
fact that Posthumus' garments fit Cloten
helps to emphasize the similarities that
coexist with the differences between
them (see the Introduction, pp. 50–1,
and the note to *spurn* at l. 17), and even
to keep Posthumus himself in the audience's mind during the long period in
which he is offstage.
3–4 **him . . . tailor** i.e. God
4–5 **saving . . . word** begging pardon for the
   expression. This was a standard way of
   apologizing for using unseemly language; here, Cloten apologizes for the
   obscene puns on *fit*.
5–6 **a woman's . . . fits** a woman's inclination for intercourse comes and goes. Cloten implies that this is a proverbial
   saying, but it is not recorded.

comes by fits. Therein I must play the workman. I dare
speak it to myself, for it is not vainglory for a man and his
glass to confer in his own chamber. I mean, the lines of
my body are as well drawn as his: no less young, more
strong, not beneath him in fortunes, beyond him in the   10
advantage of the time, above him in birth, alike conversant in general services, and more remarkable in single
oppositions; yet this imperceiverant thing loves him in
my despite. What mortality is! Posthumus, thy head,
which now is growing upon thy shoulders, shall within   15
this hour be off, thy mistress enforced, thy garments cut
to pieces before her face; and all this done, spurn her
home to her father, who may haply be a little angry for
my so rough usage; but my mother, having power of his
testiness, shall turn all into my commendations. My   20
horse is tied up safe. Out sword, and to a sore purpose!
Fortune put them into my hand. This is the very description of their meeting-place, and the fellow dares not
deceive me.   *Exit*

---

13 imperceiverant] F (imperseuerant)   17 her face] HANMER (*conj.* Warburton); thy face F
18 haply] F (happily)

6 **workman** skilled craftsman (presumably
  in encouraging Innogen's sexual inclination; see the previous note)
8 **glass** looking-glass
10 **fortunes** i.e. good fortunes, what Fortune
  has bestowed
11 **advantage . . . time** favourable circumstances
11–12 **alike conversant** equally experienced
12 **general services** military operations
  involving everyone
12–13 **single oppositions** individual com-
  bats
13 **imperceiverant** imperceptive. If Dyce's
  modernization of F's 'imperseuerant' is
  correct, this is a Shakespearian coinage,
  perhaps a 'Clotenism'. Maxwell notes
  that 'perceiverance', meaning 'perception', 'is quite common from *c*.1440'.
  Furness, however, listing numerous
  Shakespearian examples of *im-* as an
  intensifier rather than a negative, interprets F as meaning 'immovably persis-
  tent', stubborn (pp. 281–2). Either

interpretation would fit the context,
'imperceptive' perhaps corresponding
slightly better with what has gone before.
13–14 **in my despite** in spite of my qualities
  (or perhaps stronger, 'out of scorn for
  me'; compare 1.6.135)
14 **mortality** human life
16 **enforced** raped
17 **her face** F's 'thy face', perhaps yields a
  kind of sense, Posthumus witnessing
  Cloten slashing his clothes as well as
  his body; but Cloten's principal aim is
  to take revenge upon Innogen for prefer-
  ring Posthumus' 'meanest garment'
  (2.3.130–3) to him.
  spurn kick. Compare 3.5.142–3: 'knock
  her back, foot her home again'. Both
  speeches show Cloten working out his
  sadistic designs step by step; both echo
  Posthumus' threat to do Innogen violence in front of her father (2.4.147–9).
18 **haply** perhaps
19 **power of** control over
21 **sore** violent
22 **Fortune** May Fortune

4.2 *Enter Belarius, Guiderius, Arviragus, and Innogen*
     as Fidele, from the cave

BELARIUS (*to Innogen*)
  You are not well. Remain here in the cave.
  We'll come to you after hunting.

ARVIRAGUS (*to Innogen*)   Brother, stay here.
  Are we not brothers?

INNOGEN   So man and man should be,
  But clay and clay differs in dignity,
  Whose dust is both alike. I am very sick.   5

GUIDERIUS (*to Belarius and Arviragus*)
  Go you to hunting. I'll abide with him.

INNOGEN
  So sick I am not, yet I am not well;
  But not so citizen a wanton as
  To seem to die ere sick. So please you, leave me,
  Stick to your journal course; the breach of custom   10
  Is breach of all. I am ill, but your being by me
  Cannot amend me. Society is no comfort
  To one not sociable. I am not very sick,
  Since I can reason of it. Pray you trust me here.
  I'll rob none but myself; and let me die,   15
  Stealing so poorly.

4.2.0.2 *as Fidele*] *not in* F   2 after] F ; *from* OXFORD

4.2.4–36 Innogen's speeches in this episode
are curious. It is surprising, after her
rebellious disregard for court protocol at
the start of the play, that she should
emphasize distinctions of rank (ll. 3–5),
and the need to observe tradition (ll. 10–
11). Her views at ll. 35–6 are more characteristic, but the gnomic, almost doggerel phrasing is not. Perhaps these
speeches are intended to suggest someone overcome with illness, as Helen Mirren plays them in the BBC television
version, hardly aware of what she is saying.
4 **clay and clay** i.e. the substance of which
man (l. 3) is made, hence 'different
people'
  dignity nobility
5 **dust** i.e. the dust to which *man* returns at
death (probably echoing the Burial Ser-

vice's 'earth to earth, ashes to ashes, dust
to dust' in *The Book of Common Prayer*
(1559); compare ll. 263–4)
8 **so . . . wanton** such a city-bred weakling.
For the contemptuous use of *citizen*,
compare *1 Henry IV* 3.1.252, where
Hotspur criticizes his wife for using
affected oaths more appropriate to
'Sunday citizens'; and for *wanton*,
compare *Richard II* 5.3.10: 'wanton and
effeminate boy'.
9 **ere** before (I was)
10 **journal** diurnal, daily
10–11 **the . . . all** i.e. the failure to follow
accustomed forms leads to chaos
12 **amend** restore
14 **reason of** talk about
15–16 **let . . . Stealing** may I die if I steal
16 **so poorly** i.e. where there is nothing
worth stealing

GUIDERIUS   I love thee : I have spoke it ;
How much the quantity, the weight as much,
As I do love my father.
BELARIUS   What, how, how ?
ARVIRAGUS
  If it be sin to say so, sir, I yoke me
  In my good brother's fault. I know not why   20
  I love this youth, and I have heard you say
  Love's reason's without reason. The bier at door
  And a demand who is't shall die, I'd say
  'My father, not this youth'.
BELARIUS (*aside*)   O noble strain !
  O worthiness of nature, breed of greatness !   25
  Cowards father cowards, and base things sire base.
  Nature hath meal and bran, contempt and grace.
  I'm not their father, yet who this should be
  Doth miracle itself, loved before me.
  (*Aloud*) 'Tis the ninth hour o'th' morn.
ARVIRAGUS (*to Innogen*)   Brother, farewell.   30
INNOGEN
  I wish ye sport.
ARVIRAGUS   You health.—So please you, sir.
INNOGEN (*aside*)
  These are kind creatures. Gods, what lies I have heard !

17 **How . . . as much** as much and as inten-
  sely
19–20 **yoke me | In** link myself with
22 **Love's . . . reason** Proverbial (Tilley
  L517 : 'Love is without reason').
22–3 **The bier . . . die** This vividly impressionistic phrase is characteristic of this play.
  To express the intensity of his love, Arviragus imagines a situation that would
  compel him to choose between the lives
  of Belarius and Fidele. For further discussion, see Sutherland, p. 149.
24 **strain** ancestry
25 **breed** lineage, inheritance
26–7, 35–6, 54–8, 60–2 Pope in his edition
  relegated these lines to the foot of the
  page as unworthy of Shakespeare, and
  by another hand. But most of them have
  a function. In ll. 26–7, for example,
  Belarius is drawing on common sayings
  or folk-wisdom, as F emphasizes by placing them in quotation marks.

26–7 **Cowards . . . grace** people inherit characteristics from their parents, and these
  can be either bad or good
27 **meal and bran** flour and husks (i.e. good
  and bad things)
28–9 **who . . . me** who this may be who is
  loved in preference to me, is a source of
  great wonder
30 **ninth . . . morn** nine a.m.—i.e. time to go
  hunting (or, as Dowden suggests, late for
  it)
31 **So please you** A polite phrase of agreement with Belarius : 'i.e. at your service'
  (Maxwell), or 'I am ready'. The Folio's
  dash before the phrase, retained here,
  indicates Arviragus turning from Innogen to Belarius. Presumably they
  move to another part of the stage, as if
  to leave, while Innogen speaks to the
  audience, then come forward again
  while she moves away to swallow the
  drug at l. 38.

Our courtiers say all's savage but at court;
Experience, O thou disprov'st report!
Th'imperious seas breeds monsters; for the dish   35
Poor tributary rivers as sweet fish.
I am sick still, heart-sick. Pisanio,
I'll now taste of thy drug.
　　　　⌈*She swallows the drug.*⌉ *The men speak apart*
GUIDERIUS　　　　　　　I could not stir him.
He said he was gentle but unfortunate,
Dishonestly afflicted but yet honest.   40
ARVIRAGUS
Thus did he answer me, yet said hereafter
I might know more.
BELARIUS　　　　　　To th' field, to th' field!
(*To Innogen*) We'll leave you for this time, go in and rest.
ARVIRAGUS (*to Innogen*)
We'll not be long away.
BELARIUS (*to Innogen*)　　　Pray be not sick,
For you must be our housewife.
INNOGEN　　　　　　　　Well or ill,   45
I am bound to you.　　　　　　　*Exit into the cave*
BELARIUS　　　　And shalt be ever.
This youth, howe'er distressed, appears he hath had
Good ancestors.
ARVIRAGUS How angel-like he sings!

---

38 *She ... apart*] *not in* F　46 *into the cave*] *not in* F　47 appears] F; 't appears CRAIG *conj.*
(*cited in* Dowden); approves NOSWORTHY *conj.*

35–6 **Th'imperious ... fish** small rivers pro-
　　duce fish that are as tasty for eating as
　　those from the sea, which is often a
　　breeding-place for monsters
35 **imperious** imperial
36 **tributary rivers** small streams that flow
　　into larger ones (with a pun on paying
　　tribute to emperors, the *imperious* of the
　　previous line)
37–8 **Pisanio ... drug** This line reminds the
　　audience that the drug she is taking is the
　　one that the Queen gave Pisanio, which
　　the doctor told them will give only the
　　appearance of death (1.5.39–42); but
　　see note to l. 196.
38 **stir him** rouse him (to speak about him-
　　self)

39 **gentle** well-born
40 **Dishonestly** treacherously. Presumably
　　Innogen was thinking of Posthumus.
46 **bound** Both 'indebted' and 'linked'.
　　shalt ... ever always will be
47 **howe'er distressed** however unfortunate
　　his circumstances (*OED, distress, sb.* 2b).
　　A more specific sense than simply
　　'unhappy' is needed to contrast with
　　ancestors in the next line.
　　appears it seems (an elliptical construc-
　　tion)
　　hath Oxford regularizes the line by omit-
　　ting F's 'he', assuming that the composi-
　　tor mistakenly expanded *hath* to 'he
　　hath' (*Textual Companion*, p. 607). For
　　other possibilities, see the collation.

GUIDERIUS But his neat cookery!   50
⌈BELARIUS⌉
    He cut our roots in characters,
    And sauced our broths as Juno had been sick
    And he her dieter.
ARVIRAGUS   Nobly he yokes
    A smiling with a sigh, as if the sigh
    Was that it was for not being such a smile;   55
    The smile mocking the sigh that it would fly
    From so divine a temple to commix
    With winds that sailors rail at.
GUIDERIUS   I do note
    That grief and patience, rooted in him both,
    Mingle their spurs together.
ARVIRAGUS   Grow patience,   60
    And let the stinking elder, grief, untwine
    His perishing root with the increasing vine.

---

51 BELARIUS] OXFORD; *Arui⟨ragus⟩*. F; *no speech-prefix in* CAPELL, *who continues the previous speech* 59 him] POPE; them F 60 patience] ROWE; patient F

50 **neat** dainty
51 **BELARIUS** F gives two consecutive speeches to Arviragus. As Oxford notes, Belarius is the only other candidate to deliver this speech (*Textual Companion*, p. 607).
    characters letters of the alphabet (as in modern 'alphabet soup', given to children to make the food more interesting and so tempt them to eat; see the next note)
52–3 **sauced . . . dieter** made our soup more tasty, as if even the queen of the gods had been ill and he had been responsible for her diet
53–8 **Nobly . . . at** The expression may be mannered, but the picture it presents of an Innogen whose smiles are so combined with her sighs that the two are hardly distinguishable strongly recalls that given by Viola in *Twelfth Night* of her sister (i.e. herself) as one who 'sat like patience on a monument, | Smiling at grief' (2.4.114–15). Compare ll. 59–61.
55 **that** what
56 **that** because
57 **commix** mingle
58 **winds . . . at** i.e. adverse winds (unlike Innogen's sigh)
59 **rooted . . . both** both rooted in him
    him F reads 'them', which is possible, if *grief* and *patience* are thought to appear in both the *smile* and the *sigh*.
60 **spurs** tree-roots, as at *Tempest* 5.1.47–8: 'by the spurs plucked up | The pine and cedar'. These two examples are the earliest of *spur* in this sense cited at *OED sb.*[1] 9, where it is said to be Warwickshire dialect usage.
61 **stinking elder** This phrase is hyphenated in F, which suggests that it may reflect rural usage, though *OED* does not include it among the many plant-names beginning 'stinking-'. The elder gained its evil reputation from its pungent smell, and from the tradition that Judas Iscariot hanged himself on one after betraying Christ.
61–2 **let . . . vine** The idea is that the vine and elder grow together, and, 'as the vine increases, let the elder untwine his perishing root' (Dowden), and so die.
62 **perishing** deadly (perhaps with secondary sense 'dying', if the previous note is correct)
    with from

BELARIUS

　　It is great morning. Come away. Who's there?
　　　Enter Cloten in Posthumus' clothes

CLOTEN

　　I cannot find those runagates. That villain
　　Hath mocked me. I am faint.

BELARIUS (*aside to Arviragus and Guiderius*)

　　　　　　　　　　　'Those runagates'?　　　　　　65
　　Means he not us? I partly know him, 'tis
　　Cloten, the son o'th' Queen. I fear some ambush.
　　I saw him not these many years, and yet
　　I know 'tis he. We are held as outlaws. Hence!

GUIDERIUS (*aside to Arviragus and Belarius*)

　　He is but one. You and my brother search　　　70
　　What companies are near. Pray you away,
　　Let me alone with him.　　*Exeunt Arviragus and Belarius*

CLOTEN　　　　　　　　　Soft, what are you
　　That fly me thus? Some villain mountaineers?
　　I have heard of such. What slave art thou?

GUIDERIUS　　　　　　　　　　　　A thing
　　More slavish did I ne'er than answering　　　75
　　A slave without a knock.

CLOTEN　　　　　　　　Thou art a robber,
　　A law-breaker, a villain. Yield thee, thief.

GUIDERIUS

　　To who? To thee? What art thou? Have not I
　　An arm as big as thine, a heart as big?
　　Thy words I grant are bigger, for I wear not　　80

63.1 *in Posthumus' clothes*] *not in* F　72 *Exeunt … Belarius*] *not in* F

---

63 **great morning** broad daylight
64 **runagates** vagabonds
66 **partly** slightly
69 **held as** considered to be
70 **but** only
71 **companies** bands of followers, retinues
72 **let … him** leave him to me
　　Soft not so fast!
73 **villain** base
　　mountaineers mountain-dwellers
74 **I … such** *Mountaineers* were associated with robbers and outlaws because

they lived in remote places. Compare ll. 137–40.
74–5 **A thing … ne'er** I never did anything more slave-like
75 **slavish** Perhaps this answers Cloten's abusive *slave* in l. 74; perhaps he is simply calling Cloten himself a *slave*.
78 **who** For 'whom' (Abbott §274), to which F2 corrects it.
80–1 **for … mouth** i.e. he is not like Cloten, who will rather talk than fight

My dagger in my mouth. Say what thou art,
Why I should yield to thee.
CLOTEN   Thou villain base,
Know'st me not by my clothes?
GUIDERIUS   No, nor thy tailor, rascal,
Who is thy grandfather. He made those clothes,
Which, as it seems, make thee.
CLOTEN   Thou precious varlet,   85
My tailor made them not.
GUIDERIUS   Hence then, and thank
The man that gave them thee. Thou art some fool.
I am loath to beat thee.
CLOTEN   Thou injurious thief,
Hear but my name and tremble.
GUIDERIUS   What's thy name?
CLOTEN Cloten, thou villain.   90
GUIDERIUS
Cloten, thou double villain be thy name,
I cannot tremble at it. Were it toad or adder, spider,
'Twould move me sooner.
CLOTEN   To thy further fear,
Nay, to thy mere confusion, thou shalt know
I am son to th' Queen.
GUIDERIUS   I am sorry for't, not seeming   95
So worthy as thy birth.
CLOTEN   Art not afeard?
GUIDERIUS
Those that I reverence, those I fear, the wise.

---

83 **Know'st me not** do you not recognize my
rank
83–4 **tailor . . . grandfather** Guiderius
alludes to the proverb 'The tailor makes
the man' (Tilley T17), i.e. give a person
stature in the eyes of the world. The tailor
is a *grandfather* because he makes the
clothes which in turn make the man.
85 **precious varlet** arrant rascal
86 **My . . . not** Cloten is caught in a double-
bind : on the one hand, he expects respect
to be paid to his court clothes—but then
he realizes that the clothes are not his but
those of Posthumus, so of course they
would not command so much respect.

88 **injurious** insulting
thief malefactor
91 **Cloten . . . name** 'Does Guiderius
jestingly take "Cloten, thou villain"
as the name, and improve on it by his
"Cloten, thou double villain"?' (Dowden)
92 **toad . . . spider** i.e. creatures that are
poisonous, or were thought to be so
94 **mere confusion** absolute destruction
95 **not seeming** since you do not seem
96 **Art not afeard** This is clearly the first time
(and the last) that Cloten meets anyone
who is quite unimpressed that he is the
Queen's son.

At fools I laugh, not fear them.

CLOTEN   Die the death.
When I have slain thee with my proper hand
I'll follow those that even now fled hence,   100
And on the gates of Lud's town set your heads.
Yield, rustic mountaineer.   *Fight and exeunt*
  Enter Belarius and Arviragus

BELARIUS   No company's abroad?

ARVIRAGUS
None in the world; you did mistake him, sure.

BELARIUS
I cannot tell. Long is it since I saw him,
But time hath nothing blurred those lines of favour   105
Which then he wore; the snatches in his voice
And burst of speaking were as his; I am absolute
'Twas very Cloten.

ARVIRAGUS   In this place we left them.
I wish my brother make good time with him,
You say he is so fell.

BELARIUS   Being scarce made up,   110
I mean to man, he had not apprehension
Of roaring terrors; for defect of judgement
Is oft the cause of fear.
  Enter Guiderius with Cloten's head
      But see thy brother.

---

113 *with Cloten's head*] *not in* F

99 **proper** own
101 **Lud's town** London (see the note to 3.1.32)
102 **abroad** about
105 **lines of favour** lineaments of his face
106–7 **snatches . . . burst** checks . . . sudden rush ('stops and starts')
107 **absolute** certain
108 **very Cloten** Cloten indeed
109 **wish** hope
 make good time may acquit himself well (Schmidt)
110 **fell** fierce
110–11 **Being . . . man** since he is only half-developed mentally. At *Richard III* 1.1.21, Richard describes his deformity as being 'scarce half made up', and Belarius perhaps adds *I mean to man* to make it

clear that he is not describing Cloten as deformed. That phrase might alternatively refer to the young Cloten whom Belarius once knew, but that surely makes a much weaker dramatic point.
111 **apprehension** perception
112 **roaring** threatening
112–13 **for . . . fear** This seems to contradict Belarius' previous point that those with defective judgement haven't the sense to be afraid; but it is probably another of Belarius' pieces of folk wisdom: 'we must remember that fools are often afraid, though Cloten is an exception to this rule'. Several editors cited by Furness read 'cease' for 'cause' to resolve the apparent contradiction.

GUIDERIUS

This Cloten was a fool, an empty purse,
There was no money in't. Not Hercules   115
Could have knocked out his brains, for he had none.
Yet I not doing this, the fool had borne
My head as I do his.

BELARIUS   What hast thou done?

GUIDERIUS

I am perfect what: cut off one Cloten's head,
Son to the Queen, after his own report,   120
Who called me traitor, mountaineer, and swore
With his own single hand he'd take us in,
Displace our heads where, thank the gods, they grow,
And set them on Lud's town.

BELARIUS   We are all undone.

GUIDERIUS

Why, worthy father, what have we to lose   125
But that he swore to take, our lives? The law
Protects not us, then why should we be tender
To let an arrogant piece of flesh threat us,
Play judge and executioner all himself,
For we do fear the law? What company   130
Discover you abroad?

BELARIUS   No single soul
Can we set eye on, but in all safe reason
He must have some attendants. Though his humour
Was nothing but mutation, ay, and that
From one bad thing to worse, not frenzy,   135
Not absolute madness, could so far have raved
To bring him here alone. Although perhaps

---

123 thank the] STEEVENS; thanks the F1; thanks to th' F3; thanks ye JOHNSON 133 hu-
mour] THEOBALD; Honor F

114 **an empty purse** (because his outward
   show contained nothing inside)
115 **Not** not even
   Hercules A classical hero who achieved
   apparently impossible tasks; dashing
   out Cloten's non-existent brains with
   his club would have been beyond even
   him.
117 **I not doing** had I not done

119 **perfect** certain
120 **after . . . report** according to him
122 **take us in** capture us
126 **that** what
127–8 **tender | To** so meek as to
130 **For** because
132 **safe** sane
133 **humour** disposition
134 **mutation** changeableness

It may be heard at court that such as we
Cave here, hunt here, are outlaws, and in time
May make some stronger head, the which he hearing—   140
As it is like him—might break out, and swear
He'd fetch us in, yet is't not probable
To come alone, either he so undertaking,
Or they so suffering. Then on good ground we fear,
If we do fear this body hath a tail   145
More perilous than the head.

ARVIRAGUS   Let ord'nance
Come as the gods foresay it; howsoe'er,
My brother hath done well.

BELARIUS   I had no mind
To hunt this day. The boy Fidele's sickness
Did make my way long forth.

GUIDERIUS   With his own sword,   150
Which he did wave against my throat, I have ta'en
His head from him. I'll throw't into the creek
Behind our rock, and let it to the sea
And tell the fishes he's the Queen's son, Cloten.
That's all I reck.   *Exit*

BELARIUS   I fear 'twill be revenged.   155
Would, Polydore, thou hadst not done't, though valour
Becomes thee well enough.

ARVIRAGUS   Would I had done't,
So the revenge alone pursued me. Polydore,
I love thee brotherly, but envy much
Thou hast robbed me of this deed. I would revenges   160
That possible strength might meet would seek us through
And put us to our answer.

---

155 reck] F (reake)

139 **Cave** live in caves
140 **make . . . head** become a stronger force
142 **fetch us in** capture us
143 **To come** that he would come
144 **suffering** allowing
145 **tail** i.e. band of followers
146 **ord'nance** what is ordained, decreed
147 **foresay** predict
    howsoe'er however that may be
148 **mind** inclination

150 **way long forth** journey tedious
155 **reck** care
158 **So** so that
    alone pursued me would have pursued
    me only
160 **would** wish that
161 **possible strength** all the power that we
    can muster
    meet i.e. in combat
    seek us through test us

BELARIUS   Well, 'tis done.
We'll hunt no more today, nor seek for danger
Where there's no profit. I prithee to our rock.
You and Fidele play the cooks. I'll stay   165
Till hasty Polydore return, and bring him
To dinner presently.
ARVIRAGUS   Poor sick Fidele!
I'll willingly to him. To gain his colour
I'd let a parish of such Clotens blood,
And praise myself for charity.   *Exit into the cave*
BELARIUS   O thou goddess,   170
Thou divine Nature, how thyself thou blazon'st
In these two princely boys! They are as gentle
As zephyrs blowing below the violet,
Not wagging his sweet head; and yet as rough,
Their royal blood enchafed, as the rud'st wind   175
That by the top doth take the mountain pine
And make him stoop to th' vale. 'Tis wonder
That an invisible instinct should frame them
To royalty unlearned, honour untaught,
Civility not seen from other, valour   180
That wildly grows in them, but yields a crop
As if it had been sowed. Yet still it's strange
What Cloten's being here to us portends,
Or what his death will bring us.
         Enter Guiderius
GUIDERIUS   Where's my brother?
I have sent Cloten's clotpoll down the stream   185

170 *into the cave*] *not in* F   171 how] POPE; thou F

166 **hasty** rash
168 **gain** regain
169 **let . . . blood** draw blood from a whole
     parish full of Clotens
171 **thyself thou blazon'st** you proclaim
     yourself (as a coat of arms proclaims
     who its owner is; *blazon* is a heraldic
     term)
173 **zephyrs** mild, probably westerly,
     breezes (as opposed to the *rud'st wind* of
     l. 175).
174 **wagging** disturbing

175 **enchafed** heated, angered
     rud'st roughest
176 **take** seize
178 **instinct** (stressed on the second syllable,
     unlike modern prose usage)
     frame incline
180 **Civility . . . other** civilized behaviour not
     imitated from other people
181 **wildly** without being cultivated
185 **clotpoll** blockhead. It literally means
     'earth head', since *clod* and *clot*, though
     now meaning different things, were ori-

In embassy to his mother. His body's hostage
For his return.
    Solemn music
BELARIUS   My ingenious instrument!
Hark, Polydore, it sounds. But what occasion
Hath Cadwal now to give it motion? Hark!
GUIDERIUS
Is he at home?
BELARIUS   He went hence even now.   190
GUIDERIUS
What does he mean? Since death of my dear'st mother
It did not speak before. All solemn things
Should answer solemn accidents. The matter?
Triumphs for nothing and lamenting toys
Is jollity for apes and grief for boys.   195
Is Cadwal mad?
    Enter from the cave Arviragus with Innogen, dead,
    bearing her in his arms
BELARIUS   Look, here he comes,
And brings the dire occasion in his arms
Of what we blame him for.
ARVIRAGUS   The bird is dead
That we have made so much on. I had rather
Have skipped from sixteen years of age to sixty,   200

---

187 ingenious] F (ingenuous)   196 *from the cave*] not in F   *dead*] F; *as dead* CAPELL

ginally synonymous (*OED*, *clod*, *sb.*).
Shakespeare's use (coinage?) of *clodpoll*
at *Twelfth Night* 3.4.186 is *OED*'s earliest
example of *clodpoll* or *clotpoll*. The jingle
Cloten's clotpoll has been taken to establish the pronunciation of the name as
'Clotten', which is how the Folio text
usually spells it—though not, ironically,
in this scene; but the pun can be established by assonance as effectively as by
literal repetition. See Appendix A.

187 **ingenious** skilfully constructed. For
  a discussion of the music, see Appendix B.
188, 197 **occasion** cause
193 **answer** correspond to
  accidents events
194 **Triumphs** public celebrations
  lamenting toys laments for trifles. Does

Guiderius think that Arviragus is playing
the music for Cloten?
195 **jollity for apes** i.e. superficial joy
  (because apes only imitate human behaviour)
  grief for boys i.e. shallow grief (since boys
  were thought to be fickle in their emotions; compare 5.4.106–7)
196 **dead** Capell and other editors change
  the Folio's *dead* to 'as dead'; but F cap-
  tures the impact of the moment on an
  audience, discussed in the Introduction,
  pp. 44–5.
198–9 **The bird . . . on** In calling Innogen
  a *bird*, Arviragus expresses his tenderness towards her in terms of his
  rural surroundings (compare ll. 219–
  30).
199 **on** of. See note to 3.4.41.

To have turned my leaping-time into a crutch,
Than have seen this.

GUIDERIUS (*to Innogen*)   O sweetest, fairest lily!
My brother wears thee not the one half so well
As when thou grew'st thyself.

BELARIUS   O melancholy,
Who ever yet could sound thy bottom, find   205
The ooze to show what coast thy sluggish crare
Might easiliest harbour in? Thou blessèd thing,
Jove knows what man thou mightst have made; but I,
Thou diedst a most rare boy, of melancholy.
(*To Arviragus*) How found you him?

ARVIRAGUS   Stark, as you see,   210
Thus smiling as some fly had tickled slumber,
Not as death's dart being laughed at; his right cheek
Reposing on a cushion.

GUIDERIUS   Where?

ARVIRAGUS   O'th' floor.

---

203 not the] F; not POPE   206 crare] STEEVENS (*conj.* Sympson); care F   207 Might]
F2; Might'st F1   easiliest] F4; easilest F1

201 **leaping . . . crutch** i.e. youth (represented by the ability to leap about
unaided) to age (when the help of a *crutch*
is needed)
202 **lily** See note to 2.2.15.
203 **the one** Oxford, following Pope's omis-
sion of F's 'the', says that 'the' would be
'an easy interpolation', perhaps 'related
to the preceding *thee*' (*Textual Companion*,
p. 607). But if the manuscript here followed the scribe Ralph Crane's habit of
marking an elision with an apostrophe
yet still writing down the vowel to be
elided (i.e. 'the' one'), the compositor
might simply have failed to observe the
elision, in which case we should perhaps
read 'th'one'. But it is easy to mark the
verse rhythm in performance without
needing to omit *the*.
204–9 **O melancholy . . . melancholy** This
speech presents several difficulties.
Emendations have been proposed for F's
'care' in l. 206 and 'easilest' in l. 207 (see
the collation). More serious, perhaps, is
that Belarius reacts to Fidele's 'death' by
reflecting on the *melancholy* that by impli-

cation caused it, but then l. 209 introduces this point as if it were a new idea. It
is possible that the first sentence (ll. 204–
7) was a first shot, cancelled confusingly
in the manuscript (and perhaps in the
process obscuring *crare* in l. 206). If
Thou blessèd thing, rather than *O melancholy*, completes l. 204, a regular verse
line results, and fits the dramatic context
better, with both Guiderius and Belarius
directly addressing Fidele.
205 **sound thy bottom** plumb, measure,
your depths
    find probe, explore
206 **sluggish** slow-moving
    crare small trading boat
207 **easiliest** most easily. With F's form
'easilest', compare *Tempest* 3.1.15 in F:
'busie lest'.
208 **I** i.e. I know
209 **rare** exceptional
210 **Stark** rigid (as if in death)
211 **as . . . slumber** as if a fly had tickled him
while he was asleep
212 **as . . . at** as if laughing at death's
arrow

His arms thus leagued, I thought he slept, and put
My clouted brogues from off my feet, whose rudeness   215
Answered my steps too loud.
GUIDERIUS   Why, he but sleeps.
If he be gone he'll make his grave a bed.
With female fairies will his tomb be haunted,
(*To Innogen*) And worms will not come to thee.
ARVIRAGUS   With fairest flowers
Whilst summer lasts and I live here, Fidele,   220
I'll sweeten thy sad grave. Thou shalt not lack
The flower that's like thy face, pale primrose, nor
The azured harebell, like thy veins; no, nor
The leaf of eglantine, whom not to slander
Outsweetened not thy breath. The ruddock would   225
With charitable bill—O bill sore shaming

225 ruddock] F (Raddocke)

214 **His . . . leagued** since his arms were joined. Sometimes *leagued* is glossed 'folded across the breast', but I think the image is of Innogen lying curled up on the floor.
215 **clouted brogues** metal-studded rough shoes
215–16 **rudeness . . . loud** roughness made my steps echo too much, made too much noise
216 **but** only
217 **a bed** i.e. only a bed. The consoling idea of death as a peaceful sleep is much developed in the following speeches, culminating in ll. 259–82.
218 **female fairies** (presumably less dangerous than male ones, who in folklore were thought malevolent to human beings)
219–30 **With . . . corpse** This speech is discussed in the Introduction, p. 24. The impression, especially in the final lines, that the body is becoming part of the natural world, recalls *Pericles* Sc. 11.55–63, in which another apparently dead body is to be buried in the ooze (compare l. 206 of this scene), and will become a part of the seabed, where 'humming water must o'erwhelm thy corpse, | Lying with simple shells'.
222 **pale primrose** John Gerard in his *Herbal* (1597), refers to 'the common white field primrose' (p. 637); Shakespeare also associates their paleness with the pallor

of death at *Winter's Tale* 4.4.122–3: 'pale primroses, | That die unmarried'.
223 **azured** blue-coloured
      harebell In Shakespeare's day, the *harebell* was the standard name for our blue-bell or wild hyacinth, as the drawings in Gerard's *Herbal* conclusively demonstrate; but this is one case where changes to the language have actually enhanced the impact of a Shakespearian speech, for the modern harebell is a different flower, much paler, more fragile and delicate than the bluebell, and therefore matching the exquisite delicacy of Arviragus' other comparisons more aptly.
224 **eglantine** The sweet-brier, which has delicately scented leaves. Gerard's *Herbal* makes the identification (p. 1088).
      whom . . . slander i.e. not to denigrate the eglantine (by claiming that its scent is no sweeter than Innogen's breath)
225 **ruddock** A name used in Warwickshire and other dialects, according to Wright's *Dialect Dictionary*, for the robin. The folklore tradition that robins charitably cover dead bodies no doubt arises because they are so tame and apparently unafraid of human beings.
226–8 **O bill . . . monument** This parenthesis is typical of the play's style, and dramatically very relevant, since Arviragus contrasts the charity of the natural world with the ingratitude of men, a

Those rich-left heirs that let their fathers lie
Without a monument!—bring thee all this,
Yea, and furred moss besides, when flowers are none,
To winter-ground thy corpse.
GUIDERIUS   Prithee have done,   230
And do not play in wench-like words with that
Which is so serious. Let us bury him,
And not protract with admiration what
Is now due debt. To th' grave.
ARVIRAGUS   Say, where shall's lay him?
GUIDERIUS
By good Euriphile, our mother.
ARVIRAGUS   Be't so,   235
And let us, Polydore, though now our voices
Have got the mannish crack, sing him to th' ground
As once our mother; use like note and words,
Save that Euriphile must be Fidele.
GUIDERIUS Cadwal,   240
I cannot sing. I'll weep, and word it with thee,

---

229 besides, when] THEOBALD; besides. When F   230 winter-ground] F; winter-gown
THEOBALD (*conj.* Warburton); winter-green DOUCE *conj.*   corpse.] CAPELL (corse.); Coarse—
F   238 once] POPE; once to F

trait displayed by Posthumus to Innogen
and by Cymbeline to Belarius.

229 **furred** i.e. thick and protective like fur
(alluding to the close growth of moss)
230 **winter-ground** Steevens explained this
as meaning to protect a plant from winter
by laying straw (or, here, moss) over it.
Since he cited no parallel, *winter-ground*
would seem to be a Shakespearian coinage, comparable to 'weather-fends' (protects from the weather) in the
contemporaneous *Tempest* 5.1.10. The
Folio text begins a new sentence at *When
flowers are none*, and follows *thy corpse*
with a dash, so perhaps Guiderius interrupts a new thought, in which case F's
'winter-ground' may be an adjective and
a noun, linked by one of Ralph Crane's
hyphens (see Introduction, p. 70), rather
than a verb. But dashes in the Folio do not
inevitably indicate interruption (see the
note to 2.4.76); I think the speech is complete, and that *winter-ground*, as glossed
by Steevens, concludes it perfectly.

231 **wench-like** appropriate to women
233 **admiration** 'Perhaps used in the modern sense, with something also of the
sense "wonder"' (Dowden)
234 **due debt** owing, needs to be paid
shall's shall we
237 **Have . . . crack** have broken
sing . . . ground i.e. perform funeral rites
for him
238 **As . . . mother** as we once did our
mother. F's 'to our mother' is probably
a slip, influenced by the *to* of the previous
line; but F makes sense ('As once we
sang funeral rites to our mother'), and
as at l. 203, an elision (almost 't'our') is
easy in performance.
like note similar tune
239 **Save . . . Fidele** except that Fidele must
take the place of Euriphile (not implying
that either name need occur in the funeral rite, as has been suggested)
241-3 **I cannot . . . then** For a refutation of
the view that this is an interpolation to
meet a theatrical emergency, see Appendix B.

For notes of sorrow out of tune are worse
Than priests and fanes that lie.
ARVIRAGUS   We'll speak it then.
BELARIUS
Great griefs, I see, med'cine the less, for Cloten
Is quite forgot. He was a queen's son, boys,   245
And though he came our enemy, remember
He was paid for that. Though mean and mighty rotting
Together have one dust, yet reverence,
That angel of the world, doth make distinction
Of place 'tween high and low. Our foe was princely,   250
And though you took his life as being our foe,
Yet bury him as a prince.
GUIDERIUS   Pray you fetch him hither.
Thersites' body is as good as Ajax'
When neither are alive.
ARVIRAGUS (*to Belarius*)   If you'll go fetch him,
We'll say our song the whilst. Brother, begin.   255
                           Exit Belarius

GUIDERIUS
Nay Cadwal, we must lay his head to th'east.
My father hath a reason for't.
ARVIRAGUS   'Tis true.

255.1 *Exit Belarius*] *not in* F

241 **weep** i.e. he is too overcome with emotion to sing
word speak
243 **fanes** Literally 'temples'—but perhaps suggesting the oracles that issued from them, which often gave ambiguous information (hence perhaps *that lie* here).
244 **Great . . . less** Belarius draws on proverbial wisdom : 'The greater grief drives out the less' (Tilley G446).
med'cine cure. F's elision indicates the pronunciation required by the metre.
247 **paid** Schmidt says that this means 'punish', but perhaps it is simply a grim understatement : 'he was given his payment' (decapitation).
247–50 **Though . . . low** Belarius characteristically insists that traditional distinctions of respect must be paid.

248–9 **reverence . . . world** Respect is presented as a heavenly quality, embodied in an angel descending to earth.
253 **Thersites . . . Ajax** Shakespeare here takes these two characters from Homer's *Iliad* at their traditional valuation (a scurrilous coward versus a mighty hero), though in *Troilus and Cressida* he presents both satirically.
255 **say** speak
the whilst in the meantime
256–7 **to th'east . . . for't** Whatever Belarius' *reason* was, Shakespeare's was to emphasize the pagan world of the play, since Christian custom is to bury people *facing* east (so that at Christ's second coming from the east on the last day they will rise to face him).

GUIDERIUS

Come on then, and remove him.

ARVIRAGUS   So, begin.

GUIDERIUS

    Fear no more the heat o'th' sun,
       Nor the furious winter's rages.   260
    Thou thy worldly task hast done,
       Home art gone and ta'en thy wages.
    Golden lads and girls all must,
    As chimney-sweepers, come to dust.

ARVIRAGUS

    Fear no more the frown o'th' great,   265
       Thou art past the tyrant's stroke.
    Care no more to clothe and eat,
       To thee the reed is as the oak.
    The sceptre, learning, physic, must
    All follow this and come to dust.   270

GUIDERIUS

    Fear no more the lightning flash,

ARVIRAGUS

       Nor th'all-dreaded thunder-stone.

GUIDERIUS

    Fear not slander, censure rash.

ARVIRAGUS

    Thou hast finished joy and moan.

---

258 begin.] begin. | SONG. F

259–82 **Fear . . . grave** This lyric is discussed
   in the Introduction, p. 45.
262–4 **Home . . . dust** For the possible biblical
   echo, see the note to l. 5.
263 **Golden** This is a favourite term of praise
   and value with Shakespeare; other
   examples include 'golden chance' at
   5.3.226, and 'golden time' at Sonnet
   3.12 and at *Twelfth Night* 5.1.378.
264 **As** like
   chimney-sweepers These are obviously
   contrasted, in their sootiness, with the
   golden lads of the previous line; but
   there is a secondary (perhaps even, for
   Shakespeare, a private) meaning. In various dialects, including Warwickshire,

chimney-sweepers is a name for the spiky
heads of the plantain or ribwort, *Plantago
lanceolata* (Wright, *Dialect Dictionary*,
chimney 23b), which eventually disinteg-
rate—*come to dust.*
269 **sceptre, learning, physic** regal
   power, knowledge, medicine (i.e. repres-
   entative branches of human achievement)
270 **this** i.e. the process of decay
272 **thunder-stone** thunderbolt. Thunder-
   storms were thought to produce stones.
   Compare *Othello* 5.2.241–2 : 'Are there
   no stones in heaven | But what serves for
   the thunder?', and 'stones of sulphur' at
   5.4.240.

GUIDERIUS *and* ARVIRAGUS

        All lovers young, all lovers must   275
        Consign to thee and come to dust.

GUIDERIUS

        No exorcizer harm thee,

ARVIRAGUS

        Nor no witchcraft charm thee.

GUIDERIUS

        Ghost unlaid forbear thee.

ARVIRAGUS

        Nothing ill come near thee.   280

GUIDERIUS *and* ARVIRAGUS

        Quiet consummation have,
        And renownèd be thy grave.

       Enter Belarius with the body of Cloten in Posthumus'
       clothes

GUIDERIUS

We have done our obsequies. Come, lay him down.

BELARIUS

Here's a few flowers, but 'bout midnight more :
The herbs that have on them cold dew o'th' night   285
Are strewings fitt'st for graves upon th'earth's face.
You were as flowers, now withered ; even so
These herblets shall, which we upon you strow.

282.1–2 *in Posthumus' clothes*] *not in* F   286 th' earth's face] OXFORD (*conj.* Staunton) ; their
Faces F   288 strow] F (strew)

---

276 **Consign to** submit to the same terms as (according to *OED v.* 5b, a unique meaning of *consign*)

277 **exorcizer** conjuror, one who raises spirits

278 **charm** cast a spell on

279 **unlaid** not driven out by exorcism (the first use in this sense recorded by *OED*)
forbear thee leave you alone

281 **consummation** completion of life (with the implication of fulfilment). This echoes the Burial Service in *The Book of Common Prayer* (1559) : 'that we . . . may have our perfect consummation and bliss' with God.

283 **obsequies** funeral rites

286 **th'earth's face** Modifying a suggestion by Howard Staunton cited in Furness (p. 326–7), Oxford emends F's 'vpon their Faces', thus avoiding the undeniable theatrical awkwardness that the decapitated Cloten has no face. Shakespeare often juxtaposes *cold* (l. 285) and *earth*, as in 'the earth's cold face' (*Duke of York* [*3 Henry VI*] 2.3.35), and 'my cold corpse on the earth's cold face' (*Richard III* 5.5.220). 'After "on them" (4.2.285), contamination to "vpon their" would be easy, and after "their" the following noun would—at some stage—naturally be "corrected" to a plural. The punctuation is, here as elsewhere, scribal or compositorial' (*Textual Companion*, p. 608).

288 **shall** must (wither)
strow strew. (The variant spelling is needed for the rhyme.)

Come on, away, apart upon our knees.
The ground that gave them first has them again.   290
Their pleasures here are past, so is their pain.
        Exeunt Belarius, Arviragus, and Guiderius
INNOGEN *(awakes)*
Yes sir, to Milford Haven, which is the way?
I thank you; by yon bush? Pray how far thither?
'Od's pitikins, can it be six mile yet?
I have gone all night. Faith, I'll lie down and sleep.   295
    She sees the body
But soft, no bedfellow! O gods and goddesses!
These flowers are like the pleasures of the world,
This bloody man the care on't. I hope I dream,

---

291 is] POPE; are F   291.1 *Belarius . . . Guiderius*] *not in* F   295.1 *She sees the body*] *not in* F

---

289 Since this line is preceded and followed by rhyming couplets, Oxford assumes and so marks a missing line after it, conjecturing an incomplete sentence: 'apart upon our knees [we'll pray, etc.]' (*Textual Companion*, p. 608). But runs of couplets are often interrupted in Shakespeare, and this episode works well in performance: after strewing flowers on the body, Belarius has a typically reflective couplet about them. Then he issues the simple instruction *apart upon our knees* (i.e. 'let's go and pray'); perhaps (as often in performance) the three of them move away towards the 'cave' exit, and then turn back as Belarius closes the episode with a final sonorous couplet.

290 **The . . . again** For the biblical echo, see note to l. 5.

291.1 After their departure, a long silence usually follows in performance, as at 2.2.10, focusing attention in both cases upon the sleeping Innogen.

292–333 This climactic speech is carefully constructed in stages to provide the actress with a firm foundation for her performance, as Shaw shrewdly appreciated in a letter to Ellen Terry quoted in the Introduction, p. 46. At ll. 292–5, Innogen is still emerging from her dream about meeting the beggars whom she described at 3.6.8–9. At l. 296, she sees the body, but does not appear to register that it is headless (only that it is bloodstained) until l. 309, perhaps because the flowers strewn on it obscure the fact, perhaps because, Shaw suggests, it is wrapped in a cloak. At ll. 298–303, she still appears to be confused, probably by the drug, but by ll. 307–8 she is fully awake: she has not imagined the horrific situation. At ll. 309–13 she positively (mis) identifies the body, then (ll. 313–21) denounces Pisanio; but ll. 321–4 offer the opportunity to vary the outburst with a note of tenderness, lamenting the loss of Posthumus' head.

294 **'Od's pitikins** A watered-down oath, a diminutive of 'by God's pity'; *OED* says that *od*, 'a minced form of *God*', came into vogue about 1600 to avoid overt blasphemy.

295 **gone** travelled

296 **But . . . bedfellow** This is presumably an alarmed exclamation, almost recoiling from the realization that someone is lying beside her.
   O . . . goddesses This exclamation also occurs at the start of an old play, *The Rare Triumphs of Love and Fortune*, discussed in the Introduction, pp. 17–18, so perhaps it was chosen for its old-fashioned ring. Like the almost childish diminutive *'Od's pitikins* of l. 294, it differs from Innogen's usual language, perhaps to suggest her half-drugged state.

For so I thought I was a cavekeeper,
And cook to honest creatures. But 'tis not so. 300
'Twas but a bolt of nothing, shot at nothing,
Which the brain makes of fumes. Our very eyes
Are sometimes like our judgements, blind. Good faith,
I tremble still with fear; but if there be
Yet left in heaven as small a drop of pity 305
As a wren's eye, feared gods, a part of it!
The dream's here still. Even when I wake it is
Without me as within me; not imagined, felt.
A headless man? The garments of Posthumus?
I know the shape of 's leg; this is his hand, 310
His foot Mercurial, his Martial thigh,
The brawns of Hercules; but his Jovial face—
Murder in heaven! How? 'Tis gone. Pisanio,
All curses madded Hecuba gave the Greeks,
And mine to boot, be darted on thee! Thou, 315
Conspired with that irregulous devil Cloten,
Hath here cut off my lord. To write and read
Be henceforth treacherous! Damned Pisanio
Hath with his forgèd letters—damned Pisanio—

299 **so** in the same way (i.e. being a *cave-keeper* turned out to be a dream too)

301 **bolt . . . at nothing** This is a perfect image of the shiftingness of dreams: an arrow (*bolt*) that is nevertheless made of nothing and shot at nothing.

302 **fumes** vapours (thought to rise to the brain from the stomach and cause dreams; compare *Tempest* 5.1.67–8: 'the ignorant fumes that mantle | Their clearer reason')

303 **Good faith** i.e. in good faith (a mild oath, used for emphasis)

306 **As . . . eye** The wren was popularly thought to be the smallest of birds (compare *Macbeth* 4.2.9–10: 'the poor wren, | The most diminutive of birds').
a part i.e. give me a part

308 **not imagined, felt** This sharp contrast between what is imaginary and what is fully experienced usually marks the moment when Innogen is fully awake, as the realization in the next phrase suggests.

311–12 **His foot . . . face** The parts of the body are compared to those of gods and heroes: Mercury is the messenger of the gods, Mars the god of war, Hercules a hero noted for his strength, Jove (Jupiter) the king of the gods.

312 **brawns** muscles
Jovial Jove-like, Jupiter-like

313 **Murder in heaven** i.e. because such a god-like man has been killed

314 **madded** maddened
Hecuba wife of Priam, King of Troy, who saw the sack of Troy and murder of her husband by the *Greeks*

315 **to boot** in addition (literally, 'to the good')
darted hurled as if they were darts or arrows

316 **irregulous** lawless, irregular (a Shakespearian coinage, perhaps with a play on 'irreligious')

319 **forgèd letters** She is wrong, of course; but the error, and this whole episode, has the effect of purging Posthumus' betrayal from her system, re-establishing the 'old' Posthumus in her eyes.

From this most bravest vessel of the world   320
Struck the main-top! O Posthumus, alas,
Where is thy head? Where's that? Ay me, where's that?
Pisanio might have killed thee at the heart
And left this head on. How should this be? Pisanio?
'Tis he and Cloten. Malice and lucre in them   325
Have laid this woe here. O 'tis pregnant, pregnant!
The drug he gave me, which he said was precious
And cordial to me, have I not found it
Murd'rous to th' senses? That confirms it home.
This is Pisanio's deed, and Cloten. O,   330
Give colour to my pale cheek with thy blood,
That we the horrider may seem to those
Which chance to find us! O my lord, my lord!
⌈*She embraces the body.*⌉
Enter Lucius, Roman Captains, and a Soothsayer
A ROMAN CAPTAIN (*to Lucius*)
To them the legions garrisoned in Gallia
After your will have crossed the sea, attending   335

---

324 this] F1 ; his F3 ; thy HANMER   333.1 *She embraces the body*] *not in* F

320–1 **vessel . . . main-top** The body is imagined as a ship, with the head as the top
of the main-mast.
323 **at** through
325 **lucre** financial gain. Innogen uses the
word contemptuously, perhaps as an
abbreviation for 'filthy lucre', originally
Tindale's translation (1526–34) of a biblical phrase (Paul's Epistle to Titus 1:
11). Presumably in this line the *malice* is
Cloten's against Posthumus, the *lucre*
Pisanio's in Cloten's service.
326 **laid this woe** inflicted this misery
(*OED, lay, v.*[1] 55c)
pregnant clear, evident (as in an
argument, a sense that *OED a.*[1] distin-
guishes even from the figurative uses of
pregnant in the modern sense, citing
Othello 2.1.236–7: 'a most pregnant
and unforced position'. This sense
is picked up in *That confirms it home*
(l. 329).)
328 **cordial** restorative
329 **confirms it home** confirms the argument ('drives it home')
330 **Cloten** i.e. Cloten's
331 **Give . . . blood** For a discussion of how

Innogen gets the blood on her face, see
the Introduction, pp. 48–9.
332 **horrider** more terrifying
333 **Which** who
333.2 *Enter . . . Soothsayer* E. M. W. Tillyard
notes that this 'brisk and business-like
entry . . . is the effective breaking-in of
one world on another' (*Shakespeare's Last
Plays* (1938), p. 75), public affairs
intruding upon Innogen's private
anguish.
334 **To them** in addition to them (i.e. presumably the legions that Caius Lucius
brought with him from Rome, who are
at present on his *ships* (l. 336)). But
although the Romans enter in mid-
conversation, *To them* may not be the
start of the speech but the end of the
previous stage direction, implying that
the Romans join *them* (Innogen and
Cloten) on the stage: compare the stage
direction opening *Coriolanus* 1.4: '*Enter
Martius, Lartius . . . ; to them a Messenger.*'
Omitting *To them* would yield a regular
iambic line.
335 **After** according to
    attending waiting for

You here at Milford Haven with your ships.
They are in readiness.
LUCIUS   But what from Rome?
A ROMAN CAPTAIN
The senate hath stirred up the confiners
And gentlemen of Italy, most willing spirits
That promise noble service, and they come   340
Under the conduct of bold Giacomo,
Siena's brother.
LUCIUS   When expect you them?
A ROMAN CAPTAIN
With the next benefit o'th' wind.
LUCIUS   This forwardness
Makes our hopes fair. Command our present numbers
Be mustered; bid the captains look to't.
                                        Exit one or more
(*To Soothsayer*)   Now sir,   345
What have you dreamed of late of this war's purpose?
SOOTHSAYER
Last night the very gods showed me a vision—
I fast, and prayed for their intelligence—thus:
I saw Jove's bird, the Roman eagle, winged
From the spongy south to this part of the west,   350
There vanished in the sunbeams; which portends,
Unless my sins abuse my divination,
Success to th' Roman host.
LUCIUS   Dream often so,
And never false.
            He sees Cloten's body
                Soft ho, what trunk is here

337 are] F2; are heere F1; are hence OXFORD   345 *Exit one or more*] *not in* F   354 *He sees*
Cloten's body] *not in* F

337 **are in** F2 omits F1's 'heere', which was
   probably caught by the compositor from
   the previous line.
338 **confiners** inhabitants, those living
   within the confines
341 **Giacomo** This prepares for Giacomo's
   reappearance (and perhaps, by association, for that of Posthumus).
342 **Siena** i.e. the Duke of Siena
343 **benefit o'th'** advantageous
   forwardness state of readiness

346 **purpose** outcome
347 **very gods** gods themselves
348 **fast** fasted (Abbott §341)
   intelligence information
349 **winged** on the wing, flying
350 **spongy** damp
352 **my . . . divination** The idea is that
   earthly *sins* prevent one's spirit from
   communicating with the gods.
   abuse distort
354 **Soft** wait a moment, not so fast

Without his top? The ruin speaks that sometime   355
It was a worthy building. How, a page,
Or dead or sleeping on him? But dead rather;
For nature doth abhor to make his bed
With the defunct, or sleep upon the dead.
Let's see the boy's face.

A ROMAN CAPTAIN   He's alive, my lord.   360

LUCIUS
He'll then instruct us of this body. Young one,
Inform us of thy fortunes, for it seems
They crave to be demanded. Who is this
Thou mak'st thy bloody pillow? Or who was he
That, otherwise than noble nature did,   365
Hath altered that good picture? What's thy interest
In this sad wreck? How came't? Who is't?
What art thou?

INNOGEN   I am nothing; or if not,
Nothing to be were better. This was my master,
A very valiant Briton and a good,   370
That here by mountaineers lies slain. Alas,
There is no more such masters. I may wander
From east to occident, cry out for service,
Try many, all good; serve truly; never
Find such another master.

LUCIUS   'Lack, good youth,   375
Thou mov'st no less with thy complaining than
Thy master in bleeding. Say his name, good friend.

INNOGEN
Richard du Champ. (*Aside*) If I do lie and do

---

367 wreck] F (wracke)

355 **his** its
   sometime once
357 **Or . . . or** either . . . or
358 **nature doth abhor** a living creature
   would detest
359 **defunct** deceased
363 **crave . . . demanded** beg to be asked
   about (because they are so strange)
364–6 **Or . . . picture** 'Nature only took away
   the life—Who mutilated the body?'
   (Dowden)
367 **wreck** 'greatly damaged . . . person'
   (*COD* 2). The mutilated body is envisaged

   as a wrecked ship, as at ll. 320–1.
373 **occident** west
   service employment
376 **Thou . . . less** you are no less moving
   complaining lamenting
378 **Richard du Champ** This seems to be a
   private joke on Shakespeare's part, since
   it is a French translation of the name
   Richard Field (1561–1624), a fellow
   Stratfordian who became a London
   printer, and printed *Venus and Adonis*
   (1593) and *Lucrece* (1594).
378–80 **If . . . it** This aside emphasizes

No harm by it, though the gods hear, I hope
They'll pardon it. (*Aloud*) Say you, sir?
LUCIUS   Thy name?
INNOGEN   Fidele, sir.   380
LUCIUS
Thou dost approve thyself the very same.
Thy name well fits thy faith, thy faith thy name.
Wilt take thy chance with me? I will not say
Thou shalt be so well mastered, but be sure,
No less beloved. The Roman Emperor's letters   385
Sent by a consul to me should not sooner
Than thine own worth prefer thee. Go with me.
INNOGEN
I'll follow, sir. But first, an't please the gods,
I'll hide my master from the flies as deep
As these poor pickaxes can dig; and when   390
With wildwood leaves and weeds I ha' strewed his grave
And on it said a century of prayers,
Such as I can, twice o'er, I'll weep and sigh,
And leaving so his service, follow you,
So please you entertain me.
LUCIUS   Ay good youth,   395
And rather father thee than master thee. My friends,
The boy hath taught us manly duties. Let us
Find out the prettiest daisied plot we can,
And make him with our pikes and partisans

---

391 wildwood leaves] NEILSON–HILL (*subs.*; *conj.* Cambridge); wild wood-leaues F

Innogen's candour and dislike of lying.
She presumably wishes to conceal Posthumus' identity (and so her own) from
an enemy army.

380 **Say you** What do you say?
381 **approve** prove, show
    the very same i.e. 'faithful'
387 **prefer** recommend
388 **an't** if it will
390 **pickaxes** i.e. her fingers
391 **wildwood leaves** F's 'wild wood-leaues'
    perhaps reflects the characteristic
    hyphenation of the scribe Ralph
    Crane (see Introduction, p. 70). *OED*, cit-
    ing this passage, glosses *wildwood* as an
    'uncultivated or unfrequented wood',

and the stress on 'wild' fits the metre.
392 **century of** hundred. Perhaps the
    Roman context suggested this word,
    the name of a division (100 men) of the
    Roman army.
393 **can** am able
394 **leaving . . . you** This is a turning-point in
    the action: instead of giving way to des-
    pair, Innogen resolves on life and making
    the best of things; her decision to ally
    herself with the Romans leads ultimately
    to the restoration both of her marriage
    and of the alliance between Britain and
    Rome.
395 **entertain** take into service
399 **partisans** long-handled weapons with
    broad blades

A grave. Come, arm him. Boy, he is preferred   400
By thee to us, and he shall be interred
As soldiers can. Be cheerful, wipe thine eyes.
Some falls are means the happier to arise.

Exeunt with Cloten's body

4.3   *Enter Cymbeline, Lords, and Pisanio*

CYMBELINE
Again, and bring me word how 'tis with her.

Exit one or more

A fever with the absence of her son,
A madness of which her life's in danger. Heavens,
How deeply you at once do touch me! Innogen,
The great part of my comfort, gone; my queen   5
Upon a desperate bed, and in a time
When fearful wars point at me; her son gone,
So needful for this present! It strikes me past
The hope of comfort. (*To Pisanio*) But for thee, fellow,
Who needs must know of her departure and   10
Dost seem so ignorant, we'll enforce it from thee
By a sharp torture.

PISANIO   Sir, my life is yours.
I humbly set it at your will. But for my mistress,
I nothing know where she remains, why gone,
Nor when she purposes return. Beseech your highness,   15
Hold me your loyal servant.

A LORD   Good my liege,
The day that she was missing he was here.

---

400 he is] F2; hee's F1   403.1 *with Cloten's body*] *not in* F
   4.3.1.1 *Exit one or more*] *not in* F

400 **arm** take in your arms, lift up (on to
   your shoulders)
   preferred recommended
402 **can** can be, are
403 **Some . . . arise** The suggestion that this
   lowest point in Innogen's fortunes
   nevertheless contains a promise of happiness parallels Jupiter's promise at the
   lowest point of Posthumus' fortunes
   that he will be 'happier much by his
   affliction made' (5.3.202).
4.3.1 **Again** i.e. go back again

2 **with** on account of
3 **of** as a result of
4 **touch** afflict
6 **desperate bed** deathbed
8 **needful** needed
   for this present at this time
   past beyond
9 **comfort** recovery
11 **enforce it from** force it out of
14 **nothing** not at all
15 **purposes** intends to
16 **Hold** consider

I dare be bound he's true, and shall perform
All parts of his subjection loyally. For Cloten,
There wants no diligence in seeking him,   20
And will no doubt be found.
CYMBELINE   The time is troublesome.
(*To Pisanio*) We'll slip you for a season, but our jealousy
Does yet depend.
A LORD   So please your majesty,
The Roman legions, all from Gallia drawn,
Are landed on your coast with a supply   25
Of Roman gentlemen by the senate sent.
CYMBELINE
Now for the counsel of my son and queen!
I am amazed with matter.
A LORD   Good my liege,
Your preparation can affront no less
Than what you hear of. Come more, for more you're
        ready.   30
The want is but to put those powers in motion
That long to move.
CYMBELINE   I thank you. Let's withdraw,
And meet the time as it seeks us. We fear not
What can from Italy annoy us, but
We grieve at chances here. Away.   35
                                  Exeunt Cymbeline and Lords
PISANIO
I heard no letter from my master since
I wrote him Innogen was slain. 'Tis strange.
Nor hear I from my mistress, who did promise

35.1 *Cymbeline and Lords*] *not in* F

19 **subjection** duty as a subject
20 **wants** is lacking
21 **will** he will (a common Shakespearian ellipsis)
   troublesome A stronger word than in modern English, implying something like 'full of crises'.
22 **slip you** let you go (as a dog is slipped from a leash)
   jealousy anger, suspicion
23 **Does yet depend** still remains hanging (over you)

27 **Now for** if only I now had
28 **amazed with matter** overwhelmed with business
29 **preparation** prepared army
   affront no less confront an army no smaller
30 **Come more** if more come
31 **The . . . but** the only thing needed is
34 **annoy** harm
35 **chances** events
36 **no letter** Perhaps 'not a syllable'; perhaps literally a letter.

To yield me often tidings. Neither know I
What is betid to Cloten, but remain   40
Perplexed in all. The heavens still must work.
Wherein I am false I am honest: not true, to be true.
These present wars shall find I love my country
Even to the note o'th' King, or I'll fall in them.
All other doubts, by time let them be cleared: 45
Fortune brings in some boats that are not steered.   *Exit*

4.4   *Enter Belarius, Guiderius, and Arviragus*

GUIDERIUS
The noise is round about us.

BELARIUS   Let us from it.

ARVIRAGUS
What pleasure, sir, find we in life to lock it
From action and adventure?

GUIDERIUS   Nay, what hope
Have we in hiding us? This way the Romans
Must or for Britons slay us, or receive us   5
For barbarous and unnatural revolts
During their use, and slay us after.

BELARIUS   Sons,
We'll higher to the mountains, there secure us.
To the King's party there's no going. Newness
Of Cloten's death—we being not known, not mustered   10
Among the bands—may drive us to a render
Where we have lived, and so extort from's that
Which we have done, whose answer would be death

---

40 betid] F (betide)
   4.4.2 find we] F2; we finde F1

---

40 **is betid** has happened
42 **Wherein . . . false** (for instance, in dis-
   obeying his master and in lying to the
   King at ll. 13–15)
44 **to . . . King** so that the King may take
   notice of me
46 **Fortune . . . steered** Some boats which are
   cast adrift are brought to harbour by
   good luck. The phrase sounds proverbial,
   but is not recorded.
4.4.2 **lock it** shut it off
 4 **This way** i.e. by not joining the King's
   army
 5 **or for** either as
5–7 **receive . . . use** recruit us, as treacherous
   rebels (against our country) while they
   have need of us
 8 **secure us** make ourselves safe
9–10 **Newness . . . death** the fact that
   Cloten's death is so recent
10–11 **mustered . . . bands** recruited for the
   (British) army
11 **render** account
13 **answer** recompense

Drawn on with torture.

GUIDERIUS   This is, sir, a doubt
In such a time nothing becoming you   15
Nor satisfying us.

ARVIRAGUS   It is not likely
That when they hear the Roman horses neigh,
Behold their quartered fires, have both their eyes
And ears so cloyed importantly as now,
That they will waste their time upon our note,   20
To know from whence we are.

BELARIUS   O, I am known
Of many in the army. Many years,
Though Cloten then but young, you see, not wore him
From my remembrance. And besides, the King
Hath not deserved my service nor your loves,   25
Who find in my exile the want of breeding,
The certainty of this hard life, aye hopeless
To have the courtesy your cradle promised,
But to be still hot summer's tanlings, and
The shrinking slaves of winter.

GUIDERIUS   Than be so,   30
Better to cease to be. Pray sir, to th'army.
I and my brother are not known; yourself
So out of thought, and thereto so o'ergrown,
Cannot be questioned.

ARVIRAGUS   By this sun that shines,
I'll thither. What thing is't that I never   35
Did see man die, scarce ever looked on blood

---

17 the] ROWE; their F   18 fires] F; files RANN   27 hard] F (heard)   35 is't] F1; is it F2

---

14 **Drawn on** brought about
18 **quartered fires** the watch-fires in their encampment (quarters). Oxford prefers Rann's emendation 'files' (troops of soldiers).
19 **cloyed   importantly** filled (literally 'clogged') with important matters
20 **upon our note** in taking note of us
23 **then** was then
   not wore had not erased
24 **remembrance** memory
26 **Who . . . breeding** who experience because of my exile a lack of education

27 **certainty** inevitability
   aye hopeless for ever without hope
28 **courtesy** respect (to a king's children)
   cradle i.e. (royal) birth
29 **tanlings** children tanned by the sun
30 **shrinking** wincing with cold (as if from a whip wielded by *winter*)
33 **out of thought** forgotten
   o'ergrown i.e. with hair and/or beard; a long beard is mentioned at 5.3.17.
35 **What thing** i.e. what a shameful thing

But that of coward hares, hot goats, and venison,
Never bestrid a horse save one that had
A rider like myself, who ne'er wore rowel
Nor iron on his heel! I am ashamed   40
To look upon the holy sun, to have
The benefit of his blest beams, remaining
So long a poor unknown.

GUIDERIUS   By heavens, I'll go.
If you will bless me, sir, and give me leave,
I'll take the better care; but if you will not,   45
The hazard therefore due fall on me by
The hands of Romans.

ARVIRAGUS   So say I, amen.

BELARIUS
No reason I, since of your lives you set
So slight a valuation, should reserve
My cracked one to more care. Have with you, boys!   50
If in your country wars you chance to die,
That is my bed too, lads, and there I'll lie.
Lead, lead. (*Aside*) The time seems long, their blood
    thinks scorn
Till it fly out and show them princes born.   *Exeunt*

5.1   *Enter Posthumus alone, dressed as a Roman, carrying
        a bloody cloth*

POSTHUMUS
Yea, bloody cloth, I'll keep thee, for I once wished

5.1.0.1–2 *dressed...cloth*] *not in* F   1 once wished] OXFORD (*conj*. Kellner, *cited in*
Maxwell); am wisht F; wish'd POPE

37 **coward...goats** Hares were proverbially
  cowardly, goats lecherous (Tilley H147,
  G 167).
39 **rowel** small, rotating disc at the end of a
  spur
46 **hazard therefore due** danger owing to me
  as a result (of my disobedience)
47 **amen** Arviragus uses the traditional
  response to Guiderius' prayer (for Belarius' blessing).
50 **cracked** impaired (with age)
  Have with you i.e. let us go together
51 **country** country's
53–4 **their . . . born** i.e. the blood they
  shed valiantly in battle proves them

to be princes
53 **thinks scorn** disdains itself
5.1 The action from here to the end of the
  play is virtually continuous, concerned
  with the climactic battle and its after-
  math. Posthumus plays such a central
  role that the focus is almost exclusively
  upon him (usually in soliloquy) until the
  start of the final scene. Having severely
  dented the heroic image of him established in the first scene, the play now
  rehabilitates him so that he comes near
  to justifying that image (but see 5.4.229
  and Introduction, p. 58). That process
  begins in this first soliloquy, in which

Thou shouldst be coloured thus. You married ones,
If each of you should take this course, how many
Must murder wives much better than themselves
For wrying but a little! O Pisanio,   5
Every good servant does not all commands,
No bond but to do just ones. Gods, if you
Should have ta'en vengeance on my faults, I never
Had lived to put on this; so had you saved
The noble Innogen to repent, and struck   10
Me, wretch, more worth your vengeance. But alack,
You snatch some hence for little faults; that's love,
To have them fall no more; you some permit
To second ills with ills, each elder worse,
And make them dread ill, to the doer's thrift.   15
But Innogen is your own. Do your blest wills,
And make me blest to obey. I am brought hither
Among th'Italian gentry, and to fight

15 ill] OXFORD; it F   16 blest] OXFORD (*conj.* Johnson); best F

Posthumus makes it clear that he has forgiven Innogen *before* discovering that she was innocent; this expresses his love for her more convincingly than his earlier protestations and wagers.

1 **once wished** Although the odd construction 'I am wisht' in F is paralleled elsewhere, it gives the wrong sense and gets the whole soliloquy off on the wrong foot; Kellner's *once wished* has the advantage of emphasizing that he wishes it no longer.

2 **You married ones** This specific address to at least a part of the audience helps to involve his hearers in his situation, as Innogen's does in 3.6: they must now go through Posthumus' ordeal with him, as they shared hers.

3 **take this course** do as I have done

4 **much . . . themselves** This phrase is important in establishing Posthumus' forgiveness of Innogen.

5 **wrying** erring
  but only

6 **does not** does not carry out

7 **No bond but** having no obligation except

7–8 **if . . . have** if you had

9 **put on** instigate
  this i.e. Innogen's murder

12 **love** i.e. a sign of love

13 **fall** sin

13–15 **you . . . thrift** you allow some people to reinforce one sin with another, each worse than the one before, and then cause them to shun sinning, to their advantage (in contrast to Innogen, who was struck down and had no such chance to repent)

14 **elder** later (with the implication of maturing, accumulating *ills*; see the previous note)

15 **ill** Oxford's emendation of F's 'it', assuming a spelling 'il', which *OED* records, clarifies the sense of this dense passage.

16 **Innogen is your own** This idea is developed from *that's love* (l. 12); behind both lines perhaps lies St Paul's Epistle to the Hebrews 12: 6: 'whom the Lord loveth he chasteneth'. Compare Jupiter's 'Whom best I love, I cross' (5.3.195).
  blest Oxford's emendation of F's 'best' is supported by 'sacred wills' (*Winter's Tale* 3.3.7), as well as providing an apt symmetry with 'blest' in the next line (*Textual Companion*, p. 608).

Against my lady's kingdom. 'Tis enough
That, Britain, I have killed thy mistress; peace,   20
I'll give no wound to thee. Therefore, good heavens,
Hear patiently my purpose. I'll disrobe me
Of these Italian weeds, and suit myself
As does a Briton peasant.
       ⌈*He disrobes himself*⌉
                          So I'll fight
Against the part I come with; so I'll die   25
For thee, O Innogen, even for whom my life
Is every breath a death; and thus unknown,
Pitied nor hated, to the face of peril
Myself I'll dedicate. Let me make men know
More valour in me than my habits show.   30
Gods, put the strength o'th' Leonati in me.
To shame the guise o'th' world, I will begin
The fashion: less without and more within.   *Exit*

5.2 ⌈*A march.*⌉ *Enter Lucius, Giacomo, and the Roman
        army at one door, and the Briton army at another,
        Leonatus Posthumus following like a poor soldier.*

20 mistress; peace] F; mistress-piece OXFORD (*conj.* Staunton, *cited in* Furness)   24 *He disrobes himself*] OXFORD; *not in* F
   5.2.0.1 *A march*] OXFORD; *not in* F

20 **mistress; peace** Oxford's reading 'mistress-piece', recorded elsewhere and
formed according to *OED* on analogy
with 'masterpiece', seems to me exces-
sively mannered. Oxford argue that it is
not clear why Posthumus should say
peace to Britain, but since he is refusing
to make war against Britain with the
Roman army, it seems quite clear.
23 **weeds** clothes. He is probably wearing
Roman armour (or at least a breastplate
and helmet). If, as Oxford's stage direction at l. 24 suggests, he *disrobes* at this
point (and not offstage), it would be a
simple matter to remove those, revealing
the *Briton peasant* clothes, or lack of
them, underneath. In several modern
productions, the disrobing has been
very thorough, taking *naked breast*
(5.4.4) literally. In the 1988 National
Theatre version, especially, he became a
reduced figure: naked, bloodsoaked,

with the *bloody cloth* wrapped round his
head like a guerilla's balaclava (see fig.
4). This emphasized that Posthumus
undergoes a physical and spiritual purgatory like his wife's in 4.2, and made the
other characters' failure to recognize him
wholly plausible.
23 **suit** dress
25 **part** side
27 **Is...death** every breath I take is death to
me (because I killed Innogen)
28 **Pitied** neither pitied
30 **habits** clothes (i.e. those of a British peasant)
32 **guise** practice
32-3 **begin | The fashion** i.e. start a new
fashion
33 **less...within** less (i.e. the peasant's garb)
on the outside, more (i.e. his valour)
inside
5.2 The Folio text presents the battle as a
continuous sequence; Oxford divides it

They march over and go out. ⌈Alarums.⌉ Then enter
again in skirmish Giacomo and Posthumus: he
vanquisheth and disarmeth Giacomo, and then
leaves him

GIACOMO

The heaviness and guilt within my bosom
Takes off my manhood. I have belied a lady,
The princess of this country, and the air on't
Revengingly enfeebles me; or could this carl,
A very drudge of nature's, have subdued me   5
In my profession? Knighthoods and honours borne
As I wear mine are titles but of scorn.
If that thy gentry, Britain, go before
This lout as he exceeds our lords, the odds
Is that we scarce are men and you are gods.   *Exit*   10

The battle continues. ⌈Alarums. Excursions. The
trumpets sound a retreat.⌉ The Britons fly, Cymbeline
is taken. Then enter to his rescue Belarius, Guiderius,
and Arviragus

BELARIUS

Stand, stand, we have th'advantage of the ground.

0.4 *Alarums*] CAPELL; *not in* F   10.1–2 *Alarums . . . retreat*] OXFORD; *not in* F

into three short scenes, starting new ones
at ll. 10.1 and 13.3. F's continuity is
surely a theatrical advantage. The two
armies march and countermarch across
the stage without actually engaging in
combat, suggesting a stylized treatment,
with the action pausing for brief spoken
passages that focus attention on two crucial events, the Posthumus–Giacomo
duel and the defeat of the Roman army
in the narrow lane.
There are no sound cues in the Folio text.
Of those provided here, the opening
march is clearly required to accompany
the marching armies; the others are
standard directions in Shakespearian
battle scenes, and perhaps help to chart
the stages of the sequence.

0.4 *Alarums* A technical term for sounds on
trumpets and/or drums to indicate an
attack.
1 **within my bosom** weighing upon my
heart

2 **Takes off** removes
  belied slandered
3 **on't** of it
4 **carl** peasant (used disparagingly)
5 **drudge** slave
6 **my profession** It comes as a surprise
that Giacomo, who has been presented
as a machiavellian seducer, thinks of
himself as a professional soldier; but
Roman civilians were expected to turn
their hands to military service. This
is perhaps the moment when the
tension between the two views of
Rome in the play—the classical and
the Renaissance Italian—is most noticeable.
7 **but of scorn** only contemptible
8 **go before** surpass
9 **odds** chances, probability
10.1 *Excursions* A standard term in Shakespearian stage directions (though here
editorial), often with *alarums*, to suggest
both a physical skirmish and trumpet
calls.

The lane is guarded. Nothing routs us but
The villainy of our fears.
GUIDERIUS *and* ARVIRAGUS Stand, stand, and fight.

> *Enter Posthumus like a poor soldier, and seconds the*
> *Britons. They rescue Cymbeline and exeunt.*
> [*The trumpets sound a retreat,*] *then enter Lucius,*
> *Giacomo, and Innogen as Fidele*

LUCIUS (*to Innogen*)
Away boy, from the troops, and save thyself;
For friends kill friends, and the disorder's such   15
As war were hoodwinked.
GIACOMO   'Tis their fresh supplies.
LUCIUS
It is a day turned strangely. Or betimes
Let's reinforce, or fly.   *Exeunt*

5.3   *Enter Posthumus like a poor soldier, and a Briton Lord,*
          severally

LORD
Cam'st thou from where they made the stand?
POSTHUMUS   I did,
Though you, it seems, come from the fliers.
LORD   Ay.
POSTHUMUS
No blame be to you sir, for all was lost,
But that the heavens fought. The King himself

13.1 *like a poor soldier*] *not in* F   13.3 *The . . . retreat*] OXFORD; *not in* F   13.4 *as Fidele*] *not in* F
   5.3.0.1 *like a poor soldier*] *not in* F   0.2 *severally*] *not in* F   2 Ay] OXFORD (*conj.* Craig, *cited in*
Dowden); I did F

12 **routs** defeats
13.1 *seconds* reinforces
16 **As** as if
   hoodwinked blindfolded
   supplies reinforcements
17 **Or betimes** either before it is too late
5.3.2 **Ay** W. J. Craig, *cited in* Dowden, conjectured that the compositor, instead of
   reading 'Ay' (spelt 'I'), erroneously
   repeated *I did* from the previous line. If
   F1's *I did* is retained, F3's emendation of
   come to 'came' helps the sense.

4–51 Posthumus' account of the battle
   resembles a messenger's in Greek tragedy; the difference is that here the audience has already seen what he describes.
   Possible explanations of the duplication
   are considered in the Introduction,
   pp. 53 and 74. His narration is based on
   a passage in Holinshed's *Chronicles*
   which can sometimes clarify phrases
   where Posthumus' language becomes
   convoluted to the point of incoherence.
4 **But** had it not been

Of his wings destitute, the army broken, 5
And but the backs of Britons seen, all flying
Through a strait lane; the enemy full-hearted,
Lolling the tongue with slaught'ring, having work
More plentiful than tools to do't, struck down
Some mortally, some slightly touched, some falling 10
Merely through fear, that the strait pass was dammed
With dead men hurt behind, and cowards living
To die with lengthened shame.

LORD   Where was this lane?

POSTHUMUS

Close by the battle, ditched, and walled with turf,
Which gave advantage to an ancient soldier, 15
An honest one, I warrant, who deserved
So long a breeding as his white beard came to
In doing this for's country. Athwart the lane
He with two striplings—lads more like to run
The country base than to commit such slaughter; 20
With faces fit for masks, or rather fairer
Than those for preservation cased, or shame—

5 **Of . . . destitute** having lost his wings (military divisions). Holinshed, who also uses this compressed phrase, clarifies it: the Danes 'rushed forth with such violence upon their adversaries, that first the right, and then after the left wing of the Scots, was constrained to . . . flee' (Bullough, p. 48).
6 **but** nothing but
7, 11 **strait** narrow
7 **full-hearted** full of confidence
8 **Lolling the tongue** with their tongues hanging out in their eagerness (like wild beasts)
9 **tools** weapons (or perhaps more generally 'means')
10 **touched** wounded
11 **dammed** blocked (as a stream is by a *dam*)
12 **behind** in the back (as they were running away—a mark of cowardice; contrast the death of the valiant Young Siward at *Macbeth* 5.11.12–13, who 'had . . . his hurts before . . . on the front')
13 **lengthened** prolonged through the rest of their life
15 **ancient** Not just 'old', but implying 'of noble descent', as at *1 Henry IV* 3.2.104, where Hotspur is commended

for inspiring 'ancient lords and reverend bishops'.
16 **honest** worthy
   I warrant I guarantee (an emphatic phrase)
16–17 **who . . . to** This phrase has caused much dispute (summarized in Furness, pp. 360–1), but I think that *deserved* picks up from *ancient* and *honest*, and that the phrase means 'was worthy of his noble ancestry (*breeding*) which was as *long* as his beard' (*OED*, *deserve*, v. 3). Perhaps Posthumus suspects that, like himself, Belarius is not the peasant that he seems.
18 **for's** for his
   Athwart (standing) across
19 **striplings** youths
19 20 **run . . . base** play the rural game of prisoner's base (which involves running between two 'bases' or opposing camps)
21 **faces . . . masks** complexions so beautiful that, like women's, they needed to be protected by masks
22 **for . . . shame** covered for protection, or out of modesty (but, Posthumus says, they were *fairer* than those women who needed such masks)

Made good the passage, cried to those that fled
'Our Britain's harts die flying, not her men.
To darkness fleet souls that fly backwards. Stand,   25
Or we are Romans, and will give you that
Like beasts which you shun beastly, and may save
But to look back in frown. Stand, stand.' These three,
Three thousand confident, in act as many—
For three performers are the file when all   30
The rest do nothing—with this word 'Stand, stand',
Accommodated by the place, more charming
With their own nobleness, which could have turned
A distaff to a lance, gilded pale looks;
Part shame, part spirit renewed, that some, turned
          coward   35
But by example—O a sin in war,
Damned in the first beginners!—gan to look
The way that they did and to grin like lions
Upon the pikes o'th' hunters. Then began
A stop i'th' chaser; a retire; anon   40

---

24 harts] POPE 1728 (*conj.* Theobald); hearts F   her] THIRLBY (*cited in* Furness); our F

23 **Made . . . passage** blocked the exit
24 **harts** deer
25 **To darkness . . . backwards** i.e. those who desert are damned
   fleet hurry
26 **are Romans** will behave like Romans
27 **beasts** fierce animals
   beastly like (cowardly) animals
27–8 **may . . . frown** (you) may prevent simply (*but*) by turning and facing the enemy fiercely (*in frown*)
29 **Three thousand confident** as confident as if they were three thousand
30 **are the file** practically constitute the whole army
32 **Accommodated** given an advantage
   more charming winning over more men
33–4 **turned . . . lance** i.e. made a woman fight
34 **distaff** a pole used in spinning (symbolizing women, as in 'on the distaff side')
   gilded gave colour to
35 **Part . . . renewed** F's punctuation at the end of the previous line, followed here, implies a new sentence with this cryptic phrase, which would mean 'Shame motivated some, spirit others'; but F

may be wrong, and *These three* (l. 28) may be the subject of *renewed*, meaning that they renewed a sense of shame in one part of the British army and the spirit of courage in another, which perhaps makes better sense, though either is possible in this breathless, headlong speech.
36 **But by example** only because they saw others do so
37 **first beginners** i.e. the original cowards
   gan began
37–8 **look | The way** face in the direction
38 **they** i.e. *These three* (l. 28)
38–9 **grin . . . hunters** As the Britons turn and face the Romans, they are compared to hunted and cornered lions: the battle becomes increasingly ferocious.
38 **grin** i.e. bare their teeth in anger
39 **pikes** spears
40 **stop i'th' chaser** halt on the part of the pursuer. A *stop* is a technical term from riding, when a horse is checked suddenly and thrown on to its haunches.
   retire retreat
   anon immediately

A rout, confusion thick; forthwith they fly
Chickens the way which they stooped eagles: slaves,
The strides they victors made; and now our cowards,
Like fragments in hard voyages, became
The life o'th' need. Having found the back door open   45
Of the unguarded hearts, heavens, how they wound!
Some slain before, some dying, some their friends
O'erborne i'th' former wave, ten chased by one,
Are now each one the slaughterman of twenty.
Those that would die or ere resist are grown   50
The mortal bugs o'th' field.

LORD   This was strange chance:
A narrow lane, an old man, and two boys.

POSTHUMUS
Nay, do not wonder at it: you are made
Rather to wonder at the things you hear

---

42 stooped] ROWE; stopt F   43 they] THEOBALD; the F

---

41 **rout** disorderly flight (a military term:
*OED sb.*² 1)
confusion thick rapid destruction
41–2 **they . . . eagles** The Romans run away
like chickens along the same route down
which they had formerly swooped as if
they were eagles.
42 **stooped** descended swiftly (like a bird of
prey on its victim: *OED v.*¹ 6a). This
emendation of F's 'stopt', probably
caught by the compositor from *stop* in
l. 40, is made virtually certain by l. 210,
where Jupiter's eagle *Stooped, as to foot us*
(see the note).
42–3 **slaves . . . made** they retraced as
slaves the strides they had taken as
victors
44 **fragments . . . voyages** i.e. scraps of food
to fall back on as a last resort. Compare
As You Like It 2.7.39–40: 'as dry as the
remainder biscuit | After a voyage'.
45 **life o'th' need** means of life in time of
need
45–6 **Having . . . hearts** i.e. finding the backs
of the fleeing Romans unprotected
hearts Perhaps 'fellows'; or perhaps *heart*
stands for the whole body, vulnerable as
its owner runs away, or is used in its
figurative sense as the seat of courage
(*OED sb.* 11a) which no longer guards it.
46–8 **heavens . . . wave** The Folio punctuation here makes the exact meaning

uncertain. C. J. Sisson interprets: 'In the
confusion they strike indiscriminately, at
dead bodies, at dying men, and some of
these their own friends struck down in a
previous assault' (*New Readings in Shakespeare* (Cambridge, 1956), ii. 285). But
most editors treat F's 'heauens, how they
wound,' as an exclamation, and begin a
new sentence at *Some slain before* (l. 47),
which then becomes one of the subjects
of the sentence, implying that dead men
get up and fight; this is not impossible,
since it would give the battle a surreal,
nightmarish tone which would correspond to Posthumus' highly-wrought
state of mind, and lead naturally into
his equally surreal vision of his dead
family (ll. 123.1 ff.).
48–9 **ten . . . twenty** ten (Britons) who
were formerly pursued by (one)
Roman now slaughter twenty (Romans)
each
50 **or ere resist** before they would fight (*or ere*
is emphatic)
51 **mortal bugs** death-dealing terrors
field battle-field
53 **Nay . . . wonder** Editors sometimes suspect a lacuna in the sense here; but
why? Posthumus scornfully mocks the
lord for his *wonder*, adding that *wonder*
is all he is good for. No emendation is
needed.

Than to work any. Will you rhyme upon't,   55
And vent it for a mock'ry? Here is one:
'Two boys, an old man—twice a boy—a lane,
Preserved the Britons, was the Romans' bane.'

LORD
Nay, be not angry sir.

POSTHUMUS   'Lack, to what end?
Who dares not stand his foe, I'll be his friend,   60
For if he'll do as he is made to do,
I know he'll quickly fly my friendship too.
You have put me into rhyme.

LORD   Farewell, you're angry.

Exit

POSTHUMUS
Still going? This is a lord. O noble misery,
To be i'th' field and ask 'What news?' of me.   65
Today how many would have given their honours
To have saved their carcasses—took heel to do't,
And yet died too. I, in mine own woe charmed,
Could not find death where I did hear him groan,
Nor feel him where he struck. Being an ugly monster,   70
'Tis strange he hides him in fresh cups, soft beds,
Sweet words, or hath more ministers than we

64 This is] F; This OXFORD (*conj.* Ritson)   72 more] F (moe)

55 **work any** perform any deeds yourself
56 **vent** utter, proclaim (literally 'give out to the air', from Latin *ventus*, wind). Shakespeare frequently uses *vent* in this sense, usually as a verbal mannerism, mocked by Feste at *Twelfth Night* 4.1.11–16; it is appropriate to this context of satirical rhyming.
   for a mock'ry as an occasion for derision, as a joke
   one i.e. a rhyme
57 **twice a boy** i.e. in his 'second childhood' (proverbial: 'Old men are twice children', Tilley M570)
58 **bane** ruin
59 **'Lack** alack
60 **stand** confront, stand up to
61 **made** created (i.e. as a coward by nature)
62 **fly my friendship** (so that I won't have to put up with him)
63 **put . . . rhyme** made me start rhyming too
64 **going** running away

64 **This is a lord** Oxford, reading 'This a lord?', argue that 'F's extrametrical "is" adds nothing, since "This" could be used as a contraction of "This is"' (*Textual Companion* p. 608; Abbott §461). But the line cannot be said to be very regular even with the contraction, and the bald statement, with its four monosyllables, seems to me to express Posthumus' laconic irony more effectively than the emendation.
   noble misery wretched state of one who is called 'noble' (the phrase is an oxymoron)
67 **took heel** ran away ('took to his heels')
68 **too** anyway
   in . . . charmed my wretchedness causing me to live a 'charmed life' (Maxwell)
71–2 **hides . . . words** i.e. appears where you least expect him
72 **ministers** agents

That draw his knives i'th' war. Well, I will find him;
For being now a favourer to the Briton,
No more a Briton, I have resumed again   75
The part I came in. Fight I will no more,
But yield me to the veriest hind that shall
Once touch my shoulder. Great the slaughter is
Here made by th' Roman; great the answer be
Britons must take. For me, my ransom's death,   80
On either side I come to spend my breath,
Which neither here I'll keep nor bear again,
But end it by some means for Innogen.
          Enter two Briton Captains, and soldiers
FIRST CAPTAIN
Great Jupiter be praised, Lucius is taken.
'Tis thought the old man and his sons were angels.   85
SECOND CAPTAIN
There was a fourth man, in a silly habit,
That gave th'affront with them.
FIRST CAPTAIN   So 'tis reported,
But none of 'em can be found. Stand, who's there?
POSTHUMUS   A Roman,
Who had not now been drooping here if seconds   90
Had answered him.

83.1 *Briton*] *not in* F

74–6 **For . . . in** This passage has caused
  much dispute (summarized in Furness,
  pp. 366–7). Some think that death is
  the *favourer to the Briton* (by enabling
  the Britons to kill their enemies); but
  this makes the transition to *No more a
  Briton* very difficult. I think that Posthumus refers to himself, not death, at l. 74,
  and that the passage means: 'having
  recently been a supporter of the Britons,
  I am no more a Briton, but have become
  again the Roman I was at the start.' This
  follows reasonably from his intention to
  find death (l. 73), and leads logically into
  the following lines, where, as a Roman,
  he expects to be killed during a retaliatory
  massacre (ll. 78–80).
74 **now** just now, lately
  Briton the British side, Britons
77 **veriest hind** merest peasant (or perhaps
  veriest is literally 'truest', unlike Posthumus himself, who is a fake peasant)

78 **touch my shoulder** i.e. arrest me. At
  Errors 4.2.37, an arresting officer is
  described as a 'shoulder-clapper'.
79 **Roman** the Roman side, Romans
  answer retaliation
  be must be
81 **spend my breath** i.e. use it up (spend it in
  ransom?), die
82 **here . . . again** preserve here nor carry
  away with me
86 **silly** rustic (*OED a.* 3). *Silly* is a later form
  of Middle English 'seely', to which Oxford
  alters it here; but the senses given by *OED*
  under *seely* stress innocence rather than
  rusticity (though the meanings are
  related), and although 'silly' is somewhat
  misleading to a modern audience, 'seely'
  is meaningless, so it seemed best to
  retain F.
87 **gave th'affront** undertook the assault
90 **seconds** reinforcements
91 **answered him** acted as he did

SECOND CAPTAIN (*to soldiers*) Lay hands on him : a dog,
   A leg of Rome shall not return to tell
   What crows have pecked them here. He brags his service
   As if he were of note. Bring him to th' King.
      [*Flourish.*] *Enter Cymbeline* [*and Lords*], *Belarius,*
      Guiderius, Arviragus, Pisanio, and Roman captives.
      The Captains present Posthumus to Cymbeline, who
      delivers him over to a Jailer. [*Exeunt all but Posthumus*
      and two Jailers, who chain his legs and wrists]

FIRST JAILER
   You shall not now be stol'n, you have locks upon you.   95
   So graze as you find pasture.
SECOND JAILER   Ay, or a stomach.
                                             Exeunt Jailers

POSTHUMUS
   Most welcome bondage, for thou art a way,
   I think, to liberty. Yet am I better
   Than one that's sick o'th' gout, since he had rather
   Groan so in perpetuity than be cured   100
   By th' sure physician, death, who is the key
   T'unbar these locks. My conscience, thou art fettered
   More than my shanks and wrists. You good gods give me
   The penitent instrument to pick that bolt,

94.1 *Flourish*] *not in* F   *and Lords*] *not in* F   94.4 *Exeunt*] *not in* F   94.4–5 *all but . . . wrists*]
OXFORD (*subs.*); *Scena Quarta.* | *Enter Posthumus, and Gaoler.* F   95 FIRST] *not in* F
96.1 *Exeunt Jailers*] *not in* F

91–2 **a dog,** | **A leg** i.e. not even a Roman
dog or leg ('not the slightest bit of Rome')
94 **note** high rank (or 'worthy of note'; compare 4.3.44)
94.1–5 *Flourish . . . wrists* There are problems with the Folio text at this point,
which are discussed in the Introduction,
pp. 74–5. The scene as it stands is best
treated as a triumphant procession
across the stage for the victors of the
battle, during which Posthumus is
handed over to two jailers, who remain
on stage for a brief exchange while the
procession leaves—in which case F's
Scenes 3 and 4 become one continuous
scene, as here.
   legs . . . wrists See l. 103.
95–6 **locks . . . pasture** Animals had weights

fixed to one leg to prevent them from
straying when they grazed on open
land. This phrase makes it clear that
Posthumus is chained by the leg (probably to one of the pillars towards the front
of the Jacobean stage), the length of
chain giving him the freedom to move
about, and eventually to fall asleep in
the most convenient position for his
ghostly family to *circle . . . round* him
(ll. 123.7–8).
 96 **pasture** good feeding grass
     stomach appetite
103 **shanks** legs
104 **penitent instrument** penitence (seen as
     an *instrument* for picking locks) to free his
     conscience which is *fettered*, weighed
     down, by guilt (l. 102)

Then free for ever. Is't enough I am sorry?   105
So children temporal fathers do appease;
Gods are more full of mercy. Must I repent,
I cannot do it better than in gyves
Desired more than constrained. To satisfy,
If of my freedom 'tis the main part, take   110
No stricter render of me than my all.
I know you are more clement than vile men
Who of their broken debtors take a third,
A sixth, a tenth, letting them thrive again
On their abatement: that's not my desire.   115
For Innogen's dear life take mine, and though
'Tis not so dear, yet 'tis a life; you coined it.
'Tween man and man they weigh not every stamp;
Though light, take pieces for the figure's sake;
You rather mine, being yours. And so, great powers,   120
If you will make this audit, take this life,

---

110 main part] F; mainport NOSWORTHY (*conj.* A. Walker)   121 make] HUDSON 1881 (*conj.*
Daniel); take F

---

105 **free** i.e. in death
107 **Must** I if I am to
108 **gyves** bonds, fetters
109 **Desired . . . constrained** voluntary
rather than compelled
satisfy atone, make satisfaction
110 **If . . . part** if it is the most important
element in freeing me from guilt
110–11 **take . . . all** take nothing less as a
repayment than everything I have (i.e.
my life). For the force of *render* here, and
his offer of his life for Innogen's (l. 116),
compare Sonnet 125.12: 'mutual render, only me for thee'.
112 **clement** merciful
vile men This probably implies usurers,
moneylenders who take interest, in view
of what follows.
113–15 **Who . . . abatement** who only
take a third, or a sixth, or a tenth part
of their debtors' possessions, thus allowing them to earn more on what little is
left
115 **abatement** reduced amount. This line
antedates *OED*'s first example (1624) of
this commercial sense.
that's . . . desire i.e. I don't want even a
little to be left me; take everything

116 **dear** Both 'valuable' and 'beloved'.
117 **dear** valuable
coined created (sustaining the connection between human and financial
value)
118 **'Tween man and man** i.e. in business
transactions between men
weigh (to test for counterfeit coins)
stamp coin (with the sovereign's image
stamped on it)
119 **light** Both 'deficient in weight' (and so
counterfeit) and 'morally deficient' (and
so of less worth than Innogen).
take pieces accept the coins
figure i.e. the image stamped on the
coin
120 **You . . . yours** you should be the more
inclined to accept mine, since the *figure* is
of you (Posthumus is made in the image
of the gods)
121 **make this audit** settle this account. This
probably makes better sense than F's
'take this Audit' ('accept this account-
ing'). The 'take . . . take' symmetry in F's
line may be deliberate, but by the
same token error would have been
'exceptionally easy' (*Textual Companion*,
p. 609).

And cancel these cold bonds. O Innogen,
I'll speak to thee in silence.

> *He sleeps. Solemn music. Enter, as in an apparition,*
> *Sicilius Leonatus, father to Posthumus, an old man,*
> *attired like a warrior, leading in his hand an ancient*
> *matron, his wife, and mother to Posthumus, with*
> *music before them. Then, after other music, follows*
> *the two young Leonati, brothers to Posthumus, with*
> *wounds as they died in the wars. They circle Posthumus*
> *round as he lies sleeping*

SICILIUS

No more, thou thunder-master, show
   Thy spite on mortal flies.   125
With Mars fall out, with Juno chide,
   That thy adulteries
Rates and revenges.
Hath my poor boy done aught but well,

123.1 *He sleeps*] not in F

122 **cancel . . . bonds** There is triple word-play here: (a) cancel these dead financial agreements (once they are paid); (b) take my life (compare *Richard III* 4.4.77: 'Cancel his bond of life'); (c) remove these metal fetters.

123.1 *as in an apparition* Although this phrase may derive from Ralph Crane, the scribe who probably prepared the Folio text, rather than from the copy before him (see Introduction, p. 73), it usefully focuses the nature of this episode: it is and is not *an apparition*. It is on one level an externalization of Posthumus' dream: we see on stage what he is dreaming about. But it is also an 'objective' ghostly visitation, since the ghosts leave a *tablet* with him (ll. 203, 204.1–2).

123.3–4 *an ancient matron* We know from 1.1.37 that Sicilius was an old man, but since his wife died in childbirth she can't have been all that *ancient*; perhaps the adjective is Ralph Crane's (see the previous note)—or perhaps this is how Posthumus thinks of the mother he never knew.

123.5 *music before . . . after* The music is discussed in Appendix B.

124–86 **No more . . . fly** The basic rhythmic unit of the ghosts' speeches is the rhyming 'fourteener', a long fourteen-syllable line, as the Folio makes clear when it prints (for example) ll. 126–7 (*With Mars . . . adulteries*) as one line. In general, however, F sets out these long lines as two shorter ones, followed here. For further discussion, see the Introduction, p. 55.

124 **thunder-master** i.e. Jupiter, the king of the gods, and employer of thunderbolts (see l. 186.2)

125 **spite . . . flies** For the idea, compare *Tragedy of Lear* 4.1.37–8: 'As flies to wanton boys are we to th' gods; | They kill us for their sport.'
  flies i.e. insignificant things

126 **Mars** the god of war
  fall out quarrel
  Juno Jupiter's wife, with whom he was often at odds because of his affairs with mortals

128 **Rates** berates, reproves

129 **aught** anything

Whose face I never saw? 130
I died whilst in the womb he stayed,
    Attending nature's law,
Whose father then—as men report
    Thou orphans' father art—
Thou shouldst have been, and shielded him 135
    From this earth-vexing smart.

MOTHER

Lucina lent not me her aid,
    But took me in my throes,
That from me was Posthumus ripped,
    Came crying 'mongst his foes, 140
A thing of pity.

SICILIUS

Great nature like his ancestry
    Moulded the stuff so fair
That he deserved the praise o'th' world
    As great Sicilius' heir. 145

FIRST BROTHER

When once he was mature for man,
    In Britain where was he
That could stand up his parallel,
    Or fruitful object be
In eye of Innogen, that best 150
    Could deem his dignity?

132 **Attending nature's law** awaiting nature's decree (that he should be born). Compare *Winter's Tale* 2.2.62–4: 'This child was prisoner to the womb, and is | By law and process of great nature thence | Freed'.

134 **Thou . . . art** This echoes Psalm 68: 5, where God is 'a father of the fatherless'.

136 **earth-vexing smart** suffering that afflicts earthly life (compare modern 'earth-shattering')

137 **Lucina** goddess of childbirth (invoked at *Pericles* Sc. 11.10–11 as 'Divinest patroness, and midwife gentle' to a wife who then appears to die in childbirth)

138 **took** (in death)
throes labour pains

139 **That** with the result that
ripped i.e. removed by Caesarean section, like Macduff, who was 'from his mother's womb | Untimely ripped' (*Macbeth* 5.10.15–16)

140 **'mongst his foes** into a hostile world

142–3 **nature . . . fair** nature combined with his parents to create him so well

143 **stuff** substance out of which something is made (*OED sb.*[1] 3a)

146 **mature for man** grown up

149 **fruitful** promising good results

151 **deem his dignity** judge his worth. This echoes the First Gentleman's *how she esteemed him* (1.1.52), and the First Brother's speech as a whole restates the Gentleman's general eulogy of Posthumus.

MOTHER

> With marriage wherefore was he mocked,
>> To be exiled, and thrown
> From Leonati seat and cast
>> From her his dearest one,   155
> Sweet Innogen?

SICILIUS

> Why did you suffer Giacomo,
>> Slight thing of Italy,
> To taint his nobler heart and brain
>> With needless jealousy,   160
> And to become the geck and scorn
>> O'th' other's villainy?

SECOND BROTHER

> For this from stiller seats we came,
>> Our parents and us twain,
> That striking in our country's cause   165
>> Fell bravely and were slain,
> Our fealty and Tenantius' right
>> With honour to maintain.

FIRST BROTHER

> Like hardiment Posthumus hath
>> To Cymbeline performed.   170
> Then Jupiter, thou king of gods,
>> Why hast thou thus adjourned
> The graces for his merits due,
>> Being all to dolours turned?

---

161 geck] CAPELL; geeke F

---

154 **Leonati seat** This literally means 'the abode of the Leonati family', but since Posthumus is a commoner who is unlikely to have a family *seat*, it must be figurative, implying that he was disgraced by being *exiled* and deprived of the family honour due to him.
157 **suffer** allow
158 **Slight** worthless
161 **geck** dupe (a Midlands dialect word: Wright, *Dialect Dictionary*, *sb.*²). Nosworthy compares the balanced phrase

geck and scorn with *geck and gull* at *Twelfth Night* 5.1.340.
163 **stiller seats** calmer regions. They have come from the Elysian Fields (l. 191), the abode of the blessed spirits in classical mythology.
167 **fealty** allegiance owing to a lord
Tenantius See note to 1.1.29–31.
169 **Like hardiment** similar deeds of valour
172 **adjourned** deferred
174 **dolours** sorrows

SICILIUS

> Thy crystal window ope, look out,   175
> 　No longer exercise
> Upon a valiant race thy harsh
> 　And potent injuries.

MOTHER

> Since, Jupiter, our son is good,
> 　Take off his miseries.   180

SICILIUS

> Peep through thy marble mansion, help,
> 　Or we poor ghosts will cry
> To th' shining synod of the rest
> 　Against thy deity.

BROTHERS

> Help, Jupiter, or we appeal,   185
> 　And from thy justice fly.

Jupiter descends in thunder and lightning, sitting upon
an eagle. He throws a thunderbolt. The ghosts fall on
their knees

JUPITER

No more you petty spirits of region low
　Offend our hearing. Hush! How dare you ghosts
Accuse the thunderer, whose bolt, you know,
　Sky-planted, batters all rebelling coasts?   190

---

175 look] F2; looke, | looke F1

175 **crystal** transparent (like crystal)
　ope open
177 **race** family
181 **marble mansion** i.e. the heavens (look-
　ing like marble in colour or texture; see
　the note to l. 214)
182–4 **cry . . . deity** make an appeal to the
　remainder of the gods gathered in assem-
　bly (*synod*) against your justice as a god
　(as if to a higher court)
186.1 **descends** The area above the Eliza-
　bethan and Jacobean stage was known
　as 'the heavens', and usually housed
　flying apparatus operated by a winch.
　Characters descended in a chair or
　'throne'; perhaps the head, wings, and
　claws of the eagle were a façade fixed to
　the front of the chair, so that Jupiter
　appeared to be *sitting upon an eagle*. For
　further discussion, see Introduction,
　pp. 2–3, 11–12.

186.1 **thunder and lightning** These were
　probably sound effects combined with
　fireworks. The *thunderbolt* was also
　probably a firework effect, though
　Stanley Wells in his Globe Theatre
　lecture (see Introduction, p. 55, note
　1) cites a more elaborate technical
　device from a contemporary Italian
　source. The sound is discussed in
　Appendix B.
187–8 **No more . . . hearing** The lack of
　punctuation in F, followed here, may
　imply that Jupiter is not addressing
　them directly, but saying 'Let not you
　spirits . . . offend our hearing any
　more'—distancing himself, pulling rank
　on them.
187 **region low** Even Elysium (see l. 191)
　seems *low* when viewed from Jupiter's
　palace on Mount Olympus.
190 **Sky-planted** stationed in the heavens

Poor shadows of Elysium, hence, and rest
   Upon your never-withering banks of flowers.
Be not with mortal accidents oppressed;
   No care of yours it is, you know 'tis ours.
Whom best I love, I cross, to make my gift,   195
   The more delayed, delighted. Be content.
Your low-laid son our godhead will uplift.
   His comforts thrive, his trials well are spent.
Our Jovial star reigned at his birth, and in
   Our temple was he married. Rise, and fade.   200
He shall be lord of Lady Innogen,
   And happier much by his affliction made.
This tablet lay upon his breast, wherein
   Our pleasure his full fortune doth confine.
    ⌈*He gives the ghosts a tablet which they lay upon*
    Posthumus' breast⌉
And so away; no farther with your din   205
   Express impatience, lest you stir up mine.
   Mount eagle, to my palace crystalline.
                   He ascends into the heavens

SICILIUS
He came in thunder, his celestial breath

204.1–2 *He . . . breast*] *not in* F   207.1 *He . . . heavens*] *Ascends* F

---

191 **Elysium** the classical equivalent of heaven
193 **accidents** events
195–6 **Whom . . . delighted** This suggestion
  that happiness is only achieved after
  enduring great trials, thus making it the
  more appreciated, might be a summary
  of the action of the play.
196 **delighted** (the more) delighted in
198 **well are spent** Nosworthy suggests that
  well means 'well-nigh (almost) over';
  but it could equally mean that Posthumus' trials have been used to a good
  end.
199 **Jovial star** the planet Jupiter
203 **tablet** a sheet of writing within elaborate covers (see note to l. 227)
204 **full** complete
  confine enclose
207 **palace crystalline** Jupiter's palace seems
  to be made of, or as transparent as, crystal, though it is said to be marble at ll.

181 and 214. In the Ptolemaic astro-
nomical system, the 'crystalline heaven'
was supposed to be one or more spheres
next to the firmament (*OED*, *crystalline, a.*
5); in Fairfax's *Godfrey of Bulloigne*
(1600), 9.60–1, an angel with 'golden
feathers' (compare the eagle here) flies
to earth past the 'circle crystalline' and
the planet Jupiter (compare l. 199 and
note); so *crystalline* may evoke the situation rather than the material of Jupiter's
palace among the stars.
207.1 *the heavens* See note to l. 186.1.
208–16 **He . . . behest** The ghosts originally
spoke in 'fourteeners'; Jupiter used
iambic quatrains; now Sicilius speaks in
blank verse, perhaps to suggest that the
dream vision is fading, and to provide a
transition back to the 'normal' world,
and the blank verse that regularly
expresses it, just before Posthumus
wakes.

Was sulphurous to smell; the holy eagle
Stooped, as to foot us; his ascension is   210
More sweet than our blest fields; his royal bird
Preens the immortal wing and claws his beak
As when his god is pleased.

ALL THE GHOSTS   Thanks, Jupiter.

SICILIUS

The marble pavement closes, he is entered
His radiant roof. Away, and to be blest,   215
Let us with care perform his great behest.

The ghosts vanish

POSTHUMUS (*awakes*)

Sleep, thou hast been a grandsire, and begot
A father to me; and thou hast created
A mother and two brothers. But, O scorn,
Gone! They went hence so soon as they were born;   220
And so I am awake. Poor wretches that depend
On greatness' favour dream as I have done,

212 Preens] F (Prunes)   claws] F (cloyes)   216.1 *The ghosts*] *not in* F   217 *awakes*] *not in* F

209 **sulphurous** Sulphur was (wrongly) associated with thunder and lightning; Pisanio speaks of 'stones of sulphur' at 5.4.240. Perhaps this refers to the smell of gunpowder probably used in the fireworks for Jupiter's entry.

210 **Stooped . . . us** swooped as if to seize us in its talons

210–11 **his ascension . . . fields** His ascent is more calm (or perhaps more sweet-smelling, contrasting with his *sulphurous* descent) than the Elysian fields themselves.

212 **Preens** trims the feathers with its beak. *OED*, *prune*, *v.*¹ regards F's 'Prunes' as synonymous with *preen*.
claws scratches with its talons (as a dog scratches its face with its paws). *OED* cites F's 'cloyes' as its only example of *cloy*, *v.*², 'but the form seems clearly related to *cly*, *clye*, *clee*, *cloy* (*v.*¹), and *claw*, each in a range of spellings, all with variants of the same sense, and all but *claw* now obsolete' (*Textual Companion*, p. 609). Both the clawing and the preening (see the previous note) are expressions of contentment because *his god is pleased* (l. 213).

214 **marble . . . closes** It has been suggested that this is a literal description of Jupiter's

exit on the Jacobean stage, with the trapdoor in the floor of 'the heavens' painted to resemble *marble*; but as Stanley Wells points out (see Introduction, p. 55, note 1), 'perhaps the epithets are intended simply to give an impression of the splendour in which the god lives' (p. 14).

216 **behest** command

216.1 **vanish** leave the stage. Perhaps they simply glided off through the stage doors, or perhaps something more spectacular was contrived, as possibly for the witches at *Macbeth* 1.3.76.1 and 4.1.148.1. They cannot have disappeared down the trapdoor since that would provide the wrong symbolism: the area beneath the Jacobean stage was known as 'the hell', and these spirits have come from *blest fields* (l. 211).

217–20 **Sleep . . . born** Although the apparitions sequence has been criticized as an interpolation, these lines indicate one of its dramatic functions, a wishfulfilment for Posthumus: at this low point in his fortunes, he dreams of the family he has never known and longs for—only to *Wake and find nothing* (l. 223).

219 **scorn** (i.e. what a bad joke)

Wake and find nothing. But, alas, I swerve.
Many dream not to find, neither deserve,
And yet are steeped in favours; so am I,   225
That have this golden chance and know not why.
What fairies haunt this ground? A book? O rare one,
Be not, as is our fangled world, a garment
Nobler than that it covers. Let thy effects
So follow to be most unlike our courtiers,   230
As good as promise.

     He reads

'Whenas a lion's whelp shall, to himself unknown, without seeking find, and be embraced by a piece of tender
air; and when from a stately cedar shall be lopped
branches, which being dead many years, shall after   235
revive, be jointed to the old stock, and freshly grow,
then shall Posthumus end his miseries, Britain be fortunate and flourish in peace and plenty.'
'Tis still a dream, or else such stuff as madmen
Tongue, and brain not; either both, or nothing,   240
Or senseless speaking, or a speaking such
As sense cannot untie. Be what it is,
The action of my life is like it, which I'll keep,

---

223 **swerve** go astray (i.e. am wrong)
224 **dream . . . deserve** do not dream of finding anything, and don't deserve to either
225 **so am I** This picks up from *deserve*: Posthumus is still in the grip of low self-esteem.
226 **golden** See note to 4.2.263.
   chance piece of good fortune (presumably his glimpse of his dead family)
227 **book** The *tablet* (l. 203) in its covers looks like a book; but *book* could mean a single leaf (*OED sb.* 1), and may here.
   rare exceptional, exquisite
228 **fangled** foppish, obsessed with fashion (compare modern 'new-fangled')
229 **effects** i.e. what the book has to say
230 **to** as to
231 **As . . . promise** live up to their promise
232 **Whenas** when
   whelp cub
233–4 **piece . . . tender air** ' "tender air" being [Latin] *mulier*, a woman, the word "piece" is probably chosen because it was often used of persons, and often as

indicating supreme excellence' (Dowden).
236 **stock** trunk (and figuratively, line of descent)
239 **stuff** nonsense (as at *Tempest* 2.1.259)
240 **Tongue, and brain not** talk about but do not understand (or perhaps 'do not make sense'). The use of the nouns as verbs here is characteristically Shakespearian, as is the thorny complexity of the following lines, discussed further in the Introduction, p. 56.
   both i.e. dream and madness
241 **Or senseless speaking** either meaningless utterance
241–2 **such . . . untie** too cryptic for reason to work out
242 **Be . . . is** whatever it is
243–4 **The . . . sympathy** However weird the situation, it is no stranger than what has happened to Posthumus in the 'ordinary' course of his life—lines which can be applied to the play as a whole. See the Introduction, p. 56.
243 **which** i.e. the tablet

If but for sympathy.
>   *Enter Jailer*

JAILER Come sir, are you ready for death?   245

POSTHUMUS Over-roasted rather; ready long ago.

JAILER Hanging is the word, sir. If you be ready for that, you are well cooked.

POSTHUMUS So if I prove a good repast to the spectators, the dish pays the shot.   250

JAILER A heavy reckoning for you sir. But the comfort is you shall be called to no more payments, fear no more tavern bills, which are as often the sadness of parting as the procuring of mirth. You come in faint for want of meat, depart reeling with too much drink, sorry that you   255 have paid too much and sorry that you are paid too much; purse and brain both empty: the brain the heavier for being too light; the purse too light, being drawn of heaviness. Of this contradiction you shall now be quit. O the charity of a penny cord, it sums up thousands in a   260 trice. You have no true debitor and creditor but it: of

253 are as] MAXWELL (*conj.* Collier); are F   259 Of] GLOBE; Oh, of F

244 **If but for sympathy** if only because I am in the same situation

245 JAILER Since F does not bring the second jailer back on stage, there is no need to distinguish this one as 'FIRST JAILER' in the speech-prefixes.

245–98 The Jailer's prose is highly organized, its formally balanced phrases suggesting the complacent professional, the man who has frequently seen death and 'knows all about it', set against the simple phrases of Posthumus, the man who is about to experience it.

245–7 **ready . . . Over-roasted . . . Hanging** Posthumus applies the Jailer's *ready* to food with *Over-roasted*; the Jailer responds with a pun on *Hanging* (death, and hanging up raw meat to mature).

250 **dish . . . shot** the food (i.e. Posthumus) pays the reckoning (i.e. is worth what it costs)
    shot Wright says that *shot* was 'in general dialect and colloquial use' for a bill or reckoning, 'especially used of tavern accounts' (*Dialect Dictionary*, *sb.*[1] 1).

251–64 The Jailer picks up Posthumus' *shot* (see previous note) and develops it into an elaboration of the proverb 'Death pays all debts' (Tilley D148).

251 **reckoning** settling of an account

256–7 **are . . . much** i.e. punished for it (by excess of drink)

257–8 **heavier . . . light** more overwhelmed for being too thoughtless

258 9 **drawn of heaviness** emptied of what makes it heavy (i.e. money)

259 **Of** F's 'Oh, of' probably anticipates the start of the next sentence (Maxwell).
    contradiction (being both light and heavy)
    quit acquitted, freed

260 **penny** i.e. very cheap
    cord (regularly used of a hangman's rope: *OED sb.*[1] 1b)
    sums up pays the reckoning for (and 'disposes of')

260–1 **in a trice** Not just 'quickly', as now, but 'in a single pull'.

261 **debitor and creditor** reckoning of accounts. This seems to have been a catch-phrase; *OED, creditor*, 2, cites a 1543 title-page: 'A profitable treatise . . . to learn . . . the keeping of the famous reckoning, called . . . Debitor and Creditor'. The two words refer to the two columns in a ledger.
    debitor *OED* calls this 'a by-form of

what's past, is, and to come the discharge. Your neck, sir, is pen, book, and counters; so the acquittance follows.

POSTHUMUS I am merrier to die than thou art to live.   265

JAILER Indeed sir, he that sleeps feels not the toothache; but a man that were to sleep your sleep, and a hangman to help him to bed, I think he would change places with his officer; for look you sir, you know not which way you shall go.   270

POSTHUMUS Yes indeed do I, fellow.

JAILER Your death has eyes in's head, then. I have not seen him so pictured. You must either be directed by some that take upon them to know, or take upon yourself that which I am sure you do not know, or jump the after-   275
enquiry on your own peril; and how you shall speed in your journey's end I think you'll never return to tell on.

POSTHUMUS I tell thee, fellow, there are none want eyes to direct them the way I am going, but such as wink and will not use them.   280

JAILER What an infinite mock is this, that a man should have the best use of eyes to see the way of blindness! I am

---

274 or take] CAPELL; or to take F   277 on] F (one)

DEBTOR, current from 15th to 17th c., *esp.* in Book-keeping'. This 'by-form' is probably chosen because it makes the phrase more balanced, in keeping with the style of the speech as a whole.

262 **what's past . . . discharge** This phrase resembles *Tempest* 2.1.258–9: 'what's past is prologue, what to come | In yours and my discharge': there *discharge* refers to theatrical performance, here to payment.

263 **counters** round pieces of metal used for reckoning. The Clown at *Winter's Tale* 4.3.35 cannot add up without them.
   acquittance acquittal

266 **he . . . toothache** This sounds proverbial, but is not recorded.

267 **a man that were** if a man were going

269 **officer** i.e. the hangman

272 **death** death's-head, skull

273 **pictured** depicted. The skull has no *eyes*, only empty sockets.

274 **take upon them** profess
   take upon yourself undertake

275–6 **jump . . . after-enquiry** hazard the interrogation after death (or perhaps 'final judgement')

277 **on** of. Maxwell's emendation (or interpretation) of F's 'one' is supported by F's printing 'one' for 'on' at (for example) 5.4.134. Maxwell is probably right in saying that 'the sentence runs more naturally than with the rather formal "one" as object', though 'tell one' (tell anyone) makes sense.

278 **want** lack

279 **wink** shut their eyes. As Maxwell points out, this 'embroiders' the proverb 'Who so blind as he that will not see?' (Tilley S206).

281 **mock** jibe

282–3 If *blindness* is metaphorical ('ignorance'), perhaps *of winking* means 'for those who shut their eyes' (compare l. 279), but in view of the play's insist-

sure hanging's the way of winking.

Enter a Messenger

MESSENGER Knock off his manacles, bring your prisoner to
the King.   285

POSTHUMUS Thou bring'st good news, I am called to be
made free.

JAILER I'll be hanged then.

POSTHUMUS Thou shalt be then freer than a jailer; no bolts
for the dead.   ⌈*Exeunt Posthumus and Messenger*⌉   290

JAILER Unless a man would marry a gallows and beget
young gibbets, I never saw one so prone. Yet on my
conscience, there are verier knaves desire to live, for all
he be a Roman; and there be some of them too that die
against their wills; so should I, if I were one. I would we   295
were all of one mind, and one mind good. O, there were
desolation of jailers and gallowses! I speak against my
present profit, but my wish hath a preferment in't. *Exit*

5.4   *Flourish. Enter Cymbeline, Belarius, Guiderius,*
Arviragus, Pisanio, and Lords

CYMBELINE (*to Belarius, Guiderius, and Arviragus*)
Stand by my side, you whom the gods have made

---

290 *Exeunt Posthumus and Messenger*] F2 (*Exeunt.*); *not in* F   298 *Exit*] F2 ; *Exeunt.* F1
5.4] This edition ; *Scena Quinta.* F   0.1 *Flourish*] *not in* F

ence on death being like a sleep (2.2.31,
4.2.216–17), *winking* may simply mean
'sleeping'.

287 **made free** i.e. in death (Posthumus
assumes that he is being taken to execution)

288 **I'll . . . then** The Jailer uses an emphatic
catchphrase ; Posthumus takes it literally
in his reply.

289–90 **Thou . . . dead** This sounds like an
exit line, and F2 duly provides an *Exeunt*.
Oxford argue that the 'Jailer's final
speech can be spoken partly to Posthumus, partly aside, partly to the messenger, as he is unlocking Posthumus' leg-
irons' (*Textual Companion*, p. 609). But
this ignores the convention that soliloquies are spoken directly to the audience,
and the manacles can be swiftly removed
if the locks aren't real ones, as the Messenger's *Knock off* may imply.

289 **bolts** fetters

292 **prone** apt, eager (for death)

293 **verier** truer
for all even though

294 **them** i.e. Romans

294–5 **that . . . wills** i.e. despite their apparent stoic indifference to death

297 **desolation** i.e. total absence of
gallowses This might appear to be
the error of a 'low-life' character, but
OED sb. I records it as a genuine
sixteenth- and seventeenth-century
plural.

298 **preferment** promotion (either because
his 'pious wish will stand [him] in good
stead in the next world' (Maxwell) or
because a world so virtuous as to have
no need of jailers could offer him better
employment)

5.4 The theatrical *tour de force* of this final
scene is discussed in the Introduction,
p. 57.

Preservers of my throne. Woe is my heart
That the poor soldier that so richly fought,
Whose rags shamed gilded arms, whose naked breast
Stepped before targs of proof, cannot be found.   5
He shall be happy that can find him, if
Our grace can make him so.

BELARIUS   I never saw
Such noble fury in so poor a thing,
Such precious deeds in one that promised naught
But beggary and poor looks.

CYMBELINE   No tidings of him?   10

PISANIO
He hath been searched among the dead and living,
But no trace of him.

CYMBELINE   To my grief I am
The heir of his reward, which I will add
(*To Belarius, Guiderius, and Arviragus*)
To you, the liver, heart, and brain of Britain,
By whom I grant she lives. 'Tis now the time   15
To ask of whence you are. Report it.

BELARIUS   Sir,
In Cambria are we born, and gentlemen.
Further to boast were neither true nor modest,
Unless I add we are honest.

CYMBELINE   Bow your knees.
        They kneel. He knights them
Arise my knights o'th' battle. I create you   20
Companions to our person, and will fit you

---

5 targs] F (Targes)   19.1 *They kneel. He knights them*] not in F

3 **richly** nobly, to such good effect
4 **naked** unprotected by armour, as at
  Othello 5.2.265: 'naked as I am, I
  will assault thee'. But see the note to
  5.1.23.
5 **Stepped before** Either literally 'stood in
  front of' or figuratively 'surpassed'.
  targs of proof impenetrable shields. *Targs*
  is Oxford's spelling, to make it clear that
  F's 'Targes' is a monosyllable.
7 **grace** favour
13 **heir of his reward** inheriting the reward
  that should be his
14 **liver . . . brain** Supposed in contemporary

physiology to be the seats of passion,
affection, and judgement; compare
Twelfth Night 1.1.36.
15 **grant** acknowledge
16 **of whence** from where
17 **are** were
20 **knights o'th' battle** 'Knighthood con-
  ferred on the battle-field was specially
  honourable' (Dowden), as at *King John*
  1.1.53–4: 'A soldier, by the honour-
  giving hand | Of Coeur-de-lion knighted
  in the field'. The ancient Britons are here
  seen as medieval knights.
21 **fit** supply

With dignities becoming your estates.
> *Belarius, Guiderius, and Arviragus rise.*
> *Enter Cornelius and Ladies*
There's business in these faces. Why so sadly
Greet you our victory? You look like Romans,
And not o'th' court of Britain.
CORNELIUS   Hail great King!   25
To sour your happiness I must report
The Queen is dead.
CYMBELINE   Who worse than a physician
Would this report become? But I consider
By med'cine life may be prolonged, yet death
Will seize the doctor too. How ended she?   30
CORNELIUS
With horror, madly dying, like her life,
Which being cruel to the world, concluded
Most cruel to herself. What she confessed
I will report, so please you. These her women
Can trip me if I err, who with wet cheeks   35
Were present when she finished.
CYMBELINE   Prithee say.
CORNELIUS
First, she confessed she never loved you, only
Affected greatness got by you, not you;
Married your royalty, was wife to your place,
Abhorred your person.
CYMBELINE   She alone knew this,   40
And but she spoke it dying, I would not
Believe her lips in opening it. Proceed.
CORNELIUS
Your daughter, whom she bore in hand to love

22.1 *Belarius . . . rise*] *not in* F

22 **estates** (new) rank
23 **business** matter of great importance
27–30 **Who . . . too** Maxwell calls this
   speech 'ludicrous' (p. xxxv); but is it
   not explicable as the embarrassed and
   embarrassing kind of thing that
   people say when faced with the shock of
   death?
35 **trip me** catch me out, point out my

mistakes
38 **Affected** longed for
   by through
41 **but** were it not for the fact that
   spoke it dying Alluding to the
   proverb 'dying men speak true' (Tilley
   M514).
42 **opening** discharging
43 **bore in hand** pretended

243

With such integrity, she did confess
Was as a scorpion to her sight, whose life,   45
But that her flight prevented it, she had
Ta'en off by poison.
CYMBELINE   O most delicate fiend!
Who is't can read a woman? Is there more?
CORNELIUS
More sir, and worse. She did confess she had
For you a mortal mineral, which being took,   50
Should by the minute feed on life, and, ling'ring,
By inches waste you. In which time, she purposed
By watching, weeping, tendance, kissing, to
O'ercome you with her show; and in time,
When she had fitted you with her craft, to work   55
Her son into th'adoption of the crown;
But failing of her end by his strange absence,
Grew shameless-desperate, opened in despite
Of heaven and men her purposes, repented
The evils she hatched were not effected; so   60
Despairing died.
CYMBELINE   Heard you all this, her women?
⌈A LADY⌉
We did, so please your highness.
CYMBELINE   Mine eyes
Were not in fault for she was beautiful,
Mine ears that heard her flattery, nor my heart
That thought her like her seeming. It had been vicious   65

---

62 LADY] F4; *La.* F1   64 heard] F3; heare F1

---

47 **Ta'en off** killed
   delicate Both 'beautiful' and 'crafty'.
50 **mortal mineral** fatal poison
51 **by the minute** minute by minute
52 **waste** consume
53 **watching** staying awake at night (by the
   King's sickbed)
   tendance attention
54 **show** pretence
   in time eventually. Oxford, suspecting
   contamination from *In which time* (l. 52),
   reads 'in fine' ('in the end'), an idiom
   frequently occurring elsewhere in Shakespeare (*Textual Companion*, p. 609). But F

makes good sense, indeed virtually the
same sense.
55 **fitted you** shaped you, made you fit for
   her purpose; or perhaps 'disposed of you'
   (Dowden), or 'tortured, as by fits' (Nos-
   worthy, citing Sonnet 119.7–8: 'fitted |
   In the distraction of this madding fever')
56 **adoption of** being adopted (by you) as heir
   to
58 **opened** revealed
62 LADY F's *La.* is ambiguous, but it is best to
   avoid choral speaking, especially on the
   modern stage.
65 **seeming** appearance

To have mistrusted her. Yet, O my daughter,
That it was folly in me thou mayst say,
And prove it in thy feeling. Heaven mend all!

Enter Lucius, Giacomo, Soothsayer, and other Roman
prisoners, Posthumus behind, and Innogen as Fidele,
all guarded by Briton soldiers

Thou com'st not, Caius, now for tribute. That
The Britons have razed out, though with the loss   70
Of many a bold one; whose kinsmen have made suit
That their good souls may be appeased with slaughter
Of you their captives, which ourself have granted,
So think of your estate.

LUCIUS

Consider, sir, the chance of war. The day   75
Was yours by accident. Had it gone with us,
We should not, when the blood was cool, have threatened
Our prisoners with the sword. But since the gods
Will have it thus, that nothing but our lives
May be called ransom, let it come. Sufficeth   80
A Roman with a Roman's heart can suffer.
Augustus lives to think on't; and so much
For my peculiar care. This one thing only
I will entreat: my boy, a Briton born,

He presents Innogen to Cymbeline

Let him be ransomed. Never master had   85
A page so kind, so duteous, diligent,
So tender over his occasions, true,

68.2–3 *as Fidele . . . soldiers*] *not in* F   84.1 *He . . . Cymbeline*] *not in* F

65 **had been vicious** would have been reprehensible
67 **it** i.e. trusting her
68 **in thy feeling** through your experience
68.2 *behind* i.e. not clearly visible either to the audience or to those on stage
70 **razed out** scraped out (as when altering a written agreement)
71 **made suit** petitioned
72 **their** i.e. the dead Britons'
72–3 **their . . . captives** For the barbaric tone, compare *Titus* 1.1.125–6: 'die he must | T'appease their groaning shadows that

are gone', though there the barbarism is the Romans'; here it is contrasted with the 'high' Roman tone of ll. 75–83.
74 **estate** position, predicament (or perhaps 'spiritual state', about to die)
80 **called** named (i.e. the only ransom that can be allowed is our lives)
    Sufficeth it suffices
82 **think on't** (with the implication 'and revenge it', a characteristic piece of stoic understatement)
83 **peculiar care** personal concern
87 **tender . . . occasions** thoughtful of his (master's) needs

So feat, so nurse-like; let his virtue join
With my request, which I'll make bold your highness
Cannot deny. He hath done no Briton harm,   90
Though he have served a Roman. Save him, sir,
And spare no blood beside.
CYMBELINE   I have surely seen him;
His favour is familiar to me. Boy,
Thou hast looked thyself into my grace,
And art mine own. I know not why, wherefore,   95
To say 'Live, boy'; ne'er thank thy master; live,
And ask of Cymbeline what boon thou wilt
Fitting my bounty and thy state, I'll give it,
Yea, though thou do demand a prisoner
The noblest ta'en.
INNOGEN   I humbly thank your highness.   100
LUCIUS
I do not bid thee beg my life, good lad,
And yet I know thou wilt.
INNOGEN   No, no, alack,
There's other work in hand. I see a thing
Bitter to me as death. Your life, good master,
Must shuffle for itself.
LUCIUS   The boy disdains me,   105
He leaves me, scorns me: briefly die their joys
That place them on the truth of girls and boys.
Why stands he so perplexed?
CYMBELINE   What wouldst thou, boy?
I love thee more and more; think more and more
What's best to ask. Know'st him thou look'st on? Speak,   110

88 **feat** graceful
89 **make** be
92 **And . . . beside** even if you spare no one
     else
93 **favour** face
94 **looked . . . grace** won my favour by your
     looks
95 **wherefore** for what reason (simply
     underlining *why*, perhaps by drawing
     on the proverbial 'There is never a why
     but there is a wherefore', Tilley W331)
96 **ne'er . . . master** i.e. it is not his plea that
     has saved you
98 **state** rank

99–100 **a . . . ta'en** the noblest prisoner taken
103 **thing** (probably her ring on Giacomo's
     finger)
105 **shuffle** shift. This phrase is characteris-
     tic of Innogen's instinctive pursuit of
     truth even to the point of tactlessness or
     even cruelty, as Lucius' reaction attests.
106–7 **briefly . . . boys** Proverbial: 'Love of
     lads . . . is soon in and soon out' (Tilley
     L526).
106 **briefly** quickly
107 **truth** loyalty
     girls and boys i.e. mere children
108 **perplexed** distressed. See note to 3.4.7.

Wilt have him live? Is he thy kin, thy friend?

INNOGEN

He is a Roman, no more kin to me
Than I to your highness, who, being born your vassal,
Am something nearer.

CYMBELINE   Wherefore ey'st him so?

INNOGEN

I'll tell you, sir, in private, if you please   115
To give me hearing.

CYMBELINE   Ay, with all my heart,
And lend my best attention. What's thy name?

INNOGEN

Fidele, sir.

CYMBELINE   Thou'rt my good youth, my page.
I'll be thy master. Walk with me, speak freely.
         Cymbeline and Innogen speak apart

BELARIUS (*aside to Guiderius and Arviragus*)
Is not this boy revived from death?

ARVIRAGUS   One sand another   120
Not more resembles: that sweet rosy lad
Who died, and was Fidele! What think you?

GUIDERIUS   The same dead thing alive.

BELARIUS

Peace, peace, see further; he eyes us not, forbear.
Creatures may be alike. Were't he, I am sure   125
He would have spoke to us.

GUIDERIUS   But we see him dead.

BELARIUS

Be silent; let's see further.

PISANIO (*aside*)   It is my mistress.

119.1 *Cymbeline...apart*] *not in* F   121 resembles:] JOHNSON (*subs.*); resembles‸ F   lad]
HANMER; Lad: F

113 **vassal** subject
120–2 **One . . . Fidele** The general sense
is that one grain of sand does not
resemble another grain more than this
person resembles Fidele. Perhaps a
clarifying line has dropped out;
perhaps this is simply an extreme
example of Shakespeare's elliptical late
style.
126 **we . . . dead** Perhaps *see* should be

emended to 'saw' (Rowe 1714); perhaps
it is an archaic past tense (Maxwell); but
it probably means 'But we see him, who
was dead, alive again', in which case
Guiderius repeats the point made in his
previous speech, entirely understandably
in what Dowden calls 'the fluctuations of
wonder, of faith and unfaith' in the episode.

Since she is living, let the time run on
To good or bad.
CYMBELINE (*to Innogen*) Come, stand thou by our side,
Make thy demand aloud. (*To Giacomo*) Sir, step you forth.   130
Give answer to this boy, and do it freely,
Or by our greatness and the grace of it,
Which is our honour, bitter torture shall
Winnow the truth from falsehood. (*To Innogen*) On,
     speak to him.
INNOGEN
My boon is that this gentleman may render   135
Of whom he had this ring.
POSTHUMUS (*aside*)   What's that to him?
CYMBELINE (*to Giacomo*)
That diamond upon your finger, say,
How came it yours?
GIACOMO
Thou'lt torture me to leave unspoken that
Which to be spoke would torture thee.
CYMBELINE   How, me?   140
GIACOMO
I am glad to be constrained to utter that
Torments me to conceal. By villainy
I got this ring; 'twas Leonatus' jewel,
Whom thou didst banish; and which more may grieve
     thee,
As it doth me, a nobler sir ne'er lived   145
'Twixt sky and ground. Wilt thou hear more, my lord?
CYMBELINE
All that belongs to this.

134 On] F (One)   142 Torments] HUDSON 1881 (*conj.* Ritson); Which torments F

134 **Winnow** separate (as a thresher separates grain from chaff). Cymbeline, in threatening Giacomo, uses a figurative expression that Giacomo himself used to praise Innogen's perfection at 1.6.177–8.
135 **render** declare
140 **How, me** i.e. in what way would it torture me?
141 **constrained** compelled

141 **that** what
142 F's 'Which' at the start of this line is probably a slip, repeating in ll. 141–2 the *that* | *Which* of ll. 139–40; omitting it makes the line flow better, as Maxwell says.
145–6 **a nobler . . . ground** Giacomo uses the same wide-ranging expression to convey Posthumus' perfection that he had used to express Innogen's at 1.6.32–6.

GIACOMO   That paragon thy daughter,
For whom my heart drops blood, and my false spirits
Quail to remember—give me leave, I faint.

CYMBELINE
My daughter? What of her? Renew thy strength.   150
I had rather thou shouldst live while nature will
Than die ere I hear more. Strive man, and speak.

GIACOMO
Upon a time—unhappy was the clock
That struck the hour—it was in Rome—accursed
The mansion where—'twas at a feast—O would   155
Our viands had been poisoned, or at least
Those which I heaved to head!—the good Posthumus—
What should I say? He was too good to be
Where ill men were, and was the best of all
Amongst the rar'st of good ones—sitting sadly,   160
Hearing us praise our loves of Italy
For beauty that made barren the swelled boast
Of him that best could speak; for feature laming
The shrine of Venus or straight-pitched Minerva,
Postures beyond brief nature; for condition,   165

---

164 straight-pitched] F (straight-pight)

---

151 **while nature will** the rest of your natural life

153–209 Giacomo's narration contains the
most tortuous language in the play, so
that Cymbeline has to keep interrupting
to bring him back to the point. For
further discussion, see the Introduction,
pp. 57–8.

153–60 **Upon . . . sadly** The frequent dashes
here, reflecting the colons or brackets of
the Folio, indicate the impressionistic,
fragmented nature of Giacomo's speech.
The main sentence is merely 'Once at a
feast in Rome, Posthumus, sitting
sadly . . .'

153 **Upon a time** A contraction of 'once
upon a time'.

156 **viands** food

157 **heaved to head** raised to my mouth

158 **too good** Giacomo restates the First Gentleman's eulogy of Posthumus from
1.1.17–54, but now the audience is
aware of the distance between that

ideal and Posthumus' actual behaviour,
at least in the scene Giacomo is describing.

160 **rar'st** most exceptional

162–5 The rest of the speech itemizes the
mistresses' various qualities: they were
praised *For beauty*, *for feature*, and *for
condition*.

162–3 **made . . . speak** exceeded the greatest
praise of the most expert speaker

163 **feature** shape or looks
laming making seem lame

164 **shrine** i.e. body of Venus, goddess of
love, imaged as a holy *shrine*
straight-pitched *Pitched* means 'erected,
fixed', as a tent is pitched, so the whole
phrase means 'erect in bearing'.
Minerva goddess of arts and war

165 **Postures** (who have) characteristic
forms
beyond brief nature surpassing those of
mortal beings
condition character

A shop of all the qualities that man
Loves woman for; besides that hook of wiving,
Fairness which strikes the eye—
CYMBELINE   I stand on fire.
  Come to the matter.
GIACOMO   All too soon I shall,
  Unless thou wouldst grieve quickly. This Posthumus,   170
  Most like a noble lord in love and one
  That had a royal lover, took his hint,
  And not dispraising whom we praised—therein
  He was as calm as virtue—he began
  His mistress' picture, which by his tongue being made,   175
  And then a mind put in't, either our brags
  Were cracked of kitchen-trulls, or his description
  Proved us unspeaking sots.
CYMBELINE   Nay, nay, to th' purpose.
GIACOMO
  Your daughter's chastity—there it begins.
  He spake of her as Dian had hot dreams   180
  And she alone were cold; whereat I, wretch,
  Made scruple of his praise, and wagered with him
  Pieces of gold 'gainst this which then he wore
  Upon his honoured finger, to attain
  In suit the place of's bed and win this ring   185
  By hers and mine adultery. He, true knight,
  No lesser of her honour confident
  Than I did truly find her, stakes this ring—
  And would so had it been a carbuncle

---

177 cracked] F (crak'd)

166 **shop** store. Compare Sonnet 24.7: 'my
  bosom's shop'.
167 **hook of wiving** bait of marriage. The
  fairness in the next line is the *hook*, as in
  fish-hook, which lures one into marriage.
169 **matter** point
172 **hint** opportunity
176 **And . . . in't** i.e. he described her intellect
  as part of her *picture*
177 **cracked of kitchen-trulls** uttered as if
  they were simply boasting about
  kitchen-maids
178 **unspeaking sots** fools unable to speak
  (and to describe our loves)

178 **to th' purpose** come to the point
180–1 **as Dian . . . cold** as if the goddess of
  chastity herself were lustful, and Innogen
  alone were chaste
182 **Made scruple of** disputed
185 **In suit** by wooing
186 **hers . . . adultery** my adultery and hers.
  The word-order is to emphasize *adultery*.
  For the idiom, see Abbott §238.
187–8 **No lesser . . . find her** i.e. he was not
  more confident about her honour than
  was justified by her behaviour
189 **would so** would have done so
  carbuncle a precious stone

Of Phoebus' wheel, and might so safely had it   190
Been all the worth of's car. Away to Britain
Post I in this design. Well may you, sir,
Remember me at court, where I was taught
Of your chaste daughter the wide difference
'Twixt amorous and villainous. Being thus quenched   195
Of hope, not longing, mine Italian brain
Gan in your duller Britain operate
Most vilely; for my vantage, excellent.
And, to be brief, my practice so prevailed
That I returned with simular proof enough   200
To make the noble Leonatus mad
By wounding his belief in her renown
With tokens thus and thus: averring notes
Of chamber-hanging, pictures, this her bracelet—
O cunning, how I got it!—nay, some marks   205
Of secret on her person, that he could not
But think her bond of chastity quite cracked,
I having ta'en the forfeit. Whereupon—
Methinks I see him now—
POSTHUMUS (*coming forward*) Ay, so thou dost,
Italian fiend! Ay me, most credulous fool,   210
Egregious murderer, thief, anything
That's due to all the villains past, in being,
To come! O give me cord, or knife, or poison,

---

205 got it] F2; got F1   209 *coming forward*] *not in* F

190 **Of Phoebus' wheel** from the wheel of the chariot of Apollo, the sun god (described in Ovid's *Metamorphoses*, 2.107–10)
   might so might have done so
191 **all . . . car** worth his entire chariot
192 **Post** hurry
   design scheme
195 **'Twixt . . . villainous** He draws a distinction between Innogen's loving faithfulness to Posthumus and shameful behaviour, either his own or what he wanted her to do.
195–6 **Being . . . longing** having my hopes ended thus, but not my desires
196–7 **Italian brain . . . duller Britain** Giacomo exploits the stereotypes of the machiavellian Italian and the northerner whose climate was supposed to make him dull-witted.
198 **vantage** profit
199 **practice** trickery
200 **simular** simulated
202 **renown** reputation
203 **thus and thus** of this and that kind
   averring notes providing evidence
207 **cracked** broken
208 **forfeit** something which is due by a breach of contract, here Innogen's and Posthumus' wedding contract, the *bond of chastity* of l. 207.
211 **Egregious** shocking
211–12 **anything | That's due** any name which is applicable
213 **cord** rope (to hang myself). See the note to 5.3.260.

251

Some upright justicer! Thou King, send out
For torturers ingenious. It is I   215
That all th'abhorrèd things o'th' earth amend
By being worse than they. I am Posthumus,
That killed thy daughter—villain-like, I lie,
That caused a lesser villain than myself,
A sacrilegious thief, to do't. The temple   220
Of virtue was she; yea, and she herself.
Spit and throw stones, cast mire upon me, set
The dogs o'th' street to bay me. Every villain
Be called Posthumus Leonatus, and
Be villainy less than 'twas! O Innogen!   225
My queen, my life, my wife, O Innogen,
Innogen, Innogen!

INNOGEN (*running to embrace him*)
                          Peace, my lord, hear, hear.

POSTHUMUS
Shall's have a play of this? Thou scornful page,
There lie thy part.

        He strikes her down

PISANIO   O gentlemen, help
Mine and your mistress. O my lord Posthumus,   230
You ne'er killed Innogen till now. Help, help!
(*To Innogen*) Mine honoured lady.

CYMBELINE   Does the world go round?

---

225 villainy] F; villain MAXWELL   227 *running to embrace him*] *not in* F   229 *He strikes her
down*] *not in* F   help_∧] STEEVENS 1778; helpe, F

214 **justicer** judge
216 **amend** make (seem) better
220 **sacrilegious thief** Pisanio is described as
sacrilegious because Innogen is the *temple
| Of virtue*, but why is he a *thief*? Because
he robs the temple, or her of life? I suspect
that Thomas Underdowne's translation
of Heliodorus' *Ethiopica* was running
through Shakespeare's mind (see the
Introduction, p. 21) and that he echoes
his own reference to its 'Egyptian thief' at
Twelfth Night 5.1.116.
220–1 **The ... virtue** Innogen is described as
the goddess of love was at l. 164.
221 **she herself** virtue itself
223 **bay** bark at (a hunting term)
225 **Be ... 'twas** (by comparison with what I

have done). Maxwell alters *villainy* to 'villain' to improve the metre; the sense is
virtually the same.
228 **Shall's** must we
229 **There ... part** lying there is your role
He ... down For a discussion of this
climactic moment, see the Introduction,
pp. 58–9.
229–30 **help ... mistress** Most editors make
this two exclamations, but F's 'helpe,'
can equally be interpreted as here. The
same might apply at ll. 231–2, but *Mine
honoured lady* does sound as if it is
addressed to Innogen.
230 **Mine ... mistress** your mistress and
mine. See note to l. 186.
231 **ne'er** never

POSTHUMUS
　How comes these staggers on me?
PISANIO (*to Innogen*)   Wake, my mistress.
CYMBELINE
　If this be so, the gods do mean to strike me
　To death with mortal joy.   235
PISANIO (*to Innogen*)　How fares my mistress?
INNOGEN　O get thee from my sight!
　Thou gav'st me poison. Dangerous fellow, hence.
　Breathe not where princes are.
CYMBELINE   The tune of Innogen.
PISANIO
　Lady, the gods throw stones of sulphur on me if   240
　That box I gave you was not thought by me
　A precious thing, I had it from the Queen.
CYMBELINE
　New matter still.
INNOGEN   It poisoned me.
CORNELIUS   O gods!
　I left out one thing which the Queen confessed
　(*To Pisanio*) Which must approve thee honest. 'If Pisanio 245
　Have', said she, 'given his mistress that confection
　Which I gave him for cordial, she is served
　As I would serve a rat.'
CYMBELINE   What's this, Cornelius?
CORNELIUS
　The Queen, sir, very oft importuned me
　To temper poisons for her, still pretending   250

233 **staggers** A disease, usually of horses, which causes them to walk unsteadily. **Wake** recover, 'come round'. Posthumus has hit her so hard that she is momentarily unconscious.
235 **mortal joy** Either 'earthly joy', or 'a joy so great that I might die of it'. Compare *Pericles* Sc. 21.180–2: 'this great sea of joys rushing upon me | [May] O'erbear the shores of my mortality | And drown me with their sweetness!' Although F gives this speech to Cymbeline, its combination of ecstasy and violence sounds much more like Posthumus, so perhaps F's speech-prefix is wrong.
239 **tune of Innogen** Not just the sound of her voice, which he has already heard

and not recognized, but the imperious remark about *princes*. It is ironical that Innogen should be most recognizable when attacking the character who has been unswervingly loyal to her.
240 **stones of sulphur** thunderbolts (see note to 5.3.209)
244 **I . . . confessed** In performance, laughter at this line allows a relief from the intensity of the preceding episode.
245 **approve** prove
246 **confection** compound, drug
247 **for cordial** as a restorative
249 **importuned** The stress falls on the second syllable.
250 **temper** concoct, mix
　　still pretending always claiming

The satisfaction of her knowledge only
In killing creatures vile, as cats and dogs
Of no esteem. I, dreading that her purpose
Was of more danger, did compound for her
A certain stuff which, being ta'en, would cease   255
The present power of life, but in short time
All offices of nature should again
Do their due functions. (*To Innogen*) Have you ta'en
  of it?

INNOGEN
Most like I did, for I was dead.

BELARIUS (*aside to Guiderius and Arviragus*) My boys,
There was our error.

GUIDERIUS   This is sure Fidele.   260

INNOGEN (*to Posthumus*)
Why did you throw your wedded lady from you?
Think that you are upon a rock, and now
Throw me again.
            She embraces him

POSTHUMUS   Hang there like fruit, my soul,
Till the tree die.

CYMBELINE (*to Innogen*) How now, my flesh, my child?
What, mak'st thou me a dullard in this act?   265

---

261 from] ROWE; fro F   262 rock] F; lock NEILSON–HILL (*conj.* Dowden)   263 *She embraces him*] *not in* F

253 **esteem** value
254 **of more danger** more harmful
255 **stuff** substance
    cease halt
257 **offices of nature** natural faculties
258 **Do** carry out
259 **like** likely
260 **sure** certainly
262 **upon a rock** Most modern editors emend *rock* to 'lock'. A 'lock' is a wrestling hold, which would lead easily into *throw* in the next line; *OED sb.*[2] 12a gives several examples from the period, though its first instance of '*upon a lock*' is from 1650 and is metaphorical. Dowden, who proposed the reading, says that 'the action might playfully be imagined as that of wrestlers', but this seems to me grotesque rather than playful. Innogen is surely using an extravagant expression ('hurl me off a rock into the sea if you don't love me') in keeping with the extreme events of the scene. Her phrase may have been suggested by Ovid's *Metamorphoses* 9.211–19, where Hercules, driven mad by the poisoned shirt of Nessus, hurls his page Lichas from a rock into the sea. Shakespeare alludes to the story to express intense feeling at *Antony* 4.13.43–5, and it is much likelier that he is recalling Ovid here too than imagining a wrestling-match. Even if F's *rock* is wrong, it at least makes some sense for a modern audience, whereas 'upon a lock' makes none.
265 **mak'st . . . dullard** do you cast me as a dim-wit
    act performance

Wilt thou not speak to me?

INNOGEN (*kneeling*)   Your blessing, sir.

BELARIUS (*aside to Guiderius and Arviragus*)

Though you did love this youth, I blame ye not.

You had a motive for't.

CYMBELINE   My tears that fall

Prove holy water on thee!

   ⌈*He raises her*⌉

                Innogen,

Thy mother's dead.

INNOGEN   I am sorry for't, my lord.   270

CYMBELINE

O she was naught, and 'long of her it was

That we meet here so strangely; but her son

Is gone, we know not how nor where.

PISANIO   My lord,

Now fear is from me I'll speak truth. Lord Cloten,

Upon my lady's missing, came to me   275

With his sword drawn, foamed at the mouth, and swore

If I discovered not which way she was gone

It was my instant death. By accident

I had a feignèd letter of my master's

Then in my pocket, which directed him   280

To seek her on the mountains near to Milford,

Where in a frenzy, in my master's garments,

Which he enforced from me, away he posts

With unchaste purpose, and with oath to violate

My lady's honour. What became of him   285

I further know not.

GUIDERIUS   Let me end the story:

I slew him there.

CYMBELINE   Marry, the gods forfend!

I would not thy good deeds should from my lips

---

266 *kneeling*] *not in* F   269 *He raises her*] *not in* F   274 truth] F (troth)

270 **mother** stepmother
271 **naught** Both 'worthless' and 'wicked'.
   '**long of** 'along of', because of
272 **strangely** as strangers
275 **missing** absence
277 **discovered** revealed

278 **accident** chance
279 **feignèd letter** i.e. the one that Posthumus wrote to Innogen to lure her to Wales
283 **posts** rushes
287 **forfend** forbid

Pluck a hard sentence. Prithee, valiant youth,
Deny't again.   290
GUIDERIUS I have spoke it, and I did it.
CYMBELINE He was a prince.
GUIDERIUS
A most incivil one. The wrongs he did me
Were nothing prince-like, for he did provoke me
With language that would make me spurn the sea   295
If it could so roar to me. I cut off 's head,
And am right glad he is not standing here
To tell this tale of mine.
CYMBELINE   I am sorrow for thee.
By thine own tongue thou art condemned, and must
Endure our law. Thou'rt dead.
INNOGEN   That headless man   300
I thought had been my lord.
CYMBELINE (*to soldiers*)   Bind the offender,
And take him from our presence.
BELARIUS   Stay, sir King.
This man is better than the man he slew,
As well descended as thyself, and hath
More of thee merited than a band of Clotens   305
Had ever scar for. Let his arms alone,
They were not born for bondage.
CYMBELINE   Why old soldier,
Wilt thou undo the worth thou art unpaid for
By tasting of our wrath? How of descent
As good as we?
ARVIRAGUS   In that he spake too far.   310

---

303 This man] F; This boy OXFORD

---

290 **Deny't again** take it back
293 **incivil** barbarous, unmannerly
298 **am sorrow** F2 alters this to 'am sorry',
    but the phrase occurs at Webster's *The
    White Devil* (1612), 5.1.47; and for the
    idiom, compare *Tempest* 5.1.141: 'I am
    woe for't'.
300 **dead** condemned to death
303 **man . . . man** Oxford emends the first
    man to 'boy', suspecting 'contamination

from the other "man" in the line' (*Textual
Companion*, p. 609); but surely the repetition is the point, comparing Guiderius
with Cloten to the latter's disadvantage.
306 **Had . . . for** ever earned by their battle-
    scars
308 **worth . . . for** merit you are not yet
    rewarded for
309 **tasting of** experiencing
310 **spake too far** exaggerated

CYMBELINE ⌈*to Belarius*⌉
And thou shalt die for't.
BELARIUS   We will die all three
But I will prove that two on's are as good
As I have given out him. My sons, I must
For mine own part unfold a dangerous speech,
Though haply well for you.
ARVIRAGUS   Your danger's ours.   315
GUIDERIUS
And our good his.
BELARIUS   Have at it then, by leave.
Thou hadst, great King, a subject who
Was called Belarius.
CYMBELINE   What of him ? He is
A banished traitor.
BELARIUS   He it is that hath
Assumed this age : indeed, a banished man,   320
I know not how a traitor.
CYMBELINE (*to soldiers*)   Take him hence,
The whole world shall not save him.
BELARIUS   Not too hot.
First pay me for the nursing of thy sons,
And let it be confiscate all so soon
As I have received it.
CYMBELINE   Nursing of my sons ?   325
BELARIUS
I am too blunt and saucy, here's my knee. (*Kneeling*)

312 on's] F (one's)   326 *Kneeling*] *not in* F

311 **And . . . for't** If this is spoken to Belarius,
   as it seems to be (and not to Guiderius),
   Cymbeline's tyrannical wrath is reasserting itself.
312 **But I will** unless I
   on's of us
313 **given out him** declared him to be
314 **For . . . speech** give an explanation dangerous to myself
315 **haply** it may turn out
316 **Have . . . then** 'here goes'
   by leave with your permission
317 **Thou** Although he calls Cymbeline *great*
   King, Belarius addresses him with the
   impolite or familiar *Thou* rather than
   the polite *you*, perhaps responding to

Cymbeline's own tone.
320 **Assumed** attained
322 **hot** fast
324 **it** i.e. the payment
   confiscate confiscated (stressed here on
   the second syllable, unlike modern prose
   usage)
   all wholly, completely (as the Folio punctuation 'all, so soon' implies) ; an alter-
   native reading is 'all so soon | As',
   emphasizing that he will lose his payment at the very moment he gets it.
   Presumably he alludes to the confiscation
   of a condemned traitor's goods. For both
   uses of *all*, see Abbott §28.
326 **saucy** impertinent

Ere I arise I will prefer my sons,
Then spare not the old father. Mighty sir,
These two young gentlemen that call me father,
And think they are my sons, are none of mine.   330
They are the issue of your loins, my liege,
And blood of your begetting.
CYMBELINE   How, my issue?
BELARIUS
So sure as you your father's. I, old Morgan,
Am that Belarius whom you sometime banished.
Your pleasure was my mere offence, my punishment   335
Itself, and all my treason. That I suffered
Was all the harm I did. These gentle princes—
For such and so they are—these twenty years
Have I trained up. Those arts they have as I
Could put into them. My breeding was, sir,   340
As your highness knows. Their nurse Euriphile,
Whom for the theft I wedded, stole these children
Upon my banishment; I moved her to't,
Having received the punishment before
For that which I did then. Beaten for loyalty   345
Excited me to treason. Their dear loss,
The more of you 'twas felt, the more it shaped
Unto my end of stealing them. But gracious sir,
Here are your sons again, and I must lose
Two of the sweet'st companions in the world.   350
The benediction of these covering heavens
Fall on their heads like dew, for they are worthy
To inlay heaven with stars.

---

335 mere] RANN (*conj.* Tyrwhitt); neere F   336 treason. That] POPE (*subs.*); Treason that F

327 **prefer** advance
334 **sometime** once
335–6 **Your . . . treason** My offence, punishment, and treason were entirely your whim, invention.
335 **mere** whole, entire. Nosworthy retains F's 'neere', reading 'near-offence' (i.e. something that was hardly an offence at all).
337 **gentle** See the note to 1.1.38.
338 **such and so** i.e. both gentle and

    princes
339 **arts** accomplishments
340 **put into** teach
343 **moved** persuaded
345 **Beaten** having been beaten
346 **Excited** incited
347 **of** by
347–8 **shaped | Unto** suited
348 **end** aim
353 **To . . . stars** i.e. to become constellations themselves

CYMBELINE   Thou weep'st, and speak'st.
  The service that you three have done is more
  Unlike than this thou tell'st. I lost my children.   355
  If these be they, I know not how to wish
  A pair of worthier sons.
BELARIUS ⌈*rising*⌉   Be pleased a while.
  This gentleman, whom I call Polydore,
  Most worthy prince, as yours, is true Guiderius.
  This gentleman, my Cadwal, Arviragus,   360
  Your younger princely son. He, sir, was lapped
  In a most curious mantle, wrought by th' hand
  Of his queen mother, which for more probation
  I can with ease produce.
CYMBELINE   Guiderius had
  Upon his neck a mole, a sanguine star.   365
  It was a mark of wonder.
BELARIUS   This is he,
  Who hath upon him still that natural stamp.
  It was wise nature's end in the donation
  To be his evidence now.
CYMBELINE   O what am I,
  A mother to the birth of three? Ne'er mother   370
  Rejoiced deliverance more. Blest pray you be,
  That after this strange starting from your orbs,
  You may reign in them now! O Innogen,
  Thou hast lost by this a kingdom.

357 *rising*] *not in* F

353 **Thou . . . speak'st** Clearly Belarius weeps as he blesses his foster-children. The theatrical impact is discussed in the Introduction, p. 60.
355 **Unlike** unlikely, incredible (i.e. although this tale you have told is incredible, it is no more so than the victory you three have won)
357 **Be pleased a while** if you will give me leave for a little while longer
359–61 Oxford has both princes kneel to the King; if any kneeling is to be done, it is surely likelier that this fiercely independent pair should kneel to receive Belarius' tender blessing at ll. 351–3, as often in performance, than that they should observe form to a King who has ungratefully threatened them with

death, even if he is technically their father.
361 **lapped** wrapped
362 **curious** elaborate
363 **his queen mother** his mother the queen
     probation proof
365 **mole** Guiderius and his sister share a distinctive birthmark (compare 2.2.38). **sanguine** blood-red
367 **stamp** distinguishing mark
368 **end** purpose
     in the donation in giving it
369 **his evidence** evidence of his identity
370–1 **Ne'er . . . deliverance** never did giving birth cause a mother to rejoice
371 **pray** I pray
372 **starting** displacement
     orbs spheres (i.e. station in life)

INNOGEN   No, my lord,
    I have got two worlds by't. O my gentle brothers,   375
    Have we thus met? O never say hereafter
    But I am truest speaker. You called me brother
    When I was but your sister, I you brothers
    When ye were so indeed.
CYMBELINE   Did you e'er meet?
ARVIRAGUS
    Ay my good lord.
GUIDERIUS   And at first meeting loved,   380
    Continued so until we thought he died.
CORNELIUS
    By the Queen's dram she swallowed.
CYMBELINE   O rare instinct!
    When shall I hear all through? This fierce abridgement
    Hath to it circumstantial branches which
    Distinction should be rich in. Where, how lived you?   385
    And when came you to serve our Roman captive?
    How parted with your brothers? How first met them?
    Why fled you from the court, and whither? These,
    And your three motives to the battle, with
    I know not how much more, should be demanded,   390
    And all the other by-dependences,
    From chance to chance. But nor the time nor place
    Will serve our long inter'gatories. See,
    Posthumus anchors upon Innogen,
    And she, like harmless lightning, throws her eye   395
    On him, her brothers, me, her master, hitting
    Each object with a joy; the counterchange

---

379 ye] ROWE 1714; we F   387 brothers] THEOBALD; Brother F   388 whither? These,]
THEOBALD; whether‸ these? F   393 inter'gatories] MALONE (*conj.* Tyrwhitt); Interrogatories F

377 **But** anything other than
378 **but** only
382 **rare** exceptional
    instinct (stressed on the second syllable,
    unlike modern prose usage)
383 **fierce abridgement** drastic summary
384 **circumstantial branches** important
    details
385 **Distinction . . . in** should be more
    elaborately discriminated (Maxwell)
389 **your three motives** the motives of the

three of you
391 **by-dependences** side-issues
392 **chance** occurrence
    nor . . . nor neither . . . nor
393 **Will serve** are suited to
    inter'gatories interrogations. Malone's
    elision of F's 'Interrogatories' indicates
    the pronunciation required by the
    metre.
395 **throws her eye** gazes
397 **counterchange** reciprocation

Is severally in all. Let's quit this ground,
And smoke the temple with our sacrifices.
(*To Belarius*) Thou art my brother; so we'll hold thee
    ever.   400
INNOGEN (*to Belarius*)
You are my father too, and did relieve me
To see this gracious season.
CYMBELINE   All o'erjoyed,
Save these in bonds. Let them be joyful too,
For they shall taste our comfort.
INNOGEN (*to Lucius*)   My good master,
I will yet do you service.
LUCIUS   Happy be you!   405
CYMBELINE
The forlorn soldier that so nobly fought,
He would have well becomed this place, and graced
The thankings of a king.
POSTHUMUS   I am, sir,
The soldier that did company these three
In poor beseeming; 'twas a fitment for   410
The purpose I then followed. That I was he,
Speak Giacomo, I had you down, and might
Have made you finish.
GIACOMO (*kneeling*)   I am down again,
But now my heavy conscience sinks my knee
As then your force did. Take that life, beseech you,   415
Which I so often owe; but your ring first,
And here the bracelet of the truest princess
That ever swore her faith.
POSTHUMUS (*raising him*)   Kneel not to me.

---

406 so] F2; no F1   413 *kneeling*] *not in* F   418 *raising him*] *not in* F

398 **severally in all** individually in each one
   (i.e. each shares the other's joy)
399 **smoke** fill with smoke (of incense or
   sacrificial fires)
400 **hold** consider
401 **relieve** rescue
402 **gracious season** joyful occasion
404 **taste our comfort** experience our aid,
   mercy
406 **forlorn** wretched, (stressed on the first
   syllable)
407 **becomed** become
409 **company** accompany
410 **beseeming** appearance (i.e. what he is
   wearing)
   fitment making fit, preparation
413 **you finish** an end of you
414 **sinks** weighs down
416 **often** many times over

The power that I have on you is to spare you,
The malice towards you to forgive you. Live,   420
And deal with others better.
CYMBELINE   Nobly doomed!
We'll learn our freeness of a son-in-law.
Pardon's the word to all.
ARVIRAGUS (*to Posthumus*)   You holp us, sir,
As you did mean indeed to be our brother.
Joyed are we that you are.   425
POSTHUMUS
Your servant, princes. (*To Lucius*) Good my lord of
       Rome,
Call forth your soothsayer. As I slept, methought
Great Jupiter, upon his eagle backed,
Appeared to me with other spritely shows
Of mine own kindred. When I waked I found   430
This label on my bosom, whose containing
Is so from sense in hardness that I can
Make no collection of it. Let him show
His skill in the construction.
LUCIUS   Philharmonus.
SOOTHSAYER
Here, my good lord.
LUCIUS   Read, and declare the meaning.   435
SOOTHSAYER (*reads the tablet*) 'Whenas a lion's whelp shall,
   to himself unknown, without seeking find, and be
   embraced by a piece of tender air; and when from a
   stately cedar shall be lopped branches, which being
   dead many years, shall after revive, be jointed to the   440

---

436 *the tablet*] *not in* F

421 **doomed** sentenced
422 **freeness** generosity
423 **holp** helped (in frequent use up to the
     seventeenth century)
424 **As** as if
425 **Joyed** overjoyed
428 **upon . . . backed** riding on his eagle
429 **spritely** ghostly
     shows visions (with the overtone of
     'spectacular performance', sustaining
     from 5.3 the double nature of the ap-

paritions' appearance as both a dream
and an actual manifestation)
431 **label** sheet of writing (the *tablet* from
     5.3.203)
     containing content
432 **from . . . hardness** hard to understand
433 **collection of** deduction from
434, 445 **construction** interpretation
434 **Philharmonus** The Soothsayer's name
     in Greek means 'lover of harmony'.
436–43 See the notes to 5.3.232–6.

old stock, and freshly grow, then shall Posthumus end
his miseries, Britain be fortunate and flourish in peace
and plenty.'
Thou, Leonatus, art the lion's whelp.
The fit and apt construction of thy name,   445
Being *leo-natus*, doth import so much.
(*To Cymbeline*) The piece of tender air thy virtuous
    daughter,
Which we call '*mollis aer*'; and '*mollis aer*'
We term it '*mulier*', (*to Posthumus*) which '*mulier*' I
    divine
Is this most constant wife, who even now,   450
Answering the letter of the oracle,
Unknown to you, unsought, were clipped about
With this most tender air.
CYMBELINE   This hath some seeming.
SOOTHSAYER
The lofty cedar, royal Cymbeline,
Personates thee, and thy lopped branches point   455
Thy two sons forth, who by Belarius stol'n,
For many years thought dead, are now revived,
To the majestic cedar joined, whose issue
Promises Britain peace and plenty.
CYMBELINE   Well,
My peace we will begin; and Caius Lucius,   460
Although the victor, we submit to Caesar
And to the Roman empire, promising
To pay our wonted tribute, from the which
We were dissuaded by our wicked queen,

---

450 this] F; thy CAPELL

446 *leo-natus* lion-born (Latin)
  import mean
448–9 *mollis aer . . . mulier* soft air (Latin),
  an ancient but erroneous etymology for
  mulier (woman)
449 **divine** interpret (by divine inspiration)
450 **constant** See note to 1.4.57.
450 **who** This seems to refer to *wife*, but must
  in fact refer to Posthumus, who is *clipped*
  by her: hence Oxford's inserted direction

to Posthumus in the previous line.
451 **Answering the letter** fulfilling the
  terms
452 **clipped about** embraced
453 **seeming** plausibility
455 **Personates** stands for (stressed on the
  second syllable)
455–6 **point . . . forth** indicate
463 **wonted tribute** the tribute we used to
  pay

Whom heavens in justice both on her and hers   465
Have laid most heavy hand.

SOOTHSAYER
    The fingers of the powers above do tune
    The harmony of this peace. The vision,
    Which I made known to Lucius ere the stroke
    Of this yet scarce-cold battle, at this instant   470
    Is full accomplished. For the Roman eagle,
    From south to west on wing soaring aloft,
    Lessened herself, and in the beams o'th' sun
    So vanished; which foreshowed our princely eagle,
    Th'imperial Caesar, should again unite   475
    His favour with the radiant Cymbeline,
    Which shines here in the west.

CYMBELINE   Laud we the gods,
    And let our crookèd smokes climb to their nostrils
    From our blest altars. Publish we this peace
    To all our subjects. Set we forward. Let   480
    A Roman and a British ensign wave
    Friendly together: so through Lud's town march,
    And in the temple of great Jupiter
    Our peace we'll ratify, seal it with feasts.
    Set on there. Never was a war did cease,   485
    Ere bloody hands were washed, with such a peace.

                                    ⌈*Flourish.*⌉ *Exeunt*

---

470 this yet] F3; yet this F1   486.1 *Flourish*] *not in* F

465 **Whom** on whom
    hers i.e. her son
467–8 **The . . . peace** The gods' creation of
    peaceful harmony is expressed in terms of
    tuning a musical instrument.
469 **made known** explained (incorrectly, as
    it now turns out)
469–70 **ere . . . battle** before the action of this
    battle which is only just over
473 **Lessened herself** (by flying into the
    distance)

477 **Laud** praise
478 **crookèd** curling
479 **Publish** announce
480 **Set we** let us go
481 **ensign** standard, banner
482 **Lud's town** London (see note to 3.1.32)
485 **Set on there** go forward, you (that are)
    there
    Never . . . cease there was never a war
    which ended

THE CHARACTERS' NAMES

IN the First Folio text, the heroine of *Cymbeline* is called 'Imogen'; but Simon Forman's eyewitness account of the play calls her 'Innogen' (see Introduction, pp. 3–6, and fig. 11). This strongly suggests that in performance she was called 'Innogen', and that the Folio's 'Imogen' is an error. Furthermore, 'Innogen' is supported by other evidence. Shakespeare's creation of a remote ancient Britain derives from Holinshed's *Chronicles*, where the name of the legendary first queen of Britain is Innogen; so this was an obvious choice of name for Shakespeare's mythical British princess. It also has dramatic appropriateness. With its overtones of innocence, 'Innogen' gives the character a significant name corresponding to those of other late-play heroines: Marina, 'born at sea' in *Pericles* (Sc. 13.13); Perdita, the 'lost' one in *The Winter's Tale* (3.3.32); Miranda, 'the top of admiration' in *The Tempest* (3.1.38); and in *Cymbeline* itself it matches the symbolic name 'Fidele' which the heroine assumes as a page, and whose aptness Caius Lucius expounds: 'Thou dost approve thyself the very same. | Thy name well fits thy faith, thy faith thy name' (4.2.381–2). Moreover, Shakespeare had used the name before. The opening stage direction of *Much Ado About Nothing* introduces Leonato and '*Innogen his wife*', though she has nothing to say, and apart from a second entry (where she is not named) at the start of Act 2, she is dropped from the play; but the fact that Shakespeare had previously called a husband and wife Leonato and Innogen provides further evidence that Posthumus Leonatus' wife was called 'Innogen'. It is conceivable that the name was changed by Shakespeare or someone else between the performance that Forman saw and the preparation of the Folio text in 1623, but why should anyone substitute a meaningless name for one of such obvious appropriateness?[1]

If 'Imogen' is an error, who was responsible for it? It is unlikely to have been a compositor since the play was set by two of them, although, as Gary Taylor remarks, in the Second Quarto of *Hamlet* 'two different compositors consistently commit the error "Rosencraus"' (*Textual Companion*, p. 604); it probably originates with Ralph Crane, if he was the scribe who prepared the Folio copy (see Introduction, pp. 68–74). T. H. Howard-Hill points out sixteen misreadings in Crane's transcription of Middleton's *The*

---

[1] Richard A. Coates (in 'A Personal Name Etymology and a Shakespearean Dramatic Motiv', *Names*, 24 (1976), pp. 1–8) and John Pitcher ('Names in *Cymbeline*', *Essays in Criticism*, 43 (1993), 1–16; p. 8) attempt to invest 'Imogen' with such significance. I find their derivations unconvincing, but on such an important issue readers may wish to consult these arguments and decide for themselves.

11. Simon Forman's account of *Cymbeline* (Bodleian Library MS Ashmole 208, fol. 206ʳ), clearly showing the spelling 'Innogen' in lines 15 and 28.

Witch arising from minim errors—the kind of error involved in misreading 'Imogen' for 'Innogen'—which were 'rooted, probably, in the difficult[y] of Middleton's handwriting'.[1] Shakespeare's handwriting seems to have been even more difficult, particularly his later handwriting, of which the nearest example to the date of *Cymbeline* (*c.*1610) is his signature as a witness in the legal case of Mountjoy versus Belott on 11 May 1612.[2] In this, 'William' is abbreviated, either to 'Wilm' or 'Willm'; in either case, the 'm' is hardly more than a squiggle, and makes the possibility of minim confusion between 'm' and double 'n' in *Cymbeline* very plausible;[3] once Crane had misread 'Imogen' for 'Innogen' the first time, it would be natural for him to do so subsequently.

There is only one known occurrence of the name 'Imogen' before the Folio text of *Cymbeline*, again in the context of the first queen of Britain, and probably illustrating the same minim error. Ralph Higden, in his four-teenth-century history of the world, *Polychronicon*, relates the early history of Britain. Like Holinshed's, Higden's Latin account calls Brutus' wife 'Innogen'. John Trevisa's fourteenth-century translation renders the name 'Innoges'; but in an anonymous fifteenth-century translation (British Library MS Harl. 2261, fol. 112^r), the name is 'Ymogen'.[4] This is probably the same misreading error as in *Cymbeline*; but it is also possible, as John Pitcher says, 'that in the century between these medieval transla-tions, or before then, there were two or more ways of rendering the name *Innogen* (here in a Latin text) into English. *Ymogen* and *Innoges* may be the consequence of philological change rather than mistakes in transmitting the texts in manuscript'.[5] Or they may be regarded simply as *spelling variants*, as Brian Gibbons clearly regards them when he says that 'Imo-gen' shares her name with 'that of the very first queen of Britain',[6] which offers a way out for anyone who is unwilling to disregard Forman's evidence but who is uneasy about departing from the authority of the

---

[1] *Ralph Crane and Some Shakespeare First Folio Comedies* (Charlottesville, 1972), p. 58.

[2] This document is reproduced in S. Schoenbaum, *William Shakespeare: A Doc-umentary Life* (Oxford, 1975), p. 212, and the signature in E. K. Chambers, *William Shakespeare*, 2 vols. (Oxford, 1930), i, facing p. 504.

[3] Further support is provided by the reconstruction of how Shakespeare formed 'm' and 'n' by E. M. Thompson in his contribution to *Shakespeare's Hand in the Play of Sir Thomas More* (Cambridge, 1923), Plate VI, and from J. Dover Wilson's point that 'the large number of compositor's errors in words containing [mimim] letters [e.g. 'm' and 'n'] prove that [Shakespeare] must have been more than ordinarily careless in the formation of them' (*The Manuscript of Shakespeare's 'Hamlet'*, 2 vols. (Cam-bridge, 1934), i. 106.

[4] The Latin original and both translations are conveniently juxtaposed in the edition of *Polychronicon* by Churchill Babington and Joseph Rawson Lumby, 9 vols. (1865–6), ii. 444–5.

[5] Pitcher, 'Names in *Cymbeline*' (see p. 265 footnote 1), p. 4.

[6] *Shakespeare and Multiplicity* (Cambridge, 1993), p. 25.

Folio.[1] The seductive theatrical and literary associations that have accumulated around 'Imogen' make it very difficult to view this problem objectively. But with such a powerful tradition supporting the Folio reading, full weight needs to be given to the evidence against it; and although this evidence falls short of certainty, it seems to me strong enough to require an editor to depart from the Folio and to call the heroine 'Innogen'.[2]

I have followed the principles of this series in replacing the Folio's 'Iachimo' with its modern Italian equivalent 'Giacomo', though with some misgivings, since it imperils the theatrical impact of an important line. During the furious soliloquy in which he reacts to his apparent betrayal, Posthumus refers, in the Folio, to 'This yellow *Iachimo*' (2.4.166 / TLN 1352). The phrase surely invites a pronunciation which emphasizes the alliteration—'*yellow Yackimo*'—which is usually how it is delivered in performance. 'Giacomo' precludes this alliterative emphasis—though no more so than another modern reading, 'Jachimo', the form adopted by Maxwell, Riverside, and, apparently, the forthcoming New Penguin edition, following the Fourth Folio of 1685. This seems to me the worst of both worlds, neither preserving the advantages of the Folio nor fully modernizing.

The question of modernization arises again with Posthumus Leonatus. Both his names are clearly significant. The 'fit and apt construction' of 'Leonatus', as the Soothsayer points out at 5.4.444–6, is 'the lion's whelp'; and Cymbeline christened him 'Posthumus' because he was born after the death of his father and because his mother died giving birth to him (1.1.36–41). There is a case for making this clear by modernizing to 'Posthumous'; there is also a case for fully classicizing to 'Postumus'. But the form 'Posthumus' is itself a classical one in that *postumus* was 'in late Latin written *posthumus* through erroneous attribution to *humus* the earth' (*OED*, *posthumous*); and since this is the form that Shakespeare found in Holinshed, where Posthumus is the grandfather of Brutus, the founder of Britain, it is

---

[1] Pitcher, 'Names in *Cymbeline*' (see p. 265 footnote 1) attempts to explain away Forman's evidence by arguing that his account of *Cymbeline*, as of *Macbeth*, is contaminated by his reading of Holinshed, or that he 'already knew the name *Innogen*, and that when he went to see *Cymbeline* this is the form he thought he heard the players using on stage' (p. 6). Was the diction of the King's Men really *that* bad?

[2] The only modern production to adopt 'Innogen' so far (1997) was Peter Hall's at the National Theatre in 1988. Convinced by the arguments for 'Innogen', he nevertheless wanted to put the symbolic associations of the name to the practical test; so 'Innogen' was used in rehearsal on an experimental basis, and it was Posthumus' constant anguished reiteration of the name in the last act, and especially at 5.4.225–7, that clinched its appropriateness for Hall. The name becomes, he said, 'a kind of talisman for Posthumus, a symbol of innocence and integrity, the qualities he has lacked himself' (cited in my *Staging Shakespeare's Late Plays* (Oxford, 1990), p. 74).

retained in this edition. At least it makes a consistent pseudo-historical pairing with 'Innogen'.

For another major character the Folio offers conflicting evidence: he is called 'Cloten' eighteen times, 'Clotten' six times. The inconsistency cannot be attributed to the two compositors who set the Folio text, since Compositor E only set the name in full once ('Clotten' at 2.3.0.1 / TLN 961). Compositor B set 'Clotten' in the early part of the play, changing to 'Cloten' from 3.5.0.1 / TLN 1889, and reverting to 'Clotten' once, at 4.1.0.1 / TLN 2218. It is possible that the almost exclusive use of 'Cloten' in the second half of the play reflects a change of mind on Shakespeare's part that was preserved by the scribe. He may have decided that he had stacked the cards quite heavily enough against the character (and the actor) in the opening description of him (1.1.16–17), and in the Second Lord's mockery in 1.2 and 2.1, without cutting the ground completely from under his feet with his name as well. This is a character who, as argued elsewhere in this edition (see the Commentary to 2.3.64–73 and 3.5.70) is not wholly without the capacity for thought, however intermittent, or a kind of weird imagination; nor does the jingle '*Clotens* Clot-pole' (4.2.185 / TLN 2480) necessarily require the pronunciation 'Clotten' to have its effect, as is sometimes assumed (unlike the alliterative 'yellow *Iachimo*'); and in any case F has 'Cloten' at this point. But it is also possible that the spelling 'Clotten' derives from Ralph Crane, who had a tendency to double 't' in mid-word.[1] The other spellings of the name use a single 't': Simon Forman has 'Clotan' and 'Cloten', Holinshed 'Cloton'.

A less consequential decision, because it does not affect the pronunciation, is required for the name of Posthumus' host in Rome. The Folio initially calls him '*Filorio*' (1.1.98 / TLN 114), thereafter '*Philario*'. 'Filorio' might be an attempt to suggest a Renaissance Italian name rather than a classical one, but 'Philario' perhaps brings out more clearly that the name is from the Greek 'philo', meaning 'loving, dear': this character is a good friend to Posthumus, as he had been to Posthumus' father. A related modernization, 'Philharmonus' for F's 'Philarmonus' (5.4.434 / TLN 3762), emphasizes that the name in Greek means 'lover of harmony'. The other names follow those in the Folio.

---

[1] See Introduction, pp. 71–2.

THE MUSIC

Edited by James Walker

ALTHOUGH the stage directions in the Folio text of *Cymbeline* provide no cues for fanfares ('flourishes') at royal entries or for military music to mark the stages of the battle in 5.2, these must have been played as a matter of course in the original performances as in modern ones; the cues are duly supplied in this edition. The Folio text does, however, specify music at three points: for the song 'Hark, hark, the lark' at 2.3.19–25; for Belarius' 'ingenious instrument' at 4.2.187; and for Posthumus' vision of his ghostly family at 5.3.123.1–8.

(i) 'Hark, hark, the lark' (2.3.19–25)

A seventeenth-century setting survives in a collection of songs by Royalist composers[1] including Henry Lawes, John Wilson, and Robert Johnson, to whom this setting has been attributed on stylistic grounds.[2] Johnson was lutenist to James I from 1604 until his death in 1633. He frequently composed music for Shakespeare's company; Ariel's songs 'Full fathom five' and 'Where the bee sucks' in *The Tempest* and Autolycus' 'Get you hence' in *The Winter's Tale* are also attributed to him. His setting of the song proper does not actually begin until bar 3, as it is preceded by an unusual vocal flourish. Perhaps this is Johnson's response to Shakespeare's request for 'a very excellent good-conceited thing' (2.3. 15–16); alternatively, if Johnson's was the setting composed for the original production, it is possible that the phrase is Shakespeare's reaction to hearing the opening bars of the setting. Johnson omits the two lines 'His steeds to water at those springs | On chaliced flowers that lies', probably inadvertently.[3] The realization given here composes the missing lines; the song has been transposed down to allow for the rise in pitch since the seventeenth century.

---

[1] First discussed by George A. Thewlis, 'Some Notes on a Bodleian Manuscript', *Music and Letters*, 22 (1941), pp. 32–5. The collection is Bodleian MS Don. c.57.
[2] For example by Ian Spink in the standard edition of Johnson's *Ayres, Songs and Dialogues* (revised edn., 1974), p. 73.
[3] Willa McClung Evans, 'Shakespeare's "Harke Harke Ye Larke"', *PMLA* 60 (1945), pp. 95–101, argues that Johnson deliberately omitted the lines to avoid a cluster of sibilants; but Johnson has not balked at the repeated 'so sweet is she' in his setting of Jonson's 'Have you seen the bright lily grow?' This article usefully reproduces the manuscript setting of the song.

HARK, HARK, THE LARK

Attributed to Robert Johnson (*c.*1582–1633)

Realized and edited by James Walker

(ii) **'My ingenious instrument'** (4.2.187)

The sudden sounding of music here establishes a mood of strange, almost supernatural, solemnity apt to an episode which seems to hover mysteriously between death and life. Yet it is created by human agency—Belarius speaks of '*My* ingenious instrument' and Arviragus has 'give[n] it motion' (4.2.189)—as apparently supernatural effects are in the other late plays: Cerimon's revival of Thaisa (*Pericles* Sc. 12), Paulina's bringing Hermione's statue to life (*The Winter's Tale* 5.3), and Prospero's magic throughout *The Tempest*.

It would be interesting to know what was used in the original performances. Mechanically operated instruments were known in Shakespeare's time, but perhaps conventional instruments were combined and employed in an unconventional way, as they often are in modern performances. For John Barton's production at Stratford-upon-Avon in 1974, for example, the present music editor employed a high sustained cello harmonic, a low percussive rumble on piano strings played with a timpani stick, and a melismatic sound on a large glockenspiel with harp glissando.

(iii) **Posthumus' vision** (5.3.123–216)

This begins with an elaborate stage direction. '*Solemn music*' sounds, as in the previous episode discussed; then the ghosts of Posthumus' parents enter '*with music before them*'; they are followed, '*after other music*', by the ghosts of Posthumus' brothers. What do these phrases imply? Perhaps that offstage music sounds before each entry, perhaps that each pair of ghosts is preceded by its own ghostly musicians. If the latter, the instruments originally used must have been ones that could be played on the move: recorders or oboes with lute, small drum, or tabor. These instruments may also have been used to underpin the rhythm of the ghosts' speeches, or even to punctuate them, perhaps emphasizing the impact of half-lines like 'A thing of pity' or 'Sweet Innogen' (ll. 141, 156).

In the first annual Globe lecture (1990), Stanley Wells suggested that 'the representatives of the older and the younger generations should enter separately, probably through different entrances [the doors on either side of the stage?], each group preceded by musicians' (p. 12). If so, the musicians may have remained by the entrances, their contributions creating an antiphonal effect and so emphasizing the ritual nature of the scene; or they may have preceded the two groups of ghosts as they '*circle[d] Posthumus round as he lies sleeping*', enhancing the ritual in a different way.

When Jupiter '*descends in thunder and lightning*' and '*throws a thunderbolt*' (5.3.186.1–2), was the thunder simply a sound effect or was it achieved in part by musical means? The sound of the organ is specified in the stage directions of Marston's *Sophonisba* of 1606, and may have been used to intensify the impact of Jove's thunder here: thunder is compared to the sound of an organ at *The Tempest* 3.3.97–8: 'the thunder, | That deep and dreadful organ-pipe'.

(iv) **A spoken song**: 'Fear no more' (4.2.236–82)

When Arviragus asks Guiderius to join him in singing Innogen 'to th' ground | As once our mother', Guiderius replies that he cannot sing, and Arviragus answers 'We'll speak it then' (4.2.237–43). This is the plainest evidence that 'Fear no more' is to be spoken, not sung. But Gary Taylor comments: 'If anything in the canon is a theatrical interpolation due to exigencies of casting, these lines are a chief candidate. Quite apart from their evident excusing of a bad voice, they are contradicted by the [heading] "SONG"' (*Textual Companion*, pp. 607–8). The heading is not as decisive as this suggests, since it may not be Shakespeare's own but may reflect a characteristic tidying of the page layout by Ralph Crane, the scribe who probably prepared the copy for the Folio text. But if these lines do not reflect a theatrical emergency, what is their function? It is surely to draw attention to the words of this celebration of Innogen: they are to be spoken, not sung, so that there may be no risk of anything detracting from their hypnotic impact, to which almost every performance attests.

ALTERATIONS TO LINEATION

I.I.1–2   You...courtiers] ROWE; *as three lines in* F, *divided after* 'frowns' *and* 'heavens'

53–4   By...is] ROWE; *as one line in* F

54–6   I...King] JOHNSON; *as two lines in* F, *divided after* 'report'

139   That...queen] ROWE; *as two lines in* F *divided after* 'had'

142–3   Thou...baseness] ROWE; *perhaps prose in* F, *divided after* 'my'

143–4   No...it] ROWE 1714; *as one line in* F

179   About...me] ROWE; *as two lines in* F, *divided after* 'hence'

I.2.5–6   If...him] CAPELL; *as verse in* F, *divided after* 'it'

28–9   She...her] ROWE 1714; *as verse in* F, *divided after* 'reflection'

I.3.17–18   I...diminution] POPE; *divided after* 'eye-strings' *in* F

I.4.164–5   Signor...'em] CAPELL; *as verse in* F, *divided after* ' 'em'

I.5.1   Whiles...flowers] ROWE; *as two lines in* F, *divided after* 'ground'

46   Weeps...time] ROWE; *as two lines in* F, *divided after* 'sayst thou'

I.6.76–7   And...blame] POPE; *divided after* 'Frenchman' *in* F

78   Not...might] ROWE; *as two lines in* F, *divided after* 'he'

179   All's...yours] ROWE; *as two lines in* F, *divided after* 'sir'

2.2.3   I...weak] ROWE; *as two lines in* F, *divided after* 'then'

2.3.61   T'employ...queen] ROWE; *as two lines in* F, *divided after* 'Roman'

79–80   Ay...chamber] HANMER; *as one line in* F

2.4.31–2   Your...upon] INGLEBY; *divided after* 'lady' *in* F

142–3   Spare...million] CAPELL; *divided after* 'arithmetic' *in* F

164   Might...her] POPE; *as two lines in* F, *divided after* 'Saturn'

180–1   Why...vice] CAPELL; *as one line in* F

3.3.78   In...valleys] CAPELL; *as two lines in* F, *divided after* 'state'

82   They...meanly] ROWE; *as two lines in* F, *divided after* 'mine'

3.6.91   The...welcome] POPE; *as two lines in* F, *divided after* 'owl'

4.2.32   These...heard] ROWE; *as two lines in* F, *divided after* 'creatures'

191   What...mother] POPE; *as two lines in* F, *divided after* 'mean'

283   We...down] POPE; *as two lines in* F, *divided after* 'obsequies'

5.3.95   You shall...upon you] ROWE; *as two lines in* F, *divided after* 'stol'n'

124–5   No...flies] THEOBALD; *divided after* 'thunder-master' *in* F

126–7   With...adulteries] THEOBALD; *as one line in* F

150–1   In...dignity] F2; *divided after* 'deem' *in* F1

154–5 From . . . one] F2 ; *divided after 'her' in* FI
157–8 Why . . . Italy] F4 ; *as one line in* FI
159–60 To . . . jealousy] F4 ; *as one line in* FI
161–2 And . . . villainy] F4 ; *as one line in* FI
167–8 Our . . . maintain] F4 ; *as one line in* FI
171–2 Then . . . adjourned] F4 ; *as one line in* FI
173–4 The . . . turned] F4 ; *as one line in* FI
175–6 Thy . . . exercise] F2 ; *divided* 'look | look out' *in* FI ; *see collation.*
177–8 Upon . . . injuries] F4 ; *as one line in* FI
183–4 To . . . deity] F4 ; *as one line in* FI
5.4.168–9 I . . . matter] ROWE 1714 ; *as one line in* F
228–9 Shall's . . . part] HANMER ; *divided after 'this' in* F
259–60 My . . . error] HANMER ; *as one line in* F
286–7 Let . . . there] POPE ; *as one line in* F
300–1 That . . . lord] POPE ; *as one line in* F
318–19 What . . . traitor] CAPELL ; *as one line in* F
404–5 My . . . service] POPE ; *as one line in* F

INDEX

THIS is a selective guide to the annotations and the Introduction, although it does not duplicate the section headings of the latter. Citations from other texts are not included, nor are the two Appendixes, where the headings and sub-headings are self-explanatory. Characters in the play are only listed if their names are discussed. Asterisks identify entries which supplement the information given in *OED*.

The Oxford World's Classics Website

www.worldsclassics.co.uk

- Information about new titles
- Explore the full range of Oxford World's Classics
- Links to other literary sites and the main OUP webpage
- Imaginative competitions, with bookish prizes
- Peruse the Oxford World's Classics Magazine
- Articles by editors
- Extracts from Introductions
- A forum for discussion and feedback on the series
- Special information for teachers and lecturers

www.worldsclassics.co.uk

American Literature

British and Irish Literature

Children's Literature

Classics and Ancient Literature

Colonial Literature

Eastern Literature

European Literature

History

Medieval Literature

Oxford English Drama

Poetry

Philosophy

Politics

Religion

The Oxford Shakespeare

A complete list of Oxford Paperbacks, including Oxford World's Classics, Oxford Shakespeare, Oxford Drama, and Oxford Paperback Reference, is available in the UK from the Academic Division Publicity Department, Oxford University Press, Great Clarendon Street, Oxford OX2 6DP.

In the USA, complete lists are available from the Paperbacks Marketing Manager, Oxford University Press, 198 Madison Avenue, New York, NY 10016.

Oxford Paperbacks are available from all good bookshops. In case of difficulty, customers in the UK can order direct from Oxford University Press Bookshop, Freepost, 116 High Street, Oxford OX1 4BR, enclosing full payment. Please add 10 per cent of published price for postage and packing.